MILES GONE BY

William F. Buckley Jr.

MILES GONE BY

A Literary Autobiography

Since 1947
REGNERY
PUBLISHING, INC.
An Eagle Publishing Company • Washington, DC

Library of Congress Cataloging-in-Publication Data

Buckley, William F. (William Frank), 1925–
    Miles gone by : a literary autobiography / William F. Buckley Jr.
        p. cm.
    ISBN 0-89526-089-1 (alk. paper)
1. Buckley, William F. (William Frank), 1925– 2. Novelists, American—
20th century—Biography. 3. Journalists—United States—Biography.
I. Title.
    PS3552.U344Z465 2004
    818'.5409—dc22

                                                                2004007170

Published in the United States by
Regnery Publishing, Inc.
An Eagle Publishing Company
One Massachusetts Avenue, NW
Washington, DC 20001

Visit us at www.regnery.com

Distributed to the trade by
National Book Network
4720-A Boston Way
Lanham, MD 20706

Printed on acid-free paper

Manufactured in the United States of America

10 9 8 7 6 5 4 3 2 1

Books are available in quantity for promotional or premium use. Write to
Director of Special Sales, Regnery Publishing, Inc., One Massachusetts
Avenue, NW, Washington, DC 20001, for information on discounts and
terms or call (202) 216-0600.

FOR PATRICIA TAYLOR BUCKLEY
—WITH LOVE AND GRATITUDE

Contents

⌇ PEOPLE

⌇ REMEMBERING

These are portraits—of people, primarily, but also of institutional presences in my life. One such is the protagonist of ten of my novels, Blackford Oakes. Another is National Review, *the magazine I founded and edited for thirty-five years. And the third is my television program,* Firing Line.

EPILOGUE

Introduction

The design of this book is to bring together material I have written over fifty years, with an autobiography in mind.

I have published eight collections, most recently *Happy Days Were Here Again*, in 1993. In these, I reproduced material from articles, books, and newspaper columns. About one-half of what appeared in those volumes originated as columns, in which the first person is not used (or used only irregularly). And the articles and essays were, for the most part, nonpersonal in address. This time around, probably the final time around, I bring together only scenes and essays in which I figure directly. What I have attempted is in the nature of a narrative survey of my life, at work and play. There are personal experiences, challenges and sorties, professional inquiries, and memories beginning in childhood. Everything in this book puts me in play, sometimes actively, sometimes only in a passive way, but always there.

There would be no point in contriving an autobiography from scratch. Why? I have already written about the events and the people that have shaped my life; any new account would simply paraphrase these. I hope that this volume achieves the purpose, and that it will give pleasure.

CHAPTER ONE

AT HOME

Life at Great Elm

In 1923, after years spent abroad in Mexico and in Europe, my father bought a house, called Great Elm, in Sharon, Connecticut, and moved his family there. I was born in 1925, the sixth child. ⟶

Outdoors *it was very very still,* and from our bedroom we could hear the crickets and see the fireflies. I opined to my sister Trish, age twelve, that when the wind dies and silence ensues, fireflies acquire a voice, and it is then that they chirp out their joys for the benefit of the nightly company, visible and invisible.

"Why do they care if it's quiet outside?"

I informed her solemnly that it was well known to adults that fireflies do not like the wind, as it interferes with their movements. Inasmuch as I was thirteen and omniscient, my explanation was accepted.

"I just hope they bite all of *them*," she said. Her reference was to our five older siblings, whose shouts and yells we could hear through the chorus of crickets. They were still out there at the swimming pool playing games, one whole hour past bedtime for the four of us under fourteen. I consoled her. I reminded her that I had invited *her*, not one of *them*, to crew with me the next day. We would compete on my sailboat at two in the afternoon at Lake Wononscopomuc (also known as Lakeville Lake), a mile-square spring-fed crystal-clear lagoon lying five miles north of our home.

We raced every Wednesday, Saturday, and Sunday, seven hot-blooded contestants of whom I was by far the youngest, and my proclamation of whom I had tapped to crew with me the next racing day was eagerly awaited by qualified supplicants. It gave me great pain that only two of my seniors particularly cared whether they were invited or not. I handled that snub by telling Trish that they were, in fact, not truly qualified to serve.

Summers were seasons of unmitigated pleasure for us, in the late thirties, in Sharon, a small village that would be designated by the Garden Club of America as the most beautiful town in Connecticut, after Litchfield. My Texan father had brought his brood to rest there while he continued a peripatetic life in the years since he left Mexico.

One obsession governed almost all of us: horses and horse shows. There was one of these almost every week, somewhere within forty miles of us. Our groom was fiercely competitive. Whenever we failed to place in a contest, he surmised that skulduggery was on the throne. Obviously if one of us captured the blue ribbon, it meant that the judges were both honest and acute. If we captured the red ribbon, it meant that they were either honest or acute.

We would leave for the horse shows in two or three cars, the horses having traveled the night before in their trailers. We were properly dressed in riding habits—boots, jodhpurs, tweed jackets. If it was a day on which we would be competing in a jumping tournament, or running fences on the outside course, there were butterflies in my stomach, pacified by hot black coffee. But most of the equestrian events were mere "horsemanship" contests, in which you displayed your degree of mastery over your steed, first at walking or single-footing, then trotting, then cantering. There was the occasional "family" class, in which parents could enter as many of their children as they liked. Here, with six contestants in the field,

we regularly overwhelmed the opposition, if not by horsemanship, then by sheer juggernautery.

Some of the horse shows were also social occasions, calling for elaborate picnics and other forms of fraternization. Every year in Rhinebeck, New York, a few miles north of Hyde Park, the box alongside my father's was occupied by the president of the United States, who played the country squire at least once every season at the Dutchess County Horse Show. I remember the afternoon when Trish won the blue ribbon. Protocol requires the winner to ride around the ring to receive the plaudits of the spectators. When she rode by the president's box, FDR applauded lustily, whereupon Trish abruptly turned her pigtailed head to one side. A moment later, blue ribbon and riding crop in one hand, she came buoyantly to the family box.

"Why didn't you nod to the president?" my father whispered to her.

"I thought you didn't like him!" Trish's face was pained with surprise.

☙

In those days, in rural New England, only the principal arteries connecting the villages were macadamized. The side roads were dirt, so that Sharon was a network of leafy pleasure and opportunity for the horseman. No day went by at our place without two or three hours' wandering about through the woods and pastures, sometimes at full gallop. (Though never when within sight of the stables. Ed Turpin drove the point home to us: If you let a horse do that once, he will want to do it from that point on. Horses, like hunting dogs, are eager to set out, and eager to go home.) Horse sweat, for some reason, has always seemed healthier than human sweat, wholesome even. In midsummer the horse lather was white and soapy, but the emanations suggested only the earthy satisfactions of an inspiriting physical workout. The young riders, by contrast, would rush to efface the traces of their exertions, plunging into the pool. At lunch, those who had chosen to play golf or tennis in the morning would join the riders and we would plan the afternoon—though Mademoiselle (Mademoiselle Jeanne Bouchex, our governess) was there to see to it that no outing stood in the way of the forty-five minutes required of every one of us at piano practice. There were five pianos in the house and one organ. It was never absolutely clear whether the sound was worse when all the pianos were being exercised jointly or when only one of them was being played.

It was about that time that I came upon nature's dirty little secret. It was that beginning on the twenty-first day of June, *the days grew shorter*! All through the spring we had had the sensual pleasure of the elongating day, coinciding with the approach of the end of the school year and the beginning of the summer paradise. My knowledge of nature and nature's lore has never been very formal, and so, whereas my older brother Jim knew all about the vernal equinox and hummingbirds and for that matter snakes and fishes and what-makes-it-rain, I came to the conclusion from the evidence of my senses that in late July it was actually getting dark when it was only 8:30! I wondered momentarily whether we were witnessing some sign of divine displeasure. The only relief I had, during the humiliating meteorological briefing from my brother, who told me about the Earth's orbiting habits, was that Trish wasn't in the room to hear him. She'd have been dismayed by such a demonstration of my ignorance, given that I knew everything about fireflies.

I did care very much to penetrate the secrets of the wind, because my boat did moderately well in a good breeze and extraordinarily well in a brisk breeze; so that immediately upon waking on racing days I would run to the window and look out on the hundred elm and oak and maple trees visible from the bedroom, studying the movement of the leaves. Usually at that hour they were listless. I had to train myself to remember that in the foothills of the Berkshires

GREAT ELM IN THE 1930S

the winds tend to sleep late, beginning to exercise themselves only in midmorning. But whatever the wind did, the racers would be at the starting line at exactly 2:00 P.M. Eagerly, my crew and I would gulp down our lunch so that we could get to the lake a full hour before the starting gun, to do a few flashy turns when the wind was brisk; or to practice self-effacement when the wind was light—the objective was to reduce windage by lying flat on the deck or crowding inside the little cockpit. It meant exhilaration or despair, how many seconds after the starting gun went off I was safely across the line. The seven contestants fought fiercely for the trophy, which the winner got to keep for the whole winter season, returning it in the spring to the Commodore for safekeeping until it was awarded to the next summer's champion.

The trophy was a gift from the local drugstore to the Wononscopomuc Yacht Club, whose entire other assets comprised one box of stationery on which was written "Wononscopomuc Yacht Club." It was used by the Commodore, a retired naval officer with a master sergeant's temperament. Once a year, he would write to announce the season's schedule. The yacht club's annual party, at which the cup was awarded to the boat that had accumulated the largest number of points, was held at the house of one of the contenders. The grown-ups brought their own beer or paid the host fifteen cents for a bottle of his. I don't remember if I had to pay for my Coca-Cola. It is hard to think of anything I have ever coveted so much as to see the name of my boat engraved on the Wononscopomuc Yacht Club Trophy (achieved in 1940). But there are few desires so intense as the child's. Or disappointments so bitter, as when—it happened every *single* night of every *single* month between May and October—Mademoiselle clapped her hands at the swimming pool right in the *middle* of a game of Red Rover, to announce that it was bedtime for "*les petits.*"

My English setter, Ducky (it infuriated me that my oldest sister teasingly referred to him as "Unducky"), slept on his turf, between my bed and Trish's. He could come and go at will, because one part of the screen hung loose, allowing him to leap through the open window onto the porch, or back into the bedroom. But Ducky was not as content as Trish and I were, because he was waiting for the fall to come, which meant pheasant-shooting, every morning before school. Hunting with Ducky was a lot of fun but hunting meant goodbye to summer, and the change was drastic; because now it was still dark when I rose to go to the pheasant farm, and the dreadful school year had begun, and, on top of that, before the end of the year Trish and I would learn through bureaucratic family channels that she was being moved across the hall to share a room with an older sister, and my younger brother would be moving in with me.

I would in due course instruct him, age nine, about the secrets of the fireflies.

THE PATIO AT GREAT ELM, 1938

Life at Great Elm II

My father had strict ideas about musical pedagogy, for which I and (most of) my siblings were ultimately grateful. ⟶

W*hen in 1933 my father brought* his household back to Great Elm after three years in France and England, the youngest of his nine children was less than a year old, the oldest, fourteen. The time had come, my father decided, for us to "learn music," as he put it.

Before the summer was finished, the regimen had been institutionalized. On Tuesdays and Fridays, Mr. Pelaez came to us from Poughkeepsie. The voluble and lighthearted Spanish-American, about forty years old, was a professional violinist, I suspect of the hotel-high-tea school. But, for reasons never explained, none of us was burdened with studying the violin with Mr. Pelaez, which of course meant that no one had the derivative burden of having to listen to any of us playing the violin. Mr. Pelaez taught many other instruments and, in pursuit of no musical schematic that comes easily to mind, we found ourselves divided into mandolin players (two), banjo players (two), guitar players (two), and ukulele players (one) (my six-year-old sister). We were taught individually, and then made to perform jointly. Mostly we played traditional American songs ("Were you *there* in the Red River Vall-eee...") and Mexican folk songs ("Ay, ay, ay aaaay. Canta yyy no llorrres"), because my father, who had lived many years in Mexico, simply loved Mexican folk songs. We were as a matter of course regularly entered in the local amateur-hour competitions, which were everywhere during the thirties in the little country towns of New England. We gave ourselves the name "The Cannot Be Better Orchestra," an evaluation not regularly sustained by the judges, some of whom gave higher marks to the dancing sequences of our neighbors, Jayne Meadows and her sister Audrey—in those days Jane and Audrey Cotter—and to a twelve-year-old violinist from nearby Amenia, New York, a dirty little sneak who, we discovered after it was too late, was a protégé of Nathan Milstein.

My father was a retiring man who, however, saw no reason why his children needed to be retiring, and I remember even now the mortification with which, during a Christmas holiday in Grindelwald in Switzerland, we learned that Father had volunteered the services of the Cannot Be Better Orchestra (he never knew we had so named it, and if he had learned of it, he'd have quite simply forbidden it) to the management of the Palace Hotel for a little concert at teatime. There were moments when we Hated Father, who was the most admirable man I ever knew.

But teaching us the piano was his major strategic offensive on the musical front, and to that end he engaged the services of a tiny, shy, pretty, witty, endearing young woman, herself a concert-level jazz pianist, a composer, an organist, and perhaps the most captivating creature I have known in my lifetime.

Marjorie Otis (we called her, still do, Old Lady, although she was only twenty-four when she first came to us) would arrive in her convertible Dodge from Tivoli, New York—where she lived with her parents when not studying in New York City—on Monday mornings, between eleven and twelve. She would leave forty-eight hours later. In between, she would have given six of us a forty-five-minute lesson on Monday, Tuesday, and Wednesday. The

WITH OLD LADY, 1937

contract was that we should also practice forty-five minutes every Monday, Tuesday, Wednesday, Thursday, Friday, Saturday, and Sunday, except for the Fourth of July, Thanksgiving, Christmas, and our birthday, when we were excused.

Now, as anyone knows who has ever wrestled with young piano students, there are ways & ways of spending forty-five minutes practicing the piano, and it requires inventive monitoring to see to it that the slothful student does not spend his time playing and replaying easy lush passages (say, the languid early measures of the Minuet in G) over and over, neglecting his scales, his Czerny, and the tough new piece he is supposed to be working on. I remember vividly, as who would not, spending an entire half hour replaying the soft passages of the second movement of the Pathétique Sonata when I heard a rustling of the Spanish shawl that covered the little grand I was whacking away at. Out came Old Lady, who, in the exercise of what the Securities and Exchange Commission calls "due diligence," had ensconced herself under my piano, out of sight, before my practice hour, precisely to catch me in flagrante. There was steel in that woman, and the middle-aged inarticulateness of her former students when at the piano is entirely the result of their lack of talent and/or application, rather than of her lack of diligence during those years in Sharon before Pearl Harbor, and the ensuing diaspora. Two or three of us were so much in love with her that we resolved at one point to become concert pianists, more or less in her honor. And indeed my sister Patricia played the Grieg concerto at the Ethel Walker School, and a Beethoven sonata at Vassar, before highly appreciative audiences, and I, at age fifty-six, played "Twinkle, Twinkle, Little Star" (Twelve Variations. Mozart.) before twelve hundred drunken friends one summer day.

꙳

But the absolute no-nonsense figure in our musical training was called Penelope Oyen. She was a tall Scandinavian of austere features (no makeup), and she divided with a forty-year-old bachelor the duties of tutoring five Buckleys and three friends who came to Great Elm to learn along with us, in a curriculum that covered approximately grades one through eight.

Miss Oyen loved music with passion. The use of that word here is not platitudinous. Because Penelope Oyen would *weep* when listening to music. Not always; not for every composer; but almost always for J. S. Bach.

The drill was four times a week. At four o'clock we came in from afternoon recreation and entered The Playroom, as we inaccurately continued out of habit to call the room over which Miss Oyen now had dominion. My father had bought a huge phonograph, a Capehart, which, if memory serves, was the first instrument that boasted that it could handle records consecutively. This it did, not by the simple device of dropping a fresh record on the one just finished, but by actually taking the record, when finished, and convolutedly lifting it up, turning it around, and either placing its backside on the turntable, or replacing it with the next record, a quite remarkable feat of engineering executed at the cost of a broken record every two or three days; expensive fractures which, however, had as an uncharted social benefit the interruption of Miss Oyen's lacrimations.

The absolutely decisive feature of Miss Oyen's discipline was very simple: darkness in the room. Not total darkness, else we'd have ended up playing Sardines. Too much light, and we'd have managed to read—anything, anything to avoid just...sitting there, listening to what I suppose in those days we'd have called "that darned music." There was simply *no escaping it*. We just sat there, while the Capehart blared away, and the ordeal lasted *one whole hour*.

And, of course...*it* happened. I'd say it took, depending on the individual child's latent inclinations, between four and eight months. My oldest brother, John (RIP), was ejected from our tutorial system in the fifth month to go to boarding school, and the result was that he never ever got around to enjoying beautiful music. I am willing to bet that if he had stayed with Miss Oyen another two months, he'd have become an addict, which is what happened to the rest of us.

When I think back on my musical education, I tune in on two landmarks. The first was when I came gradually, inexplicitly, to the conclusion (at, oh, age eleven) that the *Scheherazade*, which had enthralled me a year earlier, was, really, a most awful bore. That is the equivalent of discovering, usually four or five years later, the same thing about much of the poetry of poor Longfellow.

The other experience was unusual. By age thirteen I too was away at boarding school, and my letters went out in equal volume to my mother, and to Old Lady. I was studying the piano at school, one lesson per week, three practice sessions (there were two pianos, eighty boys), to which I looked forward hungrily. My piano teacher offered to teach me the first movement of the Moonlight Sonata. But I told him that though nothing would delight me more, I would need the permission of my teacher back home, because she had early on warned us that playing the Moonlight before one was ready to play it was, well—wrong. If we had been older, she would probably have used the word "blasphemous." I didn't quite understand her point in those days, but my loyalty was complete; so I wrote, from the bowels of that remote little school, asking for permission to study the Moonlight.

Permission denied.

In a sweet, loving letter, Old Lady tried to explain that music was very serious business, if one wished to be good at music, good at understanding music. No one, she said, who didn't have the technical ability to play the third (difficult) movement of the Moonlight should undertake the first movement. And anyway, technique quite apart, to play the first movement of that sonata required…a certain maturity. Her phrases were kindly composed. I didn't fully understand them. But I believed her when she said that music is very serious business. As poetry is very serious business. As art of any sort is very, very serious business: that which is sublime can't be anything less. My debt to Old Lady is eternal. To her, and to dear, strange Miss Oyen; and, above all, to my father.

St. John's, Beaumont

*I strongly resisted being sent away to a British boarding school, but once
there, in the months before the world war broke out, I ruefully report, I
had only happy experiences.* ⟿

It *was during the summer of 1938* that we were given the
dreadful news. I forget at whose hands it came. Probably from
Mademoiselle—she was the authority in residence at Great Elm,
given that my mother, my father, and my three oldest siblings
were traveling in Europe. That left six children, ranging in age
from fifteen (Jim) to five (Maureen), to romp happily through the
summer at Great Elm. We were superintended by Mademoiselle
and by three Mexican nurses; fed and looked after by a cook, a
butler, and two maids; trained and entertained in equestrian sport
by a groom and an assistant; and given our music lessons by Old
Lady and Mr. Pelaez.

It might have been Mademoiselle who told us what Father had
decided, or it might have been Miss Hembdt, Father's secretary,
who lived in Yorktown Heights. Miss Hembdt regularly relayed to
us bulletins from Father—excerpts of letters he would mail her,
mostly to do with his business affairs but now and then including
something directed to one or more of his absent children, supple-
menting what we would learn from letters received from Mother
or from one of our siblings traveling with them. These notes, which

AT GREAT ELM, 1940: STANDING (LEFT TO RIGHT):
JIM, FATHER, JOHN; SEATED: TRISH, ALOÏSE, PRISCILLA, ME,
CAROL, MOTHER, JANE; SEATED ON GROUND: MAUREEN, REID

came with our monthly allowances, would usually be directives touching on this or that subject, or references to a book Father had just read that we should know about, or read ourselves. . . . That dreadful day in August the directive, however transmitted, was as horrifying an edict, my two afflicted sisters and I agreed, as had ever been sent to three healthy and happy children from their father. The directive was to the effect that the next school year we would pass in boarding schools near London, the girls at St. Mary's in Ascot, I at St. John's, Beaumont, in Old Windsor.

The news fractured the arcadian spirit of our summer. We had got used to quite another routine, where summer vacations merged almost seamlessly into a return to school, and where academics required no radical departures from our way of life and none at all from our surroundings, because we were taught by tutors right there in the same rooms in which we played when indoors during the summer. When school began for us at the end of September, we continued to ride on horseback every afternoon, we swam two or three times every day until the water got too cold, our musical tutors continued to come to us just as they had done during the summer, and some of us would rise early and hunt pheasants at our farm before school; our classes began at 8:30 and ended at noon, and there would be study hall and music appreciation between 4:00 and 6:00. Though we sorely regretted the summers' end, at our ages—Jane had turned fourteen that summer, Trish was eleven— the schooling we got was as tolerable as schoolwork could be. Now, suddenly, we were to go to boarding schools in England.

Why?

We fled to Aunt Priscilla, Father's sister. She lived with another maiden sister in a house nearby, commuting back to Austin, Texas, each fall. We went to her: *Why? Why? Why?* Aunt Priscilla was infinitely affectionate, sublimely humorous, but absolutely self-disciplined. After hearing us out, she agreed to write to Father in

Europe to put our case before him: What really was the point in going to England to school? We had all already *been* to England to school, only five years ago—it was there that Trish and I had first learned English. Jane, Trish, and I had gone to Catholic day schools in London, the oldest four to boarding schools. The two girls had gone to that same St. Mary's, Ascot, where now Jane and Trish would go.

ॐ

They hadn't liked St. Mary's, hadn't liked it one bit. Aloïse, the oldest, was fourteen, and possibly the most spirited girl the dear nuns at St. Mary's had ever come across, with her singular, provocative independence. They had got on at Ascot because by nature Aloïse and Priscilla (eleven) were irrepressible. But they had never pretended to like their school. John (thirteen) and Jim (ten) had gone to the Oratory Preparatory School in Reading. John had kept a diary at the school and was manifestly amused by his foreign experiences, which he depicted in words and drawings. But the entire family had been shocked and infuriated to learn that not once but t-w-i-c-e our brother Jim had been—caned! Called into the headmaster's study and told to bend over. The first time, he had received one "swipe." The second time, two swipes. Not quite the stuff of *Nicholas Nickleby*'s Dotheboys Hall, but news of the punishment was received as such in the family corridors, and the rumor spread about the nursery in our house in London that Father and Mother even considered withdrawing the boys. It did not come to that, but Jim was for at least a year after the event regarded by his brothers and sisters as a mutilated object. He, being sunny by nature and serenely preoccupied with his interest in flora and fauna, actually hadn't thought very much about the episode. For the rest of us, it was the mark of Cain, disfiguring our year of English schooling.

And now we were headed back for more of the same kind of thing? We needed to know—Why? Surely Aunt Priscilla would set things right.

The Word came, about two weeks later. A letter from Father. Aunt Priscilla didn't read it to us, but she explained that Father "and your mother"—this was a blatant invention, we knew; it would never have occurred to Mother to impose any such ordeal on us—believed it would be a very fine educational experience for us. "Besides"—Aunt Priscilla winked—"as you know, your father has complained that five years have gone by since he understood '*a single word*'"—Aunt Priscilla did a light imitation of Father, elongating a word or phrase to give it emphasis—"uttered by any one of his children." In England we would learn to *open our mouths* when we spoke. We moaned our dismay at one of Father's *typical* exaggerations. It is true that Father was a nut on elocution, and true that his nine children, on returning from four years in Europe, had quickly adapted to lazy vocalisms which Father, then fifty, had a progressively more difficult time deciphering in the din of the three-tiered dining room, the main table for the older children and the adults, the middle table for those roughly six to nine, the third little table for the incumbent baby(ies).

We felt certain that his objective wasn't merely to put us into Catholic schools. Such a thing, in our household, would have been supererogatory. Mother was a daily communicant. Father's faith was not extrovert, but if you happened on him just before he left his bedroom in the morning you would find him on his knees, praying. Our oldest brothers and sisters, here in the States, were not at Catholic schools. So we ruled that out as one of Father's objectives.

We dimly understood that Father had always stressed the value of cosmopolitan experience. Bilingual, he had gone to Mexico City to practice law after graduating from the University of Texas, intending to raise his family in Mexico. But he had been exiled in 1921, pronounced by the president of Mexico an *extran-jero pernicioso*—a pernicious foreigner. And indeed he was, having backed a revolution against President Obregón that, among other things, sought to restore religious freedom to Mexican Catholics. And so, pursuing business concerns, he moved the family to France, then on to Switzerland and England. It was in Paris that I first went to school, speaking only Spanish. Was Father simply seeking out further exposure to another culture?

It was much, much later, after the war, that we learned the hidden reason Father thought it prudent to have three of his children of sensitive age away from home. It was why Aunt Priscilla hadn't read to us the explanatory letter she had received from him: Mother had become pregnant again, against her doctor's advice. It was not known if she would survive the birth of her eleventh child (one baby had died at birth, ten years earlier). At the time, we knew only enough to be vaguely apprehensive about Mother. We did not know how dangerous the doctors thought the birth, due in November, could be.

But whatever speculation we engaged in, however horrified we were at the very thought of the ordeal ahead, there was never any doubt, in my father's house, what his children would be doing at any given time, i.e., what Father said we would be doing at that time. So that, on September 18, 1938, after an indulgent twenty-four hours in New York City shepherded about by our beloved young piano teacher to movies, a concert, and Horn & Hardart Automats, we—Mademoiselle, Jane, Trish, and I—boarded the SS *Europa*.

꩜

There was much political tension. We couldn't fail to note it immediately on landing in Southampton. British sentiment was divided between those who favored standing up to Hitler, who had just occupied the Sudetenland in Czechoslovakia, and those who opposed any move that might threaten war. Prime Minister Neville Chamberlain was scheduled to return the next day from his meeting with Adolf Hitler in Munich. Before boarding the train for London we were fitted out with gas masks.

In London we were greeted with Mother's distinctive affection and Father's firm embraces. Little was said, that I can remember, about where we would be taken the next day, but Father did tell me that he had found Fr. Sharkey, the headmaster of St. John's, a "fine" person, and Jane and Trish were told that the Mother Superior at Ascot was someone other than the Mother Superior so disliked by our older sisters five years earlier.

Mother drove in one car with Jane and Trish and their bags to Ascot, Father and I in another car to St. John's.

It was late on a cold English afternoon. Father instructed the driver to detour to the landing field, and we saw Neville Chamberlain descend from the airplane that had flown him from Munich to announce that he had brought "peace in our time." A half hour later, we turned into the long driveway that took us to the pillared

(LEFT TO RIGHT): MADEMOISELLE, ME, JANE, AND TRISH

entrance to the school, the whole of it contained in one large square brick three-story building.

We were taken by a maid to a primly decorated salon. Fr. Sharkey, short, stubby, his hair gray-white, came in, took my hand, and chatted with Father for a few minutes about the international situation. Tearfully, I bade goodbye to my father and was led up with my two bags to a cubicle, halfway along a line of identical cubicles on either side of a long hallway that held about thirty of them. To enter you needed to slide open a white curtain that hung down from a rod going across the cubicle's width, about eight feet up from the floor. The cubicles had no ceiling of their own—looking straight up, you saw the ceiling of the large room, perhaps ten feet up. On either side was a white wooden partition. To the right, a dresser—two or three drawers and a hanging locker. To the left, your bed. A small table stood near the bed, and on it I quickly placed pictures of my family. On the window ledge, which I could reach only by standing on my bed, I placed one end of a huge Old Glory I had bought that last day in New York, holding it down with two weights I contrived from something or another so that the United States flag could hang down behind my bed, all five feet of it. The dormitory master, Fr. Ferguson, knocked on the wooden partition, drew the curtain to one side, introduced himself and told me he would lead me to the refectory, as it was time for supper.

The dining hall was crowded with the eighty boys who boarded at St. John's. The youngest were aged nine, the oldest, fourteen. After supper, we went to the study hall. I was three weeks late in arriving for the fall term and without any homework to do, pending my introduction the next day to my form master.

I don't remember how I passed the two hours. In due course we were summoned to evening prayers. We knelt along two of the quadrangular corridors in the building, a priest at the corner, boys at a right angle to his right, and to his left. He led us in prayers, to which we gave the responses. Fr. Sharkey then materialized, and the boys filed by him. He shook hands with each of us and said good night. When it was my turn, he said, "Good night, Billy. You are very welcome at St. John's." We walked up the staircase to our cubicles and were given fifteen minutes before Lights Out. Just before the light was switched off, the dormitory master read the psalm (#129) "De Profundis," to which we gave the responses in Latin. These were thumbtacked behind one of the dresser doors. The first two verses exactly echoed my thoughts. "Out of the depths have I cried unto thee, O Lord. Lord, hear my voice: Let thine ears be attentive to the voice of my supplications."

☞

I don't remember very much about the period of acclimation. I do remember the quite awful homesickness (I had never before spent a night away from my family). It lasted about ten evenings, during which, pressing the collar of my pyjamas against my mouth so that I would not be heard by my neighbors, I wept.

I think I remember praying for war, confident that if war came, Father would take us home. Mother had warned us that we would be homesick. She added that this would go away after a while, and that until then we should offer up our pain to God in return for any private intentions. In a closed conference, back in London, Jane and Trish and I had decided we would offer up our forthcoming torment for the safe and happy birth of Mother's baby in November.

The routine was extremely severe, up against what I had been used to. Rising hour in the morning always came as a wrenchingly disagreeable surprise. I remember twenty years later reading C. S. Lewis's *Surprised by Joy*, in which he told that in thinking about his early schooldays in England he remembered primarily how tired he always was. I assume Mr. Lewis had a special problem because once awake I was all right, but getting up at 7:00 A.M. was for me then— for some reason—more difficult than rising, six years later, at 5:30 A.M. in the infantry, or, a few years after that, at 4:00 A.M. to do watch duty racing my sailboat. Once or twice every month the school Matron, as she was called, would ordain that this boy or that should have a "late sleep," which meant he would sleep an extra forty-five minutes, rejoining his classmates at breakfast, after Mass. In those preconciliar days Catholics could not take Communion unless they had fasted since midnight. For that reason alone, breakfast could not have preceded Mass.

The pews were stacked along the sides of the chapel. Twenty boys sat and knelt in the top right pew, looking down on the heads of twenty boys a foot beneath them. Then, across the narrow aisle, to the faces of twenty boys on the lower level, and another twenty above them. To view the altar one needed to turn one's head. There was no sermon, except a brief one on Sundays. The Mass lasted about twenty-five minutes. School announcements were given in the refectory.

I have always been impatient, and so it was I suppose surprising that I came so quickly to feel at ease with the daily Mass, becoming progressively more engrossed in the words and the ritual. We were studying second-year Latin and I was dreadful at it, incapable of understanding why the Romans hadn't simply settled for Spanish. But I paid increasing attention to the Ordinary of the Mass, which is to say that part of it that doesn't change from Sunday to Sunday. It was easy to follow—the right-hand column of the missal carried the English translation. The liturgy took hold of me, and I suppose that this means nothing more than that liturgy has theatrical properties. Yes, but something more, I reasonably supposed, and suppose so now. Thirty years later I would write a scorching denunciation of the changes authorized by Vatican II and of the heartbreakingly awful English translations that accompanied the jettisoning of the Latin. The Mass, in Latin, had got to me.

I had of course attended Mass every Sunday for as long as I could remember and thought myself something of a pro in the business inasmuch as I had been trained, in Sharon, to do duty as an altar boy. I had very nearly become a godfather a couple of years earlier—I remember the thrill, followed by the humiliation. Our devout black butler, Ben Whittaker (he was a first cousin of Fats Waller), became a special friend of mine at Great Elm. After his wife gave birth to quadruplets, he told me excitedly that he wished me to serve as godfather. It transpired that I could not act as godfather, not having yet been confirmed. The honor fell to my older brother John, though by the time the formal event took place, only one of poor Ben's poor babies was still alive.

It was then that I was told about emergency baptisms, extemporaneously given to anyone in danger of dying. I had once improvised on this privilege. Mother had a friend who visited often at Great Elm, sometimes bringing along her two daughters, one in her late twenties, the other a few years older. On overhearing a conversation between Mother and Mademoiselle, I learned that the two ladies had never been baptized. I thought this shocking and talked the matter over with Trish. We devised our strategy, and knocked at their guest-room door early one morning, after establishing that they had both been brought breakfast in bed, on trays. I knocked and told them that Trish and I were looking for my dog. They welcomed us in to search the room. I knelt down to see if he was under the first bed and, a drop of water on my forefinger, touched it on Arlie's forehead as if reaching to maintain my balance, silently inducting her into the Christian Communion, while Trish, emerging from under the other bed in search of the dog, did as much for her older sister.

My mother was solemnly attentive when I whispered to her the happy consummation of our Christian evangelism. She did not betray her amusement: that was a part of her magic as a mother. She would never permit herself anything that might suggest belittlement—whatever her child's fancy. And then, too, she was as devoted a child of God as I have ever known, and perhaps she permitted herself to believe that her friend's two grown-up daughters, neither one of them at death's door, had in fact been baptized. When, in England, I found myself going to Mass every day and offering every Mass for the health of my mother, I felt a closeness to her that helped diminish the pain of separation.

In those days I remember a special reverence for Our Lady, to whom I appealed as a mother herself. I hadn't the capacity (even now I am not comfortable with the abstraction) to imagine infinity. I accepted it as a gospel truth that the Mother of God was "infinitely" wonderful, which meant to me that she was many times more wonderful than my own mother, but this hypothesis I had difficulty with: How was it possible to be many times more wonderful than my mother? I never asked any of the priests for help with that one. After all, I reasoned, they did not know Mother, so they might find the question surprising, impudent even. I knew that would not be the case if they *had* known Mother. But Our Lady became in my mind an indispensable character in the heavenly cloister. A long time after that I learned that a thing called Mariolatry had been especially contemned by noisy iconoclasts like Charles Kingsley. My first instincts were not combative, but sad. That someone so much like my mother should be disdained was incomprehensible.

&

No doubt my religious ardor was stimulated by the circumstances we lived in. St. John's was run by Jesuit priests. They were, as members of the Society of Jesus tend to be, thoroughly educated. It required thirteen years to become a member of the Jesuit order, and the training was exacting, the regimen spare. Fr. Manning was our form master. At every other school I would ever encounter, a fresh master moves in at the end of the hour, to teach the class his specialty. Fr. Manning did not teach us French, for which purpose St. John's brought in a layman, whose accent I would ostentatiously mock, my own being so superior, as anyone's would be who learned

French at age four in Paris. But excepting French, Fr. Manning taught every subject in "Figures IIA"—the equivalent, roughly, of first-year junior high. Geography, History, Maths, Latin, Doctrine. Each of the six school years at St. John's (grades three to eight) had a single form master. Two of these were preordination Jesuits, climbing up the long ladder to priesthood, serving now, so to speak, as field instructors at a boys' boarding school. They were addressed as "Mr.," but they met with the priests at faculty conferences, which were conducted in Latin, and I often wondered when did they sleep, since they were always up and around before we rose, and never appeared ready to retire when our lights went out.

I remember once being handed a corrected paper by Fr. Manning in his study. I leaned over to grasp it and accidentally overturned his can of pipe tobacco. I heard the slightest whinny of alarm, and then the majestic Fr. Manning was on his hands and knees, picking up each tobacco grain, one after another, and replacing them in the can. "That is my month's allowance, Billy. I cannot afford to let any go unsmoked!" I thought this extraordinary—that this . . . seer should have less than all the tobacco he wanted.

On those rare afternoons when we did not do school sports, we would be taken for long walks in that historic countryside. We were within a few hundred yards of Runnymede, where King John had signed the Magna Carta. Striding alongside Fr. Paine, a tall, angular priest, about thirty-five years old, I'd guess—he was the administrative coordinator at the school and also its disciplinarian—I asked about Fr. Manning's tobacco. Fr. Paine told me that Jesuits took a vow of poverty and that therefore they were given a monthly allowance, which had to suffice for all their needs. I asked whether it would be permitted for a friend to give tobacco to a Jesuit priest and he said no, this was only permitted in the case of food, when it was in short supply. (After the war, for several years, meat was very scarce, and my father sent meat every month to the fathers.) Ten years later, at Trish's wedding, the Jesuit priest who officiated, a lifelong friend of the groom, told my father not to make the mistake of offering him a stipend in return for his services, "because under Jesuit rules, we cannot turn down a donation, which in any event goes to the order, not to the priest to whom it is offered." Fr. Paine told me that Jesuit priests needed to guard against the sin of pride, because Jesuits were in fact very proud of the Jesuit order and very happy in it. One inevitably wonders whether that pride is quite whole after the strains of the 1960s.

Fr. Paine would regularly check individual cubicles at night and say good night to each of the boys. When November came, I confided to him that my mother was soon to bear a child, and that I was anxiously awaiting a telegram confirming that the baby had come and that my mother was well. He leaned over and embraced me warmly. He did so again extemporaneously after the baby came, and once finally seven months later when my father wrote to say that because of the lowering clouds of war, my sisters and I would be withdrawn from our schools after the spring term.

Fr. Paine's warmth did not affect what I judged the extreme severity of the punishment I was twice sentenced to, for whatever social infraction. The first time it was a single ferule stroke, smacked down on my open hand; the second, two strokes, one on each hand, the cumulative experience with corporal punishment in my lifetime, if you leave out an unsuccessful fistfight with the strongest and biggest boy at St. John's, a rite of passage for any newboy challenger (his name was Burns—I forget his first name, though first names were universally used among the boys). Many years later, when as a magazine editor I contracted for the services of Erik von Kuehnelt-Leddihn as European correspondent, I learned from him that while I was a student at St. John's, he was teaching the senior boys down the hill at Beaumont College. He told me that on learning, soon after arriving from Austria, that the ferule was the regular instrument of discipline, he had gone to the priest-executioner and demanded to receive six strokes, the conventional ration for grave infractions, exactly as they were inflicted on student miscreants. He was reassured that, at his age, with adult, callused hands, he would hardly feel any smart. But he persisted, and after receiving the blows reported clinically that far from negligible, six ferule strokes, even for a husky Austrian in his twenties, was a singularly painful experience. I heard that for extreme acts of misbehavior the birch rod was used on the buttocks, but I never knew any boy who received this punishment at St. John's. Fr. Paine and I exchanged a half-dozen letters in the ensuing forty years, and we spoke once in London over the telephone in the 1970s. He was retired and had difficulty breathing. He told me among other things that the young rowdies in London who were disturbing the peace should be given a good beating.

When Lent came we were given a retreat by the brother of Fr. Sharkey, also a Jesuit. He was short, like his older brother, and like him radiated a singular charm on this thirteen-year-old. (I had had a birthday soon after my sister Carol was born, and Father had redeemed his promise to make me her godfather.) I thought back to this retreat twenty years later when I went to Washington with my brother-in-law for a retreat conducted by the president emeritus of Fordham University, Jesuit Fr. Robert Gannon, whose short, electrifying sermons I begged him to put on tape, eliciting an assurance that one day he would certainly do this (RIP, he never did). They were cognate skills, Fr. Sharkey's and Fr. Gannon's: their sermons were dramatic, but never melodramatic; persuasive, poignant, inspiriting.

I recall only a single parable, if that is the right word for it, from that retreat at St. John's, six months before the world war. I put it in an essay I wrote on my boat during a transatlantic sail. *Esquire* had asked me to write about where, that I had never been, I would

most wish to visit. I wrote, on that sunny, breezy day in mid-
Atlantic, that I would most like to visit Heaven because it was
there I would be made most happy. I gave Fr. Sharkey's exegesis:
He had been approached some weeks earlier, he told us, by a
devout elderly woman who asked him whether dogs would be
admitted into Heaven. No, he had replied, there was no scriptural
authority for animals getting into heaven. "In that case," the lady
had said to him, "I can never be happy in Heaven. I can only be
happy if Brownie is also there."

"I told her"—Fr. Sharkey spoke with mesmerizing authority—
"that if that were the case, that she could not be happy without
Brownie, why then Brownie would in fact go to Heaven. Because
what is absolutely certain is that, in Heaven, you will be happy."
That answer, I am sure, sophisticated readers of *Esquire* dismissed,
however indulgently, as jesuitical. Yes. But I have never found the
fault in the syllogism.

My sisters at nearby Ascot were in regular contact by mail.
Trish, with whom I had been paired since infancy, wrote me twice
every week, always—always—closing, "I hope you are well and that
I will see you soon." We did in fact see each other every week.
Father had rented an apartment (50 Portland Place, I still recall)
where Mademoiselle would stay, looked after by James Cole, a New
Orleans–born black cook-butler, a man of enormous spirit, a
devout Catholic, who normally looked after Father in New York.
Mademoiselle, driven by a chauffeur—his name was McCormack—
would come to see us every Saturday afternoon, beginning after
the two-week embargo against visiting new boys and girls. My sisters would be picked up at Ascot and driven to pick me up at St.
John's, where I could be found sitting, waiting, at the end of the
long driveway. We would all go off to Windsor, which, of course, is
where Windsor Castle and Eton College are located. I remember,
breathless with pride and pleasure, recounting to my sisters a tale
I had just been told. In 1855, five years after the founding of Beau-

mont, the headmaster had issued a challenge to the headmaster of Eton to a soccer match, and got back a note, "What *is* Beaumont?"—to which the fabled answer had been, "Beaumont is what Eton used to be, a school for Catholic gentlemen." We would eat and talk and laugh and then—sadly—go back to our schools in time for supper. We were allowed, if I remember, two hours away.

೩~

The principal extracurricular enthusiasm in my childhood having been horses, I wrote to my father as we neared the great day in March at Aintree. He and Mother had come to London in January, bringing the baby and her immediately older sister and brother and their nurse. Maureen and Reid were about the same ages Trish and I had been when we had gone to day school in London in 1932 attending the same schools they now attended. I asked my father if I might be taken to the Grand National. Camden, South Carolina, our winter home, is the steeplechase center of the region, and I would hear nothing during the first two weeks in March, from horse owners and their grooms, but talk about who would win the Grand National, in which one or more Camden thoroughbreds regularly competed. Father wrote back that I would need the permission of Fr. Sharkey. I sought it. He said, No, such exceptions to school rules could not be made. I wrote back to my father with the sad news. He then wrote a letter to Fr. Sharkey, a copy of which he sent me. Dire signs were visible on the horizon, my father wrote, and if I did not get to see the Grand National now, I might never have the opportunity again. Would Fr. Sharkey, under the circumstances, bend the rule to permit an American boy this experience?

I was summoned to his study. He had changed his mind, he said. I might go to the steeplechase.

Three days later Father's chauffeur drove up. Fr. Sharkey led me to the car and stopped me just as I was about to enter it. He reached into his pocket and withdrew a florin, a two-shilling piece.

He leaned over and whispered to me, "Billy, put this on a horse called Workman, to win."

I was driven to 50 Portland Place, where my father and his close friend George Montgomery got into the car, and together we went to the station at Euston and got into a private compartment.

I spent the three hours poring over the tabloid coverage of the thirty-six horses that would compete, carefully apportioning the ten shillings my father had given me among the horses I thought likeliest to prevail. I was startled, on reaching Aintree, by the appearance of the famous track—it seemed as though all of Liverpool squatted on the infield. It was impossible to see the horses after the first turn. They would reappear, after a minute or two, on the left turn. I was in a frenzy of excitement. Finally, they were off.

Of the thirty-six horses that competed, six finished. On none of them had I bet. The winner was Workman. He paid 18–1.

And I had neglected to place Fr. Sharkey's bet.

I didn't dare tell my father about this…egregious, unspeakable delinquency. It passed through my mind to "borrow" the thirty-six forfeited shillings from him, but I was too ashamed. I was preternaturally silent on the train ride back, and altogether silent in the car with McCormack on the hour's drive to St. John's. It was nearly midnight when we reached the door. Fr. Sharkey opened it, exultant over the news he had got on the radio about the horse that won the Grand National.

"Father," I said, looking down on the stone steps, "I forgot. I didn't place your bet."

His dismay was acute. Then, suddenly, he smiled. "Those things happen. Now get to bed."

I fell quickly to sleep, but not before praying that God would forgive me, that God would find a devious means of transmitting thirty-six shillings to Fr. Sharkey, that God would suspend the vow of poverty for long enough to permit Fr. Sharkey full and indulgent use of those thirty-six shillings. But I awoke the next morning in panic, fearing the obloquy of my schoolmates, already jealous of the privilege I had been given.

The scandal was stillborn, aborted by Fr. Sharkey. All that I heard the next day was from Fr. Manning, who wished to know what it had been like at Aintree, and had I been told that Fr. Sharkey had picked the winner? Yes, I said—just that, "Yes." We had a secret, Fr. Sharkey and I, and I wondered whether, by his confessional vows, he was bound to silence about my sin.

&

When my boy, Christopher, was ten I took him to see St. John's. I had no intention of sending him there, but I was curious about what we would now call his chemical reaction. My father was wonderful with children (up until they were adolescents; at which point with his own children he took to addressing us primarily by mail, until we were safe again at eighteen). He loved especially about them that they were incapable of deception. "You can always tell," he said to me one day in his wheelchair, after a stroke, his grandson on his lap, "whether they really like something or whether they don't." Perhaps my son, who was much taken by what he saw, was reflecting my own radiations. I had been, notwithstanding my distance from home, very happy at St. John's, and I knew absolutely—about this there simply was no doubt—that I had developed a deep and permanent involvement in Catholic Christianity. They say about alcoholics that they are never "cured." I am a senior citizen and my faith has never left me, and I must suppose that Fr. Sharkey and Fr. Paine and Fr. Manning had something to do with it. They, and the closeness I felt, every morning, to the mystical things that were taking place at the altar.

The "Distinguished" Mr. Buckley

Two decades after I took my son to see my old school, I found myself introducing him at a political affair (at the East Side Conservative Club in Manhattan) as an established author. ⟋

*L*adies and gentlemen:

I am very happy to be here again in the company of the most distinguished conservative club in the United States, unless there's a more distinguished one I haven't heard of, which is unthinkable. Which reminds me of a story told me by my late mentor, Professor Willmoore Kendall of Yale. A humble priest, calculating that the mortgage on his church would be paid up at the end of the month, called on his rather pompous bishop to ask whether he would speak at the mortgage-burning ceremony on the first Sunday of the following month. The bishop replied with a heavy sigh of self-pity that he would appear, provided the priest could not succeed in finding somebody "less distinguished" than the bishop to appear instead.

Well, the priest searched high and low, but finally was forced to redeem the bishop's pledge, and His Grace reluctantly appeared. In introducing him to the parish, the priest apologetically stuttered out the story and then said, "And so, ladies and gentlemen, having failed to find *anyone* less distinguished, I present to you our bishop."

THOMAS A. BOLAN

THE AUTHOR OF THE WHITE HOUSE MESS

The Lord specializes in humbling the proud. As a father, last spring I was ecstatic to learn that on the following Sunday, my son would visit with me on the bestseller list of the *New York Times Book Review*, where I keep a little apartment in which I reside for a few weeks every year.

The following week, looking down at the *New York Times Book Review* list, I saw my son's name—but my own was no longer there. I had been ousted. By my own flesh and blood. I knew how King Lear felt. I marched over to Dan Mahoney [the retiring Conservative Party chairman, and my own lawyer] and said, You know that will I made out a few years ago? Well, I want to make it over. Every time you see the name Christopher Buckley, substitute the name Serph Maltese [the incoming Conservative Party chairman].

But then I thought: The Lord can be wonderfully playful. I have no doubt what happened. The guardian angel of the *New York Times*, whose delinquencies we are all most awfully familiar with, was neglecting his duties one afternoon, as usual, and he picked up a copy of *The White House Mess*. He roared with laughter— uncontrollable laughter—and he pushed the button on his desk and said, "Put the author of *The White House Mess* on the *New York Times* bestseller list."

An intimidated voice came back, "But sir, there is already a Buckley on the list."

The guardian angel said, "Remove that Buckley. The one I'm talking about is more distinguished."

Well, this time, the guardian angel of the *New York Times*—just this one time—did the right thing. You will get a specimen of *The White House Mess* from my distinguished son, Christopher, here introduced by his proud father.

Wine in the Blood

My father liked to collect wine, and in doing so, had an adventure. ⁓

A t age forty, my father had never *(he said* so, and he never lied*)* tasted an alcoholic drink. But that year his doctor, after fishing around with whatever doctors fish around with to examine the heart, recommended that he drink red wine every day. It became an affair of the heart.

He tended to take on his enterprises in a big way. I have an early memory of my father doing a single thing with his own hands (he was inept at manual pursuits). He was in the large wine cellar he had had built during the twenties at Great Elm, engaged, with the help of my mother and one or two assistants, in the painstaking job of pouring wine from the barrels he had bought in France into appropriate bottles, which they then carefully labeled. I remember that it was a very protracted project, lasting several evenings. In those days serious purchasers brought their wine in barrels to America and let it rest for five or six years before decanting it. But that has changed—I suppose, as a result of cork technology. In any event, my memory of it is that by the end of the thirties Father was buying his wine already bottled, wherein lay a tale that greatly amused his children during the war years.

The last batch he had purchased was in 1939, and when the shippers were about ready to dispatch it, a world war got in the way. But though freight was suspended during the war, the mails were not suspended, and every year or so the wine broker would write from Lyons reporting that my father's wine was still securely stored at a repository in the countryside, safe from bombs bursting in air and other wartime distractions. But then in 1943 a terrible letter came—the Nazis had discovered the hidden wine in the château and consumed it! My father was stoical about these things, but he was, not unexpectedly, saddened at the loss of thousands of bottles of lovely Bordeaux and Burgundies.

The second letter on the subject was a happy surprise. By that time the German soldiers had fled, and the merchant learned that they had *not* discovered the wine, which rested contentedly in its storing place. That was good news, but sadly overtaken by the next letter, sometime soon after the Normandy landing in 1944. The American invading force had chased out the Germans—but, *en cherchant partout*, they had come upon the wine and, presumably toasting to the Allied cause, had consumed it. Well, nothing too good for our GIs was my father's philosophical position, though I knew he wished the GIs had realized what delicate wines they had got so uproariously drunk on only because they had run out of beer and bourbon.

A year later, after the German surrender, the wine broker's jubilant letter came: In fact, the GIs had drunk an entirely different lot of wine! My father's was after all secure, and would be shipped in a matter of weeks; which indeed it was.

A few years after that, for insurance purposes, my father brought in a French oenologist to assess his cellar. The Frenchman, whose English was insecure, spent a half hour surveying the wines, taking notes. After he was done he came up to my father's study and said solemnly, "Your wine is valueless."

"Oh?" my father said. "I have thought it very fine wine."

"That's what I said," the expert replied. "*Valueless!*" It was with some relief that it dawned on us what a Frenchman can do in search of the English word "priceless."

Father was devoted to his ten children, and he desired very much that he should have no estate left for the government to tax, to which end he distributed every year as much as he could of his assets. He did this with so much success that when, the year before he died, he instructed his secretary to make the usual arrangements to take him to Bad Gastein late in the summer, where he went to escape a debilitating hay fever, he was informed that he could not afford to travel to Austria with his wife and entourage (he had had a stroke and needed a practical nurse) because he had no money. He found this hilarious, and so did his ten children. Forswearing the opportunity to act like the dreadful daughters of King Lear, we provided for him. When after his death his will was probated, we each received a check for forty-four dollars. There could never have been such posthumous content as the size of those checks must have given my father.

The jolt came when, a few months after that, a revenue agent appeared. He wanted to look at the deceased's wine cellar. My father had absentmindedly forgotten to list it as an asset, or to give it away to his children.

But our consolation was prolonged. Year after year, for over twenty years, whenever we gathered at Great Elm, we would be served the wines Father had accumulated, those lovely things that had slept peacefully, gaining flavor and enhancing their power to delight, through a world war and several occupations. It is a wonderful way to remember one's benefactors, isn't it? To drink wine in their memory?

Wine: One Man's Happy Experiences

As a junior wine collector, I had my own adventures, recorded in this piece written in 1985. —○

My *father's approach to wine* collecting was quite simple and direct: he would order the best wines (of contemporary vintage) that could be bought. He used them in moderation, and his cellar, when he died, contained about 7,500 bottles—great Bordeaux, and Burgundies, and Sauternes, and Loires, a few Spanish wines, nothing from California (my father died in 1958, before which I don't remember that California grew potable wines).

Last Thanksgiving, twenty-six years after his death, we drank the last of his wine. The family rule was that Father's wines would be reserved for joint consumption. They were too valuable, too special, for routine use by any of the sons or daughters or in-laws who, in the absence of the interdict, would have needed only the energy sufficient to walk a few steps to the wine cellar.

So...we developed our own cellars.

This required a certain reorientation. Before long, we had dissipated not only most of his cellar, but also much of his patrimony, so that the question for us was, How do you find a drinkable wine that doesn't cost too much money?

The question has been addressed universally, and every third wine column one reads highlights that season's buys. But recommendations by others, we all know, while worth pursuing, are not worth betting on, for so simple a reason as that palates differ, and in the last analysis one does not care if the other nine people in the room like a particular wine: if *you* do not like it, you do not want to stock it. On the other hand, if you have enjoyed wine of different kinds frequently with someone else and your evaluations nicely correspond, year after year, then you have made not only a friend, but a wine clone. My friend Jack Heinz and I, having jointly appreciated the same wines on a hundred different occasions, made a pact in the early seventies that we would limit our purchasing to white wines we could get for three dollars a bottle, red wines for four dollars a bottle. Those who have feasted at Jack Heinz's table will believe that if this story is true, Heinz has mastered not only the art of making ketchup, but also the art of alchemy. No. He has a cellar of vintage wines he raids for special occasions. We are talking about house-wine drinking.

Well, here are the rules I have decocted from the experience, and I give them out while acknowledging that they cannot be put into universal practice. Books on how to ski are not particularly useful to those living in the tropics. But here goes:

The first rule is to make a connection with a genial vintner. Mine is a gentleman called Bill Sokolin of New York City, whose enthusiasm for wine is the animating enthusiasm of his life. I remember the description of one of the characters in Randall Jarrell's *Pictures from an Institution*. Jarrell wrote of Professor Daudier, a man of letters. "There were two things he was crazy about, the thirteenth century and Greek; if the thirteenth century had spoken Greek I believe it would have killed him not to have been alive in it." So one might say that it would positively have killed Bill Sokolin if he had been born, say, in Saudi Arabia. I suspect both his hands and both

B. BOROUGHS COMPANY   176 MADISON AVENUE
                                                        NEW YORK CITY 10016
                      RETAILERS / IMPORTERS
                       WINES AND SPIRITS

                                          Oct. 19, 1971

15	1970	BEYCHEVELLE	@ 49.	$ 735.
20	1970	BRANE CANTENAC	39.	780.
20	1970	CALON SEGUR	44.	880.
20	1970	DUCRU BEAUCAILLOU	55.	1100.
20	1970	LA LAGUNE	42.	840.
20	1970	LEOVILLE POYFERRE	42.	840.
20	1970	LYNCH BAGES	43.	860.
15	1970	LEOVILLE LASCASES	45.	675
20	1970	TROPLONG MONDOT	30.	600.
20	1964	BORGNEUF	39.	780.
20	1966	LIVRAN	14.	580.
20	1966	LEOVILLE LASCASES	@ 50.	1000.
(20)	1966	BRANE CANTENAC	45.	900.
(20)	1966	CLOS L'EGLISE	43.	860.
(20)	1966	DUCRU BEAUCAILLOU	49.	980.
(20)	1966	LEOVILLE POYFERRE	49.	980.
(20)	1966	PETRUS	220.	4400.
(13)	1966	DE SALES	36.	468
(20)	1966	FIGEAC	48.	960.
(20)		MIRASSOU CABERNET	@ 40.	800
(10)		MEURSAULT PERRIERES 69 (JOS. DROUHIN)	72.	720.
40		SOLEIL BLANC '69 (DROUHIN)	29.	1160.
(5)		MONTAGNY (LOUIS LATOUR)	40.	200.

his feet would have been amputated by the time he was sixteen, because Bill Sokolin cannot be kept from wine tasting.

When I first knew him, back in the sixties, he recommended to me that I make a serious "investment" in a wine cellar. (When vintners want you to buy a lot of wine, they will use the word "investment.") I talked myself into thinking that what I would do is buy twice as much wine as I was likely to use in twenty years. Keep it for ten years, then sell one-half of it for enough to pay for the cost of the whole. That way, I explained cheerfully to my siblings and others who would listen, I would in fact be drinking wine free for the rest of my life.

Well, of course, funny-money schemes don't work in any medium. When, after ten years, I found that indeed the dollar value of my wine had doubled, there arose the question: How could I sell it? The answer in Connecticut, where I and the wine live, is: You cannot sell it. Not a single bottle. Because if you do, you are acting as a wine merchant. And wine merchants need to be licensed as such. If you sell a bottle of wine without a license, the penalty is a fine plus the confiscation of *your entire cellar*! Accordingly, I was left with the excruciating fate of having more wine than I could drink, an oxymoron I have managed to adjust to.

So the wines I paid three and four dollars for were, fifteen or twenty years later, fine wines, some of them what my colleague William Rusher calls oh-my-God wines. Among them are some of the standbys, like Beychevelle, Brane-Cantenac, Ducru-Beaucaillou, Lynch-Bages, Troplong-Mondot, Léoville Poyferré, and Figeac. But Sokolin introduced me also to Château Livran, which until I tasted the Serradayres from Portugal I thought the best inexpensive red wine I had ever tasted. I learned from him about the Château Raspail, whose 1967 is a wine that widens the eyes of the most cosmopolitan gourmets. And some of the wines changed along the way. There was the Mirassou Cabernet from

California, which I very nearly returned on tasting it. But either I forgot about it or else I decided that since California harvested Reagan, I'd give it a second chance. Ten years later it was superb. The whites were less successful, but the Montagny was splendid, and the Soleil Blanc superb.

But the layaway private wine cellar does not answer the quotidian demands of lively social households in which a fair amount of entertaining goes on. And it is here one can hope to be useful with a simple hint. It is this: Never consent to taste wines that, should it happen that they meet the Heinz–Buckley formula (which has inflated [as of 1985] to ten dollars per bottle), you can't then go out and buy in quantity. Nothing is more frustrating than to find a good cheap wine and then discover that there are two and one half cases left of it in all of New York. I bought thirty cases of a Château Livran from Sokolin at under three dollars a bottle, and my guests have gasped with pleasure on tasting it.

White wines are harder to handle, and the H–B formula strains at the ten-dollar tether. On the whole, I begin by checking out the Portuguese inventory. The wines there are almost uniformly underpriced. Now, most of the whites deserve to be underpriced, but every once in a while you land one, as with the *vinhos frescos*, though the supply is irregular, and not copious. Then look at Italy. People tend to forget that Italy exports twice as much wine as France, and a good Italian wine tends to be cheaper than a good French wine, even with the dollar triumphant over the franc. White California wine is, or rather tends to be (there are always exceptions), out-of-sight expensive. Or out-of-sight awful. There is nothing more dismaying than to approach the bar at one of those large affairs, ask for a glass of white wine, and see that gallon jug of California Chablis tilted over a poor, defenseless glass, causing you to close your eyes and recall the white wine you had aboard the airplane that day, which was worse.

It would be a tempting profession, wine purchaser for an airline. The wisecrack that you need to begin with wines that travel well is shopworn. Never mind what travel does to them. You need to begin with wines that taste good. I have been served wines aboard fancy airlines that almost certainly cost a lot more than my budget wines, but which were affronts to the taste. It has got to be that someone is in charge of purchasing who simply does not know, or does not care. Or—I remember one wine, aboard an airline, that convinced me, on tasting it, that the man/woman/monster who had chosen it (a) hated wine and (b) hated people who drink wine. That purchaser must be very happy, as he reflects on all those wine drinkers he has succeeded in making unhappy at mealtime.

It is wonderfully comforting to reflect that the New Testament speaks other than invidiously of wine. There is always the sin of excess, and I comply with the biblical injunctions against greed by making it a hard-and-fast rule never to pay excessive prices for wine. Meanwhile, one has to acknowledge the pleasure and satisfaction it gives. And resolve to set aside just a few special bottles as a part of our patrimony. Our children should be helped to smile when they think back on us.

William Frank Buckley, 1881–1958

I wrote the obituary notice for National Review *about this remarkable man.* ⌒

The vital statistics are that he grew up *in Texas and as the old-est son undertook, upon the premature death of his father, to look after the health and welfare of his mother, and the education of his three brothers and two sisters. He did this, and supported himself at the University of Texas by teaching Spanish, which he had mastered while living as a boy on the frontier. He went to Mexico to practice law, and saw the revolution against the benevolent and autocratic Porfirio Díaz, and what followed in its wake—and learned, and never forgot, his distrust of revolutionary ideology.

There are not many alive who knew him then, but those who are remember keenly the intelligence, the wit, the largeheartedness, and—always—the high principle, which brought him a singular eminence in the community. That eminence the American government repeatedly acknowledged, as when three successive secretaries of state called on him for guidance; as when the Wilson administration offered him the civil governorship of Vera Cruz (he refused indignantly); as when he was called by the Senate Foreign Relations Committee as the premier American expert on the tangled affairs of

Mexico. And in 1921, the end of the line: exile from Mexico. At that he was lucky. For he had indeed materially aided a counterrevolutionary movement. The fact that the counterrevolutionaries were decent men, and those in power barbarians, does not alter the political reality, which is that it is a very dangerous business indeed to back an unsuccessful insurrection—and he knew it, and barely escaped with his skin.

He had married, and had had three children, and would have seven more, all of whom survive him. He launched a business in Venezuela, and his fortunes fluctuated. But as children we were never aware of his tribulations. We knew only that the world revolved about him, and that whether what we needed was a bicycle, or an excuse to stay away from school for a day, or the answer to an anguished account of a personal problem, he was there to fill the need, and when he thought the request exorbitant, or improper, he would, by a word, bring us gently to earth. He worshipped three earthly things: learning, beauty, and his family. He satisfied his lust for the first by reading widely, and by imposing on his lawless brood an unusual pedagogical regimen (recounted on pp. 11–16). The second impulse he gratified by a meticulous attention to every shrub, every stick of furniture that composed his two incomparable homes. The third he served by a constant, inexplicit tenderness to his wife and children, of which the many who witnessed it have not, they say, often seen the like.

In his anxiety for the well-being of his country his three passions fused. Here in America was the beauty, the abundance, that he revered; here in the political order was the fruit of centuries of learning; here his wife, and his ten children, and his thirty-one grandchildren would live, as long as he lived, and years after. So he encouraged us to stand by our country and our principles. To his encouragement, moral and material, *National Review* owes its birth and early life. It was only two weeks ago that, crippled and convalescent in Austria, he registered, in turn, joy, and indignation, and amusement, and sadness, as his wife read aloud to him from the latest issue of this chronicle of America's glories and misadventures.

My father died last week at seventy-seven, and we take leave of him in the pages of the journal which had become his principal enthusiasm. We pray God his spirited soul to keep.

Aloïse Steiner Buckley, 1895–1985

I also wrote my mother's obituary notice for National Review, *and then reworked it for use as the epilogue to my book* Nearer, My God, *which I dedicated to her.* ⌒

My mother worshipped God as intensely as the saint transfixed. And his companionship was to her as that of an old and very dear friend. Perhaps somewhere else one woman has walked through so many years charming so many people by her warmth and diffidence and humor and faith. If so, I wish I might have known her.

The great house where my mother brought us up in Connecticut still stands, condominiums now. But the call of the South, where she and my father were both born, was strong, and in the mid-thirties they restored an antebellum house in Camden, South Carolina, where we spent the winter months. There she was wonderfully content, making others happy by her vivacity, her delicate beauty, her habit of seeing the best in everyone, the humorous spark in her eye. She never lost a Southern innocence.

Her cosmopolitanism was unmistakably Made-in-America. She spoke fluent French and Spanish with unswerving inaccuracy. My father, who loved her more even than he loved to tease her, and whose knowledge of Spanish was flawless, once remarked that in forty years she had never placed a masculine article in front of a masculine noun, or a feminine article in front of a feminine noun; except on one occasion, when she accidentally stumbled on the correct sequence—whereupon she stopped (unheard of in her case, so unstoppably did she aggress against the language) and corrected herself by changing the article: the result being that she now spoke, in Spanish, of the latest encyclical of Pius XII, the Potato of Rome (*"Pio XII, la Papa de Roma"*). She would smile, and laugh compassionately, as though the joke had been at someone else's expense, and perhaps play a little with her pearls, just above the piece of lace she always wore in the V of the soft dresses that covered her diminutive frame.

Her anxiety to do the will of God was more than ritual. I wrote her once early in 1963. Much of our youth had been spent in South Carolina, and the cultural coordinates of our household were Southern. But the times required that we look Southern conventions like Jim Crow hard in the face, and so I asked her how she could reconcile Christian fraternity with the separation of the races, a convention as natural in the South for a hundred years after the Civil War as women's suffrage became natural in the twentieth century. She wrote, "My darling Bill: This is not an answer to your letter, for I cannot answer it too quickly. It came this morning, and, of course, I went as soon as possible to the Blessed Sacrament in our quiet beautiful little church here. And, dear Bill, I prayed *so* hard for humility and for wisdom and for guidance from the Holy Spirit. I know He will help me to answer your questions as He thinks they should be answered. I must pray longer before I do this."

There were rules she lived by, chief among them those she understood God to have specified. And although Father was the unchallenged source of authority at home, Mother was unchallengeably in charge of arrangements in a house crowded with ten children and as many tutors, servants, and assistants. By the end of the thirties her children ranged in age from one to twenty-one, and an inbuilt sense of appropriate parietal arrangements governed the

hour at which each of us should be back from wherever we were—
at the movies, at a dance, hearing Frank Sinatra sing in Pawling,
New York. The convention was inflexible. On returning, each of us
would push, on one of the house's intercoms, the button that said,
"ASB." The exchange, whether at ten, when she was still awake, or
at two, when she had been two hours asleep, was always the same.

"It's me, Mother."

"Good night, darling."

If—as hardly ever happened—it became truly late, and her mind
had not recorded the repatriation of all of us, she would rise and
walk to the room of the missing child. If the child was there, she
would return to sleep, and remonstrate the next day on the neglected intercom call. If not there, she would wait up, and demand
an explanation. I doubt she'd have noticed, half asleep, if the person on the other end of the line had been God Himself, her most
reliable friend, and lover.

☙

On my father's seventy-fifth birthday she raised her glass to say,
"Darling, here's to fifteen more years together, and then we'll both
go." But my father died two years later. Her grief was profound,
and she emerged from it through the solvent of prayer, her belief in
submission to a divine order, and her irrepressible delight in her
family and friends. Six years later her daughter Maureen died at
age thirty-one, and she struggled to fight her desolation, though
not with complete success. Her oldest daughter, Aloïse, died five
years after Maureen. And then, three months before her own
death, her son John. She was by then in a retirement home, totally
absentminded; she knew us all, but was vague about when last she
had seen us, or where, and was given to making references every
now and then to "Will" (her husband) and the trip they planned
next week to Paris, or Mexico. But when John died she sensed
what had happened, and instructed her nurse (she was endearingly

under the impression that she owned the establishment in which she had quarters) to drive her to the cemetery, and there, unknown to us until later that afternoon, she witnessed from inside her car, at the edge of an assembly of cars, her oldest son being lowered into the earth. He had been visiting her every day, often taking her to a local restaurant for lunch, and her grief was, by her standards, convulsive; but she did not break her rule—she never broke it—which was never, ever to complain; because, she explained, she could never repay God the favors He had done her, no matter what tribulations she might be made to suffer.

Ten years before Mother died, my wife and I arrived in Sharon from New York much later than we had expected. Mother had given up waiting for us, so we went directly to the guest room. There was a little slip of blue paper on the bedside lamp, another on the door to the bathroom, a third on the mirror. They were love notes, on her three-by-five notepaper. Little valentines of welcome, as though we were back from circling the globe. There was no sensation to match the timbre of her pleasure on hearing from you when you called her on the telephone, or the vibration of her embrace when she laid eyes on you. Some things truly are unique.

Five days before she died, one week having gone by without her having spoken—though she clutched the hands of her children and grandchildren as we came to visit, came to say goodbye—the nurse brought her from the bathroom to the armchair and (inflexible rule) put on her lipstick, and the touch of rouge, and the pearls. Suddenly, and for the first time since the terminal descent had begun a fortnight earlier, she reached out for her mirror. With effort she raised it in front of her, and then said, a teasing smile on her face as she turned to the nurse, "Isn't it amazing that anyone so old can be so beautiful?"

The answer was, Yes, it was amazing that anyone could be so beautiful.

CHAPTER TWO

YALE

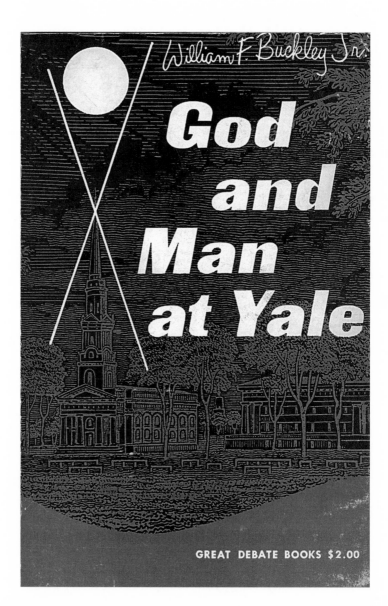

William F. Buckley Jr.

God
and
Man
at Yale

GREAT DEBATE BOOKS $2.00

God and Man at Yale

My first book, God and Man at Yale, *was widely read and rejected as something of an effrontery, or even as protofascist thought. When the publisher undertook to bring out a twenty-fifth-anniversary edition, he asked for a comprehensive introduction to the book, describing the circumstances that brought me to write it and the critical reception it was given. I spent time reviewing the heavy critical seas of 1951, which were rough, varied, and engulfing. But then literary devastation, or attempts at it, can be very readable, and here what they said, and how they said it, is preserved.*

To young inquisitive friends, I say: Don't bother to read the book, but do read the introduction. ⟿

I *was still familiar with the arguments* of *God and Man at Yale* when Henry Regnery, its original publisher, asked whether I would furnish a fresh introduction to a reissue of it. But I had not looked at the book itself since I had finally closed its covers, six months after its publication in the fall of 1951. It had caused a most fearful row and required me over a period of several months to spend considerable time rereading what I had written, sometimes to check what I remembered having said against a reviewer's rendition of it; sometimes to reassure myself on one or another point. The prospect of rereading it a quarter-century later, in order to write this introduction, was uninviting.

Granted, my reluctance was mostly for stylistic reasons. I was twenty-four when I began writing the book, freshly married, living in a suburb of New Haven, and teaching a course in beginning Spanish at Yale University. I had had help, notably from Frank Chodorov, the gentle, elderly anarchist, friend and disciple of Albert Jay Nock, pamphleteer, editor, founder of the Intercollegiate Society of Individualists, a fine essayist whose thought turned on a single spit: all the reasons why one should be distrustful of state activity, round and round, and round again. And help, also, from Willmoore Kendall, at that time a tenured associate professor of political science at Yale, on leave of absence in Washington, where he worked for an army think tank ("Every time I ask Yale for a leave of absence," he once remarked, "I find it insultingly cooperative").

Kendall had greatly influenced me as an undergraduate. He was a conservative, all right, but invariably he gave the impression that he was being a conservative because he was surrounded by liberals; that he'd have been a revolutionist if that had been required in order to be socially disruptive. Those were the days when the Hiss–Chambers case broke, when Senator McCarthy was first heard from, when the leaders of the Communist Party were prosecuted at Foley Square and sentenced to jail for violating the Smith Act. That conviction greatly incensed Kendall's colleagues, and a meeting of the faculty was called for the special purpose of discussing this outrage against civil liberties and framing appropriate articles of indignation. Kendall listened for two hours and then raised his hand to recite an exchange he had had that morning with the colored janitor who cleaned the fellows' suites at Pierson College.

"Is it true, professor"—Kendall, with his Oklahoma drawl, idiosyncratically Oxfordized while he studied as a Rhodes scholar in England, imitated the janitor—"Is it true, professor, dat dere's people in New York City who want to... destroy the guvamint of the United States?"

"Yes, Oliver, that is true," Willmoore had replied.

"Well, why don't we lock 'em up?"

That insight, Kendall informed his colleagues, reflected more political wisdom than he had heard from the entire faculty of Yale's political science department since the meeting began. Thus did Kendall make his way through Yale, endearing himself on all occasions.

Kendall was a genius of sorts, and his posthumous reputation continues to grow; but not very long after this book was published he proposed to Yale that the matter of their mutual incompatibility be settled by Yale's buying up his contract, which Yale elatedly agreed to do, paying over forty thousand dollars to relieve itself of his alien presence. Willmoore Kendall went over the manuscript of *God and Man at Yale* and, as a matter of fact, was responsible for the provocative arrangement of a pair of sentences that got me into more trouble than any others in the book. Since any collusion or suspected collusion in this book was deemed a form of high treason at Yale, I have always believed that the inhospitable treatment of Kendall (after all, there were other eccentrics at Yale who survived) may in part have been traceable to his suspected association with it and to his very public friendship with me (he became a founding senior editor of *National Review* while still at Yale).

You see, the rumors that the book was being written had got around. They caused considerable consternation at Woodbridge Hall, which is Yale's White House. Yale had a brand-new president, A. Whitney Griswold, and he had not yet acquired the savoir faire of high office (when the controversy raged, Dwight Macdonald commented that Yale's authorities "reacted with all the grace and agility of an elephant cornered by a mouse"—but more on that later). I remember, while doing the research, making an appointment with a professor of economics who privately deplored the hot collectivist turn taken by the economics faculty after the war.

At Yale—at least this was so when I was there—the relations between faculty and students (properly speaking I was no longer a student, having graduated in the spring) were wonderfully genial, though (again, this is how it was) there was no confusing who was the professor, who the student. I told him I was there to collect information about the left turn taken in the instruction of economics, and he reacted as a Soviet bureaucrat might have when questioned by a young KGB investigator on the putative hetero-doxy of Josef Stalin. He told me, maintaining civility by his fin-gernails, that he would simply not discuss the subject with me in any way. It was not so, however, in my research dealing with the treatment of religion at Yale, perhaps because I ambushed my Protestant friends. I asked the then president of Dwight Hall, the Protestant student organization, if he would bring together the chaplain and the half-dozen persons, staff and undergraduate, cen-trally concerned with religion to hear one afternoon my chapter on religion at Yale. Everyone came. I read them the chapter that appears in this book—save only the paragraph concerning Yale's chaplain, the Reverend Sidney Lovett. (I did not want to express even the tenderest criticism of him in Dwight Hall.) Three or four suggestions of a minor kind were made by members of the audi-ence, and these corrections I entered. I wish I had recorded the episode in the book, because a great deal was subsequently made of the alleged singularity of my criticisms and of the distinctive-ness of my position as a Roman Catholic. All that would have been difficult for the critics to say if they had known that the chapter had been read out verbatim to the half-dozen Protestant officials most intimately informed about the religious life of Yale, all of whom had acknowledged the validity of my findings, while disso-ciating themselves from my prescriptions.

I sent the completed manuscript to Henry Regnery in Chicago in April, and he instantly accepted it for publication. I had waited until then formally to apprise the president, Mr. Griswold, of the forthcoming event. We had crossed paths, never swords, several times while I was undergraduate chairman of the Yale *Daily News*. The conversation on the telephone was reserved, but not heated. He thanked me for the civility of a formal notification and told me that he knew I was at work on such a book, and that he respected my right to make my views known. I was grateful that he did not ask to see a copy of the manuscript, as I knew there would be eternal wrangling on this point or the other.

But a week or so later I had a telephone call from an elderly tycoon with a huge opinion of himself. William Rogers Coe is mentioned in the book. He advised me that he knew about the manuscript and had splendid tidings for me: namely, I could safely withdraw the book because he, Mr. Coe, had got the private assurance of President Griswold that great reforms at Yale were under way and that conservative principles were in the ascendancy, so why bother to publish a book that would merely stir things up? I gasped at the blend of naïveté and effrontery. But although I had observed the phenomenon, I was not yet as conversant as I would quickly become with the ease with which rich and vain men are manipulated by skillful educators. As a matter of fact, men who are not particularly rich or vain are pretty easy to manipulate also.

I did attempt in my correspondence with Mr. Coe to make one point that especially bears repeating. It is this: that a very recent graduate is not only supremely qualified, but uniquely qualified, to write about the ideological impact of an education he has experienced. I was asked recently whether I would "update" this book, to which the answer was very easy: This book cannot be updated, at least not by me. I could undertake this only if I were suddenly thirty years younger, slipped past the admissions committee of Yale University in a red wig, and enrolled in the courses that serve as ideological pressure points; if I listened to the conversation of students and faculty, participated in the debates, read the college paper every day, read the textbooks, heard the classroom inflections, and compared notes with other students in other courses. For years and years after this book came out I would receive letters from Yale alumni asking for an authoritative account of "how the situation at Yale is now." After about three or four years I wrote that I was incompetent to give such an account. I am as incompetent to judge Yale education today as most of the critics who reviewed this book were incompetent to correct me when I judged it twenty-five years ago. Only the man who makes the voyage can speak truly about it. I knew that most of my own classmates would disagree with me on any number of matters, most especially on my prescriptions. But at another level I'd have been surprised to find disagreement. Dwight Macdonald was among the few who spotted the point, though I don't think in his piece for *The Reporter* on the controversy he gave it quite the emphasis it deserved. But he did say, "Nor does Buckley claim any sizable following among the undergraduates. They have discussed his book intensively—and critically. Richard Coulson ('52) notes in the *Yale Alumni Magazine* that 'it is a greater topic of serious and casual conversation than any philosophical or educational question that has been debated in quite a few years.... In contrast to many of their elders the majority has not been blinded with surprise or carried away with rage at either Buckley or the Corporation by his claim that individualism, religion and capitalism are not being propounded strongly both in and out of the classroom. The undergraduate feels that this particular observation is correct.'"

Well then, why republish *God and Man at Yale* in 1977, if it tells the story of Yale in 1950? The question is fair. I suppose a sufficient reason for republishing it is that the publisher has experienced a demand for it. Not, obviously, from people who desire to know the current ideological complexion at Yale—they will have to probe for an answer to that question elsewhere—but from whoever it is who is curious to know how one student, a Christian conservative, experienced and reacted to a postwar education at Yale University, and wants to read the document that caused such a huge fuss; and those who are curious—the purpose of this introduction, I suppose—about what, a quarter-century later, the author might have to say (if anything) about his original contentions, and the reaction to them. I do have some thoughts about the arguments of this book (which I have reread with great embarrassment at the immaturity of my expression—I wish Messrs. Chodorov and Kendall had used more blue pencil) and about the sociology of the educational controversy. It is extremely interesting how people react to the telling of the truth. We all know that, but should not tire of learning even more about it. But the problems raised by *God and Man at Yale* are most definitely with us yet. Some of the predictions made in it have already been realized. Some of the questions are still open. Some of the arguments appear antiquarian; others fresh, even urgent.

First, something on the matter of definitions. Several critics, notably McGeorge Bundy (whose scathing article-length review in the *Atlantic Monthly* was adopted unofficially by Yale as its showcase defense), objected to the looseness of certain terms on which I relied. Throughout the book I used a term briefly fashionable after the war, commonplace a half-century before that, which however now has ebbed out of most polemical intercourse. It is "individualism." I have mentioned Chodorov's Intercollegiate Society of Individualists. Well, about ten years ago even that society changed its name (to the Intercollegiate Studies Institute). The term "individualism" was once used as the antonym of "collectivism." Today the preference is for more individuated terms.

We hear now about the private sector. About free-market solutions, or approaches. "Individualism" has moved toward its philosophical home—it always had a metaphysical usage. One would expect to hear the word nowadays from disciples of Ayn Rand, or Murray Rothbard; neo-Spenserians. In any case, if I were rewriting the book I would in most cases reject it in favor of a broader term (e.g., "conservative") or a narrower one (e.g., "monetarist"). Even so, though it is unfashionable, "individualism" is not, I think, misleading as it here appears.

Now, it was very widely alleged, in the course of criticizing the book's terminology, that the position of the authors of the economics texts cited was misrepresented. For instance, Frank Ashburn, reviewing *Gamay* (the publisher's useful abbreviation in office correspondence) in *Saturday Review*, wrote: "One economist took the trouble to extract quotations out of context from the same volumes Mr. Buckley used so freely, with the result that the texts seemed the last testaments of the robber barons." That statement puzzles me as much today as when I first read it. After all, on page forty-four I had written, "All of these textbook authors take some pains to assure the student that they have in mind the 'strengthening' of the free enterprise system. Not one of them, I am certain, would call himself a socialist or even a confirmed collectivist. Witness, for example, [Theodore] Morgan's eulogy [in *Income and Employment*]." I went on to quote Morgan:

> ...it is our general assumption that government should not do anything which individuals or voluntary associations can more efficiently do for themselves [p. 184]... succeeded very well in the Western World in raising tremendously the volume of production [p. 176].... Obviously, the American public does not want a nationalized economy or a totalitarian unity. We want to give up no segment of our area of freedom unless there is clear justification

[p. 177]....There are both economic and non-economic reasons for preserving a dominantly wide area of free enterprise [p. 193].

It is hard to understand how any critic, laboring the point that I had suppressed professions of allegiance to the free-enterprise system by the authors under scrutiny, could do so persuasively in the face of the plain language quoted above. The technique of associating oneself for institutional convenience with a general position but disparaging it wherever it is engaged in wars or skirmishes along its frontiers is as old as the wisecrack about the man and woman who got on so splendidly during their married life, having arrived at a covenant that she would settle minor disagreements, he major: "We have never had a major disagreement," the husband ruminates. In this textbook Mr. Morgan, having professed his devotion to the private sector, went on to call for means of "diminishing the inequality of income and wealth," later revealed as a tax of 75 to 99 percent on incomes over one hundred thousand dollars, the elimination of the exemption for capital gains, confiscatory taxes on inheritance "aimed at the goal of ending transmissions of hereditary fortunes," the nationalization of monopolies, the universalization of Social Security coverage, family allowances from the government, and a government guarantee of full employment. The preferences of this economist would even in 1977 be viewed as left of center. In 1950 they were very far to the left of anything the Democratic Party was calling for. To suggest, as Mr. Ashburn and others did, that there was distortion in representing Morgan et al. as "collectivist" is, simply, astonishing; but at another level it is consistent with the public perceptions. Frank Ashburn was a trustee of Yale when he wrote that review. Yale University was thought of (and still is, though to a lesser extent) as a "citadel of conservatism" (*Time* magazine's phrase). Therefore what emerges to the myth-preserver as principally relevant is not the left-salients in a book like Morgan's but the obeisances to orthodoxy. Very well. But who's misleading whom?

Now, other reviewers graduated their criticism from misrepresentation to misunderstanding. These would stress that economics is a scientific discipline; that Keynes (for instance) could no more be called a left-wing economist than Buckminster Fuller could be called a collectivist architect.

Philip Kurland, writing in the *Northwestern Law Review*, was emphatic on the point. He quotes with some relish a statement by the author of another book reviewed in *Gamay*, Professor Lorie Tarshis. "A word must be said, before we begin our analysis, about the political implications of the Keynesian theory. This is necessary because there is so much misinformation on the subject. The truth is simple. The Keynesian theory no more supports the New Deal stand or the Republican stand than do the newest data on atomic fission. This does not mean that the Keynesian theory cannot be used by supporters of either political party; for it can be, and if it is properly used, it should be. The theory of employment we are going to study is simply an attempt to account for variations in the level of employment in a capitalist economy. It is possible, as we shall see later, to frame either the Republican or the Democratic economic dogma in terms of the theory."

This point, variously stated, was not infrequently made by reviewers. But, in fact, by the end of the 1940s the analysis of John Maynard Keynes was the enthusiastic ideological engine of the New Economics. There is documented evidence that Keynes himself was unhappy about the lengths to which "Keynesians" were going, presumably under his scientific auspices. Kurland, via Tarshis, was telling us in 1951 that Keynes was all technician. As a matter of fact even that is in dispute. It is not disputed that Keynes formulated an analytical vocabulary for addressing certain kinds of economic problems, and the universalization of this vocabulary is as much a fait accompli as the universalization of Freud. But there is continuing dispute over what it is to be "a Keynesian." A long series was published in the sixties in *Encounter* magazine under the title "Are We All Keynesians Now?" One contributor to that series—to demonstrate the confusion—maintained that one could not properly qualify as a "Keynesian" unless one believed that the apparatus of the government should be used to maintain low interest rates. Others argued that Keynes had higher—indeed much higher—priorities. Richard Nixon, early in his second term, made the statement, "We are all Keynesians now." Even in 1973 that statement shocked the orthodox. For a Republican to have said such a thing in 1950 is inconceivable—as inconceivable, to quote Professor John Kenneth Galbraith, as to have said, "We are all Marxists now." Whatever a Keynesian was, at least he was the archenemy of the balanced budget, a trademark of conservative economic thought.

It is especially significant that anti-Keynesian analyses of some gravity had been published at the time the class of 1950 graduated from Yale University. These were both technical and political. But the work of Robbins, Mises, Hutt, Anderson, Roepke—to mention a few—was not called to the attention of students of economics at Yale. The operative assumption was that the business cycle was the result of an organic deficiency in the market system and that interventionism was the only cure. We know now that the factor of the money supply looms larger in causing contraction and expansion than anyone surmised at the time. The texts reviewed in *Gamay* were, I am saying, heavily ideological, and "Keynesian" was the correct idiomatic word to use to describe economists who inclined to interventionist solutions for economic problems and, while at it, social problems as well.

I do not mean to give the impression that critics were united in their disdain of my analysis of economic education at Yale. Max

Eastman, who had himself written books on socialist theory, was amusingly impatient, in his obstinate atheism, with the chapter on religion ("For my part, I fail to see why God can not take care of Himself at Yale, or even for that matter at Harvard. To me it is ridiculous to see little, two-legged fanatics running around the earth fighting and arguing in behalf of a Deity whom they profess to consider omnipotent"). But he was forthrightly enthusiastic about the economic section: "His second chapter, 'Individualism at Yale,' is by contrast entirely mature. And it is devastating." There were others, schooled in economics, who applauded the chapter, e.g., Felix Morley, Henry Hazlitt, John Davenport, Garet Garrett, and C. P. Ives.

Max Eastman's dichotomization brings up the heated reaction to a book that professes concurrently a concern over the ascendancy of religious skepticism and political statism. I spoke earlier about a pair of sentences that many critics found especially galling. When I saw the suggested formulation, written out in the margin of my manuscript in Willmoore Kendall's bold green script, I suspected they would cause difficulty. But there was a nice rhetorical resonance and an intrinsic, almost nonchalant suggestion of an exciting symbiosis, so I let pass: "I believe that the duel between Christianity and atheism is the most important in the world. I further believe that the struggle between individualism and collectivism is the same struggle reproduced on another level." The words "the same struggle reproduced on another level" were not originally my own. In my prolonged defense of the book I did not renounce them, in part out of loyalty to my mentor, in part, no doubt, because it would have proved embarrassing to disavow a formulation published over one's signature, never mind its provenance. But also in part because I was tickled by the audacity of the sally and not unamused by the sputtering outrage of its critics.

They were, no doubt, particularly spurred on to lambaste the suggested nexus by their knowledge of its popularity in certain Christian-conservative circles, my favorite of them being the American Council of Christian Laymen in Madison, Wisconsin, which quoted the two sentences in its publication and then sighed, "No Solomon or Confucius or other wise man of the ages ever spoke or wrote truer words than the sentences just quoted." It was the very first time I had been compared to Solomon or Confucius.

The widespread objection was not only on the point that to suggest an affinity between the eschatological prospects of heaven and hell and the correct role of the state in achieving full employment was something on the order of blasphemy. It was fueled by the ideological conviction of many Christian modernists that the road to Christianity on earth lies through the federal government. Although these criticisms flowed in copiously from Protestant quarters, they were on the whole most bitter in the fashionable Catholic journals; and indeed my being a Catholic itself became something of an issue. McGeorge Bundy, in his main-event review in *The Atlantic Monthly*, wrote directly on the point:

> Most remarkable of all, Mr. Buckley, who urges a return to what he considers to be Yale's true religious tradition, at no point says one word of the fact that he himself is an ardent Roman Catholic. In view of the pronounced and well-recognized difference between Protestant and Catholic views on education in America, and in view of Yale's Protestant history, it seems strange for any Roman Catholic to undertake to speak for the Yale religious tradition.... It is stranger still for Mr. Buckley to venture his prescription with no word or hint to show his special allegiance.

On this point Dwight Macdonald commented: "Buckley is indeed a Catholic, and an ardent one. But, oddly enough, this fact is irrelevant, since his book defines Christianity in Protestant terms, and his economics are Calvinist rather than Catholic. One of the wryest twists in the whole comedy is that the Catholic press has almost unanimously damned Buckley's economic views."

Macdonald exaggerated, but not entirely. "He quite unwittingly succeeds in contravening Catholic moral doctrine as applied to economics and politics on almost every topic he takes up," the Jesuits' *America* had editorialized, concluding, "Mr. Buckley's own social philosophy is almost as obnoxious to a well-instructed Catholic as the assaults on religion he rightly condemns." (Who is flirting with the nexus now?) *Commonweal*, the Catholic layman's journal of opinion, was right in there. "The nature of Mr. Buckley's heresies was pointed out again in the Catholic press, but apparently the young man remains unmoved. He continues to peddle his anti-papal economics without any noticeable changes, often under the auspices of Catholics." Father Higgins, the labor priest, objected heatedly to my "attempt to identify the heresy of economic individualism with Catholic or Christian doctrine."

I am obliged to concede at this distance that, the attacks from the Catholics quite apart, it is probably true that there was a pretty distinct anti-Catholic animus in some of the criticism of this book. The Reverend Henry Sloane Coffin, former head of the Union Theological Seminary, former chairman of the Educational Policy Committee of Yale, former trustee of the Yale Corporation, chairman of a committee commissioned by the Corporation to investigate my charges about Yale education without ever acknowledging them (see below), was so incautious as to write to an alumnus who had questioned Coffin about my book, "Mr. Buckley's book is really a misrepresentation and [is] distorted by his Roman Catholic point of view. Yale is a Puritan and Protestant institution by its heritage and he should have attended Fordham or some similar institution."

Now, there are three strands to the Catholic point. The first has to do with the allegedly distinctive Catholic definition of Chris-

tianity; the second with the allegedly distinctive Catholic understanding of the role of the university; and the third, most simply
stated, was ad hominem, i.e., an attempt to suggest that by "concealing" my Catholicism I told the discerning reader a great deal
about my deficient character and, derivatively, about the invalidity
of my criticisms and arguments. Taking the third point first, a
semantic advantage was instantly achieved by those who spoke of
my having "concealed" my Catholicism. By not advertising it—so
ran the planted axiom—I was concealing it. Inasmuch as, on writing the book, I saw nothing in the least distinctively Catholic
about the points I made, I had thought it irrelevant to advert to my
Catholicism. Even as I was criticized for "concealing" my Catholicism, I could have been criticized had I identified myself as a
Catholic on the grounds that I had "dragged" in my Catholicism as
if it were relevant. But see, for instance, Professor Fred Rodell (of
the Yale Law School) writing in *The Progressive*, probably (though
there are close runners-up—Arthur Schlesinger in the *New York
Post*, Vern Countryman in the *Yale Law Journal*, Herman Liebert in
the *St. Louis Post-Dispatch*, Theodore Greene in the Yale *Daily
News*, Frank Ashburn in *Saturday Review*) the most acidulous
review of the lot: "...most Catholics would resent both the un-
Christian arrogance of his presentation and, particularly, his deliberate concealment—throughout the entire foreword, text, and
appendices of a highly personalized book—of his very relevant
church affiliation." Ah, the sweet uses of rhetoric. "No mention" of
Catholicism elides to "concealment" of Catholicism elides to
"deliberate concealment" (a tautology, by the way). That my affiliation was "very relevant" spared Mr. Rodell the pains of having to
explain its relevance. By the same token, would it have been appropriate for a reviewer of a book by Fred Rodell on the Supreme
Court and freedom of religion to accuse the author of "deliberate
concealment" of the "very relevant" fact that his name used to be

Fred Rodelheim, and to allege that his interpretation of the freedom-of-religion clause was tainted in virtue of his lifetime's concealment of his having been born Jewish? That would have gone down—quite properly—as anti-Semitism.

If one pauses to think about it, it is difficult at once to be an "ardent" Catholic, as everyone kept saying I was, and to "conceal" one's Catholicism (unless one worships furiously and furtively). The only place in the book in which I might unobtrusively have said that I am a Catholic is on page 28, where I mention an Inter-Faith Conference held in the spring of 1949 sponsored by Dwight Hall (Protestant), St. Thomas More (Catholic), and the Hillel Foundation (Jewish). I was the Catholic cochairman of that conference, which is hardly the way to go about concealing one's affiliation. But even to have mentioned in this book that I had been cochairman would have been irrelevant, perhaps even vainglorious. Should I have mentioned that I was the son of a wealthy father, in order to explain a prejudice in favor of capitalism? With respect to the second point, I accepted as the operative definition of "Christianity" that of the World Council of Churches, supplemented by a definition by Reinhold Niebuhr—an organization and an individual never accused of being closet Catholics.

As to the remaining point—namely, the purpose of education—it is hard to know what the Reverend Henry Sloane Coffin had in mind when he suggested that I had a "distorted" understanding of Yale's "Puritan and Protestant" heritage that grew inevitably out of my Roman Catholicism; or McGeorge Bundy, when he referred to the well-recognized difference between Protestant and Catholic views on education in America. I am aware of no difference, celebrated or obscure, with reference to the purpose of a secular college. Yale was indeed founded as a Protestant institution, but the bearing of that datum on this book underscores rather than subverts its thesis. The man who was president of Yale while I was there said in his inaugural address, "I call on all members of the faculty, as members of a thinking body, freely to recognize the tremendous validity and power of the teachings of Christ in our life-and-death struggle against the force of selfish materialism." That wasn't Pope Pius IX talking. And, later, President Charles Seymour said, "Yale was dedicated to the training of spiritual leaders. We betray our trust if we fail to explore the various ways in which the youth who come to us may learn to appreciate spiritual values, whether by the example of our own lives or through the cogency of our philosophical arguments. The simple and direct way is through the maintenance and upbuilding of the Christian religion as a vital part of university life." Maybe Charles Seymour should have been made president of Fordham.

§

I have mentioned that the reaction to the publication of *Gamay* was quite startling. Louis Filler wrote in the *New England Quarterly*, "This book is a phenomenon of our time. It could hardly have been written ten years ago, at least for general circulation." He meant by that that (a) no one ten years earlier was particularly alarmed by, or interested in, ideological trends in higher education; and (b) that therefore nobody would have bothered to read a book that examined those themes, let alone one that focused on a single college.

So that the book's success as an attention-getter first surprised, then amazed. It was infuriating to the hostile critics that a man as eminent as John Chamberlain should have consented to write the introduction to it, and indeed Fred Rodell held him personally responsible for the notoriety of the book ("It was doubtless the fact of a John Chamberlain introduction that lent the book, from the start, the aura of importance and respectability"). But it was too late to ignore it. *Life* magazine did an editorial (cautious interest in the book's theme), *Time* and *Newsweek* ran news stories; *Saturday Review*, a triple review; and after a while there were reviews and news stories about the reviews and news stories. The critic Selden Rodman, although he disagreed with the book and its conclusions, had said of it in *Saturday Review*, "[Mr. Buckley] writes with a clarity, a sobriety, and an intellectual honesty that would be noteworthy if it came from a college president." (Compare Herman Liebert, from the staff of the Yale Library, writing for the *St. Louis Post-Dispatch*: "...the book is a series of fanatically emotional attacks on a few professors who dare to approach religion and politics objectively." Note that collectivist economics and agnostic philosophy suddenly became the "objective" approaches. That they were so considered at Yale was of course the gravamen of the book, which this critic, in his fustian, was witless to recognize.) Oh, yes, Fred Rodell: "I deem it irresponsible in a scholar like Selden Rodman to dignify the book as 'important' and 'thought-provoking.'" Max Eastman had written, in *The American Mercury*, "He names names, and quotes quotes, and conducts himself, in general, with a disrespect for his teachers that is charming and stimulating in a high degree.... This perhaps is the best feature of his book, certainly the most American in the old style—its arrant intellectual courage." (From the encephalophonic Mr. Rodell, his voice hoarse: "I deem it irresponsible, in a scholar like Max Eastman, to shower the book with adulatory adjectives.")

And so on, for months and months. Official Yale took no official position but was very busy at every level. The Yale *Daily News* ran analyses of the book by six professors, only one of whom (William Wimsatt) found anything remotely commendable about the book. The series was introduced by an editorial of which a specimen sentence was "When the Buckley book has succeeded in turning the stomachs of its readers and lining up Yale men categorically on the side of that great 'hoax' academic freedom, Bill Buckley will, as Professor Greene suggests, have performed a great service to Yale."

In the *Yale Alumni Magazine* the book was treated with caution, but I was offhandedly coupled with a notorious and wealthy old crank called George Gundelfinger, a gentleman who had gone off his rocker a generation earlier and periodically drowned the campus with nervous exhalations of his arcane philosophy, which heralded as the key to the full life a kind of platonic masturbation ("sublimate pumping," he called it). Copies of McGeorge Bundy's review were sent out to questioning alumni. Meanwhile, in the trustees' room, a plan had been devised to commission an inquiry by a committee of eight alumni into "the intellectual and spiritual welfare of the university, the students, and its faculty." The chairman, as mentioned, was Henry Sloane Coffin, and among its members was Irving Olds, then chairman of the board of United States Steel Corporation, thus effecting representation for God and man. The committee was surreptitiously set up during the summer, in anticipation of *Gamay's* appearance in the fall, but its clear function of unsaying what the book said was acknowledged even in the news stories.

Yale didn't have an easy time of it. Too many people knew instinctively that the central charges of the book were correct, whatever the inflections distinctive to Yale. Felix Morley, formerly president of Haverford College, had written in *Barron's*, "[Buckley's] arguments must be taken seriously. As he suggests, and as this reviewer from personal knowledge of scores of American colleges can confirm, the indictment is equally applicable to many of our privately endowed institutions of higher learning. Mr. Buckley, says John Chamberlain in the latter's foreword, is incontestably right about the educational drift of modern times." It is confirmation of Morley's generalization that, twenty-five years later, references to religion and politics that were then eyebrow-raising seem utterly bland—almost conservative, in a way. What is unthinkable in the current scene isn't that an economics teacher should come out for a 100 percent excess-profits tax, or that a teacher of sociology should mock religion. What is unthinkable today is an inaugural address by a president of a major university containing such passages as I have quoted from Charles Seymour.

So Yale had that problem—that most people suspected that heterodoxy was rampant—and an additional problem which it needed to handle most deftly (and, on the whole, did). I made the suggestion in this book that the alumni of Yale play a greater role in directing the course of Yale education: that they proceed to govern the University, through their representatives, even as the people govern the country through theirs. This suggestion had a most startling effect. Yale's challenge has always been to flatter its alumni while making certain they should continue impotent.

The purpose of a Yale education, never mind the strictures of *Gamay*, can hardly be to turn out a race of idiots. But one would have thought that was what Yale precisely engages in. Walking out of the Huntington Hotel in Pasadena during the hottest days of the controversy, I espied the Reverend Henry Sloane Coffin walking in. I introduced myself. He greeted me stiffly, and then said, as he resumed his way into the hotel, "Why do you want to turn Yale education over to a bunch of boobs?" Since Mr. Coffin had been chairman of the Educational Policy Committee of the Corporation, it struck me that if indeed the alumni were boobs he bore a considerable procreative responsibility. Certainly his contempt for Yale's demonstrated failure was far greater than my alarm at its potential failure.

He was not alone.

Bruce Barton, the anti–New Dealer at whose partial expense President Roosevelt had composed the rollicking taunt "Martin, Barton, and Fish," saw the need for reform. But by alumni? "As for Mr. Buckley's cure, letting the alumni dictate the teaching, what could be more terrifying? Are these noisy perennial sophomores, who dress up in silly costumes and get drunk at reunions, who spend their thousands of dollars buying halfbacks and quarterbacks, and following the Big Blue Team—are they to be the nation's mental mentors?" I really had had no idea the contempt in which alumni qua alumni were so generally held.

My notion, as elaborated in the book, was that alumni would concern themselves with the purpose of a university, that if mind and conscience led them to the conclusion, they would be not only free, but compelled, to decide that certain values should be encouraged, others discouraged; that, necessarily, this would give them, through their representatives, the right to judicious hiring and firing, precisely with the end in mind of furthering broad philosophical objectives and cultivating certain ideals, through the exposure of the undergraduate body to (in President Seymour's phrase) cogent philosophical arguments.

There are many grounds for disapproving the proposal of alumni control. But the description, by some critics, of the state of affairs I sought led me to question my own sanity, and then, finding it in good order, to question that of my critics. Consider the near-terminal pain of Frank Ashburn as he closed his long piece for *Saturday Review*: "The book is one which has the glow and appeal of a fiery cross on a hillside at night. There will undoubtedly be robed figures who gather to it, but the hoods will not be academic. They will cover the face."

Gee whiz. Now it is important to remember that Frank Ashburn is a very nice man. He is, moreover, quite intelligent. He founded a successful boys' preparatory school, Brooks School, and years later, in his capacity as headmaster, he invited me to address the student body, proffering the customary fee. And I did, arriving without my hood; and to the extent it is possible to do so under less than clinical conditions, I probed about a bit, and Frank Ashburn was to all appearances entirely normal. But that's the kind of thing *Gamay* did to people, especially people close to Yale. I did mention that Frank Ashburn was a trustee?

I must not let the point go, because one *has* to ask oneself *why* it is that any alumni supervision of the general direction of undergraduate instruction is so instinctively repugnant to nonjuveniles. I do not know whether Robert Hatch, who wrote for *The New Republic*, is a Yale graduate, but in terms of horror registered he might as well have been. He took pains, in his review, to try to explain what, in fact, I was really up to with my bizarre proposals. "It is astonishing," he wrote, "on the assumption that Buckley is well-meaning, that he has not realized that the methods he proposes for his alma mater are precisely those employed in Italy, Germany, and Russia. An elite shall establish the truth by ukase and no basic disagreement shall be tolerated."

It really wasn't all that astonishing that I did not spot the similarities in the methods I proposed and those of the Fascists, Nazis, and Communists, because there are no similarities. My book made it plain that alumni direction could be tolerated only over the educational institution of which they were uniquely the constituents; that alumni of institutions that sought different ends should be equally free to pursue them. Moreover, the ideals I sought to serve were those that no authoritarian society would regard as other than seditious—namely, the ideals of a minimalist state, and deference to a transcendent order.

But the notion that the proposals were subversive was jubilantly contagious. Four months after the publication of *Gamay*, Chad Walsh was writing in *Saturday Review*: "What Mr. Buckley really proposes is that the alumni of Yale should turn themselves into a politburo, and control the campus exactly as the Kremlin controls the intellectual life of Russia." "Exactly," as used here, can only be understood to mean "analogously." Obviously there are no "exact" parallels between a state directing all education and enforcing a political orthodoxy, and the constituencies of discrete educational institutions, within a free and pluralist society, directing the education of their own educational enterprises. Indeed, so obviously is it inexact to draw the parallel, the heretical thought suggests itself that conventional limitations on alumni are closer to the authoritarian model. A free association, within a free society, shaping an educational institution toward its own purpose, is practicing a freedom that totalitarian societies would never permit. An obvious example would be a German university under Hitler that prescribed that its faculty, in the relevant disciplines, should preach racial toleration and racial equality; or, in the Bolshevik model, a constituency backing a university that, athwart the political orthodoxy, insisted on preaching the ideals of freedom and pluralism.

I find it painful, at this remove, to make points so obvious. But if *Gamay* is to be republished, it must surely be in part for the purpose of allowing us to examine specimens, however wilted, of the political literature of yesteryear; and to wonder what was the madness that seized so many people of such considerable reputation; and to wonder further that such profound misinterpretations were not more widely disavowed. Were these people lefties?—shrewdly protecting their positions by theoretical incantations? Yes, one supposes, in some cases. But surely not in others: Frank Ashburn was an Establishment figure, in lockstep with the Zeitgeist, who probably shed a wistful tear or two in private over some of the departed virtues. Men like him are the enigma. The Left was of course especially scornful. When, fifteen years later, a number of our colleges and universities were given over to the thousand blooms of the youth revolution, which demanded that colleges be "relevant"—i.e., that they become arms depots for the anti–Vietnam War—many of the same people who had sharpened their teeth on *Gamay* were preternaturally silent.

They feasted on ideological reticulation. Michael Harrington was in those days a socialist and a Christian. He would in due course repeal the laws of progress by reaffirming the one faith and renouncing the second. He wrote his review for Dorothy Day's *Catholic Worker*: "The frightening thing is that Mr. Buckley is not yet realistic enough for fascism. Mr. Buckley's aims can only be secured by fascist methods—coercion in favor of capitalists—a realistic conclusion which Mr. Buckley's five years in New Haven did not educate him to make." Neither five years' education in New Haven nor twenty-five years' education outside New Haven. The case for capitalism is infinitely stronger in 1977 than in 1950, having profited in the interim from the empirical failures of socialism, as from the scholarly accreditation of the presumptions of the free market. Besides which, the word "fascism" loses its pungency when it is used to mean, pure and simple, the exercise of authority. Mr. Harrington, even then, was flirting with heresy, which would become his succubus.

Authority is licitly and illicitly acquired by the democratic canon; and, once acquired, is then licitly and illicitly exercised. The authority to apprehend, try, and punish a lawbreaker is licitly acquired in the democratic circumstances of a society that, after popular consultation, makes its own laws, prescribes its own judicial procedures, and stipulates its own punishments—all subject to the rule of law. The line between licit and illicit authority in a secular society is, however, elusive, though it is generally acknowledged in the Judeo-Christian world that there is such a line, most resonantly affirmed by Christ's distinction between Caesar and God. It is an unusual experience for a libertarian to be catechized by a socialist on the theme of the dangers of coercion. Harrington's oxymoronic formulation—"coercion in favor of capitalists"—reminds us of the fashionable jargon in the commodity markets of the Left (alas, not greatly changed). His sentence is on the order of

"coercive freedom," or "the slavery of the Bill of Rights." Unless a
"fascist method" can be distinguished from a plain old "method" by
which the will of the entrepreneurial unit prevails over the will of
the individual resolved subversively to gainsay that will, then par-
adoxically you are left without the freedom of the collectivity. The
interdiction of that modest freedom on the grand piano Mr. Harrington is used to playing on in his tireless crusade for state socialism is not only inconsistent, it is positively unseemly.

It is worth pursuing the matter yet one step further, I think, in
order to notice the review by T. M. Greene. Professor Greene was
a considerable character on the Yale campus. I think he was the
most quintessentially liberal man I ever came upon, outside the
pages of Randall Jarrell's *Pictures from an Institution.* As master of
the largest residential college at Yale (Silliman), he one day issued
an order, in the interest of decorum, requiring students who ate
dinner in the dining room to wear coats and ties. He was dismayed
by the trickle of criticism, and very soon indignantly repealed his
own order, apologizing for his lapse into dirigisme. He taught, as an
explicit Christian, a course in the philosophy of religion that was
widely attended; but I remarked in *Gamay* that in the opinion of
his students he was engaged, really, in teaching ethics, not religion.
(There's nothing against teaching ethics, but of course it isn't
exactly the same thing.)

His reaction to *Gamay,* as published in the Yale *Daily News,*
fairly took one's breath away. He fondled the word "fascist" as
though he had come up with a Dead Sea Scroll vouchsafing the key
word to the understanding of *God and Man at Yale.* In a few sentences he used the term thrice. "Mr. Buckley has done Yale a great
service," (how I would tire of this pedestrian rhetorical device)
"and he may well do the cause of liberal education in America an
even greater service, by stating the fascist alternative to liberalism.
This fascist thesis...This...pure fascism...What more could

Hitler, Mussolini, or Stalin ask for...?" (They asked for, and got, a great deal more.)

What survives, from such stuff as this, is ne plus ultra relativism, idiot nihilism. "What is required," Professor Greene wrote, "is more, not less tolerance—not the tolerance of indifference, but the tolerance of honest respect for divergent convictions and the determination of all that such divergent opinions be heard without administrative censorship. I try my best in the classroom to expound and defend my faith, when it is relevant, as honestly and persuasively as I can. But I can do so only because many of my colleagues are expounding and defending their contrasting faiths, or skepticisms, as openly and honestly as I am mine."

A professor of *philosophy*! Question: What is the (1) ethical, (2) philosophical, or (3) epistemological argument for requiring continued tolerance of ideas whose discrediting it is the purpose of education to effect? What ethical code (in the Bible? in Plato? Kant? Hume?) requires "honest respect" for *any* divergent conviction? Even John Stuart Mill did not ask more than that a question be not considered as closed so long as any one man adhered to an opposing view; he did not require that that man, flourishing the map of a flat world, be seated in a chair of science at Yale. And this is to say nothing about the flamboyant contrast between Professor Greene's call to toleration in all circumstances and the toleration he showed to the book he was reviewing. An honest respect by him for my divergent conviction would have been an arresting application at once of his theoretical and his charitable convictions.

The sleeper, in that issue of the Yale *Daily News*, was William Wimsatt. The late Professor Wimsatt, the renowned critic and teacher, was...a Catholic! Not an uppity Catholic. He was, simply, known by the cognoscenti to be one, and his friends found that charming. But under the circumstances, the pressure on Professor Wimsatt to yield to his colleagues must have been very nearly unbearable, and his conciliatory motions must be weighed charitably under the circumstances. He denounced *Gamay* as "impudent," inasmuch as its author "used the entree and confidential advantage of a student and alumnus to publicize so widely both embarrassing personalities and problems of policy which are internal to the relation between administrative officers and alumni." A so-so point, which, it happens, I dealt with in the book itself, in my discussion of the emasculating hold the Yale administration exercises over its alumni; but, in a sense, also a point gainsaid by the universal interest provoked by the book, which interest focused not at all on its gossip value involving any one or more professors (only three of the hundred reviews I have reread bother even to mention by name any individual professor named in the book).

Protected by such rhetorical cover, Professor Wimsatt went on to say some very interesting things. He began, for instance, by suavely blowing the whole Coffin–Bundy–Dwight Hall position about religion at Yale. "The prevailing secularism of the university is palpable," wrote Professor Wimsatt matter-of-factly. That's what *I* said. But lest that should shock, he added, What-else-is-new? "What else did Mr. Buckley expect when he elected to come here?" He went on to say, in effect, that a "modern" university cannot orient itself other than to fashion. "What would he expect of any modern American university large enough to be the representative of the culture in which he has lived all his life?" Mr. Wimsatt is here carefully avoiding the point. Obviously a modern, acquiescent college will tend not to buck the Zeitgeist. This begs the question whether under certain circumstances it might do so; and certainly begs the question whether idealistically active alumni are entitled to apply pressure on it to do so.

But, despite himself, Professor Wimsatt was getting hotter and hotter. "It is more fundamental to ask...what is actually right, and how far any individual may in good conscience tolerate or assist the teaching of what he firmly believes wrong. If I knew that a professor were teaching the Baconian heresy about Shakespeare, I should think it a pity. If I knew that a professor were preaching genocide, I should think it a duty, if I were able, to prevent him—even though his views were being adequately refuted in the next classroom." That buzz saw ran right through the analysis of Professor Greene, adjacent on the page, leaving it bobbing and weaving in death agony. But nobody noticed. "As Mr. Buckley so earnestly pleads, it is indeed very far from being a fact that the truth, in such matters of value, is bound 'to emerge victorious.' It would be easy to name several doctrines, not only genocide but the less violent forms of racism, for instance, or an ethics of pre-marital sexual experiment— which the present administration of no university in this country would tolerate." (From a questionnaire published in the 25th Reunion Yearbook of the Yale Class of 1950, Question #13: "Are you in favor of or opposed to: . . . People living together out of wedlock? Oppose, 42%. Favor, 43%.") Although Professor Wimsatt was hardly quotable as an endorser of *Gamay*, the passages here reproduced take you exactly as far as I go on every theoretical point. Everything else he said was in the nature of social shock absorption.

It is worth it, before making a final comment on the grander points involved, to climb out of the polemical fever swamps and look with a little detachment on the purely economic question. When I wrote this book, there were reviewers who defended the factual generalities, indeed went so far as to say the points I made were obvious. Yale's teachings were distinct from Yale's preach- ings—"this rudimentary fact of life," Dwight Macdonald com- mented, "Buckley is rude enough to dwell on for 240 pages." On the other hand, very few reviewers (certainly not Macdonald) were prepared to associate themselves with my prescriptions— though some of them acknowledged nervously that any way you looked at it there was a paradox in the circumstance of alumni agitatedly supporting the cultivation of values different from their own. I think it safe to say that no fully integrated member of the intellectual community associated himself with my position on academic freedom. In March of this year Irving Kristol, a professor, editor, author, and philosopher of unassailable academic and intellectual standing, included in a casual essay in his regular series for the *Wall Street Journal* (which space he shares with such other scholars as Robert Nisbet and Arthur Schlesinger Jr.) the comment "Business men or corporations do not have any obligation to give money to institutions whose views or attitudes they disapprove of. It's absurd to insist otherwise—yet this absurdity is consistently set forth in the name of 'academic freedom.'" The prose is an improvement on my own in *God and Man at Yale*, but the point is identical. Yet no one rose to say of Professor Kristol that he should be wearing a hood and that he was introducing fascism into American education. Indeed the educational establishment, although it rose to smite my book hip and thigh, has since then tended to find it more useful to take the advice of that class of prudent lawyers who counsel their clients to say "No comment." Even now I rub my eyes in amazement at the silence given to events—historical, sociological, and even judicial—that tend to confirm and reconfirm the factual claims of my book, and to give support to its theoretical arguments. There was, for instance, the A. P. Smith case of 1953 (*A. P. Smith Manufacturing Company* v. *Barlow*). I should like to be able to refer to it as the "celebrated A. P. Smith case." But it is not celebrated at all. It is unknown.

※

What happened was that a New Jersey manufacturer of valves and hydrants made a gift of fifteen hundred dollars to Princeton University, and a group of stockholders sued, saying in effect, What does Princeton University have to do with the fortunes of the A. P.

Smith Company? The case was tried and most vigorously defended, with star witnesses moving in and out of the witness stand. Not because of the fifteen hundred dollars, obviously, but because the precedent was deemed very important.

Well, Princeton and the management of the A. P. Smith Company won. Two courts, the Superior Court of New Jersey and the Supreme Court of that state on appeal, affirmed the corporate validity of the gift. Why then is the case not more greatly celebrated?

Because the price of victory was academic freedom as commonly understood. The A. P. Smith Company, in its defense brief, took the position that by giving money to Princeton it was advancing its corporate purposes strictly defined. The defense brief said, "The Smith Company turned to philanthropy not for the sake of philanthropy but for the sake of selling more valves and hydrants." *How's that again?*

But there was no recorded objection from representatives of Princeton University. Expert witnesses were called. One of them was: Irving Olds. Our old friend! Chairman of the board of United States Steel! Mr. Olds testified soberly on the stand that

> . . . our American institutions of higher learning can and do perform a service of tremendous importance to the corporations of this and other states, through acquainting their students with the facts about different economic theories and ideologies. With the good educational facilities provided by these institutions, the courses of instruction will and do lead the student body to recognize the virtues and achievements of our well-proven economic system; and, on the other hand, to discover the faults and weaknesses of an arbitrary, government-directed and -controlled system of production and distribution.

That testimony by Mr. Olds was given approximately on the first anniversary of the release of the report by the Yale committee investigating the charges leveled in *Gamay*, and Mr. Olds had then put his signature on a document that said, "A university does not take sides in the questions that are discussed in its halls. The business of a university is to educate, not to indoctrinate its students. In the ideal university all sides of any issue are presented as impartially and as forcefully as possible. This is Yale's policy." Now the only course in comparative economic systems being taught at Yale at that time is described in my book. The professor who taught it proclaimed himself an ardent socialist in the British tradition, and defended the socialist alternative to the free-market system, which alternative one would suppose is not the system that, in the understanding of A. P. Smith, the lower court, the higher court, and Irving Olds, promotes the "selling of more valves and hydrants."

The worst was yet to be. The lower-court judge, in authorizing the gift, wrote:

> It is the youth of today which also furnishes tomorrow's leaders in economics and in government, thereby erecting a strong breastwork against any onslaught from hostile forces which would change our way of life either in respect of private enterprise or democratic self-government. The proofs before me are abundant that Princeton emphasizes by precept and indoctrination [*precept and indoctrination!*] the principles which are very vital to the preservation of our democratic system of business and government.... I cannot conceive of any greater benefit to corporations in this country than to build, and continue to build, respect for and adherence to a system of free enterprise and democratic government, the serious impairment of either of which may well spell the destruction of all corporate enterprise.

I cannot think of a more excruciatingly embarrassing victory in Princeton's history.

Dumb judge? I invite you to find a denunciation of him by an official of Princeton University. The decision was appealed and went on to the Supreme Court of New Jersey, where another dumb judge affirmed the lower court's decision, and made it all worse. Because he reminded the "objecting stockholders" that they had "not disputed any of the foregoing testimony" asserting the service Princeton is performing in behalf of the free-market economy; and the court reminded them, paternalistically, that "more and more they [private corporations] have come to recognize that their salvation rests upon a sound economic and social environment which in turn rests in no insignificant part upon free and vigorous nongovernmental institutions of learning." Princeton didn't take its fifteen hundred dollars and go hang itself, but one can imagine the gloom in the paneled office where they all met to open that judicial valentine.

The educators were saying, in response to *Gamay*, that college is a cultural sanctuary from the commerce of life. That such concessions as periodically were made by university officials were purely rhetorical—President Seymour, at his inaugural ceremony, enjoining the faculty to cultivate the doctrines of Christ; Princeton deans, nodding their heads acquiescently when the court upholds a corporate gift on the grounds that Princeton is "by precept and indoctrination" committed to spreading the gospel of free enterprise. Actually, they were saying, no interference is possible. All ideas must start out equal. (All ideas *are* equal!) To make demands on a college is totalitarian, fascist, communist, condemned by all men of understanding, reaching back to Thomas Jefferson. How widely he was used during the controversy! "Subject opinion to coercion," Philip Kurland quoted him; "whom will you make your inquisitors? Fallible men; men governed by bad passions, by private as well as public reasons. And why subject it to coercion? To produce uniformity. But is uniformity of opinion desirable? No more than of face and stature...difference of opinion is advantageous." And, of course, who would disagree that men are fallible? But does that mean we can rely, at the margin, other than on men? On whom was Jefferson relying for remedies when in 1821 he wrote to General Breckinridge to complain of "seminaries [where] our sons [are] imbibing opinions and principles in discord with those of their own country"? Did Jefferson wish to do something about it? Or was he only describing a situation that could not be corrected, because men are fallible, dominated by passions? No. Jefferson continued, "This canker is eating on the vitals of our existence, and if not arrested at once, will be beyond remedy." If not arrested by whom? Surely not the state. We would all agree on this?

Not quite all. The state would prove to have its uses. President Seymour warned urgently and repeatedly against accepting federal aid to education on the grounds that it would bring federal interference. President Seymour retired in 1950. In the succeeding generation major private universities became totally dependent on federal funds. Remove the federal subsidy to Yale (35%), Harvard (25%), and MIT (65%), and what would happen to them? The notion of mere trustees influencing the choice of textbooks was—and is—thought scandalous: by the same people who, having called such interference fascism, backed, or were indifferent to, legislation which twenty-five years later would permit the attorney general of the United States (ironically, a former college president, in a Republican administration, executing laws passed by a Democratic Congress) to pry out of a thoroughly private association—the American Institute of Real Estate Appraisers—the promise to destroy a textbook called *The Appraisal of Real Estate*, in which appraisers are advised that the ethnic composition of a neighborhood in fact influences the value of its real estate. Under the proposed consent decree, the Institute agrees to strike from the present (sixth) edition of its textbook all the improper language. Specific textbook revisions have been prepared. These changes "will be included in the seventh edition of the text" not later than September 5, 1978. Sixty days after the decree is entered, the Institute "will commence a review of all booklets, manuals, monographs, guides, lexicons, and...other instructional material published under its auspices" to assure that they too conform with the text revisions. And they called fascistic a summons to free citizens freely associated, exercising no judicial or legislative power, to communicate their ideals at a private college through the appropriate selection of texts and teachers.

"Unless the great concepts which have been traditional to the western world are rooted in a reasoned view of the universe and man's place in it, and unless this reasoned view contains in its orbit a place for the spirit, man is left in our day with archaic weapons unsuited for the problems of the present." I don't know who wrote that sentence, which appeared in an editorial in the *Boston Pilot*, but I know I wish I had written it, because with great economy of expression it says, really, everything my book sought to say. It leaves unsaid only this: Is there a role for the nonacademician in formulating that "reasoned view"? Or if not that, in catalyzing that "reasoned view"? Or if not that, in providing favorable ground in which to cultivate that "reasoned view"? It is on this point that I declare myself, a generation after the event, on the side of the university with a mission.

In recent months I have been asked by representatives of Yale University to make a public declaration urging contributions to the University's capital fund. I dealt with the first such communication most tactfully, uttering an evasion, stuttering off like a member of the Drones Club. It did not work. A second request came in. I had, this time, to say No, but I begged off giving the reasons why. A third request came in, and there was then nothing to do—I was backed up against the wall. My correspondent had never learned Machiavelli's axiom that you should not cut off the enemy's line of retreat.

I have always held in high esteem the genial tradition, and I hope it is something other than sentimentality that inclines me to believe that one of the reasons I was so happy at Yale was that geniality is—forget, and forgive, the intemperances necessarily recorded here—as natural to Yale as laughter is to Dublin, song to Milan, or angst to *The New York Review of Books*. Mostly I prefer nowadays to contend with the slogan, rather than with the man who hoists it. But sometimes there are no alternatives (in particular as the anthropomorphization of public life proceeds—you do not talk about the Democratic Party, you talk about Kennedy, Johnson, Carter). So, in my third communication, I answered directly. "In the ideal university all sides of any issue are presented as impartially and as forcefully as possible." This was Official Yale's answer to *Gamay*. In a world governed by compromise, in which opportunism can be virtuous—such a world as our own—I am obliged to confess that I would probably settle for such an arrangement: a truly balanced curriculum, in which as much time, by professors as talented as their counterparts, in courses as critical as the others, was given to demonstrating the cogency of the arguments for God and man. *Gamay* establishes that nothing like that balance obtained twenty-five years ago. But the allocation of ideological and philosophical commitments aside, I cannot come to terms with a university that accepts the philosophical proposition that it is there for the purpose of presenting "all sides" of "any issue" as impartially and as forcefully as possible. That will not do, for the reasons Professor Wimsatt gave.

And so I was driven to write, in what I swore—until I was seduced into writing this essay—would be my last exchange on the Yale question. And what I said was: "What's the problem? Why doesn't Yale donate itself to the State of Connecticut?" The mechanical problem, as it happens, is virtually nonexistent. There is a thing called the Yale Corporation. It literally owns Yale. If the trustees of Yale were to vote tomorrow to give Yale to the State of Connecticut, there would be lots of amazement and thunderstorms of indignation—and no recourse. Obviously the State of Connecticut would accept the gift. We are talking about several hundred million dollars' worth of real property, and a half billion or so in endowments.

What then would happen?

To tell the truth, I don't know that anything much would happen. Obviously there would be changes at the corporate level. Instead of fourteen trustees, eight of them elected by their predecessors, the balance by the alumni, there would, presumably, be fourteen (or more, or fewer) trustees named by the governor of Connecticut (who is already ex officio a trustee) and confirmed by the state legislature. Would these be a scurvy lot? That is hard to say. If you look at the board of trustees of the University of California you will not find a significant difference between the profile of its membership and that of the trustees of Yale today. The University of California, particularly in recent days, has had its share of flower children; but, lo, so has Yale.

What else would be different? Standards of admission?

Why? The University of California at Berkeley is as hard to get into as Yale. A state university can be "elitist" and get away with it provided there are other universities within the system that will accept the less gifted students.

The curriculum would be less varied?

I don't think that would necessarily follow. There is a luxurious offering at Yale of courses in the recondite byways of human knowledge, wonderful to behold. But—that is also true of the University of California.

Excellence of faculty?

But the University of California has the highest concentration of Nobel Prize winners in the country. It is simply no longer true that the most gifted scholars insist on joining the faculties of privately run universities. As for the maintenance of a Yale tradition within the faculty, the incidence of Yale-educated members continues to decline, consistent with the detraditionalization of Yale.

What about the quality of undergraduate instruction?

There are a lot of complaints about the mega-university—large lecture courses; instruction of undergraduates by graduate students, not professors. But these complaints are also increasingly lodged against Yale and Harvard as well as Berkeley, and as the economic noose tightens, economizing at the expense of the undergraduate is likelier at private universities, whose resources are limited, than at public ones, whose resources are less limited.

The quality of undergraduate life?

Why should it be affected? Yale has insisted it can show no genealogical preferences—neither would the State of Connecticut; neither, of course, does Berkeley. Would state ownership interfere with undergraduate social life? How? There is only a single fraternity surviving at Yale; there are dozens at many state colleges. Yale's senior societies are unique, but they are privately owned; and, in any case, their survival (so heatedly opposed, for instance, by the recent chaplain of Yale, among others) would hardly be the pivotal justification for withholding the gift of Yale to the State of Connecticut.

And consider the advantages! Yale's painful annual deficit would be a mere added calorie in the paunch of Connecticut's deficit. Those who desire to contribute to Yale to promote specific activities within Yale could continue to do so, even as there are private endowments at Berkeley.

And—the most interesting point of all, I think—what are the philosophical objections? The sense of the swingers in the social-science faculty even twenty-five years ago was to prefer the public sector over the private sector. I cannot think what arguments most of the distinguished teachers mentioned in this book would use to oppose in principle turning Yale over to the public sector.

Now, all this having been said, let me say that *I* know why Yale shouldn't be turned over to the state. Because there are great historical presumptions that from time to time the interests of the state and those of civilization will bifurcate. Unless there is independence, the cause of civilization will be neglected. Individual professors can raise their fists and cry out against the howling of the storm; but professors so inclined are resident alike at Berkeley and at New Haven. The critical difference is the corporate sense of mission. At Berkeley that sense of mission is as diffuse and inchoate—unspecified and unspecifiable—as the resolute pluralism of California society. At the private college, the sense of mission is distinguishing. It is, however, strangled by what goes under the presumptuous designation of academic freedom. It is a terrible loss, the loss of the sense of mission. It makes the private university, sad to say, incoherent; and that is what I was trying to say when, two months after graduation, I sat down to write *God and Man at Yale*.

A Toast to the Class of 1950

Forty years later, I reflect on what we went through, and at whose hands. ⟿

S ome of us who wondered if we would ever be this old now wonder whether we were ever young.

Most of us are older today than Franklin Delano Roosevelt was when he died, five months before we arrived in New Haven.

Were we ever young?

Three weeks before matriculating at Yale I was in a little hotel bar in Edgartown with my future college roommate and two of my sisters after a day's sailing. I ordered a beer and was surprised when the waitress asked to see my driver's license. I was not quite twenty-one years old, and so was told to settle for a Coke or a 7-Up. I remember the great welling up of resentment. Should I tell her that six months earlier I had been in charge of a detachment of one thousand men at Fort Sam Houston, Texas? I thought the indignity monstrous.... But had the sense to keep my mouth shut. There wasn't a barmaid in Edgartown you could impress by reciting your war record. And anyway, it was all very good training for reaching Yale as a freshman.

There were 1,800 of us—triple the normal enrollment—because one of Yale's contributions to the war effort had been to make a comprehensive promise to matriculate, once the war was over, every single student it had accepted from the graduating secondary-school classes during the war. Never mind how many we would be: somehow Yale would find food, quarters, and teachers for us. It is a good thing the war did not go on to Peloponnesian length, given that even as it was, several hundred freshmen were forced to occupy Quonset huts, built during the war for service use, and the rest of us were forced to double up. The shortage of teachers in certain fields was so acute that in my freshman year I found myself being taught economics by a freshman in the Law School, and the following year I, along with two other undergraduates, was teaching Spanish.

There was an indistinct class structure, I remember: the veterans and the nonveterans. Formally, the administration pursued egalitarian policies in dealing with us, with only the incidental perquisites (veterans got the Old Campus, not the Quonset huts). In fact, a little winking of the eye was done at mannerisms and practices Yale would not, I think, have indulged in a class made up of eighteen-year-olds. Frank Harman (RIP), a notorious physical slouch who had spent three sedentary years in the army learning how to speak Japanese, was told matter-of-factly, at the compulsory physical exam we were all subjected to at the Payne Whitney gymnasium, that he should proceed, like the student ahead of him, to leap over a vaulting horse. He turned to the athletic examiner and said simply, "You must be joking"—and walked quietly around the obstacle, on to the next station, deciding, one after another, whether he would submit to the test or treat it as he treated the ash on his cigarette. He got away with it.

How do you handle freshmen back from Omaha Beach? I remember the tryouts for the freshman debating team. One of the applicants we'll call Henry Atterbury. Henry delivered a fiery oration. When time came for the septuagenarian historian who served as debate coach to give his critiques, he said quietly to Henry, "Mr. Atterbury. You really don't need to speak quite so loudly." He got

First day, freshman, 1946, with roommates

Last day, senior, 1950: Class Day Orator

back from Atterbury: "I'm sorry about that, sir. I got into that habit having to shout to my men over the roar of tanks." Roaring Henry Atterbury (as we ever after referred to him), a college freshman, had been a captain in the artillery, and was living now with his *second* wife.

Henry was not easily governed. I won't forget his encounter with Dean DeVane at the beginning of our sophomore year. Henry returned to New Haven one week after the semester had begun, and one of the few regulations about which Yale was inflexible, you will remember, was that all students had to be present on the first and the last day of classes. Henry was accordingly summoned to the office of that calm, courteous, scholarly Southerner, who asked why Mr. Atterbury had been late.

"Well, sir," said Roaring Henry, "I spent the summer studying the Middle Ages, and I became so engrossed in the subject I completely forgot about the Gregorian calendar change."

The response of Dean DeVane became legendary. "Ah, Mr. Atterbury. In that event, you would have arrived in New Haven one week early." Roaring Henry went into hiding for a while after that one.

My roommate Richie O'Neill (RIP) was not easily trifled with. He came early to the decision that he needed to do something to tame the fastidious dean of the Engineering School, who, an inflexible disciplinarian, required from all engineering majors attendance at all classes, unless, at midterms—which were several weeks away—they achieved the Honor Roll. When Richie slept in one Monday, he found on Tuesday a summons to the office of Dean Loomis Havemeyer. Richie was six feet two, had fought as a Marine in Okinawa, was all Irish, and had the smile of Clark Gable; every time Richie smiled I was moved to count the silver.

"Why did you miss your class yesterday, Mr. O'Neill?"

"Diarrhea, sir." Richie smiled.

He was thereafter immune to summonses from that office.

I reflect on the extent to which lines were drawn between veterans of the war, and apple-cheeked freshmen straight out of high school or prep school. At first the difference was marked primarily by dress: veterans were almost studiedly wedded to khaki pants. But after a month or so, the nonveterans, following the lead of their grizzled seniors, adopted similar dress; and, really, it was not all that easy to stare into the face of an eighteen-year-old and a twenty-year-old and discern in the latter the distinctive scars of service in the military.

For one thing, before the days of the Hollywood super-directors—who learned exactly how to atrophy the young mien in order to document service time done in Vietnam—there was no clear way to distinguish between the features of such as another of my roommates, who had taken part in the invasion of Iwo Jima, his closest friend dying at his side on the beach from machine-gun bullets, and such as me, who spent twenty-four months in the infantry, stateside—miserably uncomfortable months, but the bullets we needed to dodge, as we crawled on our bellies under barbed wire, were carefully aimed several feet above our rumps.

In part the lack of distinction between us at Yale, veterans and nonveterans, grew out of the general knowledge that, overwhelmingly, those of us who had served were draftees, not volunteers. I suppose most of us, by the time we were old enough for the draft, several years into the war, would have enlisted: the Second World War, unlike its successors in Korea and Vietnam, was a relatively popular war, causing the patriotic juices to run. But the differences between the 600 and the 1,200 gradually dissolved, and maybe all that was finally detectable was a faint air of urgency among the veterans. We were in something of a hurry to get on, get some learning, get married, get started in life. I was older when I entered Yale than my brother Jim was when he graduated from Yale.

Even so, my sense of it is that the veteran population in the class of 1950 wasn't an altogether wizening influence on normal campus activity. Money wasn't much of a worry—the GI Bill was paying our way, or substantially paying our way. There was carousing, if nothing on the scale of *Animal House*. Those of us who drank had learned two or three years earlier how to do so and when to stop doing so. Much of the time.

Eighteen hundred bright, individualistic men cultivated a lot of unusual pursuits. Fernando Valenti was practicing to become the world's leading harpsichordist. Claes Oldenburg—I guess—was dreaming of great ironwork constructions, worrying only whether museums would be large enough to house them. Jimmy Symington was wondering whether he would ever learn enough to become a Republican. I rounded up a few friends and jointly we bought an airplane, and learned to fly, and did a little crash-landing—for instance, one afternoon on the lawn of the Ethel Walker School; I was hauled out, along with my brother-in-law-to-be Brent Bozell, by three hundred girls in high hilarity at the ignominious end of the two fly-happy Yale freshmen. Friendships were instantly struck up, sometimes under the oddest impulses. I sat for the first lecture in Physics 10 alongside another freshman, a young man of grave countenance. We were two of perhaps one hundred students, and at the end of the lecture, which had been given by a retired naval captain, we turned to each other—strangers—and the extrasensory circuit was instantly completed: We burst out into convulsive, almost hysterical laughter. We had a bond. Neither of us had understood a single word uttered by the instructor. We became fast friends and copatrons of a private tutor who barely escorted us through the survivors' gate of Physics 10ab.

I think most of us, probably even including Henry Atterbury, were struck by something we had not anticipated: the awesome, breath-catching brilliance of some of our teachers. The basic course in philosophy, a survey course that began with Thales and ended with Whitehead, was taught by Robert Calhoun (RIP), a member of the faculty of the Divinity School. Remember? A tall, ruddy-faced man with crew-cut hair who wore a hearing aid. He spoke the kind of sentences John Stuart Mill wrote. Never a misplaced accent, qualifier, verb: sentence after sentence of preternatural beauty, formed as if in a magical compositors' shop, by golden artisans. Never pretentious, just plain beautiful. His learning so overwhelmed him that sometimes—and he was a man without affectation of any kind—sometimes as he traced a philosopher's thought schematically on the blackboard he would find himself lapsing into Greek, or perhaps Hebrew. When this happened there would be a quiet tittering in the classroom, but Professor Calhoun was deaf and didn't hear; so, after a while, we would just struggle to understand. He undertook, at the request of a few of us, to deliver a lecture at Dwight Hall bemoaning the Soviet coup in Czechoslovakia in 1948, and I can't believe that Demosthenes ever spoke more movingly. Yet Mr. Calhoun, at Yale, was just another professor in a department of philosophy star-studded with learning and brains.

Lewis Curtis, professor of European history, had a lecture course, and each of his lectures—they ran exactly forty-eight minutes—was a forensic tour de force. His description of the Battle of Jutland could have had a long run off Broadway. Pyrotechnics were deemed, at Yale in 1946, a little *infra dig*, so it wasn't thunder and lightning and the aurora borealis that Lewis Curtis gave his class: rather, wit and polish. We could not believe it, and I still wonder at it, that anyone could deliver, three times a week, on schedule, discrete lectures sculpted so lovingly: they came out as Renaissance statues, buoyant yet lapidary. How did they do it? I think the wonder of scholarly profundity hit us as freshmen here, even if we were destined to wonder about the uses to which learning is so often put.

Another thing that struck us was something I came to think of as a genetic attribute of Yale, and this was a distinctive sense of gentility. We were addressed as adults. And, for the most part, treated as adults—by men sharply to be distinguished from those noisy martinets we had experienced at boot camp. We had, however briefly, a vision of an entirely different order of social arrangements: a community of scholars. We would eventually learn, through experience and through reading, that no petty human vice is neglected in the academy, that fratricide does not stop at academic moats. But as students we were substantially shielded from such frictions because students are after all transient, and we were not competing with the faculty for anything. Perhaps our experience was in that sense denatured, but it is an ineffaceable part of the memory of four years at Yale: the very idea of institutional courtesy. We were never quite the same after those four years. Perhaps not better in every way, but certainly we were now men who knew something about the scales of human achievement.

℘

I think, in these mellow circumstances, of the great centrifugal forces in modern life. I sat late one night last week in the garage-study at my home in Stamford, putting these words together. My wife and I have lived there for almost forty years. Even so, I reflected last Monday, I have only twice laid eyes on the neighbor north of my property, and have yet to meet my neighbor to the south, who has occupied *his* house for fifteen years. By temperament I am content with the doctrine that good fences make good neighbors; but good fences shouldn't evolve into barbed-wire barricades, though much of this is happening: the atomistic pull of high-tech living, in a high-tech age.

It was here at Yale, forty years ago, that a professor introduced me to a book by Anton Rossi, with its striking passage that spoke of two Frenchmen, strangers at a sidewalk café, each one reading his newspaper and sipping his coffee in the late afternoon. Suddenly one raises his voice to the other:

"Say, do you like Jews?"

"No," the other man replied.

"Well, do you like Catholics?"

"No."

"Do you like Americans?"

"No."

"Do you like Frenchmen?"

"No."

"Well, whom *do* you like?"

The naysayer raised his head slightly from his newspaper. "I like my friends," he said, going back to his paper.

So do I. And most of my friends I met forty-odd years ago, met them within a radius of two hundred yards of where I am now standing. It occurs to me that forty years is a very long time. Less than forty years went by between the day Lincoln was shot and the day Victoria died. Just forty years *before* we graduated was the year the Chinese abolished slavery, the year Edward VII died, as also William James and Mark Twain. Friendships that last forty years are something. Monuments, I call them. There are few better grounds for celebration. So let's toast to the class of 1950, and to the university that brought us together.

Reflections on Life after Yale

A self-interview, for the fiftieth-anniversary yearbook. If the questions were wrong, that was my fault. ⟶

Q: *Fifty years ago, at Yale,* you were a pretty big wheel, right?

A: Yes, I was chairman of the Yale *Daily News*. That was a singular experience, because everybody *had* to read your paper and so brush up against its editorials. In the mid-sixties Yale had its cultural revolution and two things changed at the *Daily News*. First, the chairman was dethroned. For a few years, as when Stalin and Julius Caesar died, a troika came into being as successors, to guard against such concentrations of power. Eventually an editor in chief gestated, though with diminished authority. The consolidated idea being, one gathers, that "chairman" was too august a title, never mind that the revolutionists at Harvard, noblesse oblige, let the chairman of the *Crimson* survive. The other change during that period was that students who wrote for the OCD (we called it that, Oldest College Daily) no longer had to know how to write, merely to opine.

Q: You speak provocatively about the period in question.

A: As about most things. A curse. Halfway through my time as chairman we published a letter from Professor Norman Holmes Pearson protesting my editorials and instructing us to cancel his subscription. When, ten years later, a subscriber to *National Review* wrote to say the same thing, I published the letter with the editorial note, "Cancel your own goddam subscription." I have to admit it, the license to make such responses brings absolute joy to an editor's heart, but of course publishers don't like it. For under-standable reasons.

Q: Given your odd political positions, were your contacts with the Yale faculty nevertheless pleasant?

A: Oh sure, though there was some off-premise merriment at my expense. I remember hearing about Professor Tom Mendenhall, who taught European history to a big class at Linsley-Chittenden. At a fellows' dinner in the spring of 1949 he regaled his colleagues with the story of his crashing disappointment that morning. "I had prepared a lecture centering on all the delinquencies of the Catholic Church in Europe, and after I was well launched on it I looked up to feast on the expression on Buckley's face. But the son of a bitch wasn't there!" I made friends among the faculty, some of them lifelong, most notably Thomas Bergin, who was head of the Italian/Spanish Department. I taught Spanish and Bergin was my boss—great eminence; among other things, the supreme Dante scholar. We exchanged probably two hundred letters before his death in 1987 (an odd locution, "before his death"—as if you could exchange letters *after* somebody's death).

But yes, there was a little genteel consternation about the OCD's editorials, but after it was all over, Dean DeVane wrote me a terribly nice letter, which I saved. "As you come to the end of your editorial duties, you deserve the congratulations of the entire community for making the *News* the most lively college newspaper in the country, past or present. Of course, neither I nor a lot of other people agreed with your editorial position on a lot of points— but the paper was alive and could not be ignored. As a matter of fact, it was read eagerly because significant things were said, important issues debated. That, I believe, is the *summum bonum* of journalism. Heartiest congratulations."

Q: What was it that prompted you to write your book *God and Man at Yale*?

A: The catalyst was the annual Alumni Day event in February of my senior year. There was always an undergraduate speaker, and in 1950 I was selected. I wrote out my talk and gave an advance copy, as requested, to Dick Lee. He was then press secretary for Yale, before becoming the more or less perpetual mayor of New Haven. When I handed it to him he said in his captivating way, "What do you have to say in the speech, Bill? Nothing, I hope." Well, word was passed to Woodbridge Hall that the talk was unfilial. There was great static—the event was scheduled for Saturday—so I sent a message to Mr. Seymour offering to withdraw as speaker; offer accepted. But the ideas I had explored in that speech took root. I graduated, got married that July, returned to Yale in September, resumed teaching my Spanish class, and took on the book, which I finished in January. It was accepted for publication by Regnery Inc. in Chicago and was published in October—routine scheduling. It came out just as Yale was celebrating its 250th birthday, and much indignation was worked up to the effect that I had all along planned to subvert Yale's celebration, which was on the order of saying that a baby born on Christmas Day was designed, last March, to get in the way of festivities.

Q: What did you make of Yale's responses?

A: I thought them remarkably virulent, but then the book got very intensive treatment all over. *Saturday Review*, which was then the dominant litweekly, gave it no fewer than three reviews (one of them cordial, to my astonishment). The OCD's handling of it—a barrage of reviews by faculty and students—was pretty hostile. I certainly won't rehearse the arguments of that book, but I do recall with sad satisfaction what I was told by (the Reverend) David Gillespie, at our 45th reunion. He reminded me that I had read out the section on religion at Yale to him and a few others at Dwight Hall. "I thought you were wrong about religion. Unfortunately, you were right." Having said that, I add quickly that manifestly the Class of 1950 didn't end up voting the socialist ticket.

Q: You went on to found *National Review* in 1955. You began a syndicated column in 1962, and your television program in 1966. *National Review* continues, and presumably will do so on into the future. Your column continues. You folded *Firing Line* last December. Why did you do that?

A: My flippant answer, given in the press release, was that I did not want to die onstage.

There were real concerns, one of them being that raising money to finance the program was always a headache. Television stations will not put up money these days for educational fare; they expect to get it free, and usually do. That means one has to line up a foundation or other donors. I truly admire people who are willing, year after year, to go out and raise money. I've always found it agonizing. But another reason for giving up *Firing Line* is the progressive exasperation one feels over sciolistic preparation and exegesis. It was better when the show lasted a full hour. The client stations backed the one-hour format for decades, but a lot of them were very unhappy about such an egregious interruption in their way of life. And it wasn't just the philistines. When Harold Macmillan was my guest in London, after about forty minutes of shooting he turned and said, "I say, isn't this program over yet?"

When I shortened the program to a half hour, time spent on research was reduced by 80 percent. The first half hour of a television exchange on almost any subject—abortion, tax, war, Hollywood, education, God—pretty much rolls out from your general involvement in workaday discourse. But when the show goes on a second half hour you find yourself probing territory that your guest is truly expert in, while you most often are not. I remember Senator Gore (I speak of Al Gore, Senior). During the short pause for a commercial back in 1966 he leaned over to me and whispered, "You know something, Mr. Buckley?—I know more about the TVA than you do. I wrote the act."

And then, too, there is creeping fatigue.

Q: Is that something you feel distinctively? Or do you put it down to age, which all of us feel?

A: Can't answer that. The classmates I see most frequently seem pretty inexhaustible, though I remember with relish reading an interview with Vic Henningsen after I took him on my sailboat as crew in a Bermuda race. "A great experience," he told the inquiring reporter. "A once-in-a-lifetime experience." That was an Aesopian way of saying, "Dear dear Bill, it was fun, but don't invite me again!" And quite right: Vic was introducing the factor of fatigue at a slightly different level. I did four Bermuda races but would shoot myself if I had to do a fifth. On the other hand there are all those people out there, *older* than we are, who sally forth on Bermuda races every time. Has anybody ever seen Van Galbraith out of breath? Or Bill Draper? Paul Lambert?...So yes, I think I am a little tireder than the luckier few.

Q: Does it affect the quality of your work?

A: Aha, you coony old bird, I thought you'd get to that.

Let me back off, because the memory of this admonition is so searing for me. About ten years ago John Kenneth Galbraith, who is a close friend with whom I've shared a great deal, confided to me that he lived his apparently untroubled professional life with a single cloud off in the horizon, safely distant but conjecturally menacing. "My fear is that the day may come when I write less well

THERE WAS ALWAYS THE VACATION. HERE, ACAPULCO,
WITH CLASSMATES SHERIDAN LORD, TOM GUINZBURG

than I now do, and nobody will tell me, and I won't have the faculty of knowing it for myself."

Happily, there is no exact correlation between that kind of
thing—a lessening of mental skills—and biological attenuation,
which is pretty steady. After a four-month-long flu a couple of winters ago that weakened me to the point where I couldn't even ski,
I took to answering friends who asked how was I doing by reporting, resignedly if not cheerily, "I am decomposing." *However*, I
don't think my mind has suffered correspondingly. So to speak, I
can still ski on a keyboard. In addition to the other stuff, I do a
book while in Switzerland. I write quickly, a faculty that coexists
with a vexatious, antipodally slow reading speed. I could never
have got through such vast material as Bob Massie had to master

for either of his great books, nor come up with his art. Which reminds me, if you detect a decline in the quality of my writing in the years, or days, ahead, you have my license to stop reading me. Or, where applicable, to postpone beginning to read me. Maybe when I lose such powers as I have, reading me will be easier, like playing beginner's music on the piano.

Q: You speak of the piano. Do you still occasionally perform as soloist with an orchestra?

A: No. I gave up doing so after I played for my forty-fifth Yale reunion. I made so many mistakes, notwithstanding that I had practiced the Chromatic Fantasy and Fugue diligently, that I was forced to face up to it: I wasn't good enough, reliably enough, to perform publicly. That was my ninth public exposure, including one performance with the Yale Symphony in which I got through the F-minor concerto without total embarrassment, except maybe to J. S. Bach, if he was listening.

Q: You haven't said anything much about your personal life.

A: You haven't asked me anything about my personal life.

Q: All right. Let's stop playing games.

A: On July 6 I'll have been married fifty years. My wife, Patricia, is beautiful, bright, humorous, often quite impossible (as most wives sometimes are; as most husbands sometimes are), and I will love her always. My son, Christopher, is a resplendent public figure as a writer, humorist, and editor. Just yesterday I heard his first book, *Steaming to Bamboola*, acclaimed by a discriminating history professor as an enduring account of life in the merchant marine. What isn't widely known—how could it be?—is his singular warmth and grace, his tough gentility. He is our only child. The two grandchildren, aged twelve and eight, are works of art, which

requires that I acknowledge the role of their mother, the lovely
Lucy Gregg Buckley, which I proudly do.

Oh, I almost forgot. I live in a most wonderful property,
acquired in 1952, on the waterfront in Stamford, Connecticut, in
which providence perhaps accidentally, perhaps on purpose, contrived the most dazzling light changes, seascapes sometimes sleepy,
sometimes robust, even tumultuous when hurricanes come along;
cherry and birch and pine and oak trees frame just the corner of a
swimming pool by the sea embedded in old brick; little boats, sail
and power, pass by day and night, and we can see all of that from
our bedroom, with its twenty-foot-wide, 180-degree windows, or
from the music room, whose east side is all glass, with shifting light
changing the perspective and the colors every few minutes, causing this happy inhabitant to wonder at the wonder of it all.

Q: And to thank God?

A: Yes, God and Yale coexist. I wrote a book about God three
years ago, and as I think back on it I wonder that any apologetics
need go any further than the remark I ran into while at Yale, I forget at whose prompting. It recorded a crusty academic believer, his
back to the wall at the dizzy height of the Darwinian offensive a
hundred years earlier. How could he still believe in God? He
answered, "I find it easier to believe in God than to believe that
Hamlet was deduced from the molecular structure of a mutton
chop." I wish I had said that.

CHAPTER THREE

WARTIME

Army Life

*I wanted, in this autobiographical collection, to include something about my brief and bloodless experiences in the Second World War, but I never wrote directly about my time in the infantry, in Georgia, or, toward the end, as an administrative officer at Fort Sam Houston in San Antonio. So what I have done is to reproduce one chapter taken from a work of fiction (*Nuremberg: The Reckoning*). The brief scenes depict pretty exactly the weeks I spent at Officer Candidate School in Fort Benning, Georgia. It was there, while on bivouac, that we had the news that President Roosevelt had died, next door at Warm Springs. A few of us were assigned to his honor guard, which stood by when his body was carried to the train that would take him back to Washington.* ⟶*

O*n April 13, 1945, Platoon A* of Officer Candidate School Class #364 was engaged in maneuvers in the pine forest of Columbus, Georgia. Sixteen weeks earlier, when the candidates drawn in to Fort Benning from basic-training graduating classes and other army echelons numbered sixty, making up a full platoon, they had begun the stiff, competitive eighteen-week program. They were now reduced to thirty-four in number, twenty-six having been cashiered.

Most of the failing aspirants were simply judged, for any one or more reasons, less than officer material and were sent back to the field. Others, deemed potentially qualified but doing less well than acceptable, were sent back to try, from Week #1, one more time. The surviving candidates assembled now in the opening in the pine forest around their platoon leader, a first lieutenant. They had been fanning the forest for "snipers" when he blew his whistle to call them in from the exercise. They followed the whistle sound and, wearing full field packs, carrying M-1 rifles, and sweating even in the cool Georgia spring, met up with him. They eased into the pine needles, tilting their helmets up and off, many of them lighting cigarettes. It was getting warm, and the maneuver had begun at dawn. The lieutenant blew his whistle again, this time calling for attention.

He had very bad news to give them, he said. "The president of the United States is dead."

He waited a minute or two for the buzz of soldier-to-soldier reaction. There were murmurs which could be taken as expressions of grief and sorrow and shock. But the focus, quickly, was on the single question, *Might this mean an earlier end to the war?*

Sebastian Reinhard leaned over to Ed Coady. "Could be good news. FDR was the unconditional-surrender man, right?"

"Right." Coady had been drafted in July 1944, after finishing freshman year at Princeton, at which he had matriculated at age seventeen. He and Sebastian had been trying diligently, in the few minutes each day not spoken for by the Officer Candidate School, to keep abreast of the news. They sequestered the short-wave radio in the rec room at nine every night to take in the BBC broadcast, subsequently amusing themselves, while undressing for sleep in their barracks before lights-out, by mimicking what George Orwell had spoken of as the "genteel and throaty" voices of BBC newscasters. *Private Edward Cooodee was repohted seen at Fort Benning in Georgia, which is an...administrative centah of the United States...Infantry.* And Sebastian would improvise a reply built on the day's news. *And so we say goodnight to Private Reinhard, inasmuch as it is two hours pahst midnight. Sleep well, Private Reinhard. You will probably be dedd in a month.*

༽~

"Yes," Coady said now. "It was FDR at Casablanca who came up with unconditional surrender. That'll keep the German fuckers—I mean, Sebby, the Nazi—well yes, the Nazi fuckers—fighting to the last—" The whistle blew.

OCS candidates were instantly compliant with any order from their platoon leader. To be less than attentive was to run the risk of a quiet, invisible demerit in the platoon leader's ledger. Enough of these and a candidate was called before the OCS Review Board and given the news: (1) He was out, or, (2) he had to begin the whole nerve-shattering, bone-crushing eighteen-week business all over again.

The lieutenant elaborated. "The president died yesterday afternoon at Warm Springs. We are the closest army base to Warm Springs. Colonel Hayes has instructed us by radio to stand by for the selection of an honor guard for the president's removal tomorrow morning to the presidential train that will take him to Washington. The last two hours of the maneuvers today are canceled. After chow we will go back to Checkpoint Baker, where the trucks will be. At 1800 the honor guard will be chosen. Report to the assembly point and stand at parade rest at 1755."

They were there promptly, the platoon reduced, by the death sentences of the Review Board, to two files of seventeen soldiers each. They were neatly aligned at parade-rest position, their khaki shirts open at the collar, their name tags on their breast pockets. A few minutes later the major stepped down from his jeep, accompanied by a technical sergeant. The men were called to attention and the major walked by the first row, then the second. A nod of his head signaled to the sergeant, who would look at the name tag, then write the candidate's name on his pad.

Sebastian was amused by the exercise. It had happened two or three times during basic training. The criteria of the reviewing officer were never explicit, but those who had eyes to see understood what they were. At basic training in Macon, privates were selected for public viewing based upon whose appearance would be most ingratiating at the designated local function—a Veterans' Day parade, a bond-selling rally, the funeral of the senator from the Armed Services Committee. Today's men would be lined up, Sebastian supposed, to escort the coffin as it departed from the president's little retreat, or perhaps as it entered the presidential train. There would be lots of news cameramen, and the commanding general, as had been the case back at Camp Wheeler, would want the most photogenic young men to represent the infantry.

Sebastian had an eye for objective reality. He knew he would be picked; he always was—handsome, muscular, brown-eyed, appearing even younger than the nineteen years he had celebrated, or rather passed by, in the early weeks of the officer-training course. He was certain that Ed Coady would also be picked, a pleasing-faced, freckled redhead from New Bedford, Massachusetts. As the major walked by, Sebastian let himself reflect, with a smile deeply buried, on how Resplendent Young American Reinhard and Resplendent Young American Coady would have looked if a cameraman had been there to film their writhings the Saturday night before in Phenix City, the sin city just over the river in Alabama. The camera would have caught the two All-Americans in the arms of Rosita and Sally on twin beds, abandoning, after much thought and discreet planning and beer consumed, their virginity. Well, he thought, the dead, worldly president would know all about boys being boys—he had served as assistant secretary of the Navy dur-

ing the other war, and that was before the docs had invented peni-
cillin, which made nights-out-on-the-town, back then, a lot riskier.

"Paaa-*rade REST!*"

The candidates moved to separate their feet and allow arms to
rest behind their backs. The major read out loud a very long tribute
written by the general in honor of the departed commander in chief.
Then Lieutenant Bryant called out ten names. The ten Resplendent
Young Americans were told to report to company headquarters at
2000. They were told by their platoon leaders, who read from a reg-
imental order sheet, what their duties would be. The late president's departure on the train from Warm Springs was set for 0830.

At taps, the flag was at half-mast. On their return from the mess
hall, the candidates busied themselves as always. The scattering of
empty beds on the barracks floor was a stern reminder of the con-
sequences of negligence or of flagged concern for perfection. The
men labored now to clean and reclean and hunt out specks of lint
from their rifles. At any given moment, in the morning before
reveille and at night before lights-out, up to a dozen candidates
would be working on their pull-ups, using the iron pipes that
served as beams below the ceiling. Most had by now achieved the
required eleven pull-ups (and forty-four push-ups), but Andy and
Henry, who were in their late twenties, past athletic prime, hadn't
quite got there, and now their brothers-in-arms, sitting on their
beds and working on their rifles, egged them on and cheered when
Andy, straining and breathless, reached ten. The final test would
be the following Thursday—eleven pull-ups or back to the ranks.
There was little conversation about the death of the president, and
Sebastian knew nothing, after five days on maneuvers, about other
developments on the war fronts.

By the time Sebastian and the others in the special funeral
detachment dismounted their buses the next morning at Warm

Springs, the crowds were already gathering. By 0800 two thousand paratroopers from Fort Benning and three thousand soldiers from the great infantry base were massively there. The OCS detachment—in battle dress, at stiff attention, guns at their side—stood on both sides as the flag-draped green hearse inched past them, and then the honor guard on foot, led by Mrs. Roosevelt. The file stopped only when it reached the railroad car. The coffin, covered with black crêpe, was taken up the ramp. From the corner of his eye Sebastian could see the coffin slide up into the cavity of the railroad car. The crowd was silent except for the weeping, which seemed uncontrolled. There was Jim Crow in Georgia, but not early that morning, on April 13, at the Warm Springs station, where the tears were copious on black faces.

On the ride back to Fort Benning there was not much talk. Ed Coady said he would try to get through on the telephone to his mother in New Bedford. "She'll be very torn up. What about your people in Arizona?"

Sebastian said there was just his grandmother there. "My Oma—my grandmother, Henrietta—will take it stoically, she's that way."

After supper, Ed went off to the message center to try his long-distance call, and Sebastian went to the radio for the BBC news. A half hour later, Ed returned.

"How's your mother?" Sebastian asked.

"Okay. She said, Well, Mr. Roosevelt was only sixty-three. But what I want to know, Eddie, is, will *you* be alive at twenty-three?"

Ed laughed. "Either Hitler or I will be dead by then."

CHAPTER FOUR

SAILING

(AND SKIING, AND ONE FLY-BY)

We Must Sail across the Ocean!

I have sailed a lot, beginning at age thirteen on a mile-square lake near Sharon, Lake Wononscopomuc. After college, I bought first a cutter, then a yawl, then a schooner, and finally a sloop. Four times I sailed across an ocean, and raced as many times from Newport to Bermuda. In this section I offer selections acknowledging the continuing mystique of the sea, which Homer first told us of, and which will surely be written about in wonder and awe in the closing days of literary life on the planet.

The first time I sailed across the Atlantic was in 1975. Here is the genesis of that trip. ⟿

"Peter," I said, late on a white summer afternoon around 1960, to Peter Starr, who had been sailing with me and looking after my boat during the summers since he was thirteen, "let's face it. Someday we'll have to sail across the Atlantic." We were walking gingerly about the mossy rocks that surround York Harbor, in Maine, getting some exercise after a long day's sail from Gloucester, before returning to *The Panic*, moored in the Hansel-and-Gretel harbor, for dinner. The first three days of our sail we—my wife and I, Peter, and some friends—had raced with the New York Yacht Club on its summer regatta. Then we struck out to cruise in Maine.

Peter agreed. Yes, we must sail across the ocean.

I had by then acknowledged widely my unalterable affection for Peter. In the five years I had known him, he had never said No to any request I made ("Please paint the hull black by next weekend"), never implied by any inflection the implausibility of any proposal I made ("Can you get a week off from school and sail to Bermuda with us in October?"), never betrayed any lack of enthusiasm for any suggestion I made anytime, anywhere. I would think nothing of calling him at his home in Stamford, a mile from my own, at eleven or twelve at night on a Friday, late in the season.

"Peter, let's sail."

"Sure!"

"I'll pick you up in ten minutes"—Peter wasn't old enough for a driver's license when I first knew him—and in twenty minutes we would be powering out of Stamford Harbor; in another ten minutes the sails would be up. In an hour or so, depending on the wind, we would make out the little flashing red light signaling the entrance to the tortuous channel, rocks on either side, winding into the little harbor off Treasure Island. It is actually Eatons Neck Point, but we came to call it Treasure Island because it was there that we took Christopher in midsummer when he was six, with his little friend Danny Merritt, and the pirate's map that my old friend Reggie Stoops, an MIT graduate who could draft the inside of an HP-65 computer, had so painstakingly contrived the day before, marking where a chest of treasure was said to have been buried during the seventeenth century. I have a movie of Christopher, in short pants and solemn mien, counting out the steps—stretching out his legs to approximate the distance Long John Silver would have intended to suggest when writing, "Count 20 paces NNW"—treasure chart in hand, with Reggie, head bent over the hand compass, pointing the way.

"I figure it ought to be about here," Reggie said finally, reflectively, and Christopher and Danny went down on their knees and began with bare hands to shovel out the sand—two inches, four inches, eight inches . . .

"Try a little deeper, Christopher. After all, if it's still here, it's been here three hundred years." And then the yelps of joy as they spotted wood and, after furious application, hauled out, reverently, a small old chest. The padlock was conveniently rusted, and Reggie pried it open for them. They were agog. A crock of jewels. Pearl necklaces, gold brooches, huge amethyst rings, diamond bracelets: It had taken Pat an hour at Woolworth's the morning before to accumulate the treasure, and she complained of having had to spend well over ten dollars. Christopher and Danny, though they had exchanged vows of eternal fidelity, clearly did not trust each other to exclusive dominion, however temporary, over their precious burden. So, although it did not weigh five pounds, they walked off in tandem, in elated silence, four arms around the little chest.

What happened that fall is a subject we didn't bring up for a while, not until Pat's sense of humor caught up with her, which it always does. Christopher, through the balance of the summer, couldn't get over the fixation that there might be yet more treasure on "Treasure Island," and he pestered Reggie on the point until, unguardedly, Reggie divulged that indeed he had heard that some-one in New York—a great-great-great-great-great-great-great- (Reggie furrowed his brows, as though counting carefully down the generations from the middle of the seventeenth century to the pres-ent, 1959) granddaughter of a famous pirate—indeed survived, who had a chart of another buried treasure chest. When we couldn't put the second search off any longer, Reggie busied himself creating the new chart, ten times as ornamental as its predecessor. Pat, fearing that another assortment from Woolworth's might arouse suspicion, collected four or five superb Georgian silver pieces of various designs that her mother had given her and that had just arrived in a wooden crate, the contents as yet unseen by Christopher. When Christopher discovered them on Treasure Island, Pat would "buy" them from

him. Besides, the silver was safer for another reason. In a characteristic access of generosity, two days after the original discovery on
Treasure Island, Christopher asked his nurse for some wrapping
paper and ribbon, and then mysteriously disappeared. When Pat and
I went to bed, a bulky package lay under her pillow. It contained
Christopher's half of the ancient treasure, with a six-year-old's love
note. This, of course, required Pat during that long summer to wear,
whenever Christopher was anywhere in sight, which was most of the
time, a full suit of Woolworth's jewelry, which was bad enough when
just Christopher was around, but positively arresting when there
were a lot of other people around who clearly wondered what on
earth had happened to the taste in jewelry of the chic and stunning
Mrs. Buckley. Exhibiting her son's pirate collection of Georgian silver she could contemplate doing with serenity.

On Friday, Peter, Reggie, and I sailed across Long Island Sound
to Eatons Neck Point and buried the box, leaving a telltale stick to

CHRISTOPHER AND HIS MOTHER, IN SEARCH OF TREASURE ISLAND

guide us the next day, even as we would affect to be guided only by the compass markings on the chart.

Unfortunately, that Saturday we got not our happy little picnic sail across the Sound, but Hurricane Hilda. By the time Hilda had allowed the seas to settle down, three days had passed. Instantly we set out, and Christopher and Danny went through their paces, using the new chart. Two hours and six excavations later, Pat's sober expression having graduated to fixed stares of stupefaction and loathing aimed alternately at Reggie and me when the boys were not looking, we had to give up. Back on board, after the boys were asleep in the forward section, she demanded in no uncertain terms that we find her beautiful Georgian silver. "There, there," we said, "of course we'll find it." Reggie and I conferred privately and wondered what we would have to do to lease a metal detector from the Army Corps of Engineers. We tried a half dozen times over the next months to find the buried casket. It is still there, somewhere.

ॐ

"Of course, we must cross the Atlantic," Peter said, without looking up from the mossy stones he glided over. "Is there anything else we haven't done on *The Panic*?"

That was my first ocean boat, and I loved her dearly. I raced her to Bermuda and cruised her to Nova Scotia and up the St. John River, and a dozen times all along the Maine coast. One day in November of 1961 I called from Washington to the harbormaster at the Stamford Yacht Club and asked him to check the mooring lines of *The Panic*, as a hurricane was predicted. Two days later he called my house and asked me to come down. The storm had subsided, but one of the boats had come loose and was piled on the jetty at the harbor entrance. "I think it's *The Panic*." He took me, in the club launch, as close as we could get—the winds were still at gale force. I looked at her, grinding into the rocks with every onset of waves, and estimated that her steel hull must be punctured in a hundred different places. Only her single rugged mast—she was a cutter—was clearly visible in the high tide. At low tide, her broken body was fully, immodestly exposed, like a ravaged corpse with the bedsheet drawn back.

That night Peter called, enthusiastic as always, from Georgetown University, where he was a sophomore, to tell me the new spinnaker for next year's Bermuda race was ready and he would pick it up at the sailmaker's in Annapolis and bring it to Stamford, as he was coming home for the weekend in any case. I gave him the news. He had to put down the telephone after the first sob. That reaction was not only the teenager's who had grown up with *The Panic*. I gave the same news to the critic Hugh Kenner. He reacted in a letter that ended: "She had done much for her friends, in the summers before her side was stove in. She had...made for them a place of adventure and refreshment and peace; and taught them this, that beyond illusion it is possible to be for hours and days on end perfectly and inexpressibly happy."

This was what Hugh remembered about *The Panic*! Mercifully his memories of his initial cruise were less distinct; or perhaps, on the occasion, they were merely...transcended. He and his first wife (Mary-Jo, RIP) and I flew to Portland, Maine. Peter was waiting for us, having just unloaded a charter party. Though it was very late in the afternoon, and Peter had been working since six in the morning, and Hugh was exhausted from a round of lectures and meetings with publishers, we decided exuberantly to set out forthwith across the hundred-mile track of ocean to Provincetown, Massachusetts. Peter and Mary-Jo took the watch from eight to midnight. It began to storm at eleven, and Mary-Jo was blue with fear and mal de mer, while Peter was very nearly faint from having to cope, virtually alone, with the sail-shortening. But they stuck it out till watch change at twelve (an iron protocol

KNOCKDOWN AT THE START OF THE
BERMUDA RACE, 1956, ABOARD THE PANIC

aboard ship, except in case of emergency). Peter came forward and woke me, and I, grabbing every fixed object en route to keep my balance, went aft and nudged Hugh. He sat up in the bunk stark white, put on his glasses with great, silent dignity, looked at me as if I were a perfect stranger, rose, walked uncertainly forward to the head, clutched two handy pipes, leaned over, vomited a day's food into the toilet, groped his way somnambulistically back to his bunk, got in, pulled the covers over himself, and passed out. Mary-Jo, wrestling with the strange tiller, wasn't good for another ten minutes. Peter looked up at me—he looked as young as on the day, three years earlier, when he had bicycled to my house to apply for a job he hoped to find more interesting than his paper route. "I'll stay awake with you, Mr. Buckley."

"Go to bed," I told him. "I'll call you if I need you." I put on foul-weather gear, relieved Mary-Jo at the wheel, felt the boat surging at hull speed with only the No. 3 jib and reefed main, and wondered (this happens at sea as often as people who write about the sea tell you it does)—facing four hours alone, already soaked, beginning to feel the cold, the boat's erratic needs exacting every nerve of concentration, arm and back muscles taxed like a galley slave's, facing God knows what ahead, the human reserves aboard comprising one seasick poet, his incapacitated wife, and an exhausted sixteen-year-old—what madness finds me here, in these conditions, at this time. The hoariest line in the literature, which even so never ceases to amuse me, is: "Ocean racing is like standing under an ice-cold shower, tearing up thousand-dollar bills."

There was a lot to think about during that long and hectic night, but Walt Disney was in his heaven, and by the time the sun rose, the storm had abated; and I even managed to hoist the spinnaker utterly alone—sad, in the radiant early sun, the wind steady off the port quarter, only that no one was witness to this feat of virtuosity. Finally I woke the ship's company and they were all, miraculously, quite cured and ravenously hungry. As we chatted—picking up now a land speck on the horizon, the tower at the tip of Cape Cod, validating a night of navigation by dead reckoning—spirits soared, and I mentioned to Hugh that one day Peter and I would cross the Atlantic. But even though, seventeen years later, the voyage had been set, and even though the date of departure was fixed fifteen months ahead, when we did set out from Miami, on May 30, 1975, Peter was not aboard. He was thirty-three now and had discovered the well-known American phenomenon called the Business Crisis. Three days before our departure, he called to blurt out, in a voice that took me back to the phone call from Georgetown about *The Panic*, news I had known for three weeks was coming. Not intuition. Peter was president and chief executive officer of a company of which I was board chairman, and I knew something about the crisis in which, as it happened, our common sailing experience figured tangentially. I wondered, when Peter called, whether I could imagine any crisis such as would cause me to cancel the B.O., as we had come to refer to it—the Big One. I refused to let my imagination travel across that Stygian frontier.

ઌ

Having undertaken, however vaguely, to set out one unspecified day to sail across the Atlantic, I found myself focusing haphazardly on the trials of such a passage. These questions would accost me with special force during the longer sea voyages—when racing to Bermuda, for instance. When becalmed, I would think very hard about them. I thought about them while heading south from Bermuda to the Virgin Islands, as I did once on a crazy impulse. During four days of heaving, pursued by following winds and seas that roller-coastered us a thousand miles; during an overnight sail from Cuttyhunk back to Stamford, lost, drenched, blinded by fog, I wondered about crossing the ocean. The negative factors accumulated. For one thing, though I and my sailing friends are devotees of the sea, we are that in a qualified sense. We never fancied ourselves as "the everlasting children of the mysterious sea." Rather their "successors," accurately anticipated by Conrad as "the grown-up children of a discontented earth." We were "less naughty, but [also] less innocent; less profane, but perhaps also less believing." And indeed, if we had learned how to speak, we had "also learned how to whine."

Really, it came down to two basic questions. The first was: How much protracted physical discomfort can you put up with before discomfort overwhelms the memory of an ocean passage? Hugh Kenner and I sailed a half-dozen times together on *The Panic*. But only once—on that first run—in circumstances distractingly, even preemptively, uncomfortable. Almost anything is tolerable at sea, if

ON TO BERMUDA, IN CALMER SEAS

it is guaranteed to end *that very day*—at, say, cocktail time, in a quiet anchorage. A young, tough, phlegmatic friend who raced twice across the Atlantic told me that on the second passage (Newport to Sweden), beginning on the tenth day out, he had been so cold, so bitterly, awfully, gnawingly cold, day in day out, night after endless night, that he solemnly pledged to himself—days before arriving finally in Scandinavia—never, ever again to sail across the North Atlantic.

I engaged once in a polemic with a veteran seaman who teaches English to fortunate students of St. George's School. He took public issue with me over a complaint I had published against the creeping professionalization of the sport. In pointing out the mysterious inexactitude of specialized knowledge about boats and their accessories, I gave as only one of many examples the demonstrated inadequacy of foul-weather gear advertised as competent to keep a man dry at sea. With great huff, Mr. Hoyt (who, disappointedly, I subsequently discovered to be a most engaging and undogmatic man) replied, in a published article, that he had made eight transatlantic crossings and had not once—not o-n-c-e—been either cold or wet.

Now, you must understand the gravity of this kind of boast in the amateur community I write of. It is—simply—unbelievable. I wrote once about an erstwhile friend who, at age seventeen, resolved never again to make a typing mistake. Forty years later, he has yet to make one. Why should he? he asked. If Horowitz can play at hurricane speed horribly intricate pieces of music, using ten fingers simultaneously without making a mistake, why should he—Revilo Oliver, a full professor in the classics, master of seventeen tongues—make a mistake, typing at his own speed, and using, at *whatever* speed he typed, what comes down to *only one finger at a time*?

Still, they don't believe me about Revilo; even as, still, I don't really believe it about my friend at St. George's. But I must report that in his article he gave a step-by-step account of just how he handles the problem of dressing in a sailboat at sea for the cold and the wet. I have traveled to the Antarctic and, on doing so, submitted to a technician's lecture on how to keep warm, walking away with a trunkload of clothes supplied by the United States Navy, which, when I donned them, left me entirely comfortable in temperatures that brushed up against fifty below zero. But I must add that it could not have taken the Queen of England as long to dress for her Coronation as it took me to put on my costume in the mornings I was in the Antarctic; and it is a wonder that Mr. Hoyt had time left over to devote to watch duty, after preparing himself for it. But let us leave the point moot and agree to say modestly: You can keep warm on a boat, but the preparations necessary for doing so vitiate, substantially, the pleasure of the day's sail.

On the matter of keeping dry, I remain, perforce, a skeptic. My brother-in-law Firpo (my wife's brother, who got his nickname because he was born on the day that Dempsey fought Firpo) believes in attacking problems head-on. For our first race to Bermuda he designed his own foul-weather gear. It was the grandest and most elaborate piece of gear I have ever seen, not less imposing for its responsibility for keeping dry 250 pounds of human flesh. It had rubber gloves with shock-cord belts, all-directional zippers, a seamless balaclava; everything except perhaps a catheter tube.

The first hard wave that tore into *The Panic*'s cockpit left Firpo totally drenched, and, on top of that, facing twenty minutes of disassembly before he could dry his bare skin. My old friend Van Galbraith (Yale '50), who had observed with awe the design and engineering of the ultimate foul-weather suit, comforted Firpo with a practical suggestion for the next trip: "You must go to a garage, strip, and have yourself vulcanized."

It was in any case a fact that my ocean-racing friend remembered about his North Atlantic passage only the cold. Like C. S. Lewis recalling, about his first year at boarding school, primarily that he was painfully, achingly *tired, all* day, *every* day, *through* the semester.

Now it is much closer to Europe from America via the North Atlantic, and, accordingly, I hadn't ever thought of going by any other route. But that is the compulsion of genus *Americanus*: to focus automatically, and unthinkingly, on the shortest distance between two points. It was humiliating to remind myself that electing sail as a means of transportation is itself the major commitment, to which the corollaries should naturally suggest themselves. If speed were the only objective, then *sailing* across the Atlantic would be, well, perverse. This much one can accept without difficulty. But, even having grandly rejected the shortest route, making consistent adjustments is difficult—particularly if, on boarding a sailboat, you are incapable of leaving ashore a nervous system that pushes you on and on, impatient, disdainful, intolerant of delays. "Pup has it figured out," Christopher, out of a lifetime's knowledge of his father's inclination to hecticity, would write, amused and annoyed, in his journal, "how we can see all the Azores in five hours." It is one thing to decide not to take the northern passage, even if it means adding fifteen hundred miles to the trip. It is something else to calm down your metabolism to accept an unhurried trip. It is something else to tarry four days—instead of, say, two—in Bermuda; or two weeks, rather than three days, in the Azores. Or to sail on in a light wind for four hours rather than turn on your engines and help out the wind.

Racing a boat is, in this unique sense, as satisfying as army life. The rules are explicit: Under no circumstances do you turn on your engine, except to save a drowning man, preferably a member of the Race Committee. So that when a calm attacks you—as a notable one did in the 1960 Bermuda Race, when the sails flapped, the sun excreted its heat upon us, and we moved not one hundred yards in thirty-six agonizing hours—it is all strangely tolerable only because there is no alternative: save abandoning a race the preparations for which had taken hundreds of hours, dissipated thousands of dollars, and required major adjustments in the schedules of eight busy men. Where there is no alternative, the wise man has said, there is no problem. There was, of course, one major alternative in our crossing. It was exercised when we elected to take the long southerly route. The next question was whether to race across the Atlantic, or cruise across. Here again thought must be given to pleasure–pain factors.

There are other forms of discomfort aboard a boat than physical cold. When William Snaith (whose enthralling account of the transatlantic race from Bermuda to Sweden in 1960 is given in *On the Wind's Way*) gave the exhortation to his crew just before starting out, he pledged that they would "race the boat to the point of discomfort." No one who has written about modern racing has recited more vividly what these discomforts can add up to, and although his journal shows the fierce pride the author and his crew took in winning the race, sometimes, on reading him, one has the same sensation one had on reading Amundsen's account—also triumphant—of his passage to the South Pole. I wrote a brief account, in 1958, of my second race to Bermuda, recalling my first, in 1956: "My first trip and—the thought crossed my mind as I bit at a salt-soaked sandwich while tugging at the helm, heeled over thirty-five degrees; or as I grappled in the claustrophobic reaches of the forepeak with yet another sail to drag up and hang on the base of a headstay which, like a submarine's periscope, slid in and out of the water; or as I lay sleepless in my tossing bunk, lusting after the comforts of a Carthusian cell, jets of water streaming in from a leaky deck, the waves pounding two inches from my ear upon the arching bow—surely my last." That was my first long ocean trip with Van, my classmate and, until not long before, my landlocked friend. He was quite simply unbelieving. For one thing, he had been seasick. Not once, or ten times, but more or less continuously. Several times he announced himself as over the hump; and a few hours later he would arch over the rails in a movement as dexterous by now as the golf stroke of the professional. What was more phenomenal than his extraordinarily unmanageable stomach was his good humor. He lived on bouillon and Bonamine and promised to contribute a testimonial to the anti–motion-sickness company on arrival: "Bonamines I Have Barfed, Starring Van Galbraith." On landing finally at St. George's in Bermuda, he told me he intended to write an article that would consist quite simply of a minute-by-minute log of the typical hour aboard our boat during the race. The effect of the piece, he confidently predicted, would be to certify the insanity of all participants in the "sport," and very possibly, by its exposure of the real, awful nature of the ordeal, extirpate ocean racing from the civilized world. I was utterly convinced. I *am* utterly convinced. We talked about it every time we raced together to Bermuda thereafter.

I have done a lot of racing: on Wononscopomuc Lake as a boy; at sea on *The Panic* (and her successor, *Suzy Wong*), beginning in 1955. I am not absolutely sure whether I wouldn't be out there yet, had *Suzy* and I developed into a successful racing combination. Though the estrangement came gradually, I think I can trace the seeds of it to 1965. I disappeared surreptitiously from the race for mayor of New York in order to participate in the race from Marblehead, Massachusetts, to Halifax, Nova Scotia, which I had roughly the same chance of winning. Though it was a rough ride, I and Reggie, and Peter, and Van, and two other friends with whom we raced more or less regularly, managed the boat well. We made no significant errors in seamanship or navigation or strategy; but when finally we slipped across the finish line, just before 3:00 A.M., we learned that there was only a single boat that hadn't yet come in. (It was Lee Bailey's. He told me later that on learning I had finished ahead of him, he deserted ocean racing and bought a jet airplane. I comforted him that at least he had effected an economy.)

By contrast, in the very first race to Bermuda on *The Panic*, we had done quite creditably, halfway in our class. But never on *Suzy*, beautiful, all-teak *Suzy*, built in Hong Kong and sailed from there by four GIs (discharged, by their choice, in Tokyo) across the Indian Ocean, up the Red Sea, through the Suez Canal, across the Mediterranean, down to the Canary Islands, over to Antigua, and finally to Miami, where the young owners, following their design, sold her in order to launch their professional careers, get married, and muse for the rest of time on their great adventure. They turned a small profit on the sale, given the difference in construction costs in Hong Kong and the United States, and calculated, working back, that their year and a half's vacation at sea had cost them each less than two dollars per day. But *Suzy*, although designed by Sparkman & Stephens, which is like saying about a violin that it was designed by Stradivarius, could not live up to her theoretical rating. This is something called The Rule. It is as romantic an adventure in Procrusteanism as has ever been engaged in by otherwise serious men. It is designed to make all vessels that compete in an ocean race theoretically equal in speed by imposing graduated handicaps. These are calculated by such compounded anfractuosities that nowadays only a half-dozen men even affect to understand The Rule, and no one can give you your rating without feeding all the relevant factors into a computer. Not just any computer, but a monster-type bunkered somewhere in Long Island for the purpose of guiding missiles to Mars, and giving yachtsmen their ratings.

Nowadays a successful racing boat is a tangle of expensive mechanisms designed to beat The Rule. *Suzy*, with her noble teak, is probably too heavy to have profited even from such radical surgery. We raced her that fall, in the annual race from Stamford to Martha's Vineyard and back. Once again, boat and crew were in nearly perfect sync, and once again we trailed the fleet. So in due course I retired her from regular campaigning, though I would still race her, when I got around to it, for the fun of it. That was, mostly, why I raced her and *The Panic* all those years, my point (elaborated once upon a time in a chapter of a book, *Racing at Sea*) being that an ocean race is really a test of yourself and your crew; there are too many variables to permit one to conclude that this vessel, or this crew, is superior to that other vessel or crew. But no doubt the phasing out of *Suzy* as a racing boat was part of what led me to the conclusion that when I sailed to Europe, I would cruise there, rather than race there. There are considerable differences.

❧

Normally, a cruise is conceived as a daytime sail from one harbor to another. You arrive late in the afternoon (say), drop anchor, swim, hike, have a drink, cook and eat dinner, then perhaps play cards or simply talk, perhaps address yourself to a specially recalcitrant part of the boat's equipment neglected during the day. Everyone in due course turns in, sleeps soundly, wakes up rested. The whole of the ship's complement is up, and down, together.

So is it, of course, in the one-day race. It is when sailing over distances that require shifts in crew that the nature of the experience radically changes. When you race, you need more men on watch: at least three (in boats up to fifty feet long), and if you need to perform intricate work such as jibing the spinnaker or reefing the mainsail, you generally rouse a fourth. When cruising, you don't, in serene circumstances, need more than two men on watch. This means, assuming you carry the full complement of crew, that in overnight cruising you are on duty less than half the time. To go on duty for four hours, then off duty for eight hours, is manifestly more relaxing than to go back on duty after only four hours off. Moreover, since under such arrangements you have roughly sixteen hours of leisure to deploy, there is more time than otherwise to be gregarious; more time to read; more time to attend to miscellaneous projects.

I stress, however, that on a long trip even cruising cannot guarantee comfort. A few years ago I induced six classmates from Yale, only Van among them an experienced sailor, to share a trip with me from Bermuda to St. Thomas. So the professional crew, Ned Killeen as captain, brought my boat—by that time I had acquired a schooner, *Cyrano*, so named because of her eighteen-foot-long bowsprit—to Bermuda. The professionals, except for Ned, then flew back to New York, and the rest of us flew in, and took off at midnight. Not because midnight is a melodramatic time to take off, but because the sixth friend came in from South America at eleven, and we all had to be home for Thanksgiving.

The strategy was to head south (St. Thomas is exactly south of Bermuda) as fast as possible for the two hundred miles necessary to get into the trades and out of the formal limits of the North Atlantic gale area. I decided we might as well baptize the passengers into discomfort beginning at midnight, inasmuch as we had to get to St. Thomas by the following Wednesday at the latest. So there we were, excited, our gear tucked away, the shifts assigned (four hours on, eight hours off), headed out of the little cut at St. George's through which, coming the other way, I had passed so often before, exhausted, elated, at the end of a Bermuda race. We expected the worst, and were pleasantly surprised. Light winds from the northeast, quite moderate seas, and, darting in and out of the clouds, a moon that would be full in mid-passage.

A large storm front, unfortunately, was at that moment kicking up most monstrous waves north of Bermuda, and these rolled down on us beginning on the second day, and pursued us through the whole of our passage, severely taxing the equanimity of the green passengers. They looked at me, as the days went by, as at an incubus, with intensifying hatred. I remember that on the fourth day it appeared that, finally, the whale-sized waves would dissipate. The sun shining merrily, I decided at lunchtime, as my friends began to show a more than purely biological interest in their food, that the time had come to try a little R&R, to which end I brought up the big Zenith portable radio—we had heard no voice from the mainland for four days. I flicked on the switch, and the cockpit was filled with a familiar voice engaging in some solemn didacticism or another. It was mine. The Voice of America, rebroadcasting a *Firing Line* exchange. My friends all stopped eating, and for a few seconds I feared for my life; but, gentlemen songsters that they proved to be even under such duress, they caucused, and decided finally to accept my fevered assurance that the entire thing was an unholy coincidence.

During the worst of it we had up only a storm trysail and the forward staysail (that is to say, about 25 percent of the sail we were carrying). I had set out to unfurl at least a part of the genoa, which on *Cyrano* is rigged on a roller-reefing fitting that theoretically permits the exposure of any amount of it. But the main fitting on the halyard slipped overboard while I was making an adjustment, the smaller substitute swivel proved too weak, and the sail tumbled down after a few hours. I went theatrically up the masthead on the bo'sun's chair to bring down the halyard and put on yet another swivel. But this one too gave way after a few hours, and now it was too rough to go up again. The result was a heavy-weather helm which was unpleasant, and which put too great a strain on the automatic pilot, reducing us to the humility of having to steer our own boat—imagine, with only eight people aboard!

It was especially galling to lose the extra knot or two from the rudder's brake action—like driving a sports car in low gear mile after mile, day after day. If it had been a race, of course, we'd have figured out some way to get the genoa up. But the wind and the seas were relentless, and it wasn't until we got right into the harbor at St. Thomas, bruised and strained, my *Cyrano* rather weather-beaten, that we got any relief. The twelve-year-old daughter of one of my friends wrote me a letter a week or so later on some vexing political question and added the P.S., "What *did* you do to my daddy?" The wife of another of my friends, who is a very nice man even though he did run for Congress against Shirley Temple, recounted a week or so later, when we came upon them in California, that three times, at three in the morning, her husband had risen stiffly out of bed, stared fixedly ahead, and declared firmly, "*I have to go on deck!*"—whereupon he would walk straight into a closet, which sharply, but reassuringly, jolted him back into the knowledge that his nightmare cruise was over.

⤜

I mentioned one of two concerns about sailing the Atlantic, one being the tolerable measure of physical discomfort during a substantial part of the journey. The other was the sheer length of an Atlantic crossing. I am attracted by adventure, repelled by marathons. I could be persuaded to jump out of an airplane and land in a well in Death Valley; I could never be persuaded to hike across Death Valley or, for that matter, up the Matterhorn. Evel Knievel makes more sense to me than the Long-Distance Runner.

The fear of boredom is a cognate aversion. The friend who told me about the bitter cold sailing to Sweden gave me heartening news on this point. After six days on board a sailing boat, he said, perceptions change radically. You come to do routinely those things you had to force yourself to do when first you came on board, wrenched from a life different in so many rhythms. After that novitiate, he said, the hours fly by. The watches, once interminable, diminish in length; anxiety ebbs; on reaching your bunk you are instantly asleep; on being roused, you are instantly and eagerly awake. The ocean and the sky and the night are suddenly alive: your friends and your enemies, but not any longer just workaday abstractions. It is most surely another world, and a world worth knowing.

I had never sailed longer than seven days—a stormy cruise to Bermuda, into the edge of a hurricane. It was an experience, except for the three perfect days at the outset, so uniformly unpleasant, dangerous, and frightening that it qualified not at all as a countdown toward that serenity I might have expected on a seventh day. This one was spent tacking at a thirty-degree angle of heel for fourteen hours, the cockpit half submerged in water under relentless pounding from the seas. In prospect, assuming a southern run, via Bermuda, we would face a thirteen- or fourteen-day cruise, Bermuda to the Azores. What if, after two days out, I thought suddenly to myself: I am trapped! What if the hours then lengthened and I grew listless with boredom? It is all very well to say, Hell, sit down and study the *Pisan Cantos.* When you are bored at sea, and I have been bored on much shorter trips, there are suddenly no efficacious distractions, neither Pound nor Agatha Christie; not even music over the radio or on the tape recorder. There is nothing in the ship's medicine cabinet for acedia. There is only industry, that "enemy of melancholy" isolated in his diaries by Sir Harold Nicolson. But what if, *per impossibile,* everything were in working order? The weather fine? The engine room and its paraphernalia in perfect condition? I'd take a sight at eight, another at noon, another at four, and star sights at seven. Fourteen days? And what if my friends were similarly afflicted, and conversation slowly ground to a halt, and, by the seventh night out, human communication was reduced to asking for the ketchup? Boredom is the deadliest poison, and it is a truism that it strikes hardest at the most comfortable. Ivan Denisovich suffered everything—except boredom. In due course I would think about devising a few practical hedges, but it was not too soon to think about the right crew.

And so I did. And came up with Peter, Christopher, Danny, Reggie, Van. Perfect. And destined, in the preambular formulation of our Constitution, to become even more perfect when Bill Finucane, who is a woman, the only sister of my wife, and who knows as much about sailing as I know about lacrosse, told me she wanted to come. Everyone knew her. The vote was unanimous, and elated. We had our crew.

Christmastime in the Caribbean

Our first prolonged family experience with Cyrano *took place over Christmastime, 1969. I wrote about that cruise at sufficient length to convey some of the properties of cruising...on* Cyrano...*in the Caribbean...with me.* ⌒

F*riday, December 19. We arrived* at Antigua airport, and that was an achievement. J. K. Galbraith says you shouldn't use pull unless you need to. Well, I needed to get to Antigua because I had decided to go there for a Christmas aboard *Cyrano*—that was two months ago—only to find that all the airlines were booked solid for December 19 and for a day or two bracketing the 19th. I tried everybody I knew, or almost everybody I knew, and finally got Mrs. Julie Nicholson—who with her husband and family dominate Antigua more firmly than Horatio Nelson ever did—to help. She and her husband are yacht and charter brokers, and can get you a ticket from anywhere to anywhere, anytime. It was ordained only that we should make a stop at San Juan. There, waiting for us, were the three Finucanes—Bill and her husband, John, and their daughter, Kathy—who had come in from Los Angeles, joining three Buckleys and Danny, all seven of us traveling together to Antigua. At the dockside was our own Captain Ned Killeen, and a half-dozen partygoers, at the center of whom was Mrs. Nicholson herself. She greeted me warmly and, as I slipped away in the tender, demanded to know what words immediately follow *Gaudeamus igitur*—the first line of the medieval drinking song. My memory failed me, and I felt dreadful, after all the Nicholsons had done for me, that I could not oblige. However, I had not forgotten to bring her Barricini chocolates and ribbon candy, which you must not forget to do if ever you find yourself coming from where you can get Barricini chocolates and ribbon candy to Antigua at Christmastime. I have made a mental note to let Mrs. Nicholson know what comes after *Gaudeamus igitur* as soon as I find out. Let us therefore rejoice. What would follow naturally from that? At this point, I could only think: *Quam ad Antiguam pervenimus*—that we have managed to reach Antigua.

Saturday, December 20. Cyrano is nowadays based in St. Thomas, and it was Ned Killeen's idea that it would make for a pleasant cruise if he "deadheaded" *Cyrano* to Antigua, permitting us to cruise downwind back to St. Thomas. To deadhead means to take a boat without payload. It took him two long nights, into midmorning, to ferry *Cyrano* 220 miles from St. Thomas to Antigua. Ned likes daytime landfalls. I like nighttime landfalls. Ned usually prevails. Ned always prevails when I am not aboard. Interesting thought: How much should we charge charterers to deliver them *Cyrano* in Antigua, should they so desire it? Ned suggests $200 for the two days, which is less than one half the $265 per day that we get for the use of *Cyrano*; but his point is that at $100 per day we are not actually losing money, and a little noblesse oblige on the high seas is always in order. I say something dour about how I wish the bankers would show a little noblesse oblige, and acquiesce in the arrangement.

My beautiful *Cyrano*. Built in the Bahamas, in Abaco, to an old fishing-boat design. Sixty feet long, fifty-four feet at the waterline, with an extraordinary eighteen feet of bowsprit (which I reduced to twelve after poor Danny, aged eighteen, demasted *Cyrano* by going under a fixed bridge on the East River, allowing me to start ex nihilo), seventeen and one-half feet of beam, tapering back to about thirteen feet at the transom, where two stout davits hold up the tender. Acres and acres of deck space. And below, an upright piano which Art Kadey, the previous owner and skipper, banged away at to the great delight of his passengers over the three years between the construction of the boat and my purchase of her.

What was needed, I thought on first looking the boat over, was a great deal of impacted luxury, plus complete instrumentation and rerigging for ocean passages. The latter was obvious enough: running backstays, loran, radar, automatic pilot, that kind of thing. The former is, I think, less obvious. I had done a fair amount of chartering—not a great deal, but enough to come to a few conclusions. They are:

1. Sleeping quarters should be small and public quarters large. One needs in sleeping cabins only privacy and room to turn around.

2. Every cabin should have a port (I used to call them "portholes," until learning that the little rectangular kind that do not open are called nose ports), which should be situated at about eye level when your head is down on the pillow. All my life I have traveled on steamships which require that, in order to see through the port—presumably there for you to see through— you stand on tiptoe, which is hard to do while going to sleep. I got my ports. Three of them on the starboard side, one for each of the cabins, and three of them on the port side in the saloon— all of this in addition to the picture windows in the saloon.

3. Color, color, and more color. More boats are ruined by monochromatic dullness than by careless seamanship. So every room

was decorated by my wife in a chintz of a different color, of congruent patterns, so that we have the red cabin, the yellow cabin, and the green cabin; a green carpet and a glazed cotton print for the settee and couches; and a pattern taking off, in reds and blues, on an old Spanish sailing map.

4. Chairs, settees, and couches must be comfortable. I rebuilt the main settee three times, so as to make it, finally, slope back steeply enough and extend out far enough to make sitting in it truly comfortable for the slouchers of this world—who are my friends and clients. Opposite it, two club chairs, facing my three ports. Wall-to-wall carpeting is right for a boat; kerosene and electric torches, of course. Then I persuaded my friend Richard Grosvenor, the excellent New England artist who teaches at St. George's School, to do three original oil paintings of boat scenes which exactly fit the principal exposed areas I wired to receive them. So that every picture is lit as in an art gallery, the three little overhead lights providing plenty of illumination for the entire saloon, unless you want to read, in which case you snap on one of the other lights. But with the oil paintings alone, the saloon now lights up in color and comfort, a beautiful room designed for total relaxation. When you are under way in a breeze, the seas sometimes rise up, covering the ports completely for whole seconds at a time. (Sometimes the moonlight comes in to you right through the water.) Abaft the piano are the bar and refrigerator, which the former owner so thoughtfully installed to keep charterers from having to go back and forth to the galley quarters, a whole engine room away.

5. The deck area should be—well, perfect. There was no deckhouse. I had one designed and built, with, on either side, a six-and-a-half-foot-long, four-foot-wide cushion, usable as a berth. Between them, the companionway and then a well, where your feet can dangle over a luxuriously large area (larger than a stan-

dard card table) while you navigate, or look into your radar screen, or check your depth finder or a supplementary compass, and where you can even steer the ship electrically. That is, when you want to come forward from the wheel, to get out of the rain. Stepping aft, six or seven feet, an enormous settee. Once again, the accent on comfort. In the Mediterranean many boats have main cockpit settees on which you can sprawl out in any direction. The trick was to accomplish this and also convert the new deckhouse into dining quarters for fair weather. Castro Convertible came to the rescue—by the adaptation of its essential mechanism that permits the raising of a table. Then a custom-built tabletop which exactly fits the arc of the settee, so that when you are not eating, the table sinks down and three tailored cushions exactly cover the area, which now merges with the settee, giving you an enormous area of about four feet by twelve feet in which four or five people can stretch out and read or merely meditate on the splendid achievements of the settee designer. At mealtimes, remove the three cushions, pull a lever—and (hey presto!) a perfectly designed table rises elegantly into place, around which eight people can sit. At night, you can close off the entire area with canvas, giving you something of the feel of a large Arabian tent.

6. The crew must have living space. Under existing arrangements, it is never necessary for guests to occupy *Cyrano*'s old dining quarters in the after section. There the crew has its privacy, adjacent to the captain's cabin, the main navigational table, the galley, and the lazaret.

7. Noise. Somebody, somewhere along the line, told me that the biggest, most expensive generators make the least noise. Ned came up with an Onan so noiseless you can hardly tell whether it's on or off. It provides all the power you need, including 110-volt AC outlets. And finally,

8. Coolness. I know it is costly and difficult to install. Even so, air-condition, or die. I reason as follows: If you live in the Caribbean the year round, perhaps you get used to hot temperatures. But if you only visit the Caribbean, you get hot in the middle of the day—just as you can get hot in Long Island Sound in the summer. Turn on your air conditioner and life changes for you; or it does for me, anyway. I shall never be without my air conditioner. If the bankers one day descend on me, I shall go on national TV and deliver a Checkers speech about my air conditioner. They will never take it from me.

I am staring at the chart as we cruise out of the tight little entrance to English Harbor. What do you say we go to Nevis? I suggest to Ned. Nevis is about forty-five miles west, and it is already noon. The wind is as it should be, east northeast. Ned, so wise, so seasoned, suggests that perhaps we would be better off just going west along the coastline of Antigua, instead of striking out for so distant a goal so late in the day. I am glad I gave in.

Sunday, December 21. I said I was glad I gave in, and I suspect that I gave the impression that where we did spend the night, which was in Mosquito Bay in Antigua, was unique. Not really. It is a very pretty cove (there are no mosquitoes in it, by the way), shallow, and if you want to know when the tide changes, it changes exactly when it changes in Galveston, Texas, for heaven's sake; and not even Ned knew instinctively how to figure that one out. I mean, if the *Tide Book* says: "*see* Galveston, Texas," and you find that the tide begins to ebb at Galveston, Texas, at 1900, at what time does it begin to ebb at Mosquito Bay, Antigua? You will immediately see that conflicting hypotheses are plausible. You may find yourself reasoning that when it is 7:00 P.M. at Galveston, the tide also begins to change at Mosquito Bay: which means you have to figure out the time zone for Galveston. Well, figure Galveston is two hours behind New York, and we are one hour ahead of New York; ergo, it changes at Mosquito Bay at 10:00 P.M. Right? Not necessarily. Maybe it means that just as when it is 7:00 P.M. local time in Galveston the tide changes, so when it is 7:00 P.M. local time in Mosquito Bay, the tide changes—what's implausible about that?

The time has come to note a further complication, which is that when I sail in the Caribbean, I go on what we call Buckley Watch Time, the only eponymous enterprise I have ever engaged in. What you do is tell all hands on board to move their clocks up by one hour. The practical meaning of it all is that you can start the cocktail hour as the sun is setting and eat dinner one hour later, at eight o'clock. Otherwise, you start drinking at six o'clock and eat dinner at seven. The former offends the Calvinist streak in a Yankee; the latter, the Mediterranean streak in a yacht owner. Anyway, in order to avoid digging into the fine print of the *Tide Book*, we decide to fasten on the fact that, after all, the tide here is less than one foot anyway; so we throw out the hook 150 yards from the beach rather than crawl up any further, as we might have done if we had been absolutely sure that Galveston had another hour or so to go before the ebb began. No matter. The sunset was beautiful, we swam, ate—ate very well, thanks to Rawle, a native of St. Vincent, who is a superb cook, and who has the prestige of a real-life shipwreck under his belt. Then we played 21, and I won consistently. The tape player is the arena of a subtle contest between the generations. When one of us goes by it, we glide into the tape cavity something melodic. When one of the seventeen-year-olds goes by, quite unobtrusively he, or she, will slip in The Cream or The Peanut Butters, or whoever. I acknowledge to myself that the war will be formally declared by about lunchtime tomorrow. ("Will you please get those screaming banshees off the air, children?" "Mother, can we put on something that isn't Marie Antoinette?") I am right. We go to bed, and my wife and I can see, outside our port, the full moon and the speckly light it casts on the waters—our waters, because there is no one else in sight.

Monday, December 22. I must make myself plain. I am glad I took the advice that we make the shorter run rather than the longer run to Nevis because I know enough by now about other people to know what suits the general taste in a cruise. I remember, in talking with Art Kadey, the disbelief with which I heard him say that the typical charterer travels approximately four hours every other day! I thought that (and still do) rather on the order of spending a fortnight at your fishing lodge and going out to fish only every other day. It takes time to adapt, if you have taken part in ocean races, accustomed to day and night running. Some come easily to the change, and indeed find it easy to oscillate from furious, implacable racing, day after day—week after week, in such as the Transatlantic, or the TransPac race to Honolulu—to strolling about for a few hours on the same boat you often race, going perhaps no further than ten or fifteen or twenty miles in a single day. Moreover, *Cyrano* takes long sails in stride. She is a shoal-draft boat, built for the Bahamas. She hasn't even a centerboard—merely a long keel stretching the entire length of the hull to a distance of five and one-half feet from the waterline. The result is a certain stodginess in coming about, as any boat has that isn't equipped with ballet shoes; but with that great beam and with whatever it is the designer did to effect those numinous lines, she achieves a glorious seakindliness that makes ocean sailing dry, fast, and stable.

It isn't easy for everybody to relax on a boat. I adore my boat, and every boat I have ever had. But I feel, somehow, that I am always, in a sense, on duty, that I must be going from here to there. And if there is a little bad weather or whatever, well, isn't that a part of the general idea? The point, as Ned and others have patiently explained to me, is that there is the wholly other use of a boat, the use which is absolutely ideal for charterers, and that is the totally comfortable, totally unstrained cruise. So that if you decide this morning to go from Antigua to Nevis but the wind isn't right, why you simply go

CYRANO, WITH HER ORIGINAL BOWSPRIT

somewhere else! You don't have any obligation to meet the New York Yacht Club Squadron at Nevis at 1700, and nobody will tell the Commodore if, instead, you ease off to St. Kitts.

I mean, some people come to total relaxation in boats more easily than others, and they do not feel any constraint to harness their boats to an instrumental objective, like getting from here to exactly there, and There had better be a good distance away from Here in order to give you the feeling that you have accomplished a good run and earned the quiet hours of anchorage. All I say is: There are those of us who are driven, and if you are one of those, you will have to speak firmly to Ned. To say nothing of your wife.

St. Kitts is absolutely ravishing. We arrive rather late and do not disembark, simply because we cannot be bothered to register the boat. Why, oh why, don't the islands issue a triptyque, or whatever the Europeans called that document with all the coupons that facilitated car travel in postwar Europe? Instead you have to hunt down the Immigration and Customs officer, giving him (on one occasion, at Virgin Gorda) *six* copies of the crew and passenger list. Why not a bond that every boat owner could buy, the possession of which would grant free passage everywhere during a season, with a severe penalty if you are caught smuggling, guaranteed by the bonder? How easy everything would be if I were given plenipotentiary power over these matters.

The run to St. Bartholomew (St. Barts) is quite long—forty miles or so—and I suggest to Ned that we take off early, at nine o'clock, and sail under the great rock which they call the Gibraltar of the Caribbean. Surely you mean after the crew has breakfast? says Ned. What the hell, say I, why not get started under power, and then have breakfast? We weigh anchor and proceed, and two days later I notice in the ship's log the stern entry, "Got under way before the crew had breakfast." A brilliant day, strong winds just abaft the beam, poor Christopher is seasick, the only time during the whole trip, but by two o'clock we have pulled into the exemplary little harbor, so neat, so thoroughly landlocked, so lackadaisical, where the rum is cheaper than the water and the rhythm of life is such that the natives never go to work before breakfast, and not always after breakfast.

Tuesday, December 23. My materialistic family is glad to have a little time at St. Barts, because the guidebook says that the prices there are even lower than those at St. Maarten, a day's run west.

We consider, on our way to St. Mart, stopping by Anguilla, another four or five miles west, perhaps to decolonize it, now that history has taught us how easy it is to do. A hundred paratroopers from the British Navy had recently seized the island following its unilateral declaration of independence. But the iron schedule (we must relinquish the boat to charterers in four days) makes this imprudent. I feel very keenly the loss, inasmuch as during the few months of Anguilla's independence, when the rebel government took a full-page ad in the *New York Times* asking for contributions to revolutionary justice, I slipped the government a five-dollar bill in the mail and got back a handwritten letter of profuse gratitude from the Prime Minister.

The idea is to spend a relaxed few hours at St. Mart, and then make the longish (one-hundred-mile) sail to the Virgins, touching in at Virgin Gorda. St. Mart is half Dutch (the lower half) and half French. A very large harbor, with beaches and calm and lots of picturesque boats. We swim and water-ski, and then head out for dinner at the Little Bay Hotel, which is a Hilton type, with casino, triple-air-conditioned bar, so-so restaurant, and higher than so-so prices. We did not get to gamble because the casino opened at 9:00 P.M. and we forgot that we were on Buckley Watch Time; so we went back to *Cyrano* and started out on our overnight run to the Virgins.

I took the watch until 0200, along with Bill Finucane, Pat's exemplary sister, while Pat and her brother-in-law played gin rummy, and the boys and my niece lazed about on deck forward, discussing no doubt the depravities of their elders. I felt constrained (I am that way on a boat) to go forward every twenty minutes or so to make an aesthetic point—single out the moon, for instance, which was about as easy to miss at this point as the sun at dawn—and say casually, "Have you noticed the moon?" The kids are so easy to ambush, because it never fails that they will look up from their conversation, stare about, focus eventually on the moon, and say, finally, "Huh?"

It was an uneventful overnight journey, except that at 3:00 A.M. I was roused from my cabin by my wife, who reported that my apprehensive brother-in-law desired me personally to confirm that the lights off at one o'clock were not (a) an uncharted reef, (b) an unscheduled island, or (c) a torpedo coming at us at full speed. I came on deck and peered out at the lights of what appeared to be a tanker going peacefully toward wherever it was going peacefully

toward. A good chance, though, to show off my radar, which immediately picked it up at six and one-half miles away, heading toward,
approximately, Morocco. I went back to sleep, and awoke when Ned
at the wheel was past the famous Anegada Passage, down which the
Atlantic often sweeps bustily into the Caribbean, but which on this
passage had acted like a wall-to-wall carpet; and now we were surrounded by tall, hilly islands, such that by contrast we felt almost
as though we were going through a network of rivers, calm, warm,
but with breeze enough (finally) to sail. And we put in, at eleven, at
Spanish Town, in order to regularize ourselves with the government
of the British Virgins, which was most awfully obliging, after the
first mate and I completed the six forms registering the names and
affirming the nonsubversive intentions of the tired but happy crew
and passengers of the schooner *Cyrano*.

Wednesday, December 24. We head now for a bay, particularly
favored by Ned, in Virgin Gorda. Getting there is a minor problem,
requiring a certain concentration so as to avoid Colquhoun Reef. In
nonnavigational language, you proceed like up, over, down, back,
and up, so as to avoid the long reef. The rewards are great, because
after you nestle down there you see along the reef, a few hundred
yards away from the anchorage, the beautiful blues and greens you
have been missing thus far, where the water was deep. It is strictly
Bahamian here. They say, by the way, that the Virgins are vastly to
be preferred to the Bahamas "from the water level up." This is
shorthand to communicate the following: The islands are infinitely
more interesting in the Antilles—the Virgins, the Windwards, and
the Leewards. Every island is strikingly interesting and different,
both topographically and culturally. St. Kitts, for instance, has Mt.
Misery, an enormous volcano rising to 4,300 feet. Nothing of the
sort happens in the Bahamas, where the islands are almost uniformly low. But the Bahamian waters are uniquely splendid in col-

oration. The sandbars and reefs, which are so troublesome to the navigator, repay the bother to the swimmer and to anyone who just wants to look.

Anyway, Virgin Gorda is that way, and on shore is the Drake's Anchorage hostelry, which just that morning had changed hands. The previous owner of the little bar and inn had sold out to—would you believe it?—a professor at MIT. The bar and dining room were Somerset Maugham–tropical, and were all dressed up for Christmas. The talk was of the necessity to persuade somebody to come down and take over the exciting underwater tours of the departed owner, who specialized in taking adventurous spirits for scuba diving in the Anegada Passage to poke about the wrecks at Horseshoe Reef, not all of which have, by any means, reposed there since the eighteenth century. The flagpole at the hostelry is the corroded aluminum mast of the *Ondine*, which foundered there just a few years ago.

Having reconnoitered, we went back to *Cyrano*, at that point almost alone in the anchorage, just in time to see a smallish sloop come gliding toward us, brazenly avoiding the circumnavigatory imperatives of the guidebooks, treating the reef we had given such studied berth to as familiarly as if it were the skipper's bathroom. We watched in awe as a dignified lady in a sunbonnet directed the tiller to conform with the directions given by the angular, robust old gentleman up forward handling the anchor. The landing was perfect, the motor never having been summoned to duty, and they lodged down, fifty yards away from us. I discreetly manned the binoculars, peeked for a while, and said to my companions, "By George, I do believe that is Dr. Benjamin Spock."

I know the gentleman slightly, having sparred with him here and there in the ideological wars. I wondered what, under the circumstances, would be an appropriate way to greet him. I thought of sending Ned over to his sloop, instructed to say, "Dr. Spock, compliments of *Cyrano*, do you happen to have anything on board for bubonic plague?" But the spirit of the season overcame me, and instead I wrote out an invitation, "Compliments of the military–industrial complex, Mr. and Mrs. William F. Buckley Jr. would be honored to have the company of Dr. and Mrs. Benjamin Spock and their friends for Christmas cheer at 6:00 P.M." The good doctor rowed over (I knew, I *knew* he wouldn't use an outboard engine) to say, Thanks, how was I? Mrs. Spock wasn't feeling very well, please forgive them, they were pulling out anyway within the hour, come back soon, once you've sailed the Virgins you can never sail anywhere else; and rowed back. We struck out in the glasshopper (all-glass dinghy) with the kids to explore the reef, which they did for hours on end. I returned to *Cyrano* (I enjoy skin diving, but a half hour of it is fine by me), mounted the easel and acrylic paint set Bill Finucane brought me for Christmas, and set about industriously to document, yet again, my lack of artistic talent. The girls were working on the decorations, and by the time the sun went down we had a twinkling Christmas tree on deck and twinkling lights along the canvas of the dodger; the whole forward section was piled with Christmas gifts and decorations, and when we sat down for dinner—with three kerosene lights along the supper table, the moon's beam, lambent, aimed at us as though we were the single target of the heavens, Christmas music coming in from the tape player, the wine and the champagne and the flambéed pudding successfully passed around, my family there, and friends— I persuaded myself that no one anywhere could have asked for any kinder circumstances for celebrating the anniversary of the coming of the Lord.

Thursday, December 25. Intending to go to church on Christmas Day in Road Town, the capital of the British Virgins, we pull out earlyish, arriving in time for the noon Mass.

We come in European-style at the yacht basin. European-style, by the way, involves dropping an anchor, sometimes two, about thirty yards in front of where you intend to position your boat. Then you back up toward the pier (usually stone or concrete) while someone up forward, the anchor having kedged, is poised to arrest your backward movement by snubbing up on the anchor line the moment you give the signal. You back up the boat to about ten feet from the landing. At the right moment, you toss out the port stern line diagonally, and the starboard stern line ditto. Obliging passersby secure these lines on the pier, and you have—you can readily see—a very neat situation. The stern lines are acting as, in a way, spring lines, restricting the boat's sideward movement, sideward being where other boats are lined up, leaving, very often, no more than a few inches of sea room. Then, when you are safely harnessed, you motion to the gentleman on the foredeck to ease the line to the anchor, while the two gentlemen aft take up on their lines, bringing *Cyrano*'s stern gently aft until the davits are hanging quietly over the pier. You have now only to take a step over the taffrail, touch down easily on the ground, and without equilibratory gyration, stroll on toward the nearest taverna. I don't know why the custom isn't more widespread in American harbors, the economy of space and motion being so very obviously advantageous. Of course, you need to have a sheer situation off the pier, which isn't the case in many New England snuggeries. But even when there is water, the habit is not practiced by American yachtsmen. So much is it the drill in, for instance, Greece, that pleasure craft of any size carry gangways that extend from the transom to the pier, including stanchions and lifelines to serve as banisters for milady to hang onto as she descends daintily to earth. I remember a year ago in the Aegean seeing a hedonistic triumph called the *Blue Leopard*, an enormous yawl which, miraculously, ejected its gangway from just beneath the deck level, where it is stowed, like the shelf that pulls out from a desk, right down—onto the pier? No, dear. To six inches above the pier, contact with which it was protected from by two special halyards which quickly materialized and were quickly attached to the far corners. The purpose? Why, to spare the *Blue Leopard* the fetid possibility that a restless rat, seeking a tour of the Aegean, might amble up the companionway, it being acknowledged that rats tend to *board* a floating ship.

We linger only an hour or so. The gentleman who owns the bar, the Sir Francis Drake Pub, is moved by the spirit of the season and does not charge you—Merry Christmas!—for your first drink, and we feel rather sneaky ordering only a single round and then returning to *Cyrano* for lunch. Christmas lunch. Rawle could give us anything, beginning with lobster Newburg and ending with Baked Alaska. We settle on a fish chowder, of which he is surely the supreme practitioner, and cheese and bacon sandwiches, grilled, with a most prickly Riesling picked up at St. Barts for peanuts. Then we wander off to the Fort Burt Hotel, which is built around the top of the old fort, providing a three-hundred-degree view of the harbor and adjacent islands.

Off we go, to swim and to spend the night off Norman Island, which is reputedly the island Robert Louis Stevenson was describing when he wrote *Treasure Island*. It is, needless to say, just like any other island (except that it lies adjacent to fascinating grottos, complete with bats, into which you row wide-eyed). On the other hand, needless to say, like the other islands it is captivating: a beach; a fine, protected cove. I remember a few years ago when, intending to pleasure him, I took Christopher, aged fourteen and having done exceptionally well at school, with me cross-country to San Francisco and Los Angeles, where I was to record television programs. My son was the prodigy of the McLuhanite dogma, but I was determined not to raise my voice in criticism—he was at my side (a) because I adored him, and (b) because I sought concrete expression of my admiration of his academic work. But finally—after four hours of flight, during which, earphones glued on, Christopher merely stared at the ceiling, even as his overworked father fussed fetishistically with briefcases and papers—I lost control. I turned on him and said acidly, or better, acidulously, "Christopher, just out of curiosity, have you ever read a book?"

He moved his right hand slowly, with that marvelous impudence the rhythm of which comes so naturally to the bloody Kids, dislodging his right earphone just enough to permit him to speak undistracted by the musical narrative of whatever rockrolling fustian he was listening to. He replied in Peter Fonda drawl, "Yeah. *Treasure Island.*" Back went the earphones. The eyes did not need to revert to the ceiling of the plane. They had never left it.

It was our final night aboard *Cyrano* and we felt, although we did not sentimentalize on it, the little pang one always feels on approaching the end—of anything. The night was fine. Calm, peaceful. The moon made its appearance, though later; grudgingly, it seemed. I think we lingered more than usual before going below to sleep.

Friday, December 26. We stopped at Trunk Bay, St. John, to skin-dive. St. John is the island most of which was given by the U.S. government to the Rockefellers, or vice versa, I forget which. In any case, you must drop your anchor well out in the cove, because the lifeguards do not permit you to come too close. In fact, when you come in toward the beach with your dinghy, you are required, if you have an outboard motor, to drop anchor fifty yards from the beach and off to the right, away from the swimmers. If you don't have an outboard, you may beach your dinghy. But if you do beach your dinghy, you may not attach its painter (the boat word for the leash of a dog or tether of a horse) to the palm tree up from the beach, because you will be told that people might stumble over it, which indeed people might do if they are stone-blind. Then you walk to the east side of the beach, put on your face mask and fins, and follow the buoys, ducking down to read, underwater, marvelously readable descriptions of flora and fauna, the reading matter engraved on stone tablets which tilt up at a convenient angle and describe the surrounding situation and the fishes you are likely to come across.

The tablets I saw did not describe the barracuda that took a fancy to me, whose visage was fascinatingly undistinguishable from Nelson Rockefeller's, but then my face mask was imperfectly fitted. We got back to *Cyrano* and sailed on down past the Rockefeller Hotel at Cancel Bay to Cruz Bay, where we officially reentered the United States of America. Embarrassing point. My wife thought, it being the day after Christmas and all, that it would be pleasant if I took to the lady who transacts the official immigration protocols a bottle of cheer. I went to her with Ned at my side, and found her wonderfully efficient and helpful. She completed the forms, and then, rather like Oliver Twist making time with the beadle, I surfaced a bottle of Ron Ponche and, with a flourish or two, presented it to her, trying to look like Guy Kibbee playing Santa Claus. She smiled benignly, and then explained that she could not, under The Rules, accept such gifts. I was crestfallen, embarrassed, and shaken, and returned feistily to my wife to say, See, that's what you get trying to bribe American authorities! To which she replied, Trying to bribe them to do what? Which stumped me, and I took a swig of the rejected Ron Ponche, which tasted like Kaopectate, perhaps explaining the lady's rectitude.

We travel under power to St. Thomas, a mere couple of hours. Yacht Haven at St. Thomas might as well be Yacht Haven at Stamford, Connecticut, where *Cyrano* would spend next summer. Hundreds of boats, harried administrators, obliging officials giving and taking messages, paging what seemed like everybody over the loudspeaker, connecting pallid, sleepy Northeasterners with their snowflaked baggage and then with wizened boat captains. Only the bar, which opens at 8:00 A.M., made it obviously other than Yacht Haven, Stamford; and, of course, the weather. About eighty-two degrees, and sun, sun, sun; we had not been without it, except for an hour or two on either side of a squall, during the entire idyllic week.

A charterer would board the next afternoon, and the preparations were accordingly feverish. The adults obliged by taking a couple of rooms at the Yacht Haven Hotel in which to spend the final night. The boys stayed on board to help. We had yet to consummate a dinner cruise around the harbor, and our scheduled dinner guests were my libel lawyer, Mr. Charles Rembar, and his wife and son. They arrived (an hour late—a serious matter inasmuch as they had not been indoctrinated in Buckley Watch Time), and we slid out in the darkness (the moon would be very, very late), and cruised about, under power this time, bounding off the lights of the five great cruise ships that lined the harbor and its entrance. St. Thomas is not unlike Hong Kong at night, except, of course, that its hills are less high. But the lights are overwhelming, and the spirit of Christmas was everywhere, so that we cruised gently in the galaxy, putting down, finally, the anchor; had our dinner, pulled back into the slip, said our goodbyes, and left my beautiful *Cyrano*, so firm and reliable, so strong and self-assured, so resourceful and copious, and made our way back, in stages, to New York, where, for some reason—obscure, after the passage of time—our ancestors left their boats in order to settle down there, so that their children's children might dream, as I do, of reboarding a sailing boat and cruising the voluptuous waters that Columbus hit upon in his crazy voyage five hundred years ago, because he did not have Ned aboard to tell him when enough was enough.

Gulf Stream Musings

A leisurely cruise, New York–Bermuda, is the scene for musings about celestial navigation, then and now.

Somewhere between the Statue of Liberty and the Verrazano Bridge, our festivities came to an end. The sailors would leave the party boat that wished them Godspeed and cast off for Bermuda aboard *Patito,* my little thirty-six-foot sloop. My crew was Van, Christo, Danny, and Phil Hutchinson, a veteran sailor who had ten years earlier won the Bermuda Race sailing his own boat. We shuttled across on the Avon dinghy, two at a time, from the party boat, the *Petrel*, to *Patito*. *Patito* had been sailing along-side for an hour or so, in compliance with the sailors' command-ment that when there is an occasion for a party, it is profane not to have one. The *Petrel*, a seventy-two-foot yawl designed by Spark-man & Stephens, had campaigned, Newport–Bermuda, in the early thirties. Now she does matronly duties for hire for whatever parochial cruise the customer desires; in our case, broad-reaching back and forth wherever the wind commanded (it was fresh, steady; the day exuberant, emerging from a morning haze), while sharing a cheerful and bountiful box lunch with thirty guests.

All five of us were now aboard *Patito*, and we waved to the *Petrel* and powered into the southerly, cutting the engine and slid-ing into a starboard tack on nearing Ambrose Light. We were not quite fetching Bermuda for the first hour or two but soon we were doing so, and before the sun set, we could do 150 degrees magnetic on a close, companionable reach. A hundred miles to the east would be the Bermuda racing fleet, which had set out a few hours earlier. As a veteran of four Bermuda races I reflected smugly on our liberty, as a noncombatant cruiser, to start up the engine if the wind should fail us. I remembered most graphically the race when for almost thirty-six hours we had squatted down, airless and, by the end of the second day, frazzled by fifteen hours of sunlight. I remembered during those endless hours taking sun sights, one after another, to try to estimate what the current was doing to us, so that when the wind came, we might with confidence point the boat to St. David's.

What an odd preoccupation that now seems. A sailor no longer depends on celestial navigation. Yes, and students are no longer required to cope with multiplication or division; they just use their calculators. At sea, we use GPS.

I took stock as, six hours after leaving the *Petrel*, we sat about the cockpit with wine and pretzels, a fifteen-knot southwesterly easing us lightheartedly in the right direction. On the starboard bulkhead, within easy view of the helmsman, is our Trimble Nav-Graphic. It was telling us where we were, giving latitude and longitude to one one-hundredth of a mile (that's fifty feet). It told us where Kitchen Shoals was (32-26, 64-36—this was a reciprocal gesture, inasmuch as I had informed the NavGraphic that morning, typing in the coordinates, where Kitchen Shoals was); what direction to go in order to arrive at it (15.5 degrees), how far away it lay (671 miles), at what speed were we traveling toward it (5.7 knots), how far we had drifted from the rhumb line (0.4 miles east), and at what hour, at this speed, we were likely to arrive (2203, three days hence). The ocean chart was illuminated by the NavGraphic, which received signals via satellite situating our vessel exactly—a tiny, bobbing icon-sized sail.

It is proper to rejoice when reflecting on GPS, but there is a menacing factor in the enterprise, which is called Selective Availability. This means that when the Pentagon feels like it, which is... when it feels like it, the signal is degraded, up to three hundred meters. In a fog, that could make the difference between finding the channel entrance and hitting rocks. Why the "dithering," as it is generally called? Answer: national defense. But really, we have here a geostrategic affectation. The enemy is not going to target our hardened silos by GPS—they'd use inertial guidance, as we do. Moreover, the only world power capable of that kind of aggression right now is still Russia, and the irony here is that they have developed their own GPS system, called Glonass, and *it* is not degraded, giving the navigator real accuracy. A defense against unreliable signals is the system called Differential GPS. What we have here is beacons scattered along coastal waters. A fifteen-million-dollar Coast Guard operation designed to frustrate the Defense Department. But to tune in on DGPS you need—yet another receiver. As long as loran is still around, we have the option of dropping GPS and going loran when approaching menacing areas. There is talk of dropping loran, an event that would leave us at the mercy of an unreliable GPS. If that happens, the only thing to do is to exercise selective political availability at the polls.

I went below and dug up from my drawer my handheld, battery-operated little Trimble. It is called an Ensign. It doesn't display any charts, but it will give me every datum I just cited above. It incidentally also gives the user the option of receiving the data in any of eleven languages. If you decide to amuse yourself by opting for Arabic, which I once did in an excess of irresponsible curiosity, make certain you know the Arabic for "English," so that you can get back into your own tongue.

After I had fiddled with my Ensign and passed it around, Phil went down, foraged in his drawer, and came back with his Magellan

GPS, also battery-operated. So: We had three GPS units on board. I have also a new RDF, new in that it has never been used, though it is three years old. It would come in handy if a world war broke out before we came into St. George's and GPS was immobilized by the Pentagon or by the enemy. We could not then rely on loran, because my two-year-old NavGraphic has eschewed loran, which in any case, given its limited range, was never very surefooted by the time you reached Bermuda waters. If GPS were immobilized and we were out of reach of Bermuda Radio, I would need to pick up my sextant. I've made four ocean crossings. In all four, I had to rely on the sextant to come in. No longer.

પુરુ

Once upon a time, a sextant was useful only to establish (if roughly) your latitude. That's because, as we all know, it is easy to determine when the sun reaches its zenith, never mind what was the Greenwich Mean Time at that moment. And navigators were familiar with the essential movements of the North Star and could get another, reasonably accurate, latitude reading in the evening and at dawn, never mind the hour on the clock face, let alone the minute or second.

But there was no way to know your longitude, not until you could establish where at any given moment the sun would sit down if it blazed not a million or so miles in diameter, a hundred million miles away, but reduced to a dot on the surface of the earth, like your own little boat. The sun's Greenwich Hour Angle, they call it. You knew how fast the sun traveled and, every day, at what latitude; but if you reckoned it was 10:05:00 GMT when you took your sight, and it was actually 10:08:00, you'd find yourself forty-five miles east or west of your course. Risky business in those piratical, bellicose days, with shoals charted and uncharted, as Patrick O'Brian will remind you, if you had forgotten. The "search for longitude" was consummated when the chronometer was born, during the reign of George III.

But even then there was an element of instability. I remember twenty-five years ago rummaging in Gibraltar at an old watch shop and picking up for a hundred dollars a Hamilton chronometer, which was warranted to gain five to seven seconds per day exactly. People used to worry just a little bit, keeping their chronometers on gimbals and in recesses protected from wide swings in temperature. But meanwhile the radio grew up, and soon we were getting time ticks from Colorado to correct watch time. Among its offerings, GPS gives you the time exactly, lagniappe from IBM and the satellites.

Having got the time, you needed to get your sights: the sun, of course; and, if you were ambitious, if you were racing—if you were approaching your destination—the stars. This was a whole other matter, getting the star sights; and having collected them, you needed to plot them, and this required a drill, A, B, C, D, E, F, G, routine in its consecutive demands and mortally subversive if you slipped out of order. Even as, when I was learning to fly a plane, I was strictly enjoined to recite out loud the five initiating steps every single time before taking off, so the celestial navigation systems recommend that you follow a sequence, to remind you about things like semidiameters and index errors and parallax. The drill doesn't require long division or multiplication, merely adding and subtracting. But it was irksome, especially when you had to use one arm at maximum muscular exertion to keep from hurtling to leeward in one of those rolls, while simultaneously manipulating a pencil and a divider with the other as if performing brain surgery.

But whish! in the late 1970s that problem disappeared, with the advent of the handheld calculator. You gave it your sun sight, the GMT, the day-month-year, and an assumed position, and it returned you an intercept and an azimuth. That was the Model A. Within a year or two came the V-8. This model would give you a running fix. In 1983 I approached my polymathic friend Hugh Kenner—who is supposed to know more about Ezra Pound than anyone else alive, and this is true, but he also knows more about polyhedra than Buckminster Fuller—and I said to him, Hugh, if I shoot a star and I don't know what star it is, why couldn't a computer tell me? He went to work on the problem and came up with WhatStar. This program asks you to estimate within one hundred miles where you are, and give it the altitude of the star. It presumes then to tell you which was the star you shot at 23:05:05. It is beautiful, it is useful, but it is not entirely reliable, because more than one star might be plausible.

Along came PC Navigator. The concept here is reciprocal and, really, more graphic. You estimate your position and the computer will flash forward, listing on your screen the relevant navigational stars and the planets and their altitudes at the moment you contemplate bringing them down.

Listed how? *You* decide. You can ask the PCN to give you the stars and planets in the order of their brightness, or in the order of their magnitude; or alphabetically. (Only listing by primogeniture is excluded.) Moreover, you can instruct the program: Give me only heavenly bodies brighter than 1.2. And you can tell it, Show me only heavenly bodies higher than ten degrees above the horizon—below that (you bellyache), I find the angle flimsy and the star unreliable, never mind the parallax correction made by the computer. And while you are at it (you can be a fussbudget), kindly do not distract me with any star higher than thirty-five degrees, as I strain my back when I look up that sharply. The PCN screen immediately complies.

Incredible. Truly incredible.

On top of that, PCN (which, by the way, tries to do too much: you must exercise triage when you use it) will give you running fixes, never mind when last you fed it such basic data as speed and direction. That facet of the program is more useful on the *QE2*, where I used it the week before I took *Patito* to Bermuda, than it is on a sailboat sailing close-hauled. I must not leave the subject without urging the PCN people and their colleagues and competitors to spare the user the utterly needless distraction of having to insert periods, as in 68.05 degrees, or colons (16:08:04 GMT). Hugh Kenner imposes no such bureaucratic distractions. The computer, after all, can be coached to know that 6805 is 68 degrees 5 minutes, and that 160804 is the same as 16:08:04. In any case, the concept is reversed. Buckley–Kenner says, Here (roughly) is where I am; now what is the name of that star I just shot? This has the mystery and the fun of What's My Name, when you have five questions and have to guess the identity of the person described. PCN says: Here you are (roughly) and here is a layout of the stars at this moment. It's up to you to figure out, after consulting your screen, the name of the star that sits twenty-two degrees up on an azimuth of 270 degrees.

What then is left for the celestial navigator to do? The exact time is his for the asking, and the computations are done for him.

What he needs to do is take a reasonably reliable sight on his sextant.

Which body he is observing is not in question when he seeks out the sun or the moon. Which planet, or which of the brighter stars, he is looking at, he can be forewarned about by PCN or other systems. But actually bringing down a star, I submit after twenty-five years of doing it off and on, is by no means easy to do on a pitching sailboat. To set out to locate your star, it is ever so much easier to use a universal sight tube, the prismless, clear tube that gives you four times the width of vision of the magnified tube. But then having located your star, when you edge the horizon up, or the star down, it becomes flirtatiously visible/invisible. So you decide to attach the telescope. This takes a little time, requires a little light on the sextant, and temporarily disorients you. I'd like to see a sextant designed that toggles on/off the telescope or, alternatively, the universal sight tube, click click, so that you would never need to take your eyes from the star once you had pinpointed it. A wonderful, prehensile sextant. Granted, aboard a large and steady ship the problem diminishes. But you find yourself saying: Inasmuch as the only problematic left is the star sight, what exactly is the point in developing your skill aboard the *QE2* when the skill you need to develop is to catch the star on a heaving thirty-six-foot sailboat? Practicing with a canoe on a lake doesn't teach you to run the rapids.

৵

Will celestial navigation, in the future, be something like fencing? An aristocratic pastime for the dilettante? If the whole enterprise reduces simply to: Where am I?—then the answer is, Yes. Back then, fencing was a means of protecting yourself and making a point at another's expense, but it survives as a sport, and a form of exercise requiring coordination. Celestial navigation requires coordination, but doesn't use up many calories, and can be called a sport only in the sense that doing a crossword puzzle can be thought of as being that.

What celestial navigation does do is reaffirm in another medium what sailing is all about, namely, the unaggressive exploitation of nature. No sensible cruising sailboat disdains an engine, but no sailor would want to go to sea if, were his engine to fail, he'd thereupon be powerless. I'd guess that, unlikely though it now is that an adequately provisioned sailboat will ever again find itself lost at sea, something in the human spirit will remain there to impel the restive sailor to ask: "How, otherwise, would I know where I am?"—even as it is likely that some of tomorrow's scientists will doodle about and learn how to do long division all by themselves. Needless to say, any urge to return to original instruments can be carried to zany lengths: *Kon-Tiki* time. Do without a chronometer? Exchange your sextant for an astrolabe? . . .

TAKING A SIGHT

❧

Five days later we were tacking in to St. George's. It was after midnight, and the moon was nearly full. We could make out only two navigation lights, St. David's and Kitchen Shoals. On my right in the cockpit my faithful NavGraphic (but without the accompanying chart, as we didn't have on board the disk that covers Bermuda) told us all the things we wished to know. And on the left of the cockpit, my radar, giving out bold, resolute signals.

Presently a mountain range formed, stretching on our starboard from twelve o'clock diagonally to four o'clock. Phil was a little distressed because the GPS showed us a comfortable nine miles from Bermuda. But here was the radar, suggesting we were heading into the northern bight of land a mere 2.5 miles away.

What could be wrong?

I stayed at the wheel while Christo and Danny and Phil conferred, with furrowed brows, checking and rechecking the GPS, which adamantly insisted that we were nine miles away from hitting land and rocks, while the radar showed us getting closer and closer. I hurtled on toward the mountain range while waiting for the furrowed brows below to resolve the paradox.

Finally I thought to turn the radar to a twenty-four-mile range. The mountains shrank to mincing little flattened pearls, and beyond them we outlined a shore. Nine miles off. The mountain range, we could now see, was simply a tight, muscular cloud formation, not easily visible to the human eye under the camouflage of moonlight, and indistinguishable, in the eyes of radar, from land itself. All was well.

Funny. I remembered the finish to one Bermuda race in swirling fog and haze late at night, with only occasional glimpses of St. David's light, toward which we headed in the heavy wind, praying that when we approached the finish line the haze would go away. A few years ago, Ted Koppel asked me to go on his program to reiterate my view, published a few days earlier in my newspaper column, that a blind man had no business sailing his boat to Bermuda, a feat that had just been undertaken by an adventurer who, having been rescued by the Coast Guard, was now in Bermuda in a studio, spoiling to quarrel with me. I was dumb enough to agree to go on. I had incompletely learned the political incorrectness of the view that the handicapped are actually handicapped, and shouldn't deceive themselves by going to sea alone. As we roared now under sail toward St. George's absolutely confident of our navigation, it struck me that up until quite recently we were all relatively blind at sea. No longer.

But then we would not again experience quite that little delirium of satisfaction that comes at landfall time. In late June 1985 my job was to guide my yawl to Kapingamarangi, a two-mile-wide atoll in the South Pacific. And when it materialized, without the aid of loran, GPS, SatNav, or RDF, you had the feeling you could lick any man in the house, possibly excepting the blind sailor.

Meet Me at K Club

The rendezvous sounded simple, until we ran into a broken engine mount, treacherous surf, and chilly relations on dry land.

Sailing with my wife and me were older brother Jim and older sister Priscilla, and I had told them about cruising life in the Antilles and its special delights, among them the endless beach of Barbuda. This wasn't like taking the kids for the first time to Disney World. My siblings have been around. Jim spent two years in action in the navy during World War II and knew all about beaches because he served aboard an LST, which of course is designed to come up onto a beach to disgorge troops, tanks, and spare parts. Priscilla had wandered with me for several days in the Tahiti islands, including the fabulous Bora-Bora, and once we had sashayed about the most beautiful islands in the world (I insist)—the Azores. But the Azorean beaches do suffer from dusky-gray sand, in contrast to the white-white beaches of the Antilles. I remember, in my exasperation over tourists' neglect of the Azores, speculating on whether the old trick of the ad man in the thirties might work to sell the Azores to the tourist world. He was hired—remember?—by a fishery trying to unload an aberrant million pounds of snow-white salmon. He came up with the slogan, "Guaranteed Not to Turn Pink in the Can!"

Our approach to Barbuda was restricted by an event that had taken place that morning. As we bounded under sail from Antigua toward Barbuda in a happy easterly, the skipper of our chartered

Swan 65 advised me, with heroic equanimity, that the noise I had heard during the preceding half hour meant that the engine mount had collapsed. "How long will it take to repair?" I asked.

"Well, certainly not less than one week." But his young face brightened: "With the course you've set, we can sail all the way, and the generator's working just fine." Who needs an engine?

But this meant that our tack toward the anchorage area, about a hundred yards from Barbuda's spectacular beach, had to end before the outermost reefs began, which left us a half mile from land. Yet we needed to press on, not only because of the special allure of the famous two-mile-long beach, but because we had social obligations. My wife's old friends Arthur and Francisco were staying at K Club, at the north end of the beach, and had pressingly asked us to dine with them during our cruise. And then at the south end of the beach is Coco Point Lodge, founded and run by Bill Kelly, a college friend of Jim, who had promised to stop by.

"How old is Coco Point Lodge?" I asked Jim as the sails came down. He didn't remember exactly, but he said that if *I* could remember when Princess Margaret Rose was married, that was when the lodge opened, because she had honeymooned there. Well, I didn't remember exactly when Margaret Rose and Antony Armstrong-Jones had married, only that it was many *anni horribili* back for the Royal Family, so Coco Point had been around for several decades. But we were anchored at the other end of the beach, off K Club, where Arthur and Francisco awaited us. The captain said he would take the dinghy in to the beach and advise me what was involved in stepping ashore.

A half hour later he was back. "There's something of a...swell," he cautioned. "But of course, we can handle it." Since my wife has frail hips, thrice operated on, Jim and I decided to do a dry run in order exactly to evaluate the difficulty in landing on the island with our dinghy.

We approached, and the swell seemed quietly and nicely to subside. We were only feet away from shore when a rogue wavelet crashed in, and we tumbled out into crotch-level water. Pat and Priscilla, it was now clear, would not be visiting this island, but I would attempt minimally to discharge social obligations, and Jim would visit a half hour with Bill Kelly.

With my cellular phone I told Francisco at K Club that we were there, standing in the sand within sight of his hotel. In minutes he reached us.

Francisco was, as always, breathless with the amusements and vexations of life in general, and life in particular. As we trudged up toward the clubhouse, he gave us two data relevant to our plans.

Concerning Jim's destination, we should know something about the problem between K Club and Coco Point Lodge. They are both luxury resorts, but the relations between the two owners are, according to Francisco, straight-out Hatfield–McCoy. "It's like North Korea and South Korea," Francisco tells us. "So we'll have to make special arrangements," he said to Jim, "to get you over to Coco."

And then—he chatted on as we approached the lightly screened, aquamarine-and-white clubhouse, all but demolished four months earlier by Hurricane Luis, but miraculously rebuilt in time for the season—there was the problem of Princess Diana.

We had been at sea a few days and were ignorant of what the society page of every tabloid in the world was evidently whispering, in January 1996—namely, that Di was on the island of Barbuda, staying at K Club. "Alone?" I found myself asking, without malice aforethought, just spastic journalistic curiosity.

"She has her lady-in-waiting," Francisco explained. "They spend the *entire* time at the swimming pool." I found this odd, given the lascivious wonders of the beach, as also, we'd learn, the two flood-lit tennis courts, the nine-hole golf course, the snorkeling, the sailing.

But on the other hand—we were sitting in the lounge across from the bar; Jim had made off across the DMZ to Coco Point Lodge—there isn't actually that much to do, is there, on a beach? Arthur, who is a famous architect, had joined us and nodded in vigorous agreement, because when *he* goes to the beach, he says, he goes in order to get a lot of reading done, whereas Francisco is a beach nut who stretches out hour after hour, sun-worshipping. Beaches, Arthur and I agreed, are splendid to look at, not to plop down on.

But they were enjoying K Club and its 250 acres, on an island with 1,500 inhabitants. Sixty percent of the island's income is from tourists, and now they had the crown jewel, Princess Diana.

We would learn that her arrival had caused great commotion. She had slipped out of Heathrow a day or two after Christmas, with her lady-in-waiting, onto a commercial flight to Antigua, using an assumed name. But, poor dear, she was spotted by one of the dogs of the press, and by the time her private plane (Antigua–Barbuda, flight time ten minutes) had landed, a great legion of paparazzi had gathered, intending to make her stay on the island as exposed as possible.

To thwart this, the authorities in Barbuda had rallied. Among other things they closed off a half mile of the great beach. This was not accepted without complaint. The owner of a local grocery store had been quoted in the papers as saying that "legally, we can access the beach and sit right next to her. I totally object to anybody shutting off what is public property." And then Diana had not made time with the locals when, on being asked to appear at a ceremony honoring people who had played key roles in restoring the island (95 percent of the roofs had been damaged by the hurricane), she simply denied the request—which is not what was expected of someone who only weeks before had told the world she hoped to be thought of as the Queen of Hearts.

I was called to the telephone. It was my brother, speaking to me from Hanoi. He reported that Bill Kelly, the king of Coco Point, suggested that I contact the captain aboard our vessel and warn him not to approach us at the designated rendezvous point where he had landed forty-five minutes before, because, night having fallen, he might hit one of the barely submerged reefs.

But there was no way to reach the captain, I said, since I didn't have a radio with me and he was not monitoring any channel. Very well then, Jim would meet me in fifteen minutes, as previously arranged.

I returned to my rum Collins and my hosts, and a crew-cut middle-aged man in casual dress addressed me. "I'm Ken Follett," he said, "and Ed McBain is also staying here. Now that is a coincidence, isn't it—you, me, McBain?" I told Mr. Follett I thought *The Fist of God* one of the best suspense/espionage novels I had ever read, and he said thanks, but he didn't write it. I plunged into another title, but he hadn't written that one either. I told him I still winced at the review he had given one of my thrillers in the *Listener*, but he disclaimed that as well. The only thing I could do under the circumstances was to congratulate Mr. Follett on whatever it was he *had* written (*The Eye of the Needle*; the *other* person is Frederick Forsyth). We wished each other a happy New Year.

But the time had come, and Francisco and Arthur came with me to the point on the beach where we could make out the beached dinghy. We waited for Jim. He was almost ten minutes late. He had been stopped, after getting out of the Coco car and walking out to the beach to approach us, by the police guarding Princess Di's privacy. Jim was once a senator, is now a senior judge, and positively emanates sobriety. Not even Ken Follett would cast him as a terrorist.

We made it back over the reefs, and reported to wife and sister all the news of the captivating island of Barbuda.

A Quickie, Bahamas to Charleston

Constrained by busy schedules, beset by storms, dogged by a mystery boat—the sailors still counted themselves lucky. ⌒

T*he invitation was as welcome* as it was unexpected: to bring Peter Flanigan's thirty-eight-foot sloop back from Abaco in the Bahamas to this part of the world. I say "this part of the world" because the exact destination was unstipulated. The idea was to sail the boat as far north as possible toward Norfolk, Virginia, in the time we had. From Norfolk, a friend of Peter's, a professional pilot, would ferry the *Astraea* to its destination, Stamford, Connecticut.

Peter, I came to know, is skilled in every aspect of sailing, but he hasn't had much ocean experience and for that reason desired a skipper-navigator along. We have been friends lo these many years, and I have observed him using his shrewd mind and incisive tongue at home (Purchase, N.Y.), in the Oval Office (he was an assistant to President Nixon), and at the Metropolitan Opera (Peter attends, does not sing). He was born competent and along the way developed sharp executive skills (Dillon Read). Accordingly I could tell, early on, that he envisioned this passage as mine, and for that reason left it to me to put the crew together. "I should think four would be enough," he said over the phone in November.

I countered with five. "Someone may be seasick." I have almost always found it so, e.g., in all four races I did to Bermuda, sailing my own boats with eight crew on board.

But then, I explained to Peter, when racing, we'd always have three men on watch. When cruising, two are enough, with a third hand on call. Peter agreed, and in the ensuing period rough calculations danced about in my mind—it is always so, well in advance of a blue-water outing, vague thoughts given to the upcoming sail. The day comes when you cannot prudently put off the fine-tuning. I was away from my charts when that moment came, in Switzerland, and had to make do with a *New York Times Atlas* and my HP 41c computer. I wrote to Peter,

> I don't know where in Abaco your vessel squats, so in making calculations I posited Elbow Cay, at 26-15 North, 76-40 West. Our destination at Morehead City lies directly north (359.6 degrees). The distance is 508 miles. On the assumption that we can average five knots (modest, but safe) the passage would take us 4.2 days. My guess is that with the Gulf Stream working with us about 25 percent of the time, and with broad-reaching winds at fourteen to eighteen knots, we will more likely make the trip to North Carolina in about seventy-six to eighty-two hours. Now: If we leave at noon on Saturday, April 9, we should reach Morehead late on Tuesday. The approach there is easy at night, no sweat. So that it wouldn't matter if we got in at midnight plus.

As D day approaches, I always manage to feel a little like General Eisenhower. The weekend before leaving is the weekend for The List—of things to bring along, which included such conventional items as sextant, *HO 249* navigation tables, and plotting sheets; and a few nonconventional aids to life-at-sea, such as three trays of tape cassettes, a Walkman, and my laptop computer and recharging paraphernalia.

There is something to be said for maximum exertion the day preceding your first night on a cruising sailboat. The contrast between hectic cosmopolitan life and the stillness of the lagoon heightens. My radio alarm woke me at 6:15 in Los Angeles. Seven hours later, at the Eastern Air Lines gate in Miami, I met Van, Tony Leggett, and Claudio Veliz, who had come down from New York. Tony, thirty-four, was a veteran seaman and racer. He had joined the crew for my second transatlantic cruise, in 1980 (and would do so again for what I called "the final passage," in 1990). Claudio, an architect, is another old sailing companion.

Also meeting me at the airport was the pilot who would fly us to Abaco, an hour and a half away by Cessna. All that Peter, who had gone on ahead, had felt he needed to tell me was that I should take a taxi from the airport to the "water taxi" at Marsh Harbor. There a launch would be waiting to ferry us to Man o' War Cay, where the *Astraea* would be waiting.

The instructions sufficed, and we'd have arrived earlier except that, along the way, we ran into...a party! On the clubhouse lawn, not twenty yards from our awaiting launch, the Cruising Club of America was celebrating something or other, and we fell into the arms of old friends and sailing companions, including former Columbia University dean Schuyler Chapin and Betty, and Walter Cronkite and Betsy. Norrie Hoyt et ux. were there. Norrie and I had fired shots at each other in print (that was thirty years ago, and I pause to record that Norrie was unquestionably right, and I was wrong in my callow youth in mocking the exacting standards set by ocean racers, which he resourcefully defended). Cronkite told me he didn't know I was in the yacht-ferrying business, else he'd have engaged me to take his *Wyntie* back to the States. Much general jollity, compressed into twenty minutes. And then we were off, reaching the fine, spic-and-span *Astraea* just as the sun fell.

We rowed to the shore and headed to a restaurant for dinner. I reflected, on coming ashore, that it was here, in Man o' War Cay, that my *Cyrano*, which I had owned and sailed for ten years, had been built. "The last of the big boats built here," the water-taxi driver had told us. *Cyrano* was—is—wooden, and the yard that produced that lovely creature long since ran out of commissions for bulky sixty-foot schooners.

It always surprises me how the great bulk of things one brings on board (more exactly, the great bulk of things *I* bring on board: others practice moderation) has a way of disappearing, even on boats of modest size, if only one is diligent and ingenious, as Peter was. He effected, by way of two hours of hard labor, the deliquescence even of two cumbersome seabags hoarding emergency amenities, a reservoir against contingent want. We had a glass of Peter's soothing Moselle, and went to our bunks.

I picked up my night reading, and thought then and there to tell my companions the story I had heard from Walter Cronkite years before. He had been on television an endless number of hours in connection with the launch of *Apollo 9* (I think it was). It was Christmas Eve and he was dead on his feet. He had plotted forward to a week's sailing vacation and flew off to his sailboat in a Bahamian island, where, the sun beginning to descend, he sat contentedly with wife and another couple, eggnog in hand, when a trim yacht tender hove in. The mate doffed his cap and announced that he bore an invitation from the yacht *Seascape*, whose owner would be delighted if the only other cruisers in this remote lagoon would join him for a Christmas Eve drink.

"I shrugged my shoulders," Walter reminisced, "and thought, What the hell, it's Christmas Eve, we'd better be fraternal, so we all got into the launch, and went over to the large motor yacht a mile across the harbor, climbed up the companionway, and—my God, *it was Roy Cohn!*"

I read a couple of chapters of *Citizen Cohn*, by Nicholas Von Hoffman, and lazed into sleep, hoping vaguely that the predicted northwest winds would not materialize the following morning.

But they did. My experience has always been that weather reports that are not welcome eventuate. Those that are welcome do not. The trouble with a northwest wind, of course, was that northwest was where we planned to head in order to glide into the Gulf Stream in order to go north to Morehead City. Nothing doing.

꜠

Two days before leaving I had had a long telephone conversation with my oldest sailing companion, Reggie Stoops, in the hospital for abdominal surgery and for that reason not with us on this trip. Reggie likes to take correspondence courses, however supererogatory, in anything to do with sailing or flying, and had just completed, after forty years of sailing, a course on safety procedures at sea.

There were the usual Do's and Don't's, he told me, but also two novelties. The first involved recommended procedures in the event of a man overboard.

(1) Toss him a life cushion or two (time allowed: two seconds). (2) Assign a member of the crew to keep his eyes on the man overboard (time: one second). Then (3) come about, leaving the headsail tethered exactly where it was, so that now it is aback (time: five seconds). (4) Sail on a broad reach for the few seconds required to put yourself abeam of the "victim"—as the Coast Guard refers to him. (5) Then downwind past the victim. Then (6) upwind, bringing down the sails as you coast up toward him. At this point, to bring him up, you need either a sling, attached to your main halyard, or else a floating line to your fixed stern boarding ladder.

And second (said Reggie), you should test your EPIRB emergency radio transmitter. The way to do this, he explained, is to wait until the hour (any hour). Between the hour and five minutes past, Coast Guard monitors ignore all distress signals, on the understood assumption that they are hearing sailors' sets being tested. That is your opportunity to test yours.

"Where do you check to see if the signal is being received all right?" I asked.

"Channel 15."

For a startled moment I thought Reggie was talking about television, but of course he was talking about VHS radio. We went through the motions on the *Astraea*, and Peter showed us how to flash on the signal. At exactly 9:00 A.M., Peter broadcast the SOS signal, and Van twiddled the radio dial. Ah, but what the dial gave us was Channel 12, 13, 14, 16. No 15. I would need to ask Reggie if he wanted to take another course, after leaving the hospital, on how to find Channel 15. The stipulated exercise is akin to the reading of inscrutable instructions. Best to wait, until a tutor materializes.

ॐ

We set out—and promptly ran aground, never mind that we were well within the channel markers. I felt very much at home, running aground in the Bahamas, as I had done on *Cyrano* for a full decade. A cheerful couple in a small motor launch hauled us out, and we were off on our westward passage, under lee, one hundred miles due west to Walker Cay, unless the wind changed and gave us leave to slip out into the ocean earlier on our northerly course.

Van Galbraith—to examine the schedule from the other end— had to deliver a speech at a luncheon meeting in Paris on Thursday. He was the former U.S. ambassador to France. It was now near-sunset, Sunday. Earlier that afternoon I had told him soberly, sadly, dividers and calculator in hand, that perhaps he should disembark at Walker Cay, to be absolutely protected against the possibility of a late arrival in Morehead.

I was vaguely familiar with the facilities at Walker Cay, having visited there in 1970, summoned by Richard Nixon in the golden days before Watergate. The president was relaxing with two friends after the congressional election and was pleased by the success of my brother Jim as the new senator from New York. Getting to Walker Cay had been a wild flurry of Air Force One, small jets, and helicopters, to the insular preserve of the president, courtesy of his friend Robert Abplanalp. But the following day my wife and I relied on conventional transportation to take us from Walker Cay to West Palm Beach and back to New York. I told Van there was commercial airline service to Florida, but then Peter aborted the suspense by saying that he did not mind if we made an emergency stopover at Charleston, in the event time did run out; so, happily, Van stayed aboard.

The question now was whether to head directly for the Gulf Stream on a course of about 280 degrees, or to take the hypotenuse (due north) and meet the Stream later. I opted, by feel, for the first course, and proceeded on it. Van gives earnest attention to any challenge that might shorten by ten minutes life at sea, so he went down to the chart table. A half hour later he informed me that I was correct: he had calculated we would save one hour by going directly to the Stream.

Which we did, happy as the sails filled out. As we sat about the cockpit before dinner, watching one of those transfixing Bahamian sunsets, I delivered my lecture (it lasts about two minutes, twenty seconds) about my Pacific epiphany: the rediscovery of wing-and-wing sailing on my voyage from Honolulu to New Guinea. At lecture's end, we went to work, bringing out the pole onto which we'd fasten the genoa clew.

I thought it unwise to raise the spinnaker, as night was falling, and forecasts from Ft. Lauderdale radio were of brisk winds during the night. Accordingly, Peter gave us the ship's protocols for lowering the spinnaker boom from the main mast and positioning it for the genoa clew—in every boat the procedure is just a little bit different ("You *have* to get the end of the pole down first, touching the head-stay," Peter demonstrated).

But even after we had completed the maneuver, the *Astraea* wobbled, denying us a steady downwind course. I then remembered, aboard another boat, the *Sealestial*, hoisting the Yankee in place of the big genoa. The fit was thereafter tight, secure—perfect. Ah, and the *Astraea* has a roller furling gear. Bringing in eighteen inches of genoa gave us just that desired tightness, and the good ship settled doggedly on its dead-downwind course, holding there under the gentle prodding of the little Autohelm automatic steering device. We went below for dinner and a nice Burgundy Peter had got in Abaco.

The moonless night was uneventful save for the truly garish luminosity of the parting seas as we barreled down at 7.5 knots toward the Gulf Stream. We hit it sometime after midnight, a junction instantly decipherable from the leap in the loran speed. (When and if I reach St. Peter's gate, I will ask to see the man who invented loran, so I can say, "Thanks.") Having hit the Stream, we changed course and hugged the axis of the current, loping along at a speed of nearly ten knots.

ॐ

The following day was bright and sunny, but the winds were freakish. At one point we had practically none, so we stopped to swim. I contemplated the fixed boarding ladder and recalled the awful tale told me last November by a man who had been called to Atlantic City a few months earlier to help a friend in critical psychological shock. Four men had been sailing to New York from Cape May. Opposite Atlantic City, ten miles out, one of two brothers pitched overboard while tending a sail in rough weather. He was thrown a line and grabbed it. The other three then tried for a heartbreaking hour to lift him back on board. But, finally, in the swirling sea, they lost the fight. If they had had a fixed boarding ladder they could have managed easily. If they had had a sling and a tackle, rigged to the main halyard, they'd have managed. A grisly story, the implications of which I hastily shook off, on mounting the *Astraea*'s boarding ladder.

The balance of the day was of the sort that, however apprehensively, one simply gets used to at sea. Something is telling you that there is confusion in the elements, and odd things are likely to happen. Not hurricane-odd—there is nothing on the barometer, or on the radio, that indicates any such danger. The weather report is still talking fifteen to twenty knot winds from the southeast. But in fact the winds are coming and going, the sun is coming and going, the clouds are ditto, as also squall patterns, off in the distance. A careful examination of navigational particulars suggests that, yes, we can probably be in Morehead City by midmorning Wednesday—but there is a chance we won't be, and Van would need, in any case, to travel from Morehead to Charlotte, to LaGuardia, to JFK to make his Wednesday-evening flight to Paris. By dinnertime, we resolved to head to Charleston, two hundred miles closer. But no course change was indicated until four or five in the morning, so we more or less uniformly battened down.

I came on watch at 2300, and instantly undertook an extra reef on the mainsail. The genoa had already been furled. We were on a broad reach with southeast winds, and these were coming in gusts which a half hour later were reaching forty-five knots, with shafts of driving rain in bursts that lasted fifteen or twenty minutes.

I spotted a light at about eleven o'clock on our course. More exactly, two tiny blurs of light visible with binoculars. Tony, though off duty, came up to the cockpit (sleep below was all but impossible, as we rolled and tossed). Tony suggested in his quiet way that the ship was bearing down on us and that he thought it would be appropriate to come about to avoid any possibility of collision. I recited my philosophy in such matters (I approach oncoming ships until quite close, and only then make course changes, definitive in nature). We watched in the blinding rain and howling wind the ship, making out both its running lights. It didn't change in its bearing to us, which put us on a collision course.

What spooked us was that the ship seemed to get no closer, after twenty minutes. I doubt it was traveling at four knots, let alone sixteen. Finally I came about, primarily to ease the mounting psychological pressure in the cockpit, in the anarchic circumstances of eccentric and screeching winds. An hour later Tony was on watch with me (my watch system specifies social rotation), and suddenly, *there* was that same vessel again, this time coming at us from astern. Again we watched for fifteen or twenty minutes, wondering why it did not pass us. Again, I came about, with the purpose primarily in mind of losing our pursuer. We had a little bit the feeling that a rudderless pursuer was stalking us, awaiting the auspicious moment to pounce.

A logical next step would have been to power up the radio and ask, "What-in-the-hell are you nice people dogging us for?" Tony allowed himself to speculate that the Spookship was out here awaiting a drug drop. If so, would it react against a thirty-eight-foot sailboat out there in the wild seas that had spotted it? The stuff of post-midnight fantasies in stormy weather. I cannot even now explain the behavior of the SS *Spook*. Finally, though, we successfully distanced ourselves from it.

৵

The wind began to quiet down at four in the morning, and by daybreak we were under power. A dull day, cloudy, as we headed now toward Charleston. There came—along with the altered course, the gray skies, the reduced speed as we pulled away from the Stream—a detectable lesion in the ship's morale. Nothing serious, but nonetheless palpable. After a long day, at sunset, it was time to close in on the first marker in the long (twelve-mile) channel to Charleston Harbor. One reaches, finally, the harbor opening and then zigs and zags another ten miles, past the fort where the Civil War began, before finally reaching the marina.

Now, that inland leg proved rather an ordeal. It took five hours from the first marker to our berth. The wind was back: thirty-five knots on the nose. The current (foul) was over three knots. And the temperature dropped, during that period, from about sixty-five to about forty degrees. We gunned up to 2,200 rpm to get an extra half erg of energy, and powered—and powered—and powered away. The range lights were not easy to line up. The eyes, after several hours facing the wind, become inordinately dry. When the marina finally materialized, I tried to berth against a beam wind of thirty knots into a narrow slip. This did not work, and so we puttered anxiously about, looking for a berth with a more hospitable axis to the wind; finally found it and, sometime after midnight, tied up. I left the wheel and went below to the head to remove my contact lenses. Only to find that I could not bring my thumb and index finger together to grip them. It required a full five minutes, my hands nestled in my underarms, before the fingers would work again.

Everyone who has sailed in blue water knows two sensations, exhilaration and exhaustion. We had more of the latter at that moment than we had had of the former. If we had been greeted at the berth with the news that we had come in first in the great Abaco–Charleston race, we'd have experienced the two emotions, synaesthetically. Instead we just sat down, had a glass of wine, and crept into our bunks.

I closed my eyes and thought of Harvey Conover at the end of the 1956 Newport–Bermuda Race, addressing us in his capacity as commodore of the Cruising Club of America. "Fellow maniacs," he began. Eighteen months later Conover was dead, drowned off his palindromic *Revonoc*, voyaging on New Year's Day from Key West to Miami. But then it happens, even before you go off to sleep, that the mind turns to other moments in the passage—for instance, Sunday night driving wing-and-wing downhill at hull speed through the lambent water—and you are prepared to smile, when they tell you you are a maniac, going to sea in a sailboat. You can't see the expression on your face, in the drowsy mists, but you know that the smile is a patronizing smile. Pity them, not us.

Pleasure on Skis

After sailing, skiing is my next enthusiasm in the world of sports, and has been for nearly fifty years.

My *lunch companion at Gstaad* that Friday, early in March, is one of those women so cosmopolitan one never quite knows in which language she will address you. Easy in my case, but it would not surprise you if she handled five different languages in the course of an hour, though probably, when sleeping, she does her logarithms in French. She has a perfect set of children (three), all beautiful and beautifully trained. Her husband owns much of this and that in several countries, though his base (sometimes he has to concentrate to remember) is in Brussels. Anyway, it didn't surprise me, when I asked where she was spending Easter, to hear her reply, "In the Himalayas." Oh. So she was now taking up, or else accepting, a fresh challenge, mountain climbing. So? If she had said she was going to glide in Santiago I wouldn't have been fazed. But no. She was going to the Himalayas—to ski!

I thought this a bit much, and told her so. Skiing, I said, is a quite understandable infection. But to take your husband, your three children, your governess, and your ski teacher to the Himalayas to *ski* suggests a sense of proportion that has got out of hand. Writers (notoriously, P. G. Wodehouse) have written stories documenting, or caricaturing, the extent to which some people become prisoners of golf: those people who live for golf, who wake up in the morning well inclined or not depending on whether a round of golf is in store for them, and who will relive the day, stroke by stroke, at dinner.

It is perfectly natural to welcome the first snow that permits you to look forward to a day's skiing. But to go to the Himalayas in order to ski?

I write as I do in part because skiing got late into my blood. My boyhood winters were spent where there was no snow (South Carolina) or else where snows of the kind that encourage skiing were infrequent (southern New England); besides which, the whole uphill machinery that delivered skiing from the drudgery of the prelift generation hadn't been fully developed. So that I was nearly thirty when I first traveled to Vermont with my wife and sisters, bought a pair of skis, and at the end of the day thought seriously of abandoning journalism, my vendetta with the Soviet Union, my music, and my sailing, and settling down in Vermont, working five years to qualify as a ski instructor, and spending the balance of my life on the slopes.

These romances hit you, and of course they mostly go away. But not entirely. Some grown people, even though they have been skiing for thirty years, decided last spring to go to the Himalayas to have an extra run or two.

I was a friend of Arnold Lunn. Sir Arnold Lunn. The "sir" was given to him by Queen Elizabeth in recognition of the work he had done as a chronicler of mountaineering in Switzerland. He was the bard of mountain climbing, and an entire generation of young Brits followed him up the big mountains, from one of which he fell at age twenty-one, permanently shortening one of his legs. In the twenties, he devised a downhill swivel-hipping routine they came to call the "slalom." I know people who wonder that one could think kindly of anyone who invents new forms of torture. But he was exuberantly witty and devoted and generous.

Sir Arnold first skied with me when he was seventy years old. Because of his decrepit leg he wasn't very good at it, but that bothered him not in the least. The very idea of spending an afternoon on a couple of long two-by-fours and letting gravity glide you down a mountain was for him, as for so many others, a bit of paradise.

When he turned eighty, his wife gave him an ultimatum: he was to put his skis away permanently. Since he and she were never physically separated, he found it difficult to evade her orders. But one day Lady Phyllis's sister fell ill in London and she was forced to leave her husband alone in Mürren, where they lived. She did so only after reiterating her order not to go near the great ski slopes. He reaffirmed his vows of obedience. Ten minutes after he bade her goodbye on the funicular, he was in the lobby of the hotel importuning the steward to fetch up his skis. After an hour or two in the cellar, the steward reported that he could not find the skis. The following morning he appeared at Lunn's apartment, tears in his eyes. He had, he said, told Arnold a lie. In fact the skis *were* there, but he had promised Lady Phyllis that should her husband ask for them, he would pretend that they could not be found. Arnold faced a dilemma. If he put on his skis, he would betray the steward, as also his word to his wife. Reluctantly, grumpily, he recognized that he would never ski again. He died at eighty-six.

Young people can't imagine giving up skiing. Many elderly people—of my age—have the same difficulty. I know people who have abandoned skiing notwithstanding that they are, at sixty, or seventy, perfectly competent. There is some little inward sign. One reaches for an analogy. Toscanini put down his baton permanently when at age eighty-seven he suddenly didn't remember what music came next—he hadn't depended on a score since his world premiere in Rio at age nineteen. In the competitive world, people stop playing baseball when, to their dismay, they find that their batting average is lowering to levels both humiliating and economically traumatic. In tennis and golf one finds many men and women who keep remembering how hard they smashed the ball in days gone by, or what their handicap used to be only ten years ago. True, the links are full of senior citizens who play golf, and in tennis it helps to play doubles. And then golf is, after all, the calmest of sports, and the level of the player's exertion is greatly reduced by the golf cart and, before that, the caddie.

࿎

Skiing is different. The moment comes when you are on two slivers of wood or plastic or titanium or whatever, and you look down and see that you are three thousand feet higher than where you are supposed to end up. And that if you do something foolish, it is entirely possible that you will descend three thousand feet as plausibly as a pretzel would descend a steep staircase. It does give one pause.

But by the time you become a senior citizen, if you have skied for a while you have developed certain techniques which should permit you to exercise critical control. Not necessarily as much as you might want, in order to handle blithely this challenge or the other. But enough to give you a certain sense of operative security. The critical difference between skiing, say, and performing on the piano is that you cannot derive much pleasure from a Mozart sonata whose speed is designated as presto if you play it andante. And if your fingers simply lose their power, so does the lure of the music they once transcribed. I have maintained over and over again to elderly skiers who wonder whether they will resume next year that the *pleasure* of skiing is not a function of the speed of your performance. If, in your prime, you handled that three-thousand-foot run at the Videmanette mountain in Rougemont, Switzerland, over five miles of snow, in fifteen minutes, and now it takes you twenty minutes, or twenty-five—so what? If you want to risk something, for the pleasure of it, it is no problem at all to point your skis down a little closer to the fall line and pick up speed. I know of no sport, no hobby, no avocation, as indulgent as skiing in giving you exactly the combination you wish of challenge, relaxation, thrill, exhilaration.

Another thing. I don't know why, but it is unfailingly the case that there is *always* something to relate after an afternoon's ski. Something *unusual* happened, which you can tell your wife about or your cook or your grandchild, or, in desperation, you can write Arnold Lunn's granddaughter and tell her—*she* will understand. The ski tow stopped halfway up the hill. *You were stranded for twenty minutes!* An avalanche over on the left, where you usually ski, had hurtled down the night before, very nearly ambushing your former ski instructor! There is a new ski out, some people call it a Fat Boy, and you tried it, and I mean, there is *nothing* you cannot do using the Fat Boy!

There are the great personal adventures, like the one your sixty-year-old friend told you about when you visited him in the hospital. He is a tough-talking type, a publisher who does not mince words, and he said he was coming down from the top, turned the corner, and ran into an unexpected mogul that caught the front end of both his skis. Over he plopped, as though preparing himself for a proctological examination. At just that *second* a skier—a *mad, stupid, maniacal, bloodletting* skier—whizzed by and guess what! "He sliced both my Achilles' tendons as a surgeon might do! I was able to bear the pain and the continued immobilization only because I thought of the *enormous* joy I would take in turning my lawyer-tiger loose on that uncaged monster—when I noticed that the son of a bitch was slowly climbing back up towards me, least he could do, the bastard, visiting his frozen victim with the two ex-feet. And then ... And then! He came within sight of me and ... *It was my lawyer who had done it to me!*"

You cry on the outside, laugh on the inside. Skiing is always doing that kind of thing to you. As though nature begrudged any absolutely uninterrupted day of sheer joy sliding down the mountain at any speed you choose, treating the snow like hired gravity as it lets you glide over its softness, cooling your face and balming your spirit and reminding you day after day and year after year of the singular pleasure that issues from a mountain height, two simple planes of tough springy texture, and snow under your feet. One wonders what we would have had from Coleridge and Wordsworth and Keats if only they had been given what we take for granted.

Alta, My Alta

Thanks to Junior Bounous and his Fat Boy skis, Milton Friedman and I learned to ski powder—through the trees—and love it. ⁓

Three of us go to Alta every year, Wednesday through Sunday. Lawry Chickering and Milton Friedman come in from San Francisco, I from New York. When the three of us first skied with Junior Bounous, which is like saying when we played tennis with Bill Tilden, Junior (who has grandchildren) addressed our Nobel laureate as "Milt," which is the Mormon way, in and around Alta, Utah. "That's like addressing Einstein as 'Al,'" I whispered, awestruck, to Lawry. I thought at least to pass along the word to Junior, a half hour later, when we found ourselves sharing a lift, that our little (5'2") companion had won a Nobel Prize. "For what?" Junior asked, though I think he put the question to me to be polite—Junior Bounous doesn't really care if Milt got a Nobel Prize for ichthyology, or for that matter, if he got any prize at all. He cares only whether Milt is a nice guy (he is), and whether he is getting something out of what Junior is teaching him (he is).

Alta, forty-five minutes from Salt Lake City, is famous for its abundance of snow (five hundred inches every year) and for its saturated affability. It is quite another world, and that is probably why we've had sixteen reunions there. My first time at the Alta Lodge was in 1961. I had written an essay for *Esquire* called "Why

Don't We Complain?" (see p. 558) and I remember complaining to my wife that it was awfully tough going, generating indignation in such a place as the Alta Lodge.

Just so nobody will think me sycophantic on the matter of the Alta Lodge and Alta, I leap to a couple of things that drive me crazy. We are 8,500 feet above sea level, and this is not an altitude you get used to in a couple of hours. As a matter of fact, in three days you do not get used to 8,500 feet of altitude. It's okay if you are sliding downhill, or walking on level ground—walking, say, over to the Rustler Lodge. It is a mean, draining bore when you have to walk up (or, for that matter, down) sixty-three steps, which is what it takes to go from where the car leaves you to where the Alta Lodge begins.

If you arrive, as some of us do, with five or six mounds of baggage, you look with genuine awe at the young men in their late teens who are sent to cope with several hundred pounds of disorderly weight. But year after year it is so, sixty-three icy wooden steps (covered, to be sure, but icy just the same), down, and up. "Do you know," Lawry said last time we were there, as, climbing up to the road, we paused for breath at a landing, "this stairway has really got to be an affectation." Lawry—a lawyer, author, and think-tanker—is of course right. It reminds you of climbing about at Machu Picchu; on the other hand, the Incas *had* to do it, because they never thought up the wheel. We take our usual vow never to return to the Lodge unless they get an elevator, and a silent vow to repeat that vow when we come next year.

And then there is a complementary idiocy, only this one is the responsibility of the Alta Ski Lifts Company. In order to reach the two main lifts that take you to the 2,200 skiing acres, you need to climb up a steep little hill. It is a coincidence that sixty-three side-steps are (at my height) required to get up it. Why isn't there some sort of escalator to spare you the breath-consuming ordeal?

The answer to that question is that there is something just a little self-satisfied about Alta, and the humbling feature of the whole place is that they have pretty good reason for self-satisfaction. The good cheer is earned. It is the kind of thing you'd expect to find in the manner of the gardeners who tend the lawns at Windsor Castle. One of these was asked by an American GI during the war how they managed to cultivate so beautiful a lawn. The gardener gladly gave the information: First, he said, you plow the land using a very shallow plow. Then you water it for seven hundred years.

Alta hasn't been around for seven hundred years, but then neither, as a sport, has skiing. Alta is, in fact, one of the oldest ski resorts in the American West, but that means, really, postwar. The Alta Lodge is fifty years old, but way back then they had a few rope tows, very different from today's eight chairlifts, some triples, some doubles, each with a vertical drop of two thousand feet. There was

PRESENT AT THE CREATION: WITH MILTON FRIEDMAN
AND THE CHICKERING BROTHERS

concern a few years ago when the great Snowbird resort opened, just one mile away on the road to Salt Lake City. Snowbird has an aerial tram that will lift 125 skiers three thousand vertical feet, and two or three floors of bazaars selling everything; that, and a six hundred-room high-rise with gymnasia, and suites, and saunas. For that matter, if you head down toward Salt Lake and then do a turn and go back up on the other side of the range, you get luxurious Deer Valley. "But you know," Chick said to me—Chick Morton was for many years the manager of the Alta Lodge, and remains a high potentate in the little cadre that runs Alta—"a lot of them come *here* to ski. Then they go back to Deer Valley for the night life, and the fancy stuff." That troubles the Alta people not one bit: nightlife glitz is for other ski centers, and Snowbird helped to reduce the traffic, which was just what Alta's owners wanted.

Onno Wieringa, who manages the lift association, is young, ever so perceptive, knows avalanches the way Henry Ford knew engines, and incarnates bright self-satisfaction. He describes with some pride the new rope tow that takes you a mile or so along the all-but-level slope leading back to the Lodge from one of the outer runs. The objective was to replace the old tow that required you to take your hand off the rope when you came to each of the dozen pylons. That, and to permit the pylons to rise as required, after last night's snowfall.

Last night's snowfall at Alta is not to be compared with that gentle little carpet that nestles down on Mr. Blandings's dream house on Christmas Eve. Four days before we arrived, this last time, the day's snowfall was sixty inches. One night, a few years ago, the telephone rang in my room at 2:00 A.M. Would I kindly repair to the basement of the Lodge? Half asleep, I wondered whether the Lodge had come up with some concentrated gemütlichkeit for its guests, and I found myself asking, "Is this compulsory?" The answer was a gentle but unambiguous Yes.

Before our release, two hours later, I had read an entire issue of *Time* magazine from cover to cover in the cellar where the ski lockers are, in the company of fifty-odd fellow guests, whose impatience subsided when we were reminded that the avalanche the year before had swept away a whole wing of the Lodge. But the science of preemptive well-aimed artillery shells has diminished such climacterics, and I haven't been roused from my bed, by avalanches, since then.

℘

What is it like, a day at Alta, staying at the Lodge? It is absolutely unregimented, in sharp contrast, for instance, with Zürs, in Austria. There your ski-learning group is the center of life. You are appraised by the reigning ski czar, who matriculates you in whichever of the twenty classes (1A, beginners; 10B, experts) he thinks appropriate for your skills. At the end of the day, on his skis, he will stretch out his arm and point at you, his thumb either raised or lowered; and, accepting the finality of his judgment, you check in the following morning at the class next more advanced than where you were, or next lower. Such a regimen would strike the folks at Alta as absolutely Hitlerian, which, as a matter of fact, it is.

At Alta you do as you like. What we do is convene at 8:00 for breakfast, which is about as far removed from continental breakfast as a breakfast can be. If you like, you can start with orange juice, then take cereal with or without yoghurt, en route to a Spanish omelette with sausage and/or bacon, to tide you over until the French toast and pancakes come in. Milton has the *Wall Street Journal*, Lawry *USA Today*, I the *New York Times*. We will convene at 10:00 in the basement/avalanche room, put on our equipment, and make our way outdoors, skiing fifty yards down to the awful uphill slope, then up one of the two lifts ($23 per day) to Mount Baldy. From there there are combinations of every kind, including some very rough stuff (High Rustler), but most of it is perfect for intermediate skiers. (The runs were named when Stephen Vincent Benét was not around. E.g., we have Mambo, Blitz, Taint, Stimulation, Warm-Up, Stone Crusher, Extrovert, Secret Access, and Rabbit.) At about 12:00 we are back at the Lodge, and for lunch there is always a specialty, always satisfying. We knock off after lunch and reconvene along about 2:30 and go another hour, or hour and a half. After skiing, we sleep, or read, or do our homework. Lawry and I meet at the Jacuzzi (there are two, one hotter than the other) at 6:30, and at 7:00 we congregate in my mini-suite. I serve wine and pretzels, or whatever, and we join in animated conversation on such questions as whether intellectual property is the cause or the substance of progress, what is generally missed about Lord Keynes's economics, how creepy-crawly are the ways in which the state regularly intervenes in more and more of the freeman's life, what is the point in the tax deductibility of mortgages, how is Lawry's think tank doing, how is it that the *San Francisco Chronicle* consents to publish his atavistic columns, and how are Milton and his wife, Rose, sharing the duties of their ongoing memoirs. After so many years of total immersion in one another's company, over a period of time so brief, it is remarkable what confidences one finds oneself willing to share. It is to be compared with night watches on a sailing boat: the intimacy is of the kind that generates true pleasure in one another's company.

We eschew the Lodge at dinner, occupying a booth at the Shallow Shaft steak house, in tribute to which we undergo the sixty-three-step rite of passage. The conversation is unabated, and after dinner we walk a lazy half-dozen blocks in the cold, then wend our way down: Milton, generally, to his own room, Lawry to mine for a nightcap and maybe some music (I bring my own tapes). Then Lawry goes off to his room, and the day is ended. Elsewhere at the Lodge there is the Sitzmark Club, a television room where movies are shown, and the lounge. If fraternization is what you want, it is there abundantly.

౼

I have previously remarked the singular blessings of skiing for men and women getting along in years. It may well be that that advantage will be less noticeable as we begin to take skiing for granted, with the result that more and more Americans are learning to ski at a young age. It is as fruitful an investment of time as learning a language when you are six or seven: absolutely no effort is required; and as we observe the skiers from the lift traveling up Mt. Baldy we distinguish instantly those who began young from those who began later on.

The demarcation is perfectly exemplified in our little group. Lawry grew up skiing in California, and his touch and style are expert. I began at thirty, Milton at forty. If Lawry is ranked at, say, seventeen (out of twenty), I'd come in at about thirteen, Milton at eight.

I have observed that people do not need to give up skiing when they get older; all they need do is slow down, as much or as little as suits them. I hadn't observed, until my years with Milton, that it is possible not only to improve in your seventies and eighties, but to do so dramatically. When Junior began giving us his yearly tips, Milt glowed with the satisfaction that comes from making observable progress. And then, one year ago, on our last day at Alta, Junior said, Would we like to try out the new skis? Milton is very conservative about trying out anything new, but he consented, as did I, and we were introduced to the Atomic Powder Plus Fat Boy skis.

They are, as is pretty widely known by now, half again as wide as ordinary skis, and shorter. Indeed they come in only two lengths. Milton put on the 163s, I the 183s. Out on the mountain, Junior said, "Follow me." We looked at each other incredulously. Junior was wafting down at a relaxed speed through a pretty dense forest, in powder. The very thought of engaging such a path in such conditions was preposterous—Milton avoids powder like poison ivy, and I submit to it once or twice every season only to remind myself of my limitations.

But Junior is not to be denied, so, hesitantly, I advanced on his trail, Milton on mine. And lo!—neither of us fell, and we found we could turn in every situation. It was a liberating experience, and this last year we arrived with rented Fat Boys. They are catching on, and the superstition that they are inadequate for piste skiing is just that, a superstition. Junior told us this time around that he would recommend against using Powder Plus skis only to the skier who was bent on racing.

I asked Milton if he intended to race, before he puts away his skis. This was the week when it transpired that the person who smashed Ms. Nancy Kerrigan on the knee to keep her out of the Olympic ice-skating competition was very close to Ms. Tonya Harding, her chief rival. I dropped a note to Rose Friedman to the effect that Lawry and I were thinking of engaging some hood in Salt Lake to come and have a go at Milton's knee before he outpaced us.

Ah well, I exaggerate, but I don't when I say that Lawry and I skied with someone who at eighty-one was three times the skier he was at seventy-eight.

Is there no end to these effronteries of skiing in orderly old age? The very first thing Milton did on Day 1 was report to the ski center to get the free pass given out to skiers who are eighty or over. The lady at the desk chatted that probably Alta would have to modify this perk for the elderly, given the number of people who were qualifying. "We're thinking of giving the pass only to people over ninety," she said. A voice behind Milton rang out robustly. "That wouldn't bother me. I'm ninety-two."

Every now and again, not often, Milton will observe that sometime in the future he simply won't be up to coming to Alta. I tell
him the mere thought of a skier being superannuated is...subver-
sive, liberal-Democratic-socialist hogwash, and if he brings it up
again, Lawry and I will campaign for the Clinton Health Plan, and
then everybody will die young.

Milton laughs, and the subject of being too old to ski goes to
sleep for another couple of years.

Six Freshmen and an Ercoupe

My brief, harrowing career as an airplane pilot. ⌒

I had no fear of flying when I matriculated at Yale, but a very considerable fear of my father's learning that I had taken up a sport which, in 1946, he was as yet unprepared to concede was anything more than rank technological presumption, fit only for daredevils. It turned out that several of my coconspirators had fathers with similar prejudices, so that when our little syndicate was formed, we all agreed that communications among ourselves on the subject of our surreptitious hobby would go out discreetly, lest they be intercepted. During the Christmas holidays it was my duty to send out the accrued bills from the little grass-strip airport at Bethany, Connecticut, where we lodged Alexander's Horse (as we called our little Ercoupe). My problem, envelope in hand, was that I could not remember whether a particular one of my five partners was a junior. With a name like T. Leroy Morgan, I felt he must surely be a junior—was there any other excuse? On the other hand, if I wrote "Jr." after his name, and my friend was in fact III, then his father would open the letter. I assumed his father must be formidable, since who else would live at One Quincy Street, Chevy Chase, Maryland? So, to play it safe, I addressed the letter to: "T. Leroy Morgan—the one who goes to Yale/ 1 Quincy Street/ Chevy Chase, Md." It happened that at the breakfast table, distributing

AN ERCOUPE BETTER CARED FOR THAN OURS

the mail among the family, Mr. Morgan, père, was provoked by this designation, and displayed an imperious curiosity about the contents of a letter so manifestly intended to be seen by no other eyes than his son's.

I will contract the suspense, and say that in no time at all the word passed around a circle of fathers, reaching my own. Whenever my father was faced with rank transgression by any of his ten children, he replied to it in one of two ways, sometimes both. His first line of attack would be to announce that the child could not afford whatever it was my father disapproved of. He tried that for an entire year in his running war against cigarettes, but the effect was ruined when we all saw *The Grapes of Wrath*, where Henry Fonda, between heaves of hunger, kept smoking. Father's second line of attack would be to ignore the delinquency, pretending it did not exist. Thus one of my brothers, who hated to practice the piano, was relieved from ever having to play it again by the simple expedient of being held up by my father in discussions of the matter as the most exemplary pianist in the family.

I received a brisk memorandum (Father's reproachful communications were normally rendered in that mode) advising me that he had "learned" that I was "flying an airplane" at college, and that, the distractions to my academic career quite apart, I clearly could not afford such an extravagance. One didn't argue with Father, who in any case would never return to the subject, except in a vague, sarcastic way. Three years later he would write my prospective father-in-law, "You will find it very easy to entertain Billy when he visits you. You need only provide him with a horse, a yacht, or an airplane."

And so for the few months of our joint venture at Yale, we continued to pass around the bills quietly, like tablets in pre-Christian Rome. They were not, by current standards, frightening. Our capital was eighteen hundred dollars—three hundred apiece. We paid that exactly for the secondhand airplane. We decided, after getting quotations from insurance companies, to insure ourselves, with a three-hundred-dollar deductible payable by the offending partner. Anyone using the plane would pay his own gas, oil, and instructor. All capital improvements would have to be approved unanimously. Anybody could sell his one-sixth interest to anyone at any time. Reservations to use the airplane would be filed with the secretary of the Yale *Daily News*. These, we satisfied ourselves, were surely the most informal articles of association in modern corporate history, though I suppose it is appropriate to add that the association turned out to be one of the briefest in history.

I was off to a very bad start. My experience was akin to arriving at a casino for the first time at age twenty and winning a dozen straight passes at the craps table. When Bob Kraut—a dour, hungry ex-army pilot and mechanic, owner of the starveling little airport, who would sell you anything from a new airplane to a Milky Way—took me up for an hour's instruction, I could not believe how easy it all was. I remember it to this day (or have I forgotten something?): Check the oil. Check the gas. Turn your wheel, check ailerons, pull and check elevator. Run your motor at 1,500 rpm, check one magneto, then the second, then back to "both magnetos." Then gun her up to 2,250. Then depress the knob that says "Carburetor Heat." Then head into the wind (or as close as possible at the single-strip field), pull the throttle all the way back, and roll down the strip. When you reach sixty mph, ease the wheel back, and after the plane lifts off, push the wheel back to level until you reach eighty mph. Then adjust your trim tab to maintain a speed of eighty mph. Rise to six hundred feet on your course, then turn left until you get to eight hundred feet. Then do anything you want.

Landing? Go back to approximately where you were when you hit eight hundred feet, and proceed downwind the length of the field and another length, while descending to six hundred feet. Then turn left descending to four hundred feet. I forgot something. You should pull *out* your Carburetor Heat when you begin your descent. Then turn in toward the field, reducing your throttle to idling speed, coast down, glance sideways, which helps perspective, don't let your speed fall under eighty mph till you are over the field, then, throttle down, keep easing the wheel back until your tires touch down, at which point *immediately* set your wheel right down, because, you see, Ercoupes have no separate rudders, the wheel incorporating that function—a nice advantage except that you cannot cope easily with crosswind landings, and one or two other things.

The first lesson with Bob Kraut consumed an hour, the second a half hour, and that very evening I was speaking to a forlorn junior who grieved greatly that he could not the following day be at dinner with his inamorata in Boston. Why could he not? Because his car wasn't working, and no train would get him up in time, since he could not leave until after lunch. I found myself saying, as though I were P. G. Wodehouse himself, "Why, my dear friend, grieve no more. I shall fly you to Boston."

My friend had been a pilot during the war and, with two thousand hours' flying time, he navigated us expertly to Boston, landed
the airplane, and waved me a happy goodbye. I was left at Boston
International Airport, headed back to Bethany, Connecticut,
never having soloed, and having flown a total of three times.

Well, the only thing to do was to proceed. I remembered that
the plane came equipped with a radio of sorts, and that my friend
had exchanged arcane observations and sentiments with the tower
coming in, so as I sashayed to the end of the runway, I flipped the
switch—and found myself tuned in to an episode of *Life Can Be
Beautiful.* I truly didn't know how to account for this, and I
remember even thinking fleetingly that when the traffic was light,
perhaps the tower entertained area pilots by tuning in to the air
controller's favorite program. This bizarre thought I managed to
overcome, but it was too late to stop and fiddle with a radio I
hadn't been instructed in the use of, so I went through my little ritual, looked about to see that I wasn't in anybody's way, and
zoomed off, toward Providence, Rhode Island.

I was flying not exactly contentedly that bright autumn day. I
felt a little lonely, and a little apprehensive, though I did not know
exactly why. I was past Providence when suddenly my heart began
to ice up as I recognized that either (a) I was quickly going blind
or (b) the sun was going down. I looked at my watch. We should
have another hour and a half of light! Ah so, except that I had neglected to account for the switch, overnight, away from Daylight
Saving Time. I had put back my watch dutifully at midnight. But
today I thought in terms of light until about 7:00 P.M., same as yesterday. I looked at the air chart, so awfully cluttered and concentrated by comparison with those lovely, descriptive, onomatopoeic
ocean charts you can read as easily as a comic book. I discerned
that the New York, New Haven & Hartford railroad track passed
within a few hundred yards of the airport at New London. I

descended, lower and lower, as the light began to fade, as from an overexposed negative soaking up developing solution. By the time I reached New London I was flying at one hundred feet, and when I spotted the lights on the runway of the airfield, I was as grateful as if, coming up from asphyxiative depths, I had reached oxygen.

I approached the field, did the ritual turns, and landed without difficulty, my first, exhilarating, solo landing; my first night landing; on the whole, the culmination of my most egregious stupidity. But there we were: plane, and pilot, intact. I hitchhiked to the station, waited for a train, and by ten o'clock was sitting at a bar in New Haven, chatting with my roommate about this and that. I never gave a thought to Mr. Kraut.

~

I have been awakened by angry voices, but by none to equal Robert Kraut's the following morning. He spat out the story in volleys. While helping us climb into the plane, an assistant at the airfield had overheard us conversing excitedly on my impending first solo flight from Boston to New York. In the internalizing tradition of New England, the assistant had said nothing to me about my projected violation of the law. But he spoke about it later in the afternoon to his boss, who exploded with rage and apprehension. Kraut called the tower at Boston, which told of an Ercoupe having landed, and then taken off at 4:07, without communication with the tower. Kraut calculated that I would arrive in the Bethany area in total darkness, and thereupon began frantically collecting friends and passersby, who, in the tradition of the flying cowboys, ringed the field with their headlights, providing a workmanlike illumination of a country strip. Then they waited. And waited. Finally, at about 10:00, Kraut knew I must be out of fuel and, therefore, on the ground somewhere other than at Bethany. Whether alive or dead, no one could say, but at least, Kraut growled into the telephone, he had had the pleasure of hoping out loud I was dead. *Why hadn't I called him?* I explained, lamely, that I did not know that he even knew about my flight, let alone that he had thought to provide for my safe return. He consoled himself by itemizing lasciviously all the extra charges he intended to put on my bill for his exertions and those of his friends, which charges the Executive Committee of Alexander's Horse Associates voted unanimously and without extensive discussion would be assessed exclusively to me.

I got my license to solo, and, twenty flying hours later, my license to take passengers. I am compelled to admit that I cheated a little in logging those twenty hours, giving the odd half hour's flight the benefit of the doubt, listing it at one hour, and I feel bad about this. But I did achieve a limited proficiency, and would often go out to the field and take up a friend for a jaunty half hour or so in my little silver monoplane, though I never felt confident enough to do any serious cross-country work, having no serviceable radio (in those days radios were not required, except to land at the principal fields, which I routinely avoided).

I remember two experiences before the final episode. In the early spring I invited aboard a classmate, a seasoned navy pilot. We roared off the lumpy field in an overcast which the mechanic on duty assured us was 1,200 feet high. It wasn't. The Bethany airport is at four hundred feet, and at seven hundred feet we were entirely enveloped in cloud. I had never experienced such a thing, and the sensation was terrifying, robbing you, in an instant, of all the coordinates of normal life, including any sense of what is up and what is down. We would need, I calculated, to maintain altitude and fly south until we figured ourselves over mid Long Island Sound. Then turn east, and descend steadily, until we broke into visibility, unencumbered by New England hills; then crawl over to the New Haven airport, which is at sea level. I willingly gave over the controls to my friend Ray, who assumed them with great competence as we began our maneuver. Then suddenly there was a hole in the clouds, and he dived for it, swooping into the Bethany strip, landing not more than three minutes after our departure. I stayed scared after that one, and resolved never again to risk flying in overcast.

Then there was the bright spring day with the lazy-summer temperature. My exams, it happened, had been banked up during the first two days of a ten-day exam period—four hours Monday morning, four Monday afternoon, four Tuesday morning, four Tuesday afternoon. In between I did not sleep but crammed for the next test, taking Benzedrine. Walking out of the final exam at 5:00 P.M., I was numb with fatigue and wild with liberty. I knew I must stretch my limbs in the sky, and so drove out to Bethany, pulled out Alexander's Horse, and zoomed off by myself, heading toward downtown New Haven and east, and climbing to four thousand invigorating feet. There I fell asleep.

I have ever since understood what they mean when they write about the titanic intellectual/muscular energy required to keep one's eyes open when they are set on closing. What happened was that the Benzedrine had suddenly worn off, and the biological imperative to sleep was asserting itself with vindictive adamance. It was, curiously, only after I landed that I found it relatively easy to summon the adrenaline to stay awake for long enough to make it back to my bedroom. In the tortured fifteen minutes between the moment I first discovered myself asleep and the moment I landed, my eyes closed a dozen times. It is safer to learn these things about the human body aboard a sailboat than an airplane. Boats can be dangerous, but they don't sink when you go to sleep at the wheel.

～

My final flight, like so many of the others, was propelled by a certain mental fog. My best friend at Yale had become engaged to my favorite sister. All my siblings had met Brent Bozell save my poor sister Maureen, cloistered at the Ethel Walker School in Simsbury, Connecticut. I would instantly remedy that! I wrote to my sister, age fourteen, telling her to send me a map of the huge lawn that rolls out from the school (which I had many times seen while attending the graduations of older sisters) and the immediate environs. By return mail it arrived. On all accounts, the most nonchalant map in the history of cartography. At the east end she drew vertical lines marked "Trees." Running parallel from the top and bottom of that line to the west were two more lines, also marked "Trees." At the extreme left end of the paper she marked "Main Schoolhouse." Armed with that map and my future brother-in-law, I set out on a bright late-spring afternoon for Simsbury, about an hour's flight.

I found the school, and flew around it a couple of times with mounting agitation. My sister having advised her classmates of my impending arrival, the entire school was out on the lawn. On spotting us, the girls let out a great cheer, which reached us through the roar of the little engine. The problem was that the trees at the east side of the lawn were indeed "Trees." They happened to be the tallest trees this side of the California redwoods. I buzzed them a time or two. Could they really be *that* tall? I estimated them at a couple of hundred feet. That meant I would have to come over them and then drop very sharply, because although the lawn is long, it is not infinite in length, and a normal landing approach would have had me three-quarters of the way down the length of it before touchdown. "Well," I said to my stoical friend, "what do you say?" Fortunately, he knew nothing about flying.

I was terribly proud of the way I executed it all, and wished Mr. Kraut had been there to admire the deftness with which I managed to sink down after skimming the treetops, touching down on the lawn as though it were an eggshell. I looked triumphantly over to Brent as our speed reduced to thirty mph. The very next glimpse I had of him was, so to speak, upsidedownsideways. We had hit a drainage ditch, unmarked by my carefree sister, which, invisible from the air, traversed the lawn except for a twenty-foot-wide bridge, also unmarked, over which the school's lawnmowers or whatever moved. The problem now was quite straightforward. The aircraft was nosed down absolutely vertically into the ditch, into which we had perfect visibility. We were sustained by our seat belts, without which our heads would have been playing the role of our feet. We were there at least a full minute before the girls came. I am not sure I recall the conversation with Brent exactly, but it was on the order of:

"Are we alive?"

"I think so."

"What happened?"

"Ditch."

"Why did you run into it?"

"Very funny."

"Well, why didn't you fly over it?"

"We had landed, goddammit. We were just braking down."

"This isn't going to be easy to get up from."

But the girls, with high good humor, giggles, and exertion, managed to pry us out. We dusted ourselves off outside the vertical plane, attempted languidly to assert our dignity, and were greeted most politely by the headmistress, who said she had tea ready for us, in anticipation of our arrival. We walked sedately up the lawn to her living room, accompanied by Maureen and two roommates. The talk was of spring, Yale, summer plans, the Attlee government, and General MacArthur, but Maureen and her friends would, every now and then, emit an uncontainable giggle, which we manfully ignored. It all went moderately well under the circumstances until the knock on the door. An assistant to the headmistress arrived to ask whether her guests had any use for— "this," and she held forth Alexander's Horse's propeller, or, rather, most of the propeller. I told her thank you very much, but broken propellers were not of any particular use, and she was free to discard it.

Eventually we left, having arranged by telephone with Mr. Kraut to come and fetch the corpse at his convenience. We returned to New Haven by bus. Brent, who had a good book along, did not seem terribly surprised, even after I assured him that most of my airplane rides out of Bethany were round trips.

℘

Oh the sadness of the ending. The plane was barely restored when, during a lesson, one of my partners—his brother, it occurs to me, is the congressman from New Hampshire; another partner became senator from New York; another was the son of columnist Marquis Childs; another had a brother who founded Donaldson, Lufkin & Jenrette; the other was the Morgan who went to Yale— was pleased to hear his instructor say as they approached the strip for a landing, "You're hot!" My friend figured that, in the idiom of the day, this meant he was proceeding splendidly, so he nosed the ship on down, crashing it quite completely. As he later explained, what reason did he have to know that, in the jargon of the trade, to say you were "hot" meant, "You're going too fast"? He had a point. The estimate to repair Alexander's Horse was an uncanny eighteen hundred dollars, exactly what we had paid for her. Mournfully, we decided to let her rest, selling the carcass for one hundred dollars. Father was right, as usual. I couldn't afford to fly.

The Angel of Craig's Point

I sold Cyrano *in 1978,* Suzy Wong *in 1981, as the problems of main-taining wooden boats and of making them pay their way in the charter business became too demanding. But not having a boat of my own was not an option, and so I commissioned Christo and Danny to look for a smaller boat, made of relatively carefree fiberglass.*

They quickly came up with Patito, *a thirty-six-foot sloop, and I have loved the little boat. For our inaugural cruise on* Patito, *we chose the St. John River in New Brunswick. Christo and Danny and I were joined by an old friend, historian Tom Wendel.* ⌐

O*ur last day on the river,* after sailing briskly downwind with only the headsail for two or three hours, during which we lunched, we thought to take a little exercise—a good walk—and, while at it, to get rid of two sackfuls of garbage, neatly tied up in plastic bags and riding in the dinghy we were towing.

I spotted a little private wharf on Craig's Point and glided in toward it, intending to ask the owner's permission to use his garbage container and perhaps even to tie up the boat on his dock for an hour while we walked. As we approached the dock, Christo leaned forward, a docking line in his hand ready to toss to the man in his early sixties who approached us. We assumed he was doing so in the usual manner in which boats are approached when com-ing in for a landing—i.e., prepared to receive the bowline and to cleat it to the dock. I signaled Tom to make the request from amidship. He said, "Is it okay if we tie up here for a few minutes? We'd also like to get rid of the garbage, if that's all right."

To our astonishment, the man answered, "It is not all right. Go away. This is private property."

I intervened. "How far from your house is the public road?"

He pointed in the general direction of his own house. "It's back there."

"Well," I said, "could we just walk across your property to find a public place to leave the garbage?"

"You may not. Go away."

To put it calmly, sailors are not used to being treated that way. To begin with, our anxiety to put the garbage on an assembly line to the city dump presumptively indicated our concern for the cleanliness of the water that ran by Craig's Point, where the gentleman lived, not Wallacks Point, where I live, three hundred miles away. But of course there was no alternative but to retreat from his dock area. We consulted hastily, calculated the probable extent of his shoreline property, went safely beyond it, and threw out a hook, and three of us went ashore. At least we could get our walk. The garbage could continue to accumulate until we reached the yacht club the next morning.

After our walk we sailed another hour, spotted a seductive mini-cove nestled among tall cypress trees, and let down the anchor for our last meal aboard *Patito* on that trip. Christopher and Danny set about preparing a gourmet dinner while Tom played an entire Bach toccata on the Casio portable keyboard. I felt an ungovernable urge, and reached for my typewriter. Before we sat down to dinner, I announced that I wished to read to my crew a letter I had written to the editor of the afternoon paper at St. John. I had intended a catharsis for the unpleasant experience at Craig's Point, and achieved it.

Four days later, back in New York, my secretary, Frances Bronson, told me that the editor of the *Telegraph-Journal* of St. John, New Brunswick, was on the line and wanted to speak to me.

I was stuck. Journalists should always take calls from other journalists (my rule). But I knew that there was no way I could take this phone call and speak the truth without undermining my own enterprise. So I instructed Frances to tell the editor, "Mr. Buckley has nothing to add to the letter he addressed to your paper a few days ago at St. John, and sends his best wishes."

A few days later, someone sent me in the mail a copy of the *Telegraph-Journal* for July 16, 1982. On the right, there was a large picture of me, smiling. The headline read:

BILL BUCKLEY LOVES HOSPITALITY IN N.B.

An editor's note began the story...

(Editor's note: William F. Buckley, editor of National Review, *a conservative magazine published in New York, and host of the popular* Firing Line *program on the educational television network, was in New Brunswick recently with his family. They had a few problems but were delighted with the help they received. And he wrote to us to say so.)*

Dear Sir:

Indulge, if you will, a vacationing American journalist with Canadian connections (my wife, even after thirty years' marriage, is obstinately Canadian) a word or two about our recent voyage in my small sloop with three companions, from Stamford, Connecticut, to St. John, via Nantucket.

1. Near Lepreau Point, west of St. John some twenty-five miles, we ran out of fuel—and there was no wind. My son and his companion took the dinghy, approached the nearest house, and explained our predicament. The gentleman conveyed them to

the nearest gas station, where they filled two five-gallon containers, returned them to the beach, wished them Godspeed, and rejected most amiably a proffered bottle of champagne.

2. At St. John, while waiting for the current's equilibrium in order to make the passage across the falls, a resident volunteered to drive us in his work truck to the restaurant where we lunched. En route he spotted our five-gallon container, ascertained that we intended to buy some diesel fuel, and volunteered to do so for us while we lunched, and to place the container in our dinghy; where, an hour later, we found it, together with the receipt from the gasoline station.

3. The following day, heading up the river, I radioed to my office to ascertain whether the details had been completed involving the ferry crew retained to bring my sloop back to Connecticut. After the telephonic exchange had been completed, the operator said to me: "Excuse me, sir, but I heard your secretary give the telephone number of the hotel where she booked your crew. She gave you an area code of 709. That is the area code for St. John's, Newfoundland, not St. John, New Brunswick." I quickly called back to New York, explained the confusion, and thanked the marine operator whose merciful intervention spared us a geographical solecism that would have qualified for the annals of, well, something.

4. But I must close by mentioning the man my shipmates have come to refer to as "The Angel of Craig's Point." That may really be overstating it, but the gentleman who owns the house on Craig's Point, at latitude 45° 23.5, longitude 66° 12.3, is certainly very special. We had accumulated some garbage, and went by dinghy to the gentleman's little wharf, where he met us with open arms, guiding us to a disposal point, complimenting us effusively on the thought we took to preserve the ecological purity of your beautiful river. Such ardent attention

Bill Buckley Loves Hospitality In N.B.

(Editor's note: William F. Buckley, editor of National Review, a conservative magazine published in New York and host of the popular 'Firing Line' program on the educational television network, was in New Brunswick recently with his family. They had a few problems but were delighted with the help they received. And he wrote to us to say so.)

***

Dear Sir:

Indulge, if you will, a vacationing American journalist with Canadian connections (my wife, even after 30 years' marriage, is obstinately Canadian), a word or two about our recent voyage in my small sloop with three companions, from Stamford, Connecticut to Saint John, via Nantucket.

1) Near Lepreau Point, west of Saint John some twenty-five miles, we ran out of fuel — and there was no air. My son and his companion took the dinghy, approached the nearest house, and explained our predicament. The gentleman convoyed them to the nearest gas station, where they filled two five gallon containers, returned them to the beach, wished them godspeed, and rejected mostly amiably a proffered bottle of champagne.

2) At Saint John, while waiting for the current's equilibrium in order to make the passage across the Falls, a resident volunteered to drive us in his work-truck to the restaurant where we lunched. En route he spotted our five-gallon container, ascertained that we intended to buy some diesel,

volunteered to do so for us while we lunched, and to place the container in our dinghy; where, an hour later, we found it, together with the receipt from the gasoline station.

3) The following day, heading up the River, I radioed to my office to ascertain whether the details had been completed involving the ferry pilots retained to bring my sloop back to Connecticut. After the telephonic exchange had been completed, the operator said to me: "Excuse me, sir, but I heard your secretary give the telephone number of the hotel where she booked your pilots. She gave you an area code of 709. That is the area code for St. John's, Newfoundland, not Saint John, New Brunswick." I quickly called back to New York, explained the confusion, and thanked the marine operator whose merciful intervention spared us a geographical solecism that would have qualified for the annals of, well, something.

4) But I must close by mentioning what my shipmates have come to refer to as "the Angel of Craig's Point." That may really be overstating it, but the gentleman who owns the house on Craig's Point, at Latitude 45 degrees 23.5, Longitude 66 degrees 12.3, is certainly very special. We had accumulated some garbage, and went by dinghy to the gentleman's little wharf, where he met us with open arms, guiding us to a disposal point, complimenting us effusively on the thought we took to preserve the ecological purity of your beautiful river. Such ardent attention he gave us that we soon

WILLIAM F. BUCKLEY

gathered that he devotes himself substantially to welcoming any yachtsman or passers-by who have garbage or any form of detritus to dispose of. Such heartening concern for nature, and such hospitality evidenced to strangers, prompts me to send a copy of this letter to the editor of the famous Cruising Guide to the New England (and Canadian) Coast, so that future editions will assure that no yachtsman will pass by Craig's Point without paying respect to its Angel, and leaving him their garbage.

We are all very much in debt to citizens of Saint John for your hospitality.

WILLIAM F. BUCKLEY, JR.

New York, N.Y.

he gave us that we soon gathered that he devotes himself substantially to welcoming any yachtsmen or passersby who have garbage or any form of detritus to dispose of. Such heartening concern for nature, and such hospitality evidenced to strangers, prompt me to send a copy of this letter to the editor of the famous *A Cruising Guide to the New England* (and Canadian) *Coast*, so that future editions will assure that no yachtsmen will pass by Craig's Point without paying respect to its Angel, and leaving him their garbage.

We are very much in debt to the citizens of St. John for your hospitality.

WILLIAM F. BUCKLEY JR.
NEW YORK, N.Y.

The following day I received a copy of the *Telegraph-Journal* of St. John for July 17, 1982. The headline was too good to be true.

The Angel of Craig's Point Strikes Back

On the left of the boxed story, another headline:

More About Bill Buckley's Garbage Bags

Then:

By Jim White
Associate Editor

Where is William F. Buckley's garbage?

That's the big question facing residents of the Craig's Point area on the St. John River north of Westfield.

Mr. Buckley, the well-known American writer and editor of the *National Review,* wrote a letter to the editor of the *Telegraph-Journal* which was published yesterday, complimenting New Brunswickers on their hospitality during a recent visit.

But the vituperative Mr. Buckley struck out at one resident of Craig's Point in a seemingly innocent passage, and that resident wants to set the record straight once and for all.

Mr. Buckley in his letter referred to the "Angel of Craig's Point," who assisted him in disposing of his accumulated "detritus" from his "small sloop."

Mr. Buckley went on further to suggest passing yachters should not miss the opportunity to deposit their garbage at Craig's Point.

But the so-called "angel" has an entirely different recollection of the encounter.

Aubrey Pope, a retired St. John businessman, remembers the July 1st encounter with Mr. Buckley's party very well.

The Buckley sloop had spent the night in the shelter of a cove off Craig's Point, Mr. Pope said.

The next morning, Mr. Pope's wife noticed "three chaps in a rubber dinghy heading toward the shore."

The Angel Of Craig's Point Strikes Back

More About

Bill Buckley's

Garbage Bags

By JIM WHITE
Associate Editor

Where is William F. Buckley's garbage?

That's the big question facing residents of the Craig's Point area on the St. John River north of Westfield.

Mr. Buckley, the well-known American writer and editor of the National Review, wrote a letter to the editor of The Telegraph-Journal which was published yesterday, complimenting New Brunswickers on their hospitality during a recent visit.

But the vituperative Mr. Buckley struck out at one resident of Craig's Point in a seemingly innocent passage and that resident wants to set the record straight once and for all.

Mr. Buckley in his letter referred to the "angel of Craig's Point" who assisted him in disposing his accumulated "detritus" from his "small sloop."

Mr. Buckley went on further to suggest passing yachters should not miss the opportunity to deposit their garbage at Craig's Point.

But the so-called "angel" has an entirely different recollection of the encounter.

Aubrey Pope, a retired Saint John businessman, remembers the July 1st encounter with Mr. Buckley's party very well.

The Buckley sloop had spent the night in the shelter of a cove off Craig's Point. Mr. Pope said.

The next morning, Mr. Pope's wife noticed "three if-ats in a rubber dinghy heading toward the shore."

Mr. Pope, who is well known up and down the river, went out to greet the landing party.

By the time Mr. Pope arrived at the shore one of the men was standing on the wharf and the others were handing out two boxes and a couple of bags of garbage.

"If they had only asked permission, I would have been happy to give them a hand," Mr. Pope said.

But the party arrogantly went about their work and told Mr. Pope they

were going to dump the garbage beside the road.

When Mr. Pope told the group there was no roadside pickup they insisted they wanted to get rid of their unseemly cargo.

At this point Mr. Pope informed them they were trespassing on his private property and were no longer welcome. They could pick up their garbage and return to their boat.

"They got in their boat and rowed into the river," Mr. Pope said. "Then they put into shore a little way's down river. They walked ashore with the boxes. I don't know where they dumped it, but they didn't have their garbage when they came back to the boat."

Attempts to get through to Mr. Buckley at his New York office failed. But Mr. Buckley's assistant, Frances Bronson, said Mr. Buckley had submitted the letter for publication and had no further comment.

Kempton Pope, son of the owner of Craig's Point, said the rudeness of the Buckley party was what really riled his father.

WILLIAM F. BUCKLEY

"If they had introduced themselves he probably would have been proud to have Mr. Buckley's garbage," he said with a chuckle.

Because of his actions in writing the letter, Mr. Pope suggests Mr. Buckley confine his cruising to the Love Canal.

Meanwhile the search continues at Craig's Point for Mr. Buckley's garbage.

Mr. Pope, who is well known up and down the river, went out to greet the landing party.

By the time Mr. Pope arrived at the shore, one of the men was standing on the wharf and the others were handing out two boxes and a couple of bags of garbage.

"If they had only asked permission, I would have been happy to give them a hand," Mr. Pope said.

But the party arrogantly went about their work and told Mr. Pope they were going to dump the garbage beside the road.

When Mr. Pope told the group there was no roadside pickup they insisted they wanted to get rid of their unseemly cargo.

At this point Mr. Pope informed them they were trespassing on his private property and were no longer welcome. They could pick up their garbage and return to their boat.

"They got in their boat and rowed into the river," Mr. Pope said. "Then they put into shore a little way's down river. They walked ashore with the boxes. I don't know where they dumped it, but they didn't have their garbage when they came back to the boat."

Attempts to get through to Mr. Buckley at his New York office failed. But Mr. Buckley's assistant, Frances Bronson, said Mr. Buckley had submitted the letter for publication and had no further comment.

Kempton Pope, son of the owner of Craig's Point, said the rudeness of the Buckley party was what really riled his father.

"If they had introduced themselves we probably would have been proud to have Mr. Buckley's garbage," he said with a chuckle.

It had been ages, Tom Wendel wrote me from California, since he had seen such a farrago of misinformation as that given to editor White by Aubrey Pope. But we had had our laugh, and I resigned myself to living with the consolation that misrepresentations of *Patito*'s behavior were limited to a modest circulation centered on Craig's Point, New Brunswick.

Not so.

On September 6, *People* magazine (circ. 2,854,000) ran an item in its Chatter column, written by Josh Hammer.

DUMPING ON THE LOCALS

After a recent cruise down New Brunswick's picturesque St. John River, writer-skipper William F. Buckley, Jr., sent a letter to the St. John *Telegraph-Journal* praising a fellow whom he dubbed "the Angel of Craig's Point." According to Buckley, the man had helped his crew dispose of its shipboard garbage. Aubrey Pope, 67, a local businessman, recognized his description but surfaced with a somewhat different version of Buckley's tale. As he told it to an editor at the *Telegraph-Journal*, three of Buckley's crew members had indeed sought to unload their trash—by dumping it all on Pope's private dock. Pope happened to intercept them and ordered them off. "I'm not very big, but I can get ugly," he said, adding that he "would have been glad to help"—if it hadn't been for their "arrogant attitude." Buckley's response was to dump his trash without permission at a scenic spot farther down river and then fire off his sarcastic missive, in which he "thanked" Pope for his help, gave the exact location of his dock and advised mariners passing through not to cruise by Craig's Point "without paying respects to its angel" by dropping off their garbage there.

Oh dear, I thought. It was all really getting out of hand. Not only had we obstreperously arrived at Mr. Pope's dock, landed on it without his permission, and (in effect) threatened him, we had actually thrown our garbage into a scenic spot next door. So, of course, I needed now to write to *People*. I did so, patiently straightening out the story. *People* did not publish the last half of the sentence that began, "It would not occur to us to dump garbage on private property without permission"—which sentence went on to say, "or to publish a story to the effect that Mr. Hammer [the author of *People*'s Chatter column] had done so, without first calling him up and asking him whether so bizarre an allegation was correct."

And then, on top of all that, I had a pleasant letter from Roger Duncan, the editor of *A Cruising Guide to the New England Coast*, the bible of New England sailors. I hadn't actually sent him a copy of my letter to the St. John paper, but somebody else had done so. And now he was writing to thank me for thinking to send him such random information about cruising experiences as I was collecting. He advised me that his own experience with Canadians, like mine, reaffirmed that they were the most hospitable breed of people on earth. He finished:

> I appreciate your thinking of the *Guide*. It is only with the help of cruising men who write in their experiences of various harbors that we can possibly keep the book current. I visit a great many harbors and so does [my associate] John Ware, but we could never accomplish the project without help. Any other information of interest to cruising yachtsmen will be welcome, either now or later.

I needed to straighten Mr. Duncan out in a hurry.

And then, on reading the correction published in *People*, the editor of the St. John paper wrote to remind me that he had tried to reach me over the telephone but I had not taken his call. He added that Mr. Pope was now asserting that his own story of what had happened was confirmed by someone who had used binoculars from the other side of the river. I replied:

Dear Mr. White:

Thank you for your amiable letter. You will perhaps have reflected on the reasons why I did not take the telephone call from you that day in July. Obviously my letter, while composed three parts of genuine praise of Canadian hospitality, was composed one part of sarcasm at the expense of Mr. Anti-Pope. I could hardly have talked with you over the telephone without giving away the show, and obviously I wouldn't have wanted to do that.

On the astonishing point that there was a live witness via binoculars: That would suggest, given that the verbal exchanges with Mr. Pope were exactly as described by me, that the binoculars disposed of facilities for picking up the sound of human voices several hundred yards away. Since to my knowledge such powers as these are limited to the CIA and KGB, then you have more to worry about than my inaccessibility. If your reporter advised you that we proceeded to dump the garbage ashore, why he is just plain wrong, and if it were necessary to prove the point, you could have four sworn affidavits. My own guess has been that Mr. Anti-Pope is industrious in elaborating circumstances that vitiate his rudeness. I note that *People* magazine edited my letter, leaving out the last sentence, which was the only trenchant remark on their own misbehavior. Ah well. Could it be that journalists are also human?

Exactly one year later, Tom Wendel, Danny, Christo, and I found ourselves once again on the St. John River. We had planned to cruise to the Bras d'Or Lake in the northern part of Nova Scotia, but a tight schedule plus head winds rerouted us, and now we were at anchor within sight of the Angel's spread, a few hundred yards upstream. We had consumed, with dinner, a magnum of fine Bordeaux, a cruising gift from a friend, which greatly animated us. Accordingly, we typed out a note, stuck it in the bottle, corked it tightly, and let it float downstream. The note read:

IMPORTANT... REWARD...

The finder of this bottle can claim a fifty-dollar reward by presenting the bottle to Aubrey Pope, Esquire, at Craig's Point, Morrisdale, NB. The reward will be payable on saying to Mr. Pope, "This bottle represents the gratitude of the Canada Beautiful Society, Ltd, Garbage Collection Division, W. F. Buckley, Corresponding Secretary, Care Editor, St. John *Telegraph-Journal.*"

Somewhere in the oceans of the world that bottle is floating about. That, or else it has been presented to the Angel for the promised reward.

A Sail across the Pacific

My friends and I had sailed across the Atlantic twice, in 1975 and 1980—years that coincided with anniversary celebrations of National Review. *When 1985 loomed, I raised with Danny the subject of a third crossing. No, he said, he really didn't think he wanted to cross the Atlantic again on a sailboat.*

"How about the Pacific?" I said without premeditation.

"That's different," said Danny, and so that is what we decided to do.

Patito, holding four sailors comfortably, was obviously not the boat for this cruise, and so I chartered the Sealestial, *a seventy-one-foot ketch, for our 4,400-mile journey.*

S ome years ago *National Geographic* ran a piece about a seventeen-year-old boy who set out to sail across the Pacific single-handed on a small boat—a thirty-two-footer, as I remember. His capital consisted of the boat and its gear, drinking water and canned goods for a couple of months at sea, and fifty dollars his father had endowed him with. A haunting and exotic story, I thought, but my curiosity focused finally on a picture of the boy taking a shower aboard his boat halfway between, oh, Tahiti and Fiji. The picture depicted the showering subject, the entire sailboat, and stretches of endless sea all about them. Question: How was that picture taken? Did the magazine send out a passenger pigeon trained to take pictures at sea? Did NASA contribute the

use of a Peeping Tom satellite—the kind that can read the classi-
fieds in *Pravda* from eleven thousand miles above Moscow?

A grain of skepticism entered the system that day, and guides me
now to Full Disclosure. That commitment to disclosure compels me
not to say that crossing an ocean on a sailboat can be made effort-
less. Or that it is always fun. Or that there is no discomfort. Or even
that there is no danger. But it does compel me to say that there are
ways of crossing an ocean on a sailboat that hugely lessen the exertions, physical and mental, of the experience, and the loneliness and
the boredom and the tedium, and that I've become proficient, after
two runs across the Atlantic on a sailboat, in fingering them.

So that when, at 4:00 P.M. on the second of June, we set out from
Honolulu, bound for Papua New Guinea, 4,400 statute miles away,
we were about as well insulated from the vicissitudes of life-at-sea
as one could reasonably hope to be. To begin with, we had Liz,
maybe the finest sea cook afloat. Blindfolded you would not know
whether you had eaten on a sailboat making its lonely way across
an endless ocean, or at the Four Seasons restaurant in New York.
As first mate we had Noddy, who notwithstanding his truculent
Rastafarian hairstyle is a gentle and ingenious young man from
Barbados, where his father is chief of staff of the army, his uncle,
the prime minister. Maureen was there to serve meals and make
beds and, primarily, to smile indulgently whenever asked for anything, which she would forthwith fetch up from the galley. And
Allan Jouning, the finest skipper of my acquaintance, to help
whenever help was most crucially needed.

And I and six carefully selected companions. Our job was to sail
the *Sealestial*, to ascertain where we were, to hold the course, to
cope with squalls, to forecast the weather, to write our journals,
and carefully to steer our way without human abrasion through a
thirty-day retreat from cosmopolitan lives of hectic texture far
removed from the rusticity of life-at-sea.

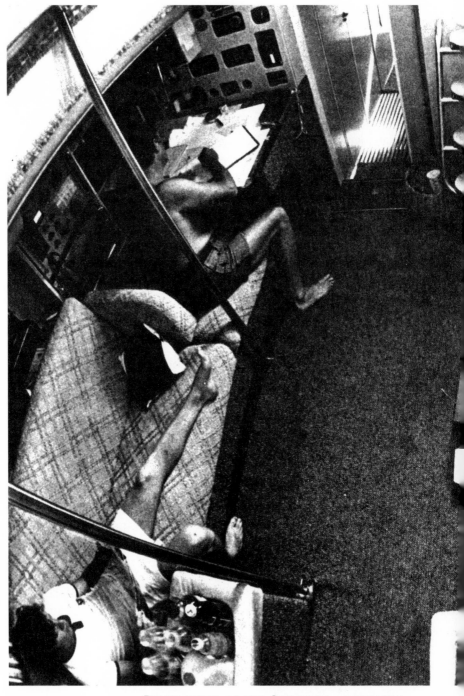

BELOW DECKS ON THE SEALESTIAL: OFF WATCH

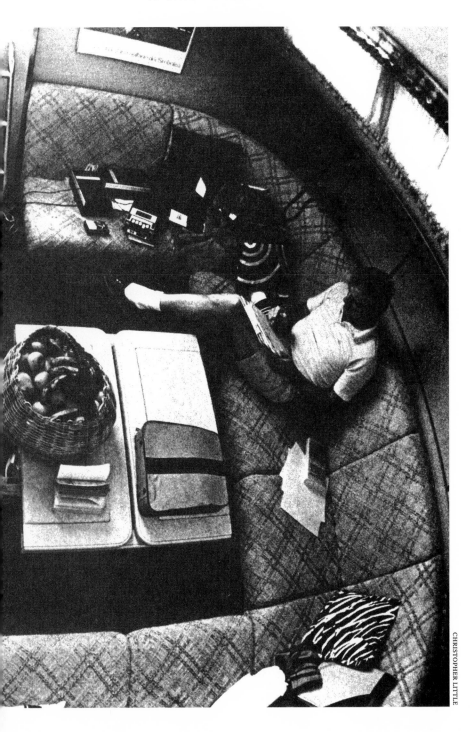

Christo, age thirty-two, took time off from his writing to take charge of R&R, and every morning he would post the day's extranavigational doings in the saloon, on the mirror we used as a bulletin board. A typical notice: *"Tonight:* Bonnie and Clyde! *The melodramatic adventures of the century's most sizzling bank robbers! At* Sealestial-*Odeon, 8 P.M.*!" We trolled two fishing lines and twice had exciting catches, one of them a fifty-five-pound mahi-mahi. Once it was landed into the after-cockpit, Allan Jouning dispatched it by the novel contrivance of pouring a jiggerful of vodka into its gills, bringing on, to our astonishment, instant death: death rapid and ostentatious enough to satisfy the most apocalyptic evangelist for the WCTU. We had a .410 shotgun aboard and did a little skeet shooting, and a .223 Ruger rifle with which to discourage sharks while we swam during the periodic lulls, and also to beat up on beer cans tossed overboard as targets.

Occasionally Christopher would set up a miniature Ping-Pong table. The tournament was scheduled below, in the saloon, if it was rocky. But when the seas were especially calm, the contest was played on the foredeck, under the sunny sun. Oh yes, speaking of vodka, we had fifty cases of beer, a like amount of ginger ale and Coke and Pepsi, thirty cases of wine, and a little of this and that of the other stuff. One hundred audiocassettes with (very) heavy emphasis on baroque. Christopher and Danny had Walkman headsets so that, on the Midnight Watch (post-movie to 1 A.M.), they could listen to Bob Dylan or The Screeches, or whomever. Jarsful of cookies and candy to keep the Post-Midnight Watch (1 A.M. to 5 A.M.) from undernourishment in the dead hours. Thermosfuls of coffee and soup for prebreakfast revival on the Early-Morning Watch (5 A.M. to 9 A.M.). Four computers (two Kaypro 2000s, two Epson PX-8s) for the scriveners on the Late-Morning (9 A.M. to 1 P.M.) and Early-Afternoon (1 P.M. to 5 P.M.) Watches (one of us was revising memoirs of his three years as ambassador to France;

another was surveying the first 25,000 words of an ambitious book on the press and public controversy; a third was readying to proof-read a political comedy, a novel which will be called *The White House Mess*; another had just done a spy novel and was collecting ideas from his companions, who read the manuscript in turn, for a final revision, due a couple of weeks after the end of the cruise). And, during twenty minutes of the Late-Afternoon Watch (5 P.M. to 7 P.M.), we listened every evening to recorded episodes from the two autobiographies of David Niven, *The Moon's a Balloon* and *Bring On the Empty Horses*, over drinks and hors d'oeuvres.

That was followed by star-taking time, and I had in my Epson Professor Hugh Kenner's wonderful WhatStar program. The idea is: You feed the computer the time of your sight, the sextant angle of the observed body, your assumed position at sea, and Whrrrr!—the computer reveals that you were just now looking at Arcturus! That you are therefore somewhere on a line of position that stretches east to west seventeen miles north of where your Assumed Position is. The succeeding shot tells you that *that* body was Spica, and you are somewhere on a north-south line eight miles west of your Assumed Position. You post these data on your plotting sheet and proceed to the cockpit, to announce noncha-lantly to your companions that we are 1,236 miles from Majuro (our destination in the Marshall Islands on the second leg), that our course should be corrected three degrees east to 232; and that, this being Monday, we should get there maybe on Tuesday week, if the winds stay about where they are. We go down to a splendid dinner, watch the movie, and resume watch duty, which is ours twenty-two hours per day, Allan's and Noddy's during the period the *Sealestial*-Odeon tracks the most sizzling bank robbers of the century.

Cool stuff.

But there is the downside.

Twenty minutes after leaving Honolulu I was at the wheel, while
Noddy and Van and Reggie were hoisting the spinnaker. A gust of
wind caught the great sail, whose sheet had been prematurely
secured, so that it bellowed out, causing a sudden pull of maybe
two, three thousand pounds on the halyard. Struggling to take an
extra loop on the winch, Noddy let two of his fingers get caught
between line and winch. In the five seconds before Van, tailing the
line, could let go of the halyard—the alternative being to sever two
or more fingers from Noddy's hand—the great sail was in the water,
Noddy's hand was crippled, and two hundred feet of line were
destroyed, shaved in pieces by the sheave at the masthead.

And so we limped back to Honolulu. Emergency ward for Noddy;
two hundred feet of line purchased from another boat. Three hours
later, chastened in spirit, we set out again. We have been lucky:
Lucky we were close to land when it happened. Lucky that Noddy's
fingers were not broken. Lucky that the doctor authorized him, his
hand bandaged, to resume the journey. Lucky that we could find a
replacement for our halyard on a Sunday afternoon.

The first leg was 850 miles, the next 1,450, the third 975, the
fourth 740, the fifth and last 350. During the whole run we did not
see a single other boat, sail or power, except in port. Our main
genoa, a sailboat's workhorse, fell to pieces after two days...it was
old and tired. The mainsail twice split half its seams, under the
downwind pressure of sail against shrouds (Danny was hoisted
almost to the masthead to insulate the spreaders). The spinnaker
boom we were using to keep the Yankee to windward (we were sailing wing-and-wing) showed deterioration—corrosion. We had to
make do with a substitute rig. The clew of the Yankee ripped out,
making that sail inoperative. During the last two legs we had maybe
fifty squalls, with gusts reaching to fifty-five mph, and we were
drenched great stretches of the time. If anyone had fallen overboard
during one of those squalls he'd have had, in effect, a burial at sea.

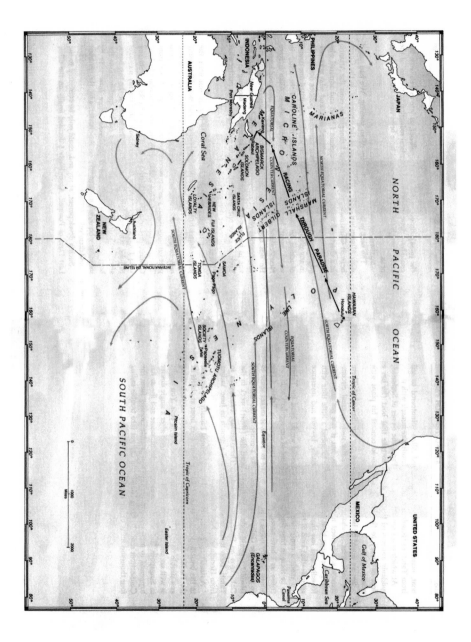

You need to be careful about fire (after boredom, the single greatest hazard at sea), and there were four smokers aboard, names not to be revealed (one of them had taken a public and publicized pledge to swear off). We had wind most of the time and, on the (cumulative) three or four days we didn't have it, the engine worked just fine, except when a trailing line wrapped itself around the propeller, requiring underwater disentanglement by Allan. Celestial navigation brought us in, which was providential, since the SatNav didn't work. Lucky, too, that the days of overcast came when we were hundreds of miles away from land or shoals, not when we needed urgently to know where we were so as to fine-tune our way to our next step, at one point to the tiny atoll of Kapingamarangi, the size of a grain of sand on a great beach.

☙

There is something residually defiant—I often reflect on this—about flying in an airplane. The whole enterprise is a studied effrontery, isn't it? Soaring at six hundred mph within an aluminum carapace, smiling condescendingly at an altimeter that keeps telling you just how many thousand feet gravity would drop you if it had its solemn, natural way—which, sometimes, it does. It is the same feeling some of us get at sea when in a vessel that weighs a small fraction of some of those waves that come thundering by when the ocean is exercised.

Just to begin with, everything depends on the integrity of your hull. And on the lines that maintain your sail at propitious angles, which sails are attached to a mast, the combination rescuing you from squatting down, immobile, helpless, one thousand watery miles from land. You rely on a fiberglass or wooden rudder that you must constantly keep turning—a centimeter's net deviation can mean one hundred miles off course, after a few lazy, negligent days. And the compass. Sailors have relied on it for a thousand years, ever since someone discovered, or rather intuited, the existence of the great emancipating deposit up there near true north of a mountain of magnetic material that directs the compass needle toward it. These are the contingencies of sailing across an ocean, a distance the equivalent of Maine to Dakar, of Capetown to Suez: from the westernmost state of America to the easternmost of the great Asian islands, just north of Australia.

You can't, then, ever know for sure what will happen, and so you rely on the odds. These are tidily reassuring (two hundred dollars will buy you a million dollars of life insurance). And anyway, you don't neglect to stock your cellar or your library just because you might be struck by lightning, do you? If the odds were conclusively intimidating—why, they would intimidate! A college classmate of mine recently ascended Mt. Everest, and in doing so exposed himself to danger and hardship I probably would not survive, and would most certainly not court. You can fetch up all the cushions in the world but, if you step recklessly out of the airplane, you will still have a rough landing. ("What I admire about the astronauts," Phil Harris once said, "is that they do it without safety nets.") Even as, at sea, one can always be overpowered, and the unfortunate sailor is regularly overpowered; but then so is the unfortunate urban pedestrian overpowered. There has to be a reason for it all. It took us thirty active days, six watches per day, to get there; and we got back to where we had started in a mere eleven, sedentary hours of flying. So what is it?

Have you ever experienced the cockpit of a sailing ship, sails set, propelling you at eight knots, the water parting, poutful but, at the margin, submissive, as you charge along all but noiselessly—with only the sound of water hissing to get out of your way? The moon is out and you see shafts of silver lighting up a third of all the globe you can see, all the globe that matters. Or else the moon isn't up: it is black-black, but the tiny, dim red light in your compass confirms,

when you look down at it, that you are on a steady course. You are
steering by the star over there—there, just to the right of the upper
shroud, the star that beckons you along; ceding gracefully, as the
celestial tapestry slides by, to its successor, down by the spreader,
which in turn yields, after fifteen or twenty minutes, to the succeeding star—this one just up by the masthead, and though you
need constantly to manipulate the wheel, you are making a fairly
steady course along the calculated way. It is warm, and you remove
your light sweater and feel the tender air.

Or—it is chilling up, and you slip a foul-weather jacket over your
sweater, and feel the warmth of your own body, added now to your
inventory of protections against the eccentric impositions of nature.

But always, on reflection, you are awed by the greatest imposition of all, which is that *you* are making *headway* by manipulating
craftily the carefree endowments of nature. The wind is propelling
you: one hundred thousand pounds of hull, equipment, human
beings, and Goo-Goo candy bars; and notwithstanding where the
wind is coming from, you are making headway toward the destination of your own choosing. We could in roughly as many hours
have doused our sails finally at Yokohama in Japan, at the Canal in
Panama, at Anchorage in Alaska; same ocean, same winds, just set
your sails accordingly, and steer the course you want, and ask the
sun and stars to guide you.

It adds up to a whole lot, in a world that specializes, even in the
freer societies, in straitening rules and regulations. It is, all by itself,
a sensation of a singular order to know that everything you will
need for thirty days, everything from bread to medicine to music to
literature to navigational almanacs, lies less than seventy feet away
from where you are standing. That you can take all of this, and
yourself, and your companions, and move without permission from
the FCC, the SEC, the FDA, or the *New York Times*, from one hemisphere to another. Look in on the atoll you casually fingered, sur-

veying the charts one night last winter in Switzerland—it hasn't seen another sailboat in three years, it transpires. There you were greeted warmly and guilelessly by a cigar-smoking prime minister and by bare-breasted young mothers, by children of wide eyes and Polynesian warmth and inquisitive smiles looking at that exotic white vessel that brought these strangers to their necklace of little palm-lined islands. It is an experience, above all else, in living, at such very close quarters, with the same people for a whole month. You test the bonds of companionship, stretch them sometimes until tight, but they don't snap, and it reassures to know how wonderfully strong fraternity can be. Always you are aware that it doesn't necessarily work. There can be tragedy, for which nature or dereliction can be responsible. And there can be what amounts to tragedy, for which human nature is responsible. But neither happened to us.

And when, after thirty days, we arrived at Kavieng harbor and tied down, for the last time, we knew intuitively that it had worked. Late that night, strolling along the tropical shore three degrees south of the equator and twenty-nine degrees into the eastern hemisphere, a few of us experienced the smells and scents of land, the dislocating stability of settled ground. I stopped and picked up a hefty little branch I spotted, lying by the faintly luminous road among the solemn deadwood trees, and used it as a walking stick. It helped to steady legs unaccustomed to the equilibrium of level earth. At sea your legs are always working to compensate for the constant motion. The muscular adaptations become instinctive, automatic. Back on land you are suddenly relieved of the need for them. It is the sea's momentum that puts you off balance. And, gradually, you become aware of all those other synchronizations you will need quickly to make, from which, for thirty days, we were suspended, making our long, slow, steady, isolated way across the vast ocean, savoring the heady experience of the explorer.

Aweigh

It had to end at some point. I thought about it. ⟶

C*onsequential decisions can be* triggered by inconsequential causes. *She leaned over, picked up the phone—and I knew then that I'd be filing for divorce.* But later, introspective curiosity sets in. And the search for self-justification. So we poke about dormant gray matter trying to bring out a plausible teleological narrative. All this has been happening to me since I decided to sell my boat.

Selling a boat one has spent happy decades on isn't the awesome equivalent of filing for divorce, but it is a fateful decision. It can be likened to a decision to stop skiing, or playing the piano, if one has skied a lot, and played the piano a lot. The sequence here is critical to the effort to explain a self-inflicted privation.

 ❧

What brought it on? It wasn't that I decided to do away with my boat after narrowly surviving the storm I took her through. I wasn't making a gesture of despair and remorse after losing a companion overboard.

Dramatic forerunners engender sequels that are self-explanatory, most of the time. There was none such here to account for my decision. If there had been a catalytic event, you would be looking for something quite simple, on the order of resolving to file for divorce after finding your wife in bed with another man; a banality. It's the inconsequential factor that I searched for.

What did happen is that the summer first mate I had retained— as always—to crew for me one day every week, and ten days in August, had had to pull away when a mortal cancer seized his mother, quickly killing her. *Of course* he would leave me for a period, to be in Canada with his father. But after two or three weeks I expected him back. Instead, he now reported that he had contracted an episodic malady of sorts which would keep him away for the balance of the sailing season. He would be returning directly to Yale to get on with his graduate work in molecular biology. My summer schedule was put awry.

A few weeks later, my plans reconstituted, I was sailing off Cape Cod with three very old friends. I blurted it out to them at dinner on the fourth night that I had decided to sell my boat, on which, as on its predecessors, they had all sailed with me over many years, and to distant places. Their stupefaction was gratifying, in that it confirmed the felt gravity of my own decision. I had acted on impulse but not, I tried to explain to them, impulsively.

છ

In September 1938, two of my sisters and I received (as recounted on pp. 17–18) the distressing news that, two weeks hence, we were to embark for England, where for one academic year we would attend boarding schools. This disruption of happy lives, being home-schooled in northwest Connecticut, we found unbearable. My father had given no reason for his arbitrary move beyond that the experience of foreign schooling would be educational for us, never mind that, living in Europe five years earlier, we had all already been to British schools. Age twelve, I wrote to him resignedly (there was no alternative to complying with my father's decisions) about the impending extra-territorialization, and took sly and arrant advantage of his predictable defensiveness—he owed us one, and he had a very tender heart. I told him that when we got back from the English ordeal, I pined to have a sailboat.

And so, nine months later, in June 1939, I beheld my own sailboat on the neighboring lake. It was a torrid affair, from the moment I sighted her. I thought it a filial gesture to name her *Sweet Isolation*, reflecting my father's political leanings in the prewar years. My little (seventeen-foot) conventionally rigged Barracuda (sailing class extinct) took me around the triangular course on Lakeville Lake twice every Wednesday, Saturday, and Sunday, mid June to Labor Day. I contended in the no-handicap marathon against six other boats of different designs, all of them captained by aged men and women in their twenties and thirties. We struggled hugely to acquire the trophy. You needed to win it three times before acquiring permanent ownership of it. An exact replica of it could be seen at the local drugstore, for sale for twenty-one dollars.

I would rise early on racing days to stare at the wind's preliminary dispositions, and to contemplate a strategy for that afternoon. I would be driven the five miles to the lake, arriving an hour before race time to practice my starts and coach my crew (usually one of my siblings). We had three summers of this, but the Wononscopomuc Yacht Club races were a casualty of Pearl Harbor and did not revive after the war. The spring-fed, one-square-mile lake is still there; on it, when the winds are still and the sun is low, you can discern the bricked profile of the Hotchkiss School. On the opposite rise, in the low Berkshires, Wanda Landowska could view the lake from her house, where, for RCA, she performed her historic harpsichord renditions of the Well-Tempered Clavichord. One afternoon she had advised the state police, by telephone, that they must close off to traffic the whole road on the eastern side of the lake so that she could have the total stillness she wished for the recordings. No one had ever before made such a request, no one else ever will, but the police, dumbfounded by the high Teutonic voice of the lady who had been on the cover of *Time* magazine, complied.

There was no sailing for me during the war years, but I was discharged from the army in May 1946 and had *Sweet Isolation* back in the water a week later. In July, I contrived a cradle on a four-wheeled trolley. Attached to a station wagon, it took my boat to Edgartown. We sailed, my sisters and the childhood friend I'd be sharing a room with at Yale a month later, in those glamorous waters. One afternoon, off Chappaquiddick, our mast was disabled in a strong wind, my sister Trish swept into Nantucket Sound. For harrowing minutes, as we struggled desperately to bring our boat about, we knew she was at risk of drowning. But a Coast Guard vessel spotted the flailing arms, and picked her up, and then us and my crippled boat, towing the bedraggled lot back to a marina.

That night, silent, we looked at the dinner menu at an inn overlooking the harbor. We were woozy from the afternoon's trauma and unstimulated by alcohol (I wasn't twenty-one, and management would not serve me a beer). My eyes idled over to the cruising boats slipping into the harbor in the falling light, the red and green running lights twinkling off the cozied water. There was shelter here from the heavy winds that continued to roil the Sound outside. One vessel, especially imposing, was identified for our benefit by the waiter, a college student doing summer work and crewing in the afternoons on one of the racing boats. That boat going by—he pointed—was *Manxman*, a surviving Class J boat, 136 feet long, created to compete for the America's Cup in the 1930s. I counted twelve or more crew in the dimming light, fastening down sails, with two or three of them, wearing yellow jackets and khaki shorts, crowded about the skipper. The sight of that long dark beauty especially, and of all the sloops and yawls and cutters and schooners nestling about the harbor, many of them secured now on their moorings, paralyzed me with longing. *A cruising sailboat!* That was now the object of my desire. For several years I read the yachting magazines as a window shopper, praying that, one day, I would put my foot in the door, and sail into Edgartown harbor as captain of my own boat.

੪

I did that in 1954, having conscripted my brother-in-law Firpo, who had never before sailed, into a joint purchase of *The Panic*, the name we gave to the Dutch-built forty-two-foot steel cutter. It was the most misbalanced sailing vessel ever created. In a hard wind, making way close-hauled, you needed all the strength of both arms to hold the tiller to the desired angle.

But she was all ours, including the tiny captain's cabin, not much bigger than the berth it housed, and we gave it an enormous ice box in which, for the long hauls, we could store as much as 250 pounds of ice. We laughed a lot on *The Panic*, cruising on most summer weekends, my wife presiding over a remarkable cuisine that she produced using three sterno stoves that hung down from individual fixtures: multi-gimballed, they were indifferent to any motion of the boat fore and aft or side to side. One night in Maine, Pat's imaginative dinner was prolonged in preparation and I announced that in order to celebrate appropriately the wind the sun the stars and the moon, and the harbor in Maine—there is always a reason to celebrate aboard a boat—I would pour myself a third drink, and went to the bottle of premixed margaritas she had brought on board. I wondered whether, having already drunk two, I would be courting tipsiness with a third, but I poured it anyway. I thought to ascertain the strength of the drink and so tilted the kerosene light to read the fine print on the label. It described the ingredients and then gave directions: "Pour two ounces over ice.

Then add tequila." I had been near tipsy drinking lime juice, causing my crew mates and my wife to be tipsy with amusement.

Cruising in October to Bermuda we had to make our way through the eastern end of a hurricane, and after a very hard day's combat using only storm jib and trysail I finally hove to for a long night of furious wind. This capitulation at sea is achieved by adjusting the reduced sails to vie against one another in such fashion as to induce relative immobility.

The next day, the crew, shaken after the prolonged struggle of the day before and the shriek of the wind against the shrouds during the sleepless night, was somnolent and detached. The dishes from the day before were unwashed. No one had moved to make breakfast. There was cloud cover and we were too far distant from the island to take radio bearings on Bermuda's commercial radio station. I had to tell my companions that I simply didn't know where we were. Demoralization was setting in. I revived the crew by serving hardtack and port. The sweet alcoholic potion revived the spirit, the chewy hardtack gave sustenance. The sun soon crept out, giving me a sight, and on we slogged in a forty-knot wind, eleven hours close-hauled on a starboard tack, ocean water taking up one third of the cubic space of the cockpit in that tipsy boat, arriving finally at St. George's Harbor.

Earlier the same year we had raced *The Panic* with the Newport fleet to Bermuda. On arriving I heard at the festive cocktail party the hairy tale of the metallurgist. He had raced in his brand new thirty-eight-foot aluminum boat on which, forty-eight hours out, was heard a thwack unrelated to the conventional creaks and groans of boats hard pressed under way. The thwack came again forty minutes later. The owner took a professional interest in what was happening. He disclosed after the fourth thwack—these were coming in decreasing time intervals—that when the interval reduced to one minute, that meant that the vessel had at most one remaining minute to stay afloat: an entire aluminum bulwark on the port side would at that point simply fall away. When that boat arrived in Bermuda, thwack time intervals had reduced to four minutes. The owner sold the boat and never sailed again.

But for all that that was a singular experience, his decision to get rid of the boat after undergoing it is hardly inexplicable, never mind that the Swedish builders flew in an engineer, and presumably a lawyer, to cope with the derelict. I would soon be reminded of the psychological impact of a boat loss, not only on the owner, but on others. *The Panic* was destroyed by a hurricane in 1961, so to speak, in my backyard, uprooted from her mooring in the Stamford Yacht Club and splayed across the stony breakwater at the harbor's entrance. The shock of her loss was felt by others who knew her. Hugh Kenner, the uneffusive critic, let out a full-throated jeremiad. Here was the end, he wrote to me, of a boat which had "done much for her friends, in the summers before her side was stove in. She had taken them all around the Sound and along the New England coast, and even to Bermuda (thrice), and shown them Wood's Hole, and the Great Fish that eats taffrail logs, and the Kraken, and the strange men of Onset with their long faces, and perfect Edgartown; and lapped them at night gently to rest; and given them the wind and sun and made for them a place of adventure and refreshment and peace; and taught them this, that beyond illusion it is possible to be for hours and days on end perfectly and inexpressibly happy."

೮౿

Boat owners tend to upgrade, and I had now the insurance money and very quickly bought, sight unseen, a forty-foot yawl (Nevins 40) of illustrious design (Sparkman & Stephens) from its four owners in Miami. It was offered with a piquant story. The sailors had served together in the army in Japan and, aged twenty to twenty-two, had dreamed of owning a sailboat and taking it around the world. They could put together only just enough money to buy the bare boat and engine from the American Yacht Yard in Hong Kong. It was all teak—teak wood was cheap in that part of the world—and they flew there joyfully upon their discharge, men with varied skills learned as civilians and in the army. There they sanded and painted the hull, mounted the rigging, installed the plumbing and electrical systems, and finished the deck. Two months later the boat was ready and they set out, westward, for Miami, arriving eighteen months later, flat broke and happy. They calculated that they had spent, per person per day, $1.75. That updates to about twenty dollars.

I paid them thirty thousand dollars for *Suzy Wong*, and sailed her for nineteen years, some weekdays, most summer weekends, here and there cruising on blue water, two races to Bermuda and one to Halifax, very contented until I found *Cyrano*, a very big upgrade, though purchased for the same thirty thousand dollars I would eventually realize on selling *Suzy*.

There was much to do to make that sixty-foot schooner with its eighteen-foot bowsprit habitable; indeed, to transform it into the dream boat I sailed for ten years, taking her across the Atlantic, Miami–Bermuda–Azores–Gibraltar, with son, sister-in-law, sailing friends, a cook, a hand, and a mate. I built a dodger (this shields the deckhouse from the wind), situated a circular sofa with a matched circular table which, when lowered and covered with cushions, made room for four, even five flopped-out sailors to rest or read; when lifted—cushions removed—provided dining surface for eight people. Two long berths at either side of the navigation table proved handy, and now the rudder could here be electrically controlled when the helmsman sought shelter. Protective canvas could be rolled down on all sides to seal in the entire area. While standing in the navigation well, examining the almanac, the ship moving in a moderate following wind, I spotted the Pico light off

Horta, landfall after eleven days of sailing. I shouted back to Christopher at the wheel. Danny, sitting alongside on the taffrail, stood up and peered excitedly in the direction I signaled. I wrote a book (*Airborne*) about that passage, but the next year, sailing *Cyrano* from Ft. Lauderdale to Cozumel, again with my son and Danny, I reflected hard on the running costs, tucked into my brief-case by the bookkeeper. The figures spoke out to me unanswer-ably—I had to sell her. There was only that single reason for doing so, but it was decisive. *Cyrano* cost too much money to maintain, my grand plan to subsidize her through chartering having failed, after ten years of trying. If anybody (rich) is looking for a perfect boat, track her down, and live happily ever after.

Three years later I sold *Suzy* as well. It was then that I bought *Patito*.

॰॰

I left the purchase of the new boat in the hands of Christopher and Danny. They thought to call it *Patito*, which is the diminu-tive, in Spanish, of duck, a term I use when addressing my wife, as does she when talking to me. I knew that they would find the right boat, this time in fiberglass, to succeed the wooden boats they had wearied of maintaining. I beheld *Patito* for the very first time after giving a lecture at Trinity College in Hartford and driving for almost an hour to Essex. I arrived at the dock in the cold April evening at about eleven, and my new boat was there, lit up below with candlelight, a flicker or two of snow falling down into the cockpit, the saloon well warmed with a kerosene heater. Christo and Danny, in high spirits, had the wine bottle open. *Patito* is thirty-six feet, and the most intimate of my boats since *Sweet Isolation*. I have written about her that she is perfect with four aboard, and that five are—three too many. She has been with me full time ever since. I have been faithful to her except for

two more transoceanic sails, these on a boat I skippered but did not own, the ketch *Sealestial*.

On transocean runs the rule was that I and my friends would do the sailing, and the (paid) crew, the maintenance. It was a good arrangement, giving us, at work and at play, eating and sleeping, a privacy beyond even the gross privacy of living on a little boat in a great ocean. On the 4,300-mile Pacific run (Hawaii to New Guinea) we did not once, in thirty days, see a single other ship at sea, or plane overhead. Such apparent alienation sharpened the miniaturization of it all. I calculated that from the starting point in Hawaii, by altering the rudder a mere eighteen degrees, one twentieth of the orbit of possibilities, I could have directed the boat to land in the Philippines instead of New Guinea. On that passage we had the run of experiences at sea, recounted in another book, *Racing through Paradise*.

It was good that my sea books featured mostly the same friends, given that one's memory is of a boat incorporating the company aboard it. That essential factor of human pleasure—a small crew, with repeat companions—struck me most vividly when, walking by the fleet of boats that had just completed the Annapolis–Bermuda Race, I spotted and spoke to a friend who had crewed aboard what they call a "maxi," i.e., a boat longer than the seventy-two-foot limit permitted during my own racing years. I asked if he had got on with the rest of the crew. He replied that half of them (there were eighteen) he had not even met during the passage.

The convention for summer weekends did not change when I acquired *Patito*. The operative day was Friday. We would convene at my house for a drink, and sometimes a look at the Weather Channel, though we could see the waters of Long Island Sound by looking through the glass doors of the same room. The mate would have the boat ready, and soon after 6:30 we would set out for Long Island, usually Eatons Neck or Oyster Bay. In a hard southeaster, we would stay on the Connecticut side of the Sound, sailing east to Norwalk, or west to Greenwich. Depending on the wind, the sail would take an hour and a half or two hours. Lately we had got used to a dry martini on arrival. Music was instantly at hand. *"The Entertainment Committee never sleeps"* was my mantra, as I slid in a tape of Dick Wellstood or Claude Debussy. A half hour later, the meal began to arrive, prepared at home but cooked by the mate. The mates changed every year, handily recruited mostly from nearby Yale, young men who lived in the area, knew how to sail and were anxious to do so, and welcomed the stipend. They were quickly integrated socially by *Patito* into a Friday routine that usually ended with a game of poker and a swim.

Patito ventured out from the Sound from time to time—twice to Bermuda, to Nova Scotia and Cape Breton, to the St. John River in New Brunswick and thereabouts—but the Friday evening sail, twenty years of it, was simply an organic part of my home schedule, and of my life, and the bonds to friends deepened.

$\wp$

What happened when Michael told me he couldn't persevere with his duties was that everything I had correlatively planned for the August sail changed. I could not ferry the boat east, where I had thought to pick it up and sail in Passamaquoddy and over to Digby in Nova Scotia, and back to St. John and up the enchanted river.

The crew needed recomposition. As I assimilated these alterations in plan, minuscule under the aspect of the heavens, my mind turned to the composite administrative infrastructure of owning a boat. Such concerns not only *seem* exiguous, they *are* that, really, especially if you can get some help. For some, boating is incomplete without the foreplay of sanding and painting and lubricating and all that. Satisfactions got from doing such things yourself, if ever you had them, reduce as you get older. And then up there, up over the clouds, toward which you are gradually climbing, is the mountain top from which, looking down over it all, you see for the first time ever the whole scene. And you have risked asking yourself that mortal question: Is the ratio of Pleasure to Effort holding its own? Or is Effort creeping up, Pleasure down? I mentioned giving up the piano. That actually happened to me, after a dilettante's lifetime of playing, even with nine (spotty) performances onstage as harpsichord soloist. The fingers get rusty, the dividends more laboriously achieved, the memory shakier; one can putter on. Or quit.

Piano playing (at normal speed and for normal lengths of time) is not a physical exertion, and as the master and commander progressively offloads the physical work at sea, exertions are minimal except when visibility attenuates, and wind and seas assert themselves. Then there is concentrated work and thinking to be done, and a measure of anxiety: but these aren't physically taxing, unless I have missed something that Freud et al. passed along. I resist the word "tedium," because sailing can have so many rapturous moments, and there are the accompanying pleasures. When you are in the harbor, four congenial people around the table, eating and drinking and conversing, listening to music and smoking cigars, the wind and the hail and the chill outside faced up to and faced down, in your secure little anchorage—here is a compound of life's social pleasures in the womb of nature. So the decision that the time has come to sell *Patito,* and forfeit all that, is not lightly taken, bringing to mind the step yet ahead, which is giving up life itself.

CHAPTER FIVE

PEOPLE

Ten Friends

Here are ten mini-portraits, commissioned in 2000 by my son, Christopher, the editor of FYI *magazine. He asked me to describe, in a few hundred words each, ten friends who are also public figures. (*FYI *was celebrating its tenth anniversary, and the theme of the entire issue would be "Ten"—wines, books, countries, friends.) My Ten all gave pleasure, not for identical reasons.*

I chose the device of starting each piece with my first encounter with the subject. ⟿

DAVID NIVEN

The first time...On the telephone was John Kenneth Galbraith. He had under his wing Jacqueline Kennedy, who was trying to get a week's vacation, skiing. It had been more than three years since the assassination but she was followed everywhere, and now Professor Galbraith had undertaken her protection and was looking out, too, for her social life. Did I want to join them for dinner at the chalet of David Niven and his wife, Hjördis?

David was a radiant host, attentive to every need and whim; indeed after a while my wife (who became, arguably, his closest friend) suspected that his magic was to induce a whim, so that he could gratify it. What Jackie most needed, during that extended period of shock, was to laugh. Making people laugh was a specialty of David's.

I remember an evening with him years later in Monaco. We were to have drinks in the palace with Prince Rainier and then dinner at a restaurant as David's guests. There was one problem. We had hit Rainier in one of his grumpy moods. That kind of situation was, for our old friend and neighbor David Niven, a challenge.

Waiting for the first course to arrive, David launched into an account of his seduction at age fifteen by an accomplished lady of the night. He imitated sundry accents. The words spoken were lightly ribald, amusing, evocative. Before the second course was served, the prince was a rollicking companion. In Niven's company, nobody had a *chance* to live very long as a wallflower.

He continued, in the sixteen years of our friendship, to make movies, of uneven quality, and we once collaborated on a documentary (never aired) on the Sistine Chapel, along with Malcolm Muggeridge and Grace Kelly and Charlton Heston (see p. 277). But his life was heavily taken up with domestic traffic. He would drive his two little girls to school and bring them back to their chalet after skiing. Every two or three days he would come to our place with its huge playroom, one half of it my writing quarters, the other half an improvised studio built around a Ping-Pong table.

He was greatly skilled at painting, and seldom spoke during the hour or two devoted to the canvas at hand. His six paintbrushes were carefully positioned in his left hand. He washed and cleaned them meticulously and proudly recalled that he had bought them in his earliest days in Hollywood, even before his first wife, Primula, was killed in that crazy accident—David and Primula were playing hide-and-seek with their two young boys; in the dark, Primula opened what she thought was a closet door and fell down a long staircase, breaking her neck.

In the last winter of his life he came to us to paint more frequently, because what he mostly didn't want, at that point, was to have to talk: his disease (Lou Gehrig's) was creeping up on him, and it was a strain to talk through its strangulations. He would just come, set up his paints, and leave after about an hour because, he explained to me, the turpentine fumes soon overcame him.

I remember, one afternoon, coming back from skiing to go to work. He was there with his paintbrushes and hailed me. He wanted to tell me something.

His face choked up with laughter. It was hard to make out what he was saying, but I managed. He had been in his car and was stopped by a traffic light. An old friend who knew nothing about the illness was coincidentally stopped next to him, headed in the opposite direction.

The other man leaned out the window. "What have you got?" he called out to David.

"I tried to get out to him"—he had difficulty pronouncing the words—"that I had *amyotrophic lateral sclerosis*. He could hear me well enough but couldn't make out what I said. He yelled back just as the light changed. 'Oh? Well *I've* got a Lamborghini 500S!'" It hurt David to laugh, and that was the truly unbearable burden.

Ronald Reagan

The first time? My speech in Beverly Hills was scheduled for 7:30, and I ate in the restaurant across from the high-school auditorium with my sister-in-law Bill Finucane. When the time came, two other diners also rose. They had been at the far end of the room, and their faces hadn't been visible in the dim light. "I'm Ronald Reagan. This is Nancy. I just finished your book [*Up from Liberalism*]. The passage on Eleanor Roosevelt is very funny." He quoted it and laughed.

His assignment was to introduce me to the assembly (mostly doctors). But entering the hall we came upon a huge bump in the road: not only was the sound system not on, the room where you turned it on was locked! They couldn't find the kid who was supposed to have turned it on, or the janitor who had the keys. And even Ronald Reagan, using his golden repertoire and tranquilizing voice to placate the large hall, was running short of diversions.

That's when I espied True Grit in the future president. He ascertained that the window at the end of the stage overlooked a parapet about a foot wide, which extended, at the far end of the building, to the window of the control room. So he climbed out the window, arms outstretched for balance, and edged his way above the roaring traffic to the critical window, broke it open with his elbow, climbed into the room, found the switch, and flipped it—and the show was on.

That was a dramatic first meeting, and a friendship was kindled. He was, in those days (1961), edging his way out from political company he had grown up with as a young Democrat. He had been fighting the Communists in the Screen Actors' Guild and was now looking for company on what we would call the Barry Goldwater side of the political world. He gave a famous speech urging the support of Goldwater. Goldwater didn't win, but Reagan soon found himself with a political career shaping up. A coterie of Republicans grouped about him, seeking a figure large enough to hang their shattered hopes on. During that period I visited often, and when he confided that he was deliberating a bid for governor of California, I took to referring to him sotto voce as "Guv"—"How's the Guv doing?" I'd jest with Nancy over the phone. But I was way behind in apprehending his potential. Governor Nelson Rockefeller, at our first private meeting (at his apartment in 1967), asked me how to account for the sounds beginning to come out of California—Why not Reagan for president? "There's no way," I found myself opining on politics to a four-term governor of New York, "a former actor could go for president."

"Anybody who wins the California election with one million votes is presidential material" was Rockefeller's answer.

We stayed good friends but quarreled openly—in a two-hour televised debate (see pp. 367–388)—on whether to ratify the Panama Canal Treaty. And then in 1980 it turned out that Rockefeller had been right: Reagan proved invincible. But nothing got in the way of a friendship maintained via phone calls and correspondence and visits to successive residences in California.

Yes, there was the legendary aloofness, but this was forgivingly accepted, in the context of his overwhelmingly emphasized priorities. Nancy came first, but Reagan was zestfully concerned for the company of others. He was with my wife and me in Connecticut over one Thanksgiving weekend, and the first night we consumed a dinner of leftovers in the kitchen. He sat at one end of the table with sandwiches and a glass of wine telling stories, one after another, making Thanksgiving especially credible for his friends at hand. It's hard to imagine him alive yet out of action, and best not to dwell on it.

Henry Kissinger

The first time was at Harvard, where he was conducting his summer seminar on international politics, a class which, one later had the impression, was taken only by students who intended to become prime minister or emperor.

This happened in the 1950s, and I had weighed carefully the invitation from an unknown professor. (Kissinger hadn't yet scored with his book on nuclear politics.) I had launched *National Review*, and, in his letter, Professor Kissinger asked me to talk to his seminar about the conservative movement in America.

He was captivatingly bright and engaging, and we were from that moment on in regular touch. Henry Kissinger was an important arm of Nelson Rockefeller, Inc., and over ten years, as governor of New York, Rockefeller had it definitely in mind to win the White House. His first obstacle, in 1964, had been Senator Barry Goldwater, the soul of that year's Republican Convention. Even though it seemed progressively more certain that in 1968 in Miami the GOP would nominate Richard Nixon, Rockefeller made a last-minute dramatic entry into the race. He lost to Nixon in a head-to-head primary contest in California, but there was always the possibility that there'd be an upset in Miami: (1) Nixon would stumble; (2) Reagan would be bypassed; (3) Rockefeller would be nominated.

An immediate and vital objective would be to appease American conservatives. It wouldn't benefit Rockefeller to achieve the nomination and face a postconvention array of bereft conservatives bent on revenge.

We never discussed it in exactly that way, but in Miami, in those critical days, Henry Kissinger lunched and dined with me three days in a row—just in case I'd be called upon to minister to conservative wounds.

His company was then, as now, scintillating—he was amusing, curious, ever-so-lightly irreverent. He was obsessed by the ongoing misadventures in Vietnam. When three months later Nixon was elected, outgoing president Lyndon Johnson seemed desperately anxious for a quick deal with the North Vietnamese. Kissinger called me on the telephone: Would I—most urgent!— get word to Nixon about what Kissinger construed as the subversive designs of the North Vietnamese at the expense of Saigon? "If their maneuver works, it will be known to the world that it is perhaps dangerous to be an enemy of the United States, but fatal to be its friend." I got the message through to John Mitchell, Nixon's right hand. Intrigued, he invited Kissinger to New York to meet the president-elect. That evolved into the closest association ever arrived at between a president and his counselor in foreign affairs.

It was a golden road, the thirty years ahead, notwithstanding unending criticism and mockery from opponents and factionalists who, year after year, felt dispossessed or shortchanged. There was jealousy and resentment. It was wounding, for many, to contemplate Henry's extraordinary successes as man of affairs, historian, writer, and informal consultant to the high and the mighty. And then too he had contracted a (second) marriage to a dazzling, amusing, opinionated woman, a corner of whose eye focuses on his health and disposition, while warmly welcoming the endless line of guests.

He sits there now in his chair, in New York or in Kent, Connecticut, engrossed by the conversation on any point of current controversy, comprehensively contributing his commentary, his laughter—less often, his smile. I asked myself publicly (the occasion was an intimate celebration) whether I had ever had a longer or more rewarding friendship with a public figure, to which the answer was, No.

CLARE BOOTHE LUCE

The first time was at her apartment on Fifth Avenue, shared with her husband, Henry Luce, founder and supreme overlord of the empire whose name would for a while begin with the initials AOL. Clare Luce was a renowned beauty and man of affairs (a feminist, she stoutly resisted the stylistic effronteries of she-speech). Thus she was also a congressman, an ambassador (to Rome), a journalist, a playwright (*The Women*), and a wit (one thousand public appearances). Her cause of the moment, back then in 1963, was Madame Ngo Dinh Nhu, the so-called Dragon Lady of South Vietnam.

Our policy in Vietnam was in chaos. The villain of the day, in the liberal press, wasn't anybody in Communist Hanoi. It was President Ngo Dinh Diem of South Vietnam, together with his brother and his sister-in-law, the outspoken, provocative Dragon Lady. The

JAN LUKAS

demand, most ardently made by self-immolating Buddhist monks in South Vietnam, was to replace Diem. *National Review* was loyalist on the Vietnam question, and one October morning, in mid-battle, arrives in the mail, unsolicited, a manuscript from the great Mrs. Luce, a fiery article defending the Diem government. Its title: "The Lady *Is* for Burning."

It was time to meet Clare Luce. I was there at the appointed hour. She opened the door herself. Had I ever painted? she wanted to know.

No, actually.

"I paint with acrylics. Would you like a quick lesson, before we take on world affairs?"

I learned a fair amount about painting, and a lot about Clare Boothe Luce. She loved to analyze the public scene. Always there was the bad guy in sight. On this occasion, it was her old friend Henry Cabot Lodge, who was our ambassador to Saigon and whom she suspected—correctly, it turned out—of forwarding to President Kennedy and the Pentagon subversive recommendations. Two weeks after our meeting, Diem and his brother were assassinated. Three weeks after that, JFK was shot.

Clare Luce interwove, with her instructions on how to paint, recollections of her experience with canvas and oils. Just after the war she and her husband went to England and spent the weekend as guests of Winston Churchill at Chartwell. "I tried to be especially ingratiating because Harry wanted U.S. rights to Churchill's war memoirs for *Life* magazine. So passing through one gallery I said, 'These are wonderful paintings.' Churchill said, 'I'm glad you like them, but only one of them is painted by me.'"

Clare flashed her sly, infectious smile, and then a little snort of laughter. "I thought, Oh dear, that makes me sound very sycophantic. I asked which one was his, and he pointed to a pastoral scene, a field of some sort. I thought I'd better do something to establish my critical independence. I said I liked it but I thought it was too—placid; lacking in movement.

"Three weeks later in New York that painting arrived, but on it were three sheep bouncing about. His note read, 'Is that any better?' Harry told me later that my effrontery probably ended up costing Time, Inc., one million dollars more than they'd otherwise have had to pay for his memoirs."

A close political and social collaboration ensued. She was master of ceremonies at a gaudy celebration of *NR*'s tenth anniversary, with Barry Goldwater and John Dos Passos as cohosts. Now I saw her regularly. After Henry Luce's sudden death at their winter home in Phoenix, she instructed the architect who had designed their as yet unbuilt house in Honolulu to revise the scale of it drastically—"I wouldn't be needing anything that vast. People always traveled to see Harry, not me. I'm a lame duck."

I heard later from the architect: "Clare said to me, 'If, when the house is completed, I can't sit on my lanai with a dry martini watching the sun going down over my oceanfront, there's going to be one less architect in Honolulu.'"

She entertained with brilliant charm, wrote for sundry publications, painted, and stared life in the face, including bad personal habits. "How did I get to stop smoking? I was playing bridge and the woman sitting opposite, whom I truly loathed—a very rich gal—she was also trying to stop. Suddenly she looked up and said, 'Clare, let's do this: The first one of us who smokes a cigarette after midnight is honor-bound to pay ten thousand dollars to the other.'

"The next morning I reached for my cigarettes. And I froze. I couldn't care less for the money, but the idea of giving ten thousand dollars to *her* was inconceivable—so I stopped smoking."

Whenever I traveled to Honolulu, which I did regularly on lecture and television jaunts, I stayed with her. One night was especially vivid. Her gardener, Tom, a native Hawaiian, collapsed while lighting the garden lights as the dinner guests were having drinks on the terrace. The paramedics arrived and whisked him away. Clare gripped my arm and whispered, "What shall I do?" I counseled her to continue the party and withhold from her guests the terminal news she expected to hear at any moment from the hospital; the news she did receive, before the dessert course was served, and she did suppress it, and her pained reaction to it, until her guests had left. Clare Boothe Luce never permitted a show of which she was the choreographer to falter.

Among other things, life was entertainment, and at this she was very gifted. She loved it when the rumor floated about that she was thinking of accepting a proffered invitation to run for governor of New York on the Conservative Party ticket (in 1970). "Would you believe it? Nelson Rockefeller has called me on the telephone for the first time since Harry died."

She was now a listless Roman Catholic, though remaining in that faith since her celebrated conversion in 1946. "The church I joined isn't the same church I now attend." In her will she designated me as one of her two eulogists. I recalled that at the end of her formal indoctrination, Monsignor Fulton Sheen had told her the time had come to undertake a plenary confession. Did she have in mind a particular priest she'd be most comfortable hearing her confession? "Just bring me someone who has seen the rise and fall of empires" was her daredevil reply, received by Fulton Sheen with his characteristic verve. Not even Clare Boothe Luce could surprise God, who was, among other great things, her maker.

TOM WOLFE

I don't remember the first sight of him, which is odd, because Tom Wolfe is of course memorably dressed. But in the mid-sixties, he was so widely celebrated on so many fronts—as a virtuoso humorist, a chronicler, a critic—that a visual exposure to him and his ensemble was unremarkable (even though it was and remains unusual, the double-breasted suit, the high starched collar, the rakish white fedora). We would be surprised if he appeared differently, as we'd be surprised to see Henry VIII dressed other than by Holbein. Well, how *was* Henry VIII dressed? How would you describe *his* appearance?

> He was an extremely rich man and showed it. Note the turned-back silk lining of the outer garment, the chamarre (gorgeous silks were harder to find and more fashionable than the older fur linings), the bejeweled flat hat with its ermine trim, the passe-menterie on the front, the sleeves of the doublet, the rings on his finger, the jewels in his shoulder chain and medallion and garter, his brocaded satin duckbill slippers and woven-silk nether hose; he was physically powerful, note the virile, potent, highly procreative codpiece, the beard; very much the warrior—note the dagger in its sheath, hanging from a barely visible cord, the short military tunic, which Henry wears stylized, to allow the codpiece to poke through and to show the ornate doublet—see the soldier's simple (macho) rope around the tunic, the chain that girds the shoulders—the *warrior*, since back then there was no separation in symbolism between the warrior and the aristocrat, until a century later there would be no figure of the mere aristocrat—the aristocrat who was *not* a warrior (e.g., Thomas Jefferson).

There . . . I had played a trick here. Tom Wolfe had no idea what I was up to when I asked if as a personal favor he would give me a "one-sentence description" of how Henry VIII dressed, based on the Holbein portrait I sent along. What arrived, above, is one example of his skill as stylist and observer, and of his noblesse oblige.

How would you expect Tom Wolfe to dress? It was many years later that I invited him to join me for a few days at the Bohemian Grove. I hadn't really pondered what this would mean for him, but you just can't dress his way in an outdoor setting when everybody else is dressed in camp clothes. We drove out from San Francisco after lunch and he was modifying his dress already, though I think he still had on a tie. I had gotten used to his manner. Tom Wolfe is as modest in his conversational mode as he is volatile and florid in writing. He has a trace of a Virginia accent, and of course there is the renowned diffidence, the matador taking tea with his mother.

It happened that on that weekend there were three or four astronauts at the Grove. Tom had just written *The Right Stuff*, and the movie had been made. Although it is almost impossible for a public figure to attract attention in the company of the two thousand campers who visit the Grove, Tom was lionized by the men he had written about and made famous. I remember thinking it would be fine to read a description *by* Tom Wolfe of the treatment given *to* Tom Wolfe by the heroic daredevils, who spoke to him as though they had traveled together to the moon.

We usually meet at dinners or celebrations, but one time I said I had something serious I wanted to talk with him about, and we met at the Carlyle Hotel. He was dressed as I'd have expected. My assignment was to forward an invitation to an offbeat affair. But I had come upon Tom Wolfe, the arduous novelist, in mid-labor. He had spent seven of what would be eleven years on his novel. And he was recovering from an experience he described colorfully but with clinical concern. A few months earlier he had been exercising at a gymnasium when he felt the pain. He was quickly taken to the local hospital, where he was told he had a heart problem and needed an elaborate operation, doable only in New York City. Arrived there, he was placed in the hands of a middle-aged, prepossessing heart expert to whom he took an instant liking. "I said to my doctor, How can this happen to me? I don't smoke, hardly ever drink, exercise three times every week." How can you explain, the doctor observed, that some people are born left-handed? Tom went into the operation, emerged whole and hearty, to learn that his doctor had died the night before of a heart attack.

He lives modestly, in New York City and in the country, with his gifted wife (she is a graphic artist) and two children. Some years ago I retained Sheila Wolfe to redesign *National Review*. It was a big job, and the time came eventually to discuss a fee. "How much," she asked, "does it take to buy word processing?—the whole she-bang, computer, printer, modem?"

I said, Well, to do it right, about ten grand. (That was true in 1983.) We agreed: I would order the whole assembly, and one afternoon when Tom was gone speaking somewhere, she'd have it all installed in his office.

A wonderful idea, wonderful surprise! And Tom was very grateful, she reported. But he didn't even cut the ribbon. He was still with his Underwood electric. The big news, unnoticed by the frenzied world, is that in April 2000, Tom Wolfe succumbed to the modern era.

VLADIMIR HOROWITZ

The first time astonished me. I was sitting on the Washington–New York shuttle, a typewriter on my lap, and this man walked up the aisle, a wide grin on his pointed face, in his breast pocket a striped silk handkerchief matching his bow tie. He was so familiar (this happens sometimes) that it took me a minute to realize I was talking with Vladimir Horowitz, the most celebrated musician alive. He spoke with great animation of having seen me a day or two before on television and of approving heartily of something I had said about the Soviet Union. "You muss meet Vanda!" He turned and brought from her seat the formidable daughter of Arturo Toscanini. They fought life together from their marriage in 1933 until his death in 1989.

"*Tu penses c'est bien?*" he called out to her from the piano onstage at the Metropolitan Opera House. Wanda had been posted at the very rear of the hall, to check out the sound. "*Autrement je vais annuler!*" If she didn't think the sound was up to his standards, he'd cancel the concert. There was near-panic among the dozen executives standing about, because the whole of the proceeds from this concert by Horowitz—the first ever done by a single artist in the vast opera house—he would be donating to the Met. But here he was, trying out the piano onstage a mere week before the scheduled concert and finding things wrong with the acoustics. The personally invited audience of a few dozen friends sweated along with the Met, as stagehands experimented, moving here and there great wooden panels that affected the sound. Vladimir did his magic, in bits and pieces, on the piano, and Wanda, at the back of the hall, listened, finally calling out her approval.

I had a glimpse of the maestro's famous eccentricity. Mike Wallace, filming a segment for *60 Minutes*, asked him why, since 1953, he had rarely left his house in New York.

"You dohn like my house?"

Stifling laughter, Mike had to explain that however much he liked Vladi's house, it was nevertheless odd that he had hardly moved from it for twelve years.

The first time we dined with him at his house in Connecticut I plotted with my friend and fellow guest James Burnham. Our objective was to get Vladimir to play for us. After dinner, winking at Burnham, I said, "Volodya" (he had asked to be called by his nickname), "why are you playing Clementi at your concert next week?"

"Yes, I've wondered the same thing," chimed in Burnham, as plotted.

"You dohn like Clementi?" His expression was at once sad and combative.

"Well, sure, I *like* him." I managed to sound unpersuaded.

He rose and strode to the piano. Burnham and I smiled triumphantly as Vladimir proceeded to play six Clementi sonatas. And when Horowitz plays Clementi, Clementi becomes my favorite composer.

Sometime later we were there again for dinner. During meals both Vladimir and Wanda often absent themselves, she to check the kitchen, he for whatever reason, including watering his cat. There were five of us. At one point, while both the Horowitzes were out of the room, a fellow guest, their interior decorator, told us of the crisis of a week earlier. "It was midmorning, Horowitz was over there"—he pointed to a corner of the living room—"fussing with his music. I was measuring the couch when the man doing the curtains walked in and I asked him how much the new curtains would come to.

"His name was Nicola Righini. He took a pad from his pocket and said it would come to $575. And then, without looking over at him, he said, 'unless Mr. Horowitz would play a concert for me and my wife. Then it would be free.'"

"I froze. I didn't dare look up at Vladimir. He might have grabbed a shotgun. But then I did. He was standing with his music in his hands. There was a second's pause. Then he looked at Nicola, and bowed his head deeply. 'I would be honored to perform for you and your wife.' On Sunday afternoon they both came in, after church, all dressed up, and Vladimir played the whole two hours of his upcoming Met concert."

Now *that* was noblesse oblige.

Horowitz had a temper, and took offense easily. One evening in New York, a few years later, he did one of his disappearing acts in the middle of dinner, and I, after a very heavy day, signaled to my wife and said good night to Wanda.

That proved an egregious offense, and we never heard again from either of them. Too bad. But Horowitz was beautiful to listen to—very nearly incomparable. And, actually, we adored Wanda.

ROGER MOORE

The first time was at the Eagle Club in Gstaad, where Roger Moore was lunching with his ski teacher. The club is a small eyrie, founded in the mid-fifties for the benefit of affluent skiers who want to celebrate the exercise they have just finished taking, or are about to take, with a rewarding lunch. On the Eagle Club's Buffet, you have a choice of about seventy-five hors d'oeuvres.

Roger was always an attractive, desirable, shrewd, amiable, and often comic presence. He is by nature at once shy and a performer, his observations hilarious, the commentary sometimes ribald. I've seen him entertaining as lustily as Jay Leno, engaging his guests or his audience with a talent one doesn't connect with James Bond, from whom one expects mostly programmatic levity.

In the first twenty years of our friendship he lived with Luisa, his beautiful longtime Italian wife, in a château in Gstaad that might have been created by Walt Disney. Chalet le Fenil didn't have stuffed sheep grazing in the hallway, like the chalet belonging to Roger's neighbor, Valentino, but all else was as Swiss as a Tiffany version of a cuckoo clock, with here and there expressions of wry artistic humor as well as art pieces imaginative and enticing.

Roger made his way, during his teen years, as a cartoonist in London. He retains his skills. When we painted together at my studio nearby, sometimes he would ask the person on his right to give out a number, any number (six, let us suppose), and request as much of the person on his left (four). Then he would draw a six and an imaginative four appended or digested; and around the whole he would do an oil painting, the numerals always surviving whatever else materialized: a flower, chalet, mountain, candlestick maker.

It isn't easy to ask Roger Moore for a favor involving heavy use of his time or imagination, because he seems invulnerable to any such imposition. But twice I did so. Could we schedule a private lunch? I asked. Over lunch I sketched out to him the plot of the novel I was working on (*Stained Glass*) and told him I'd be grateful for his reaction to theatrical third-act alternatives. He didn't enjoy the assignment, but gave interesting advice. And fifteen years later I made him sit down and watch a two-hour filmed version of that novel, done as a play in Louisville, Kentucky.

His mind is naturally critical, and he can be vehement in his reactions. (*Life Is Beautiful*? "The finest movie of the year." Wallace Beery? "No wonder everybody hated him. He worked overtime at it.") It was a protocol at his house, as at David Niven's, that mention was not made of any of his movies—moviemaking was another life for Roger Moore. Gstaad was for the dashing bon vivant, sportsman, and wit.

He resists enterprise in fields other than those he has mastered. But he did confide, one January, that he intended to take the lead part in the upcoming world premiere of Andrew Lloyd Webber's *Aspects of Love*. He'd leave Gstaad for stretches of two or three days in London in order to rehearse. Late one afternoon, when we were alone in the painting studio, he permitted himself a few arpeggios—he was, after all, practicing to do a singing role, something he had never done. But one dramatic day, in London, he announced abruptly that he would not go through with it. To this friend he explained: There are two or three points in the musical where the lead has to come in at the correct pitch without any prompting from the orchestra. Roger Moore decided that that was something not even James Bond should undertake.

The marriage fell apart. The beautiful, voluble, emotionally demonstrative Luisa became someone for the sake of whose absence from his life he would give up even his cherished chalet. "You will love Kristina," he promised (prophetically), talking about his new wife-to-be. Everything else had also changed, and he agreed to become a goodwill ambassador for UNICEF, to which he has given the last several years. His charitable activities keep him traveling endlessly. But he has another chalet, in another part of Switzerland, where he skis and from which he sometimes travels to visit his affection on old friends. And though not as accessible as back in the days of the Eagle Club and Gstaad, he has taken up e-mail, facing bravely the remorseless technological birth pains, the price of admission. It is great joy to see evidence of it at work. "What a relief to know that it is all working. I now have visions of myself going to Cyber Cafés around the world sitting with Bangla-deshis and Thais trying to log on and retrieve my junk mail... Love from us both to the two of you... as always, Roger."

ALISTAIR COOKE

The first time was—lunch.

Nothing pleases an author more than a favorable book review, especially from an unexpected source. My book was a collection, and I stared with dumb gratitude at a marvelously hospitable review by the great, discerning Alistair Cooke in the *Washington Post*. I characterize as "discerning" any complimentary book reviewer. But it was welcome, from so august a figure, more widely known in his native England than any American except the president. Moreover, Cooke—I had gathered, from his writing, and from certain intimations in his famous introductions on *Masterpiece Theatre*—was something of a liberal, so that the surprise was especially great. I expressed my gratitude in a letter. He wrote back immediately and said, Let's lunch.

That was in 1971, and at the end of the lunch we made another lunch date for three months later. There was the usual reaching-for-the-check, but soon we agreed to alternate. And then that was followed by a date for another lunch—three months later. The schedule is unbroken, though interrupted by his recent illness.

What's it like, lunching with Alistair Cooke?

For one thing, there's his memory. He's ninety-one, and I'd be surprised if he has forgotten anything. I amuse myself every now and then by asking, when the check comes, "I forget, Alistair, is it your turn to pay or mine?" He remembers instantly. He is a resolute Scot.

His memory extends to improvisational powers. He doesn't tell of his accomplishments, but by probing I learned how he did those *Masterpiece Theatre* introductions. He would concentrate on the play or the dramatization and its author and the circumstances of its writing. Then he would arrive at the studio and sit down in his armchair, and the perfectly phrased ninety-second introduction would flow from his lips. He'd speak the improvised lines as confidently as if called upon to give the Lord's Prayer—which, come to think of it, I've never asked him to do. Next lunch I'll try to remember.

His cachet, beginning many years before *Masterpiece Theatre*, has derived from his weekly fifteen-minute report on America for the BBC. In America, we know him for his television work; among the cognoscenti, he is celebrated for his fine writing style and memorable portraits. His friends know him for his humor and geniality.

"Is there anybody you *haven't* known?" He pauses, his white hair framing the famous face, the eyebrows that lift for a moment, the smile. He is thinking.

"Not really, I guess I'd have to say." I make it a point not to ask him who out there, among the thousand public figures he has met, he didn't like. He'll get to that, if he wants to; one doesn't press. Though I did nag him about his legs. For Cooke, golf comes in just after good reading and writing. But finally the anxiety ended. At one memorable lunch (we meet at the Carlyle Hotel) he surprised me on arrival by saying, "Ask me to dance around the buffet."

"To *what*?"

"Watch." He did a jig around the collection of trays and sat down with a triumphant smile. "That's what the operation has done for me." He had had two knee replacements, and now could go back to his golf without pain.

Alistair Cooke has never sounded old-fashioned, let alone out of date, but certain ways of doing things are unalterable, including his love of jazz (he was a fine pianist) and his devotion to an old type-writer, with its distinctive, falling-apart-old font. "A young grandson came to see me the other day. He's seventeen. He said, 'Grandfather, is it true you have a *typewriter*?' Yes, I said. 'Could I *see* it?'"

He loved that: genuine innocence. It had better be genuine, though, because Alistair Cooke sees through everything and everybody. His geniality and bounce are always there, but his light blue eyes are penetrating. What a piece of luck, lunching with Alistair Cooke for thirty years.

PRINCESS GRACE

I first met her as a fellow guest of David Niven, at Château d'Oex in Switzerland. She would spend a few weeks in neighboring Schönried for the skiing, accompanied some of the time by Prince Rainier, some of the time by children Caroline and Albert and lit-tle Stephanie—aged sixteen, fourteen, and seven. Her skiing was more dutiful than hedonistic. The two or three times I was with her on the slopes she wore that lightly determined look she was famous for, marking the spirit with which she took on Hollywood, royalty, and the dramatic loss of her stunning career when she married Prince Rainier. She laughed heartily, that first evening, at David Niven's unrelenting bonhomie. She encouraged Jackie Kennedy to ignore the paparazzi who were surrounding her. And she spoke eagerly about sharing an evening with the Nivens painting in oils at our studio in nearby Rougemont.

Her beauty was always captivating. Three years later, before dinner and the studio, I impulsively read out loud a review in the *Washington Post* I had received that morning of my new novel, *Saving the Queen*. The momentum in my reading didn't let me stop in time to avoid reading the sentence "Mr. Buckley's dazzling queen puts the reader in mind of the young Grace Kelly." David yelped his protest against my act of aggression—recalling, in 1976, the Grace Kelly of 1951. But she laughed it off, though she'd as soon not have been reminded that any face would be expected to show traces of the passage of time. It had been twenty years since she had left the marquee to become a reigning presence in the half-square-mile principality in the southeast corner of France.

But her character fortified her in all matters. Daughter Caroline was now the attraction, and Stephanie was a burgeoning jet-set presence, spirited, challenging, and not naturally pious. One would never know whether, driving back to their chalet at the end of the evening, Princess Grace would lecture to her children about manners and morals. There proved to be a lot to lecture them about, as they began their marital high jinks. Grace was disconsolate over Caroline's first marriage, which she correctly predicted wouldn't last. (It was over in two years.)

In 1981 I told her I had an urgent and serious matter to bring up, and drove over to her orderly chalet. I had been asked to oversee two experimental documentaries featuring the Sistine Chapel, which the sponsor had got permission to occupy for thirty-six hours with a television team. The philanthropist, a wealthy Canadian who had found uranium and was looking for a devout gesture of reciprocity for his good fortune, placed the entire enterprise in my hands. I thought to commemorate two of the parables: the first, that of the prodigal son; the second, the good Samaritan. I sensed a need for some five-star participation and undertook to persuade David Niven and Charlton Heston and Princess Grace to appear in each of the two segments. Their mission was to give from their own reading evidence of the continuing applicability of the lessons of the two biblical episodes.

Princess Grace listened, with the kind of patience I'd have expected. What would be required, I explained, was thirty-six hours in Rome, and two or three minutes before the camera in each episode. (The fee would be fifteen thousand dollars.) She asked me to call her back later in the day, after she had checked her schedule "and that kind of thing."

A problem, I learned from her, was that the (well-known) writer on whom she had relied to compose "every public word I have ever uttered" needed to be asked whether he could cooperate in this venture. The answer—not for reasons antithetical to the idea—was No. I told her I would gladly write her lines. She agreed, and two weeks later performed before the camera for the first time since leaving Hollywood—an enterprise that was stillborn. The two documentaries were completed, and my collaborators did their roles well, but the producer finally concluded that the mix was self-defeating: viewers would be distracted by what they saw of the chapel, and attention to what was being said by the players would be lost. Even Grace Kelly could not compete with the paintings in the Sistine Chapel.

Immediately before boarding a plane, in September of the following year, I sent her a flippant get-well-soon telegram, having just learned that she had had a car accident. On reaching San Francisco five hours later, I was told she was dead. We watched on television the searingly tragic funeral, the camera so exploitatively focused on the weeping, disconsolate prince. We keep in our bedroom the dried-flower collage she gave my wife, spelling out the simple word "Love." Here was an operatic ending to an operatic life, and I can't help thinking how splendidly she'd have acted out her real life if it had been put on the screen. She'd have done it with panache, and her grit would have shown through the whole of it.

John Kenneth Galbraith

The first time was on an elevator. We were in the Plaza Hotel in 1966, going up to Truman Capote's Black & White Ball. Galbraith was The Enemy, professional and personal. Professional, because he was the standout political liberal in America; brilliant and influential teacher of teachers in the economics and the politics of centralization. Personal, because I had visited just months before a professor whose work I wanted regularly in my magazine. I learned from him that Professor Galbraith, on seeing the one article he had written for us, wired him to say he should ostracize *National Review*.

I introduced myself, as the elevator filled and began its climb, and said, "I understand you're instructing Professor [I gave his name] not to write for *National Review*."

He looked down from his great height, his eyes meeting mine, and said in his clipped tones, "I regret that."

He had reacted to an article in *National Review* that reached the Harvard Club the day after President Kennedy was assassinated. He had winced on seeing the byline of a distinguished colleague in a magazine that had been irreverent and even antagonistic to John

Kennedy, whom Galbraith had taught, befriended, counseled, and finally loved. His entirely uncharacteristic call on the colleague to boycott a dissident journal was corrected now with a simple apology.

Two months later, in Switzerland, he invited me to ski with him. After viewing his descent down the slope I asked him how long he had been skiing.

"Thirty years," he said.

"That's as long as you've been studying economics," I commented. Thirty-one years later, at his ninetieth birthday party, he recalled the gibe delightedly, in the company of the liberal political and intellectual elite whose muse he has been. His son Jamie, on the same occasion, correctly compared his influence on his times to those of Adam Smith, Ricardo, and Keynes in theirs.

And he's not modest about it. "I learned to write at *Fortune* magazine," he told me. He credits Henry Luce and his enterprises with having been the great teachers of readable prose. He and his wife, Kitty, have lived in a small apartment in Gstaad for two months each winter, and it was there that he wrote the critically influential *The Affluent Society*. "When I decided to take the whole semester away from Harvard, I thought I'd protect myself against criticism for neglecting my teaching duties by turning over the proceeds of the book I was writing to Harvard." He smiled ruefully, reflecting on the success of the book. "It made Harvard rich!"

Every year we visited, skied, argued. We exchanged letters and polemics. I read his books, and reviewed for *Life* magazine his marvelous memoirs of his stay in India as ambassador. Once again, with his Scottish concern to account for time spent/income earned, he wanted a point made clear for the benefit of anybody who criticized him for taking an hour off every morning, while on the federal payroll, to write his memoirs. "I've calculated that the tax I paid on those memoirs exceeded my salary as ambassador."

We debated from time to time, on television and on the road. Flying one afternoon to our third consecutive day's engagement, this one at Texas A&M, he looked up from his book, his long legs stretched out in the aisle, and said, "You know something? I have never in my entire life missed a professional lecture engagement." That night, at the lavish guest quarters at College Station, the phone rang in my room at midnight.

"Is this Professor Galbraith?"

"No," I said.

"Well could you find him and wake him?"

"No—I wouldn't want to do that at this hour."

"Well, this is the White House. Mrs. Gandhi has been shot." I got out of bed, went down the hall, and knocked on his door. President Reagan, it transpired, wished him to represent the United States at the funeral. Professor Galbraith had to cancel the next evening's scheduled lecture, first time ever.

He does very nice things, even for people who have not been assassinated. He consistently writes pleasant tributes to my own books, inevitably advising the reader that my political opinions should be ignored, my fiction or accounts of life at sea appreciated. His friends and admirers are numerous and profuse, and he doesn't mind that at all. He is amused and amusing about it. I was a speaker at his huge eighty-fifth-birthday party, my four-minute talk interrupted halfway through by the master of ceremonies. *Is there a doctor in the house?* The acoustics at Boston Public Library were bad, and the next day I sent Galbraith the text of my talk. A week later I had his acknowledgment. It read, "Dear Bill: That was a very pleasant talk you gave about me. If I had known it would be so, I would not have instructed my friend to pretend, in the middle of your speech, to need the attention of a doctor."

I'm preparing a speech for his ninety-fifth.

Five Colleagues

The following are portraits of my principal editorial collaborators, written for National Review*'s twenty-fifth anniversary issue, in 1980.* ⌁

WILLI SCHLAMM

Willi Schlamm became conspicuous to those of us who dissented, and hungered for style and flavor. We became aware of him when he began to contribute regularly to *The Freeman,* then edited by Henry Hazlitt, John Chamberlain, and Suzanne La Follette.

Willi had come back to life, after the most implausible retirement in professional history, at age forty-seven, following a decade with *Time* magazine. There he had had a relationship with Harry Luce so complicated, historians seem never to want fully to plumb it. He left *Time* after losing a major bout of office politics; bought a house in Vermont with his wife, Steffi, more or less expecting that it would evolve into a northeastern Aspen, a sort of watering hole for wanderers in search of holy water, and perhaps even liturgical emancipation from the current orthodoxy. His single commission, on leaving *Time,* was to write a more or less official biography of Clare Boothe Luce, who had gone off to Rome as ambassador. This commission, after the one year Willi devoted to research but before he had begun writing, was terminated, Harry Luce having decided that a penetrating biography, published at a time when diplomatic priorities should for conventional reasons prevail, would be inappropriate. Willi needed work, and began to write a culture column for *The Freeman,* and occasional political pieces.

His style was exuberant, colorful, witty, and iconoclastic, and he attracted a considerable following. When *The Freeman* suffered its civil war, the mass resignations included Willi's; and he went back to rustication in Vermont, undertaking an occasional editorial chore, which included a commission by Henry Regnery to go over, shorten, and write an introduction to the manuscript Brent Bozell and I had written on the controversy surrounding the public career of Senator Joseph McCarthy. (The book appeared in 1954, *McCarthy and His Enemies.*)

The collaboration on the McCarthy book took me several times to Vermont, and Willi to Stamford. A correspondence began. It was Willi's notion that I should launch a weekly conservative journal of opinion, by which he meant nothing less than that I should raise the capital for it, own the voting stock, and serve as editor in chief. These suggestions issued not out of any recognition of precocious talents (I was twenty-eight), but out of a conviction that my youth would prove precisely the catalytic agent, and I think Willi was correct in this. I doubt that, if I had been twenty years older, I'd have succeeded in engaging the attention, let alone collaboration, of the starting team at *National Review*, whom, with the exception of Willmoore Kendall, I didn't know well, certainly not intimately.

When the magazine was finally launched, it became clear that Willi's personality would become a major factor. Having, however briefly, served as *éminence grise* to Harry Luce, he would not gladly serve in any lesser capacity to a new boy in journalism, whom he had, after all, established. Our relations, at a personal level, were affectionate, but very soon it became plain that his analytical style was incompatible with that of James Burnham. Willi would have led the charge of the Light Brigade. Jim would calmly have organized the slaughter. The tension mounted, and Jim, in a brief memo whose reticence and self-effacement wonderfully contrasted with a strategic intelligence robust, daring, and self-assured, suggested that, in deference to Willi, he—Jim—should pull out of the magazine, promising to make no theater whatever of it all.

But Willi's usefulness to the enterprise had, in fact, declined. After three months, he stopped writing editorials, in tacit protest over my editing of them. Willi's mastery of English was phenomenal, but his pitch was not absolute. So he took over the editing of the book section from Willmoore Kendall, who had found it administratively burdensome; but the work Willi then put in on the book section was perfunctory, and his attention to it distracted. At one editors' meeting, which lasted most of one day, at my home in Stamford (the high point of it, in my memory, was Willmoore Kendall's declaiming that he had no objection whatever to certain proposed reforms provided that we would agree to change the denomination of *National Review* on the cover from "A Weekly Journal of Opinion" to "A Journal of Jacobinical Thought"), it was amicably resolved that Frank Meyer would take over the book section, which he insisted he could easily administer from his eyrie in Woodstock, New York. Willi was now reduced to writing a weekly culture piece; in short order, a fortnightly piece, even before indigence forced us to go from weekly to fortnightly publication.

At this point, unhappily, personal relations deteriorated. When Bill Rusher signed on as publisher, a year and a half after *National Review*'s founding, it seemed to me obvious that he would need to occupy the only other habitable office than my own (which was barely that)—the rest were cubicles. Willi was at that point coming in to the magazine only a few hours a week. As tactfully as I thought it possible to do, I explained the circumstances to Willi by letter, and got back from him, postmarked in Vermont, his resignation.

Five years later I had a note from him, and there followed a rapprochement of sorts. During the sixties he wrote a half-dozen pieces for us. Meanwhile, back in Europe, he had become a considerable success as a highbrow anti-Communist rabble-rouser, the center of much attention. He died, in 1978, in almost ideal professional circumstances—as publisher, editor, and principal contributor to his own journal, *Die Zeitbühne*. He died in the course of an exercise in office politics, which always stimulated him. It was an irony that Willi—at his best—would have laughed over: shortly before his death, an attempt was made to take his journal from him. Willi's trademark was exuberance and passion. These are traits almost always tempered in maturity: but if ever I feel the need to repristinate my fires, I have only to go back and read a column or two by Willi Schlamm from the fifties. ("Scientists are people who first build and then buy the Brooklyn Bridge.") The kind of thing that brings down the walls of Jericho.

WILLMOORE KENDALL

Willmoore Kendall was hired by Yale University right after the war, on the dreadfully mistaken presumption that he was a manageable liberal. He proved to be not only something other than a liberal (he actually defended Joe McCarthy) but also a most unmanageable human being. This institutional judgment of him by so many of his colleagues (Dwight Macdonald once characterized Willmoore as "a wild Yale don who can bring an argument into the shouting stage faster than any man in town") surprised the undergraduates who had experienced him, because, with them, there was always that air of elegant civility that disarmed even the most hostile ideological adversaries in the classroom. I studied under him, and assert that no graduate of his courses would impute to him brutality of manner, or

pedagogical sleight of hand. I came to know him most fearfully well.
It is probable that during the decade of the fifties I received one
thousand letters from him (he loved to write letters, among other
reasons because they served as anodyne for his delinquencies in getting on with his formal academic work). His dialectical brilliance
was undisputed; but although he wrote a dozen memorable scholarly pieces (most of them gathered together in two volumes), his
doctoral thesis on *John Locke and the Doctrine of Majority Rule*
remains the only book he wrote, start to finish, as a book.

He took great pleasure in the column he formulated for us called
"The Liberal Line." I have seen provocative prose in my life, but
there are liberals who went off to Skid Row to die from vexation
and fury after reading some of Willmoore's columns, the operative
thesis of which was that *somebody* (he would *never* reveal the identity) was telling the editors of the *New York Times,* the department
heads at Yale, and most other men of influence and power *what to
think*! He wrote columns about some of liberalism's pet institutions
(*"This week the* Christian Science Monitor, *the Liberal Establishment's soft-throated daily . . .*"; *"Last week at Arden House, which by
the way why doesn't somebody burn it down? . . ."*). When Yale's
provost complained to Willmoore that he was spending too much
time at *National Review*, Willmoore answered that he spent somewhat less time on *National Review* than at playing chess, his other
relaxation, and would the provost kindly mind his own business.

In 1961 Willmoore and Yale got rid of each other. The cost to Yale,
forty-five thousand dollars; the cost to Willmoore, a tenure contract—and off he went to teach at Stanford, as a visiting professor.

There he antagonized his regular ration of people, plus a few others, testimony to his accumulating skills; and so, after two years, he
went joyfully off to UCLA. I had a happy evening with him there in
1963, returning a day or two later to New York, where at one of our
periodic editors' meetings it was suggested that if Willmoore was

really going to have to cut down on his work for *NR* as drastically as he had done for the previous two years, he should be resituated on our masthead as a "Contributor" rather than as a "Senior Editor"—a proposal I routinely sent off to Willmoore as reasonable. He replied with a sundering blast; followed by a silence he maintained right up until his death (heart) in 1967, at which point he had been happily installed for several years at the University of Dallas. The single exception was a telegram from him in 1964 asking me "GODSON TO GODFATHER" (I was his sponsor when he joined the Catholic Church, shortly after I graduated from Yale) to pray for him on the day, now announced, when the annulment of his two previous marriages would be forthcoming, legalizing sacramentally his marriage to Nellie, who is very much with us.

The scholars will be reading Willmoore's fragmentary writings for a long time. Historian George Nash thinks him the most important political theorist of the postwar period. His contribution to *NR* was a relentlessly rigorous textual analysis (the kind of thing the Eisenhower crowd simply could not survive); a dazzling and eclectic prose style, one part Edmund Spenser, one part Will Rogers. And, of course, the unforgettable person. I think I wrote about him once that Willmoore made it a practice never to be on speaking terms with more than one friend at a time. I was sorry for my long exile.

FRANK MEYER

When Frank Meyer first approached us, he was writing book reviews as a regular feature for the *American Mercury*. He was eager to be involved in our enterprise, and to press his notion about the overarching compatibility between libertarianism and traditional conservatism. But the book section was spoken for, so he began with a philosophical column ("Principles and Heresies") once a month, a hermeneutic exercise he continued until his death in 1972.

A few months earlier, Frank had written, for *The Freeman,* a derogatory review of Russell Kirk's book on academic freedom; and I think that about one half of such diplomatic talents as I dispose of were regularly exhausted in editing a magazine that regularly published both Frank Meyer *and* Russell Kirk. Russell I considered indispensable to the health and prestige of *National Review,* and his name is indissolubly linked to the journal; but, living in Michigan, he was never a part of our administrative apparatus. The book section, which began under Willmoore Kendall and went on to Willi Schlamm, soon ended in the hands of Frank Meyer—at which point he became a senior editor, it being the rule at *NR* that a senior editor has to perform administrative work for the magazine (the point Willmoore blandly failed to recognize). The natural geographical reclusiveness of both Frank Meyer and Russell Kirk made unlikely any social contact between them, so that the two men could exercise their lively minds cheek by jowl between our covers without, so to speak, bumping into each other.

Frank's personal and professional habits became legendary. He would rise sometime in midafternoon and begin his working day, most of it over the telephone. His network included, without limitations on the basis of race, color, or previous condition of servitude, a spectrum beginning (roughly) with British Marxist philosophers, and stretching over to teenaged Goldwaterite scholarship applicants. When he died at Woodstock, two days after joining the Catholic Church (I was with him during his last days; at one point, his wife, Elsie, and I convened in the bathroom, to weep together, and I heard him complain, in his physical agony, that the only remaining intellectual obstacle to his conversion was the collectivist implications lurking in the formulation "the communion of saints" in the Apostles' Creed), there cannot have been, anywhere else, a more disparate group of mourners. The very young, the very old, and in between; politicians, journalists, poets. All of us—over many months—had felt the coming of the night; because while Frank was alive, nightfall never, ultimately, came; he was always there, eager to answer the telephone, and to talk about matters light or heavy; and although he regularly accentuated the negative, he knew that the gates of hell—a collective enterprise— had, finally, to fail.

His distinctive editorial contribution to the magazine came from his eclectic contacts; and, philosophically, his was the massive insistence on the point that that which bound together the Founding Fathers had its roots in a vision of man burdened by his flawed self, and movable primarily by appeals to his conscience, and to the derivative civil sense of obligation—if necessary, to die for his country. Frank had another distinctive contribution to make, and that was to communicate the totality of the Communist appetite. Having himself attained relatively high standing in the Communist Party, he knew from personal experience what it is that the Party expects of its followers: nothing less than what St. Ignatius Loyola expected of his. And the two visions were, of course, ab initio at war with each other.

JAMES BURNHAM

James Burnham withdrew from active participation in the affairs of *National Review* only a year ago, after suffering a stroke. Beyond any question, he has been the dominant intellectual influence in the development of this journal. He brought to it widely advertised qualities as a scholar, strategist, and veteran of the Cold War. He had been a practicing philosopher and an editor, and the author of seminal works on the nature of the current crisis.

Other qualities he brought to the magazine are almost certainly the primary reason for its survival. He had, to begin with, a (totally self-effacing) sense of corporate identification with it. He devoted, over a period of twenty-three years, more time and thought to more problems, major and minor, than would seem possible for an editor resident in Kent, Connecticut, who came to New York only two days a week.

But every aspect of the magazine interested him. Its typography— just for instance. He cared always for what he would only call "tone." He believed in "sentiment" but not in "sentimentality." At the regular editorial meetings, which by tradition began with his recommended list of issues about which we should write that week, his comments were always made calmly, with the kind of analytical poise that is the trademark of the professional philosopher. Notwithstanding the gentleness of his manner, he brought great passion to his work: not ungovernable passion, because Jim didn't believe that passion should be ungovernable. But his commentary, during such crises as are merely suggested by mentioning Budapest, Suez, Berlin, the Bay of Pigs, Vietnam, was sustained by the workings of a great mind.

Although he once told me that twenty years of teaching was enough—he was twenty-four years professor of philosophy at New York University before going to Washington to serve as a policy consultant—his natural instincts were always pedagogical. Probably fifty writers have in the past twenty-five years had editorial experience in the offices of *National Review*. I don't think any of my colleagues would question that the figure for whom they had the greatest respect, to whom they felt the greatest sense of gratitude, was Jim Burnham, who was never too busy to give reasons for thinking as he did, or too harassed to interrupt his own work to help others with theirs. His generosity was egregiously exploited by one person, whose only excuse, now, is that at least he has documented his gratitude by penning these words.

PRISCILLA BUCKLEY

Priscilla will not see these words until they are printed, because her juniors have conspired with me to accomplish something very nearly inconceivable, namely to insert into the magazine copy not first reviewed by the managing editor.

Priscilla, who attended Smith College with Nancy Davis (Reagan), went directly to journalism, on the radio news desk of the United Press. She worked the graveyard shift (midnight to eight) five days a week for $18.50 per week. That was the bad news, the good news being that every six months she received a fifty-cent-per-week raise. She was directed to cover sports, and so, at age twenty-two, she saw her first professional baseball, basketball, football, and ice hockey games, rushing to the typewriter to report the results of the quotidian melodramas to a panting world.

In due course she was in Paris, the first woman to be put in charge of an entire editorial shift. Among her assignments was interviewing Princess Soraya after the Shah bounced her for not managing to produce a son; covering the wedding of Olivia de Havilland; and tracking the war in Indochina. In one of her stories, she gave to the ministering lady during the great siege the title "The Angel of Dienbienphu"—which stuck. That was a pity, because the lady, when back in France, proved less than angelic. Priscilla quit after three years, anxious about her father's failing health and the strain it put on her mother. She dropped by *NR*'s office a few weeks after we began, just to help out for a month. A couple of years later she was the managing editor.

She does everything. For the magazine, for its editors and staff, for her friends. She writes "For the Record" and many editorials, including *all* the editorials on French sports. Without her, life at *NR* is, well, unimaginable. On top of everything else, at *NR* we don't have to worry when the lights go out, because Priscilla is smiling.

And a Sixth

*This portrait of William A. Rusher, Princeton B.A., Harvard LL.B., is
taken from a toast at a dinner in his honor.* ⟶

S ome of you have known Bill Rusher much longer than I have,
although I daresay not so intimately. To know anyone intimately it requires that he have the authority to question your
expenditure of money. In this respect I am certain that you will all
be glad to know that the guest of honor is the quintessential
Republican. I don't mean to say that he is tiresome about it, merely
that he is thorough. And unrelenting. Even on Sundays. I remember the legend of Congressman Rich of Pennsylvania, who was
elected to the House of Representatives sometime before the First
World War, and served there until his death, approximately forty
years—should we say long years?—later. During the first thirty-
nine of those years he uttered only a single declamation—the same
declamation, on a dozen or more occasions each year. The debate
on a spending measure would take place and, after it became obvious that it would be approved, Congressman Rich would raise his
hand and, recognized, would say, "Gentlemen, where are we going
to get the money?" and sit down. It is recorded that in his declining years, following a debate which had gone on for three weeks
and had kept his colleagues at their desks night after night, the
moment finally came for a vote on the controversial measure. At

which point, nearing midnight, Congressman Rich raised his hand. The entire chamber groaned. But under the rules the Speaker was powerless. Grumpily, he recognized the member from Pennsylvania, who, struggling against his great age, rose to his feet, looked around at his colleagues, and said, "April fool!"

Bill Rusher is not that versatile.

Our friend is a man of most meticulous habits, and it is a miracle, of the kind which providence less and less frequently vouchsafes us, that he should have endured for so long the disorderly habits of his colleagues. When so many years ago, in 1957, I asked him timidly whether he would consent to accept the responsibilities of publisher, he instinctively reached into his pocket and pulled out his notebook, presumably to see whether his notebook had any objections. Having passed that hurdle, *National Review* was subjected to a methodical probing over a period of three or four weeks. A few very close friends were directly consulted, and in due course the decision was reached. Shortly after that, he began to impose order on our affairs.

To this end he began his famous graphs. We have graphs at *National Review* charting every quiver in the organization's metabolism. We have graphs that show us how we are doing in circulation, in promotion expenses, in political influence. We have graphs that chart the fidelity to conservative principles of most major, and all minor, public figures in America. We have a graph that will tell you at a glance whether Lauren Bacall is more or less conservative than Humphrey Bogart. Our late friend and late colleague, the late Professor Willmoore Kendall, once dumbfounded Bill Rusher by telling him, "Bill, there is no proposition so simple that it cannot be rendered unintelligible to me by putting it on a graph." But the graphs go on: and, for those who have the stomach for it, they will give you a synoptic understanding of the financial record of *National Review* over the last twelve years.

Occasionally his admirers show their envy of him, as when, while he was away on a lecture tour, we tiptoed into his office and exactly reversed every reversible physical accoutrement. Thus the picture of Lincoln hung now, at our mischievous hands, where the picture of Washington had hung from time immemorial, and the picture of Washington hung where the picture of Lincoln had hung. Thus when he depressed Button One, instead of his secretary, the bookkeeper would answer; and when he depressed Button Two, instead of the bookkeeper, his secretary would answer. When he turned over the leaves of his calendar, he would find himself moving not toward the end of the month but toward the beginning of the month; and when he opened the drawer where his graphs were kept he would find not his graphs but his pills; and so on.

On entering his office and exposing himself to the pandemonium, he quickly decided that he had had enough. We had tried hard to substitute the door leading out of his office for the door leading into his bathroom but found that the problem was metaphysically insoluble. So he left, returned to his apartment, telephoned his secretary on the outside line, issued a few crisp instructions, and retired to his club for the rest of the day, pending the restoration of order.

Such have been his tribulations at *National Review*, in spite of which, I suspect, it could not have come as a great surprise to him that tonight his colleagues have rallied so enthusiastically to the idea of coming together to celebrate his achievements and his person. The most exasperating people in the world are so often the most beloved, and he is no exception. Sometimes, at the weekly editorial conference, to which he descends with his notebook and his clippings to pour vitriol on the ideologically feeble—sometimes he looks about him and no doubt feels as Congressman Rich felt surveying the expressions of those whom he would summon to fiscal rectitude. But Bill Rusher's performance at those meetings is one of the great running acts on the ideological stage.

His scorn is not alone for those in public life whose activities during the past week he finds contemptible, but also for those who lag a bit behind in exhibiting a similar scorn. For them, for his colleagues, his scorn is especially withering. "I notice," he wrote me recently after enduring an editorial conference during my absence and running hard into the opposition of some of our younger colleagues, "the difficulty in planting my views against the opposition of Merrill Lynch Pierce Fenner and Smith sitting at the opposite side of the table. I find that Merrill seldom disagrees with Lynch, who seldom disagrees with Pierce, who always disagrees with me. Perhaps you will find an opportunity to suggest a good basic reading list to our younger members." Such a reading list, I gathered, as would be everywhere useful nowadays, including in the White House.

But all is not lost; all is never lost. There is always next week's editorial conference, next month's financial crisis, next year's election: and on he marches, gyroscopically certain, ever in command of himself, whether communicating his pleasure, or registering his doubts, or metronomically tut-tutting his disapproval. Always a presence, always a performance; and always—I speak for myself and for those others who know him best—a friend.

CHAPTER SIX

REMEMBERING

WITNESS _Whittaker Chambers_

Whittaker Chambers, 1901–1961

In 1948, he gave his testimony against Alger Hiss. In 1952, he published his classic autobiography, Witness. *I went to see him at his farm in 1954, and we became friends. He died in 1961. I published his letters to me* (Odyssey of a Friend) *in 1969.*

"Where is Renoir's *Girl with the Watering Can*?" I asked the attendant at the entrance to the National Gallery. I walked up the flight of stairs, turned left through two galleries, and spotted her near the corner. It was only 12:25 and I had the feeling he would be there at exactly 12:30, the hour we had set. I could see through the vaulted opening into the adjacent galleries. I saw him approaching. It could only have been he, or Alfred Hitchcock.

The Sunday before, he had told me he was to be in Washington on the eighth of June. I was surprised—he loathed Washington, and probably had not been there three times in ten years, although he lived only two hours away. I had told him I would schedule my own business for the same day. He had asked me to keep the evening open, and we agreed to meet for a private lunch.

"You've guessed what's up, haven't you?" he said, his face wreathed in smiles.

"I haven't the least idea."

"John!" he said proudly. We went off talking excitedly. His son would be married that afternoon, and I was to go to the wedding and the reception. We lunched somewhere, and talked and talked for the hour and a half we had.

We met again at seven, in the blistering heat, at the church in Georgetown where a few months earlier John Fitzgerald Kennedy Jr. had been baptized. There were Whittaker and his wife, Esther, slight and beautiful, with her incomparable warmth; their daughter, Ellen, and her husband; a genial couple, old friends of the Chamberses from Baltimore; with his wife and sons, Whittaker's steadfast friend Ralph de Toledano, who met Whittaker during the Hiss trial, and wrote *Seeds of Treason*; the bride's parents, a sister of the bride, and a friend of the groom. We went from there to a private room at the Statler, where we drank champagne (for the first time in my life, I saw Whittaker take a drink) and ate dinner. Whittaker was quiet, but I think he was very happy. I thought back on a letter several years old. *"John's parents live for John, and for little else. In 1952, I sat and reckoned—so many years I must live to get John to his majority. It seemed an impossibly long course. Now each day is subtracted from the year that is left....I have found myself inwardly smiling because only a few months of that span are left. I have been saying to myself: I am free at last...."*

I went out with the Toledanos. As we stepped into the elevator I saw Whittaker framed by the door, his hand and Esther's clutched together, posing while his son-in-law popped a camera in his face; a grim reminder of all those flashbulbs ten years before. I never saw him again. He died a month later, on July 9, 1961. Free at last.

ॐ

I first met Chambers in 1954. An almost total silence had closed in on him. Two years earlier he had published *Witness*. When the preface of *Witness* appeared as a feature in the *Saturday Evening*

Post, that issue of the magazine sold a startling half million extra copies on the newsstand. The book came out with a great flurry. The bitterness of the Hiss trial had not by any means subsided. For some of the reviewers, Hiss's innocence had once been a fixed rational conviction, then blind faith; now it was rank superstition, and they bent under the force of an overwhelming book. But the man was not grasped by the reviewers, who treated *Witness* as a passion play acted out by archetypes. "I am a heavy man (*ernst Mensch*)," Chambers once wrote me, to apologize for staying two days at my home. There is a sense in which that was true. But he never appreciated, as others did, the gaiety of his nature, the appeal of his mysterious humor, the instant communicability of his overwhelming personal tenderness; his friends—I think especially of James Agee—took endless and articulate pleasure from his company.

Witness was off to a great start. But, surprisingly, it did not continue to sell in keeping with its spectacular send-off. The length of the book was forbidding; and the trial, in any case, was three years old, and the cold sweat had dried. Alger Hiss was in prison, and now the political furor centered on McCarthy. Those who did not know the book, and who were not emotionally committed either to Hiss's guilt or to his innocence, seemed to shrink even from a vicarious involvement in the controversy, to a considerable extent because of the dark emanations that came out of Chambers's emotive pen, depressing when reproduced, as was widely done, in bits and snatches torn from the narrative.

> It had been my impression [Hugh Kenner wrote me recently], before reading *Witness,* that his mind moved, or wallowed, in a setting of continuous apocalypse from which he derived gloomy satisfactions, of an immobilizing sort. The large scale of *Witness* makes things much clearer. It is surprisingly free from rhetoric, and it makes clear the genuine magnitude of the action which was

his life; a Sophoclean tragedy in slow motion, years not hours. I think Communism had an appeal for him which he doesn't go into; the appeal of a large-scale historic process, to which to surrender the self. The self awoke and fought its way clear by a superbly individual action (look how his attention comes awake when he is itemizing his essentials for escape; a weapon, a car, etc.). As a Communist he sleepwalked to heavy Dostoyevskian music...the constant note was surrender to a process larger than himself; and the heroic quality comes out in the interplay between this essentially musical mode of existence (the terminology is Wyndham Lewis's) and his constant awareness of the possibility, the necessity, of equilibrium, choice, the will poised freely amid possibilities. It's in the texture of the *Witness* prose, the narrative line making its way freely through the rhythms, sonorities, declarations; through the organ tones of plight.

In 1954 I asked if I might visit Chambers. He had written a long-standing friend, Henry Regnery, the publisher of my and Brent Bozell's book on Senator McCarthy, to praise the book, while making clear his critical differences with McCarthy. ("...*for the Right to tie itself in any way to Senator McCarthy is suicide. Even if he were not what, poor man, he has become, he can't lead anybody because he can't think.*") A few months after the book was published, Chambers was struck down by a heart attack, and it was vaguely known that he spent his days in and out of a sickbed, from which the likelihood was that he would never again emerge physically whole. I had every reason to believe that I would be visiting Jeremiah lying alongside a beckoning tomb.

I found him in bed. The doctor had forbidden him even to raise his head. And yet he was the liveliest man I think I ever met. I could not imagine such good humor from a very sick man, let alone a man possessed by the conviction that night was closing in all over the world, and privately tortured by his continuing fear that the forces aligned against him would contrive to reorder history, impose upon the world the ghastly lie that he had testified falsely against Alger Hiss, and so erase his witness, his expiation for a decade and a half's complicity with Communism. We did not, of course, speak of Hiss, nor did we for several months; though later Chambers spoke of him, and of the case, with relaxation and candor. But we must have talked about everything else, and I left later than I should have, hustled anxiously to the door by a wife who knew she was all but powerless to enforce the doctor's rules.

As he began to recover he was, for a while, greatly renewed by physical and spiritual energies which were dialectically at odds with his organic ill health and his intellectual commitment to the futility of all meliorative action. I talked with him about the magazine I proposed to publish and asked whether he would join the staff. To my overwhelming surprise the answer was, Yes—he might do just that. But not, he warned, if the journal was to be a sectarian enterprise, intended for a semiprivate circulation. We corresponded through the summer. He was to make up his mind definitely during the fall, after we visited again. I made the mistake in one of my letters of expressing exorbitant hopes for the role *National Review* might play in human affairs. He dashed them down in a paragraph unmatched in the literature of supine gloom, even though finally resisting despair.

It is idle [he rebuked me] to talk about preventing the wreck of Western civilization. It is already a wreck from within. That is why we can hope to do little more now than snatch a fingernail of a saint from the rack or a handful of ashes from the faggots, and bury them secretly in a flowerpot against the day, ages hence, when a few men begin again to dare to believe that there was once something else, that something else is thinkable, and need some evidence of what it was, and the fortifying knowledge that there were those who, at the great nightfall, took loving thought to preserve the tokens of hope and truth.

The tokens of hope and truth were not, he seemed to be saying, to be preserved by a journal of opinion, not by writers or thinkers, but only by activists, and I was to know that he considered a publication—the right kind of publication—not a word, but a deed. Though Chambers was a passionate literary man, always the intellectual, insatiably and relentlessly curious, in the last analysis it was action, not belletrism, that moved him most deeply.

In time I began to understand why in 1929 he resigned from the Communist *Daily Worker and New Masses*, where he had already earned an international reputation as a writer, to go scurrying about the streets of Washington, Baltimore, and New York, carrying pocketfuls of negatives and secret phone numbers and invisible ink.

One of the great failures of Witness *is that there was no time or place to describe the influences, other than immediate historical influences, that brought me to communism," he wrote me. "I came to communism ... above all under the influence of the Narodniki. It has been deliberately forgotten, but, in those days, Lenin urged us to revere the Narodniki—"those who went with bomb or revolver against this or that individual monster." Unlike most Western Communists, who became Communists under the influence of the Social Democrats, I remained under the spiritual influence of the Narodniki long after I became a Marxist. In fact, I never threw it off. I never have. And, of course, it was the revolutionary quality that bemused Alger*—mea culpa, mea maxima culpa.

Activism. From the Narodniki to the Republican Party, in one defection. During that period, Chambers believed that there was only a single man, among all those who had the slightest chance to succeed Eisenhower in the White House (Eisenhower was down with his heart attack, and it was generally assumed he would not run for reelection), who had any idea of what Communism was all about. I drove down to Westminster with a friend we had in common to get from him—it was on the eve of the publication of our first issue—his final word. The word was No. There were several reasons why he declined to leave his farm in Westminster and trudge back to New York to resume his professional life. But the predominant reason was that he would not associate himself with a journal that might oppose Eisenhower's reelection, in the unlikely event he were to run again, or even one that might be indifferent to his prospects for winning; let alone any magazine that might oppose Nixon's nomination in the event Eisenhower withdrew. Chambers the activist reasoned that under the existing circumstances, a vote for Eisenhower was actually a vote for Eisenhower's vice president. He puffed away at his pipe.

It was an awesome moment. A climaxing disappointment. It was rendered tolerable by one of those masterstrokes of irony over which Chambers and I were to laugh convulsively later on. My companion was Willi Schlamm, an old friend of Chambers from the hard anti-Communist cell at Time, Inc., and a colleague of mine, from the very beginning, in the *National Review* enterprise. Schlamm is a Viennese, volatile, amusing, the soul of obduracy, and a conversational stem-winder. He had been in on the negotiations with Chambers from the very first, and was modestly certain he could bring his old pal Whit along by the terrible cogency of his arguments. But as we drove down to Maryland from New York, Schlamm got progressively hoarser. Two minutes after we arrived, laryngitis completely closed in. Whittaker was wonderfully attentive—aspirin, tea, lemon, whiskey, bicarbonate, all that sort of thing. But at one point he turned to me, when Willi was out of sight, and gave me a huge, delighted wink.

So he stayed on his farm, and worried. He had a great deal to worry about. There was a pending libel suit against him by a minor actor in *Witness*, and Chambers felt that he had been fighting completely alone. And Alger Hiss had come out of prison arrantly proclaiming his innocence. *"Alger came out more fiercely than even I had expected.... His strength is not what it was. But that it exists at all is stunning. Every time that, in the name of truth, he asserts his innocence, he strikes at truth, utters a slander against me, and compounds his guilt of several orders.... It is this which squirts into my morale a little jet of paralyzing poison."*

His son, John, was having the normal son's difficulties at college. *"There come moments, even with a beloved son, when we are moved to nod assent to what Karl Brandt once said to me: 'Don't you know that boys at that age are poisonous, simply poisonous?'"*

Chambers's broken health, together with a grim financial situation, contributed to a great restlessness. *"I do not even have the capital to farm halfheartedly, and I cannot, as in the past, make good the capital by my own labor power. This inability to work the place is perhaps the greatest burr in my mind at that angle. It torments me, since, among other disabilities, I have no talent for being a country gentleman.... But we have long been as poor as rats."*

And then, during that period, he reached the psychological low point of his later years, as he sweated over philosophical bedrock, gathering his thoughts: *"I have been splashing about in my private pool of ice water."* Again, *"I have ceased to understand why I must go on living."* Again, *"The year was, for me, a long walk through the valley. No one but me will ever know how close I came to staying in it."* What was the trouble? *"It had to do with my inability to fix the meaning of the current period of existence in some communicable way. I knew the fault lay in me. So that, all the while I was trying to write, I was simply trying to grow."*

But he came out of it.

Between Christmas…and New Year, I woke, one dawn, from a
dream in which I had been singing (in German, but not aloud, of
course) a marching song. In my half-waking state, I continued to
sing the song to the end, which goes: "Bright, from the darkness of
the past/Beacons to the future." From what depths had this song
risen, which I had not sung (or heard sung) for decades? But the
song was only a signature. What was wonderful, incredible, was
the sense of having passed from one dimension into another; a
sense of ordered peace, together with an exhilaration ("at last I am
free"). I had touched bottom and was rising again to the surface;
and, to rise, I had cut loose a drowning weight of extraneous this
and that.… The dream was, in fact, the turning point of my late
years. I take it that such a dream is a recapitulation; it prepares
itself, as Camus says of suicide, "like a work of art, secretly, in the
heart" without the artist's being aware of the process.

ঝ

Eisenhower ran and was reelected. Nixon was safely vice president. Six months later Chambers wrote me to say he wanted to sign up with *National Review*. Having made the decision, he was elated. After years of isolation and introspection, he was like a painter who had recovered his eyesight. He felt the overwhelming need to practice his art. How many things he wanted to write about, and immediately! Mushrooms, for one thing. Some gentleman, in an act of supreme conceit, had recently published a ten-dollar book on mycology, heaping scorn on one of Chambers's most beloved species of toadstools. Camus. What a lot of things needed to be said instantly about the *Myth of Sisyphus*! Djilas's *The New Class* was just out and most of the critics had missed the whole point.…

I rented a single-engine plane and swooped down on him at Westminster to make our arrangements. For my own reasons I had to make the round trip in one day, and I wanted to act immediately on Chambers's enthusiasm. He met me, and we drove in his car to his farm. He told me that the last time a guest of his had arrived at the little grass strip at Westminster, on which reckless pilots ventured occasionally to land, it was Henry Luce, who had soared in from Washington to pay him an unexpected visit some months after Hiss's conviction. I remarked that such, obviously, is the traveling style of very important publishers. If he would not acknowledge that common denominator between me and Mr. Luce, I added, then he might recognize this one: such is the style of publishers who employ Whittaker Chambers. He laughed, but told me my manner was grossly imperfected. When Luce arrived, he said as we bounced about on the dusty dirt road in his open jeep, he had waiting for him at the airport a limousine to drive him to Chambers's farm. I made a note for my next landing....

He would not go to New York after all. To do so would be not merely to defy his doctor's orders, which he did regularly almost as a matter of principle, but to defy Esther's wishes, which was something else again. He would work at home. I begged him to desist from what I had denounced as his sin of scrupulosity. During the preceding eighteen months, since the Laryngitis Conference, he had twice volunteered to do a piece for *National Review*. One, I remember, was to be an answer to Dwight Macdonald's unbalanced attack on *National Review* in *Commentary*. He had suggested a deadline of two weeks after we spoke. Ten weeks later he abandoned the project. Meanwhile he had done thirteen drafts. He would not show me any of them.

He wrote on yellow copy paper, by hand, in pencil. Then he would rewrite and rewrite. Then—sometimes—he would type out a third or fourth draft. Then, after a few days, he would often destroy that. "Let *us* judge whether what you write is publishable," I pleaded. "You have no judgment on such matters. There should be a constitutional amendment forbidding you to destroy anything you write, without the permission of a jury of your superiors, to which I hereby nominate myself." He chuckled. Underproduction would not be his trouble any more, he said: the way he was feeling he would bury us with copy, and before long I'd be sending him literary tranquilizers.

But five weeks later, he wrote me to say he must resign: he could not bring himself to submit to us what he had written. I cajoled him, and one day a five-thousand-word manuscript arrived, "Soviet Strategy in the Middle East." (*"Talk, here in the farmlands,"* it began, *"is chiefly of the heaviest frost of this date in a decade, and what it may have done to stands of late corn. Yet it cannot be said that we are wholly out of touch with the capitals of the mysterious East—Cairo, Damascus, Baghdad, New York. . . ."*)

Two months later, after struggling with the book for eight weeks, he submitted a long review of Ayn Rand's *Atlas Shrugged*. (*"Somebody has called it 'excruciatingly awful.' I find it a remarkably silly book. . . . In any case, the brew is probably without lasting ill effects. But it is not a cure for anything. Nor would we, ordinarily, place much confidence in the diagnosis of a doctor who supposes that the Hippocratic Oath is a kind of curse."* Miss Rand never forgave me for publishing it. (For the rest of her life, she would walk theatrically out of any room I entered!)

A few months after that, he wrote about the farm problem, clearly as an insider:

Perhaps [in the future the socialized farmer] will not be able, in that regimented time, to find or frame an answer [to why he lost his freedom]. Perhaps he will not need to. For perhaps the memory of those men and women [who fought socialism] will surprise him simply as with an unfamiliar, but arresting sound—the sound of spring-heads, long dried up and silent in a fierce drought, suddenly burst out and rushing freely to the sea. It may remind him of a

continuity that outlives all lives, fears, perplexities, contrivings,
hopes, defeats; so that he is moved to reach down and touch again
for strength, as if he were its first discoverer, the changeless
thing—the undeluding, undenying earth.

And then a piece defending the right of Alger Hiss to travel abroad, while denying that Hiss could be said to have paid his debt to society. Chambers knew that his absolute endorsement of the right of anyone to travel would bring criticism from certain quarters on the Right. No matter. (*"As one of my great contemporaries put it: 'Anybody looking for a quiet life has picked the wrong century to be born in.' The remark must be allowed a certain authority, I think, since the century clinched the point by mauling with an ax the brain that framed it."*)

That piece was noticed by the *New York Times*, which also ran a paragraph calling attention to Chambers's joining the staff of *National Review*, a story picked up by AP. He bore the publicity he got with resignation, though it clearly upset him. If Chambers could have taken a bath in invisible ink, I have no doubt he'd have done so.

But notwithstanding his desire for privacy and his temperamental dislike for New York (*"New York you need to exploit, and I never learned how"*), Chambers decided in the summer of 1958 to come here every fortnight to spend two days in the office, writing editorials and short features for *National Review*. He would arrive on the train from Baltimore at noon and come directly to the editorial lunch, always out of breath, perspiring in his city clothes. He was always glad to see his gentle friend John Chamberlain, a longtime colleague from Time, Inc. He liked his little cubicle at *National Review*, which, five minutes after he entered it, smelled like a pipe-tobacco factory. He puffed away ferociously, grinding out his memorable paragraphs. Everything he wrote had intellectual and stylistic distinction and, above all, the intense emotional quality of the man who, fifteen years before, had written of the Negro spiritual: *"It was the religious voice of a whole religious people—probably the most God-obsessed (and man-despised) since the ancient Hebrews.... One simple fact is clear—[spirituals] were created in direct answer to the Psalmist's question, 'How shall we sing the Lord's song in a strange land?'... Grief, like a tuning fork, gave the tone, and the Sorrow Songs were uttered."*

Yet anyone meeting Chambers casually, without preconception, would say of him first that he was a highly amusing and easily amused man. The bottomless gravity seldom suggested itself. He was not merely a man of wit, but also a man of humor, and even a man of fun. Often, in his letters, even through his orotund gloom, the pixie would surface. (*"Would that we could live in the world of the fauves, where the planes are disjointed only on canvas, instead of a world where the wild beasts are real and the disjointures threaten to bury us. Or do I really wish that? It would take some nice thinking for, perhaps, [to contradict Gertrude Stein's famous sentence], toasted Susie is* not *my ice cream."*)

On Tuesday nights we worked late, and four or five of us would go out to dinner. By then he was physically exhausted. But he wanted to come with us, and we would eat at some restaurant or another, and he would eat hungrily, and talk hungrily about everything that interested him, which was literally everything in this world, and not in this world. He often talked around a subject, swooping in to make a quick point, withdrawing, relaxing, laughing, listening—he listened superbly, though even as a listener he was always a potent force. He was fascinated by James Burnham's method and by the scope of his interests, and the sureness of his analytical mind, though Chambers's own thoughts were so resolutely nonschematic that he tended to shrink from some of Burnham's grandiose constructions, even while admiring the architecture. They made for a wonderful dialectic, Burnham's sostenutos and Chambers's enigmatic descants.

The next morning, press day, he was at his desk at eight, and we would have a sandwich lunch. At five he was on the train back to Baltimore, where Esther would meet him. And on reaching his farm he would drop onto his bed from fatigue. Three months after he began coming to New York, he collapsed from another heart attack.

Six months later, in the summer of 1959, he felt well enough to indulge a dream, more particularly his gentle wife's dream, to visit Europe. She had never been there, and he had been there only once, in 1927, the trip he described so evocatively in *Witness*. We drove them to the airport after a happy day. I noticed worriedly how heavily he perspired and how nervously his heavy thumbs shuffled through the bureaucratic paraphernalia of modern travel, as he dug up, in turn, passports, baggage tags, vaccination certificates, and airplane tickets. His plans were vague, but at the heart of them was a visit to his old friend Arthur Koestler.

They were at Koestler's eyrie in Austria for a week, an unforgettable week.

Alpach, where AK lives, is some four hundred meters higher into the hills than Innsbruck.... There in Alpach we spent some days about which I cannot possibly write fully.... Then K. had the idea to write Greta Buber-Neumann:... "Come quickest. Good wine. In addition, Whittaker C." In case you do not know, Greta Buber-Neumann is the daughter-in-law of Martin Buber, widow of Heinz Neumann, most dazzling of the German CP leaders (shot without trial), sister-in-law of Willi Münzenberg (organizer of the Münzenberg Trust, killed by the NKVD while trying to escape the Gestapo). Greta herself spent two years as a slave in Karaganda. By then, the Moscow–Berlin Pact had been signed, and the NKVD handed her (and many others) over to the Gestapo on the bridge at Brest-Litovsk. Then she spent five years in German concentration camps, mostly at Ravensbrück.... Impossible to tell here this story of her lifetime, which makes the Odyssey, *for all its grandeur, somehow childish.... So there we sat, and talked, not merely about the daily experiences of our lives. Each of the two men had tried to kill himself and failed; Greta Buber-Neumann was certainly the most hardy and astonishing of the three. Then we realized that, of our particular breed, the old activists, we are almost the only survivors.*

They went on to Rome (*"In Rome, I had to ask Esther for the nitroglycerine. Since then, I've been living on the stuff."*), Venice (*"I came back to Venice chiefly to rest. If it were not for my children, I should try to spend the rest of my life here. Other cities are greater or less great than something or some other city. Venice is incomparable. It is the only city I have ever loved"*), Berlin (*"I feel as though I had some kind of moral compulsion to go at this time"*), Paris (*"You will look up Malraux?"* I wrote him—I remembered the gratitude Chambers felt on receiving a handwritten note from Malraux, who had just read *Witness*: "You have not come back from hell with empty hands." *"Malraux is busy,"* Chambers replied. *"If he wants to see me, he will know where to find me"*).

Within a few weeks he got sick again, and abruptly they flew back; and again he was in bed.

He wanted to resign from *National Review*. It was partly that his poor health and his unconquerable perfectionism kept him from producing a flow of copy large enough to satisfy his conscience. Partly it was his weltanschauung, which was constantly in motion. Chiefly he resisted *National Review*'s schematic conservatism, even its schematic anti-Communism. *"You ... stand within, or at any rate are elaborating, a political orthodoxy. I stand within no political orthodoxy.... I am at heart a counter-revolutionist. You mean to be conservative, and I know no one who seems to me to have a better right to the term. I am not a conservative. Sometimes I have used the term loosely, especially when I was first called on publicly to classify myself. I have since been as circumspect as possible in using the term about myself. I say: I am a man of the Right."* Chambers, the individualist, believed strongly in organization. He believed, for instance, in the Republican Party. *"I shall vote the straight Republican ticket for as long as I live,"* he told me. *"You see, I am an Org-bureau man."*

But the day came, as I knew it would. "This is my resignation from *NR*," he wrote sadly toward the end of 1959. "This is a retype of the beginning of a much longer letter."

~

He had made up his mind to do something else. He enrolled at Western Maryland College as an undergraduate. *"Most people incline to laugh. I think they feel that it is such a waste on all sides since I shall not be around long enough to put it to any use of the kind people call 'good.' I've considered that. I do not wish to die an ignoramus."*

Several reasons why he should take this course were instantly clear to me. He had quit *National Review*. He had failed to complete the book that Random House had been expecting for six years. He did not want to sit at home, half crippled and denied the life he would, I think, have liked most to lead, the life of a dawn-to-dusk farmer. Chambers was all Puritan about work. Idleness was utterly incomprehensible to him.

But there was another reason. In Europe, Koestler, whose book *The Sleepwalkers* Chambers had read just before leaving, had said to him sharply, "You cannot understand what is going on in the world unless you understand science deeply." Very well, then, he would learn science.

He threw himself into his work. Science courses galore. And, for relaxation, Greek, Latin, and advanced French composition. Every morning he drove to school and sat between the farmers' sons of western Maryland, taking notes, dissecting frogs, reciting Greek paradigms, working tangled problems in physics. After school, immediately to the basement to do his homework. Everything else was put aside. He signed up for the summer session, of course, but in the interstice between terms (*"First day of summer break, and I am wild with liberty. I was still standing by hanging onto the ropes, when the final bell sounded"*) he drove north to see his daughter, and came over to visit with us on a hot summer afternoon. How do you get on, my wife asked him, with your fellow undergraduates? "Just fine," he said. He had an admirer. A young lady, aged about nineteen, who shared with him the carcasses of small animals, which the two of them proceeded, in tandem, to disembowel. "For months while we worked together she addressed me not a word, and I was afraid my great age had frightened her. But last week, all of a sudden, she broke silence. She said breathlessly: 'Mr. Chambers?'

" 'Yes,' I answered her anxiously.

" 'Tell me, what do *you* think of "Itsy-Bitsy Teenie-Weenie Yellow Polka-Dot Bikini?" ' " He broke down with laughter. He hadn't had, at the critical moment, the least idea that the young lady was talking about a popular song, but he had improvised beautifully until he was able to deduce what on earth it was all about, whereupon he confided to his codissector that it happened that this was absolutely, positively, indisputably his very favorite song, over all others he had ever heard. Her gratitude was indescribable. From that moment on they chirped together happily and pooled their knowledge about spleens and livers, kidneys and upper intestines.

I imagine he was a very quiet student, giving his teachers no cause whatever for the uneasiness they might have expected to feel in the presence of so august a mind. Only once, that I know of, was he aroused to take issue with one of his teachers.

An incident from my Greek class, which has left me in ill favor. We came on a Greek line of Diogenes: "Love of money is the mother-city of all the ills." Opinions were invited; and when my turn came, I answered with one word: "Nonsense." That was too vehement, but there was a reason. Behind me was sitting a junior, who manages on a scholarship or grant or something of the kind, and whose college life has been made a misery by poverty. To say in the presence of such a case, "Love of money is the mother-city of all the ills"— is why I answered, "Nonsense."...I offered in Greek: "A lack of money is the root of many ills."...I thought I could speak with some freedom since there can scarcely ever have existed a man in whom love of money is as absolutely absent as in me. I don't even get properly interested in it. Oh, I also offered (while authority was being bandied) St. Thomas Aquinas's "Money is neither good nor bad in itself; it depends on what is done with it." But St. Thomas seems not to be in good standing. So, down the generations go the blinded minds, blinkered minds, at any rate. But I wonder what Master Jones, the impoverished junior, thought about it. I did not ask. He, like the other Greeks who were doing most of the talking, is a pre-divinity student—pre-Flight, as they call it happily here.

During examination weeks he was in a constant state of high boil. He slaved for his grades. And he achieved them, even in the alien field of science; nearly all A's, or A–'s; once, as I remember, a humiliating B+. After the winter, his fatigue was total, overwhelming. *"Weariness, Bill,"* he wrote in the last letter I had from him, shortly before John's wedding, *"—you cannot yet know literally what it means. I wish no time would come when you do know, but the balance of experience is against it. One day, long hence, you will know true weariness and will say: 'That was it.' My own life of late has been full of such realizations."*

He learned science, and killed himself. Those were the two things, toward the end, he most wanted to do.

ঞ

"Why on earth doesn't your father answer the phone?" I asked his daughter, Ellen, in Connecticut on a Saturday afternoon, July 8.

"Because," she said with a laugh, shyly, "Poppa and the phone company are having a little tiff, and the phone is disconnected. They wanted him to trim one of his favorite trees to take the strain off the telephone line, and he put it off. So ... they turned off the phone."

I wired him: WHEN YOU COME TO TERMS WITH THE PHONE COMPANY GIVE ME A RING. But he didn't call. The following Tuesday, I came back to my office from the weekly editorial lunch—I had thought, as often I did, how sorely we missed him there in the dining room. As I walked into my office the phone rang. I took the call standing, in front of my desk. It was John Chambers. He gave me the news. A heart attack. The final heart attack. Cremation in total privacy. The news would go to the press later that afternoon. His mother was in the hospital. I mumbled the usual inappropriate things, hung up the telephone, sat down, and wept.

> *American men, who weep in droves in movie houses, over the woes of lovestruck shop girls, hold that weeping in men is unmanly [he wrote me once]. I have found most men in whom there was depth of experience, or capacity for compassion, singularly apt to tears. How can it be otherwise? One looks and sees: and it would be a kind of impotence to be incapable of, or to grudge, the comment of tears, even while you struggle against it. I am immune to soap opera. But I cannot listen for any length of time to the speaking voice of Kirsten Flagstad, for example, without being done in by that magnificence of tone that seems to speak from the center of sorrow, even from the center of the earth.*

For me, and others who knew him, his voice had been and still is like Kirsten Flagstad's, magnificent in tone, speaking to our time from the center of sorrow, from the center of the earth.

Murray Kempton, 1917–1997

We met in the quarrelsome circumstances of the fifties, and became friends. He was the most thoughtful and amusing and resourceful journalist in town. I recall him as a friend, and at work. ⟜

T*he death of a single person* routinely overwhelms just the family, while at the other end of the scale the whole world is seemingly overwhelmed, as when, one year after the turn of the century, the Victorian age died along with its Queen. In between are the deaths of local, regional, and national divinities. San Francisco stood still the day Herb Caen died, and then Chicago spent the day mourning Mike Royko. In New York, on May 5, Murray Kempton died. The *New York Times* observed his death on its front page with a photograph of the recognizable figure with his indispensable pipe, and inside gave its readers a brilliant and moving ("Murray Kempton never sought a job at the *Times*. For him, the *Times* took itself too seriously") page-length obituary by Richard Severo. *Newsday*, the daily for which Kempton wrote until he fell ill, devoted the whole of its front page to his photograph ("MURRAY KEMPTON, 1917–1997. A HALF-CENTURY OF ELEGANCE AND TRUTH") and ran five stories. The *Daily News*'s Jim Dwyer remarked the death of "the greatest newspaperman of the 20th century," and the *New York Post*, with which Kempton was for so many years associated, ran several features.

Murray Kempton had been ailing for several months. In January, pancreatic cancer was diagnosed. After surgery he spent weeks in a hospital in Princeton, going then to a nursing home on the West Side of Manhattan for continuing treatment under the auspices of Sloan-Kettering. There, very early Monday morning, his heart stopped.

ॐ

My own reaction, on hearing the news, was the spastic It's-for-the-best. I had a friend who took two bad years to yield, finally, to that affliction. Ten days before Murray died, lying, white-haired and emaciated with a tube or two in his arm, he said, "Do you *know* what my medical expenses have been?—*me*, without any claim to any value in the free market? *Three hundred thousand dollars!*" I whistled, and shared, with Murray's son David, noisy and indignant astonishment at so gross a figure for eleven weeks' care. Without exactly delving into the question of resources, the conversation proceeded on the assumption (generally safe, though not always) that somebody, somewhere, would handle the cost of the illness, however long it lasted. Whatever the clinical prospects, there was no impulse in that little room by the Hudson River on 87th Street to pack it all in. In 1995 Murray's wife, Beverly, had died after a long ordeal. He wrote me, "I'm sure you have no end of those dear friends, Job's counselors, who describe the worst things as for the best as if to congratulate you for release from inconveniences. The day before she died one such reminded me that it might be better so, and I was grateful for the impulse that welled up and impelled me to reply that my views are the Pope's and we both prefer life to death."

He spoke now, his voice weak but resolute, of activity he would undertake in the weeks, indeed years ahead. "I don't think it's absolutely decided that I won't be able to work." He had given me

to see, in December, the opening chapter from a proposed autobiography. "I think I can get it done in eight or nine months." The
chapter I saw dealt with combat experience in the Pacific and
ended, as only Kempton and St. Sebastian could have done, with
an expression of pity and compassion for the Japanese soldiers who
hours before had tried to kill, and very nearly succeeded in doing
so, Private Kempton and his squad. Suddenly, on that tumultuous
hot humid topsy-turvy afternoon, Murray's unit discovered that
they actually outnumbered the Japanese.

"There could not have been more than six of them, and there
were never fewer than twenty of us; and our advantage in metallic
weight was far crueler than in numbers. I myself carried more
killing power on my shoulder than all of them could summon up
with their .25 caliber single-shot carbines."

Was that then the end of the enemy unit? Certainly that alternative, in a hot sticky war, suggests itself. "It would be by no
means unreasonable to inquire as to why, instead of withdrawing
in order, we did not respond as patrols are expected to and simply turn our weapons on these overmatched enemies and transform their ambush into their terminal disaster. I have once or
twice asked myself the same question. Respect for your betters
perhaps; and in any case rather more than just, as well. They had
made out of us the stuff of what must have been the last clear
Japanese victory in the Pacific, and they deserved the satisfactions of a pride that had outlasted what may or not once have
been their arrogance."

It sounded unreal—spare the enemy, else run the risk of an
affront to their pride. But it sounded, also, very much like Murray
Kempton, who in his career lacerated us all, but scorned only the
hypocrites and the arrogant. In March 1945, on the island of Aglao
in the South Pacific, Murray had no personal evidence that the six
Japanese whose ambush had failed really deserved to be killed.

In 1989, *Newsday*'s publisher decided to celebrate the paper's three Pulitzer Prize winners by turning the stage of the 92nd Street Y over to each of the three recipients, on successive nights, for an evening of public banter with any journalist of their choice. Kempton tapped me.

My job was to introduce the prizewinner commodiously ("ten to fifteen minutes. After that, you cross-interrogate"). I gave some thought to the assignment. The audiences at the Y are sophisticated, and in any case, nothing would have vexed Murray more than ten minutes of serial idolatry.

I told the audience that twenty-seven years earlier, in 1962, I had been asked by the quarterly *Monocle* (now extinct) to do a profile of Murray Kempton, already the toast of New York's Left-literati. I told the editor that the assignment was too burdensome, given that Kempton wrote three columns every week and had been doing so for ten years—there was no way I could do a comprehensive analysis of his writing and his views. What I would agree to undertake, under the stress of raw economy, was an essay based on the columns by Murray Kempton published in the three weeks before I wrote.

My stunt (which worked) was to demonstrate to the audience at the Y that after thirty years, Murray Kempton hadn't changed. He never did change. In what ways was he unchanged?

I began by saying (The First Law) that Murray really did not understand elementary economics.

"What would happen, one wonders," I had written back in 1962, and now said to the audience at the Y, "if the Devil should take the scales from Kempton's eyes, and let him see into the world of economics? I say the Devil, because the Lord would not do so fiendish a thing. What a terrible end! Murray's muse would dry up, and the pagan love song to humankind which he has been trilling for so many years would get all hung up, under the discipline of keys, and measures, and clefs. A calamity, in a word: Because Kempton, though he does not realize that theory is as liberating in social science as dogma is in theology, nevertheless is as necessary to humane industrial organization as Sam Goldwyn to idiomatic English. But even as linguistic solecisms remain solecisms, so is it with economic solecisms."

Later in the evening Kempton did not deny his formal ignorance of the dismal science. He took, instead, wry satisfaction from it.

My second finding about Murray Kempton, 1962, was that he was perversely compassionate. I quoted from his column on the defeat of Carmine De Sapio, the last Tammany baron of Manhattan.

"One of the most satisfying things about Kempton," I had written, "is his impartial iconoclasm. I remember his writing, when Roy Cohn was finally and ignominiously forced out of Senator McCarthy's committee, 'So help me God, I feel sorry for Roy Cohn'—which I am sure he did, as well he might have, having for months galloped miles ahead of the posse (never did so many supererogate upon so little!). It is as distasteful to use a machine gun to deliver the coup de grace as it is to wait for the fourth coda to terminate a Tchaikovsky symphony. In 1960 Kempton didn't want to go to the Republican Convention in Chicago. 'If I do,' he told me, 'I'll knock Nixon—it's like junk. But I *like* Nixon!' He does feel sorry for the mangled corpse; but it is also for artistic reasons that he feels the need to back away.

"Today he goes after Tammany-killer Mayor Robert Wagner again. Kempton, of course, immediately saw through the phoniness of the anti–De Sapio frenzy of the summer and fall of 1961, of which Ed Koch was the beneficiary. Kempton passed the day of the execution in the company of the failing leader De Sapio, following him around everywhere, closely observing his manners, and reacting prodigally to his remarkable personal gentility. 'I sometimes think,' he wrote, 'that if Carmine De Sapio were running against Lucifer he would consider it ungentlemanly to mention that little trouble in heaven.' When it was finally evident that De Sapio had been over-thrown, there were still the conventional and poignant rituals to go through. After midnight, Kempton wrote, 'His visitor'—Kempton's wonderfully unobtrusive way of designating himself in all his inter-views—'left him and walked into the streets and noticed that there were no slums any more, and no landlords, and the Age of Pericles had begun because we were rid of Carmine De Sapio. One had to walk carefully to avoid being stabbed by the lilies bursting in the pavements. I wish the reformers luck—with less Christian sincerity than Carmine De Sapio does. I will be a long time forgiving them this one.'"

The Second Kempton Law: He would help anyone who was down.

My succeeding law was to the effect that nobody in the entire world had a shrewder eye than Kempton for political mischief, or had—or gave—greater fun in setting it down.

Why had John F. Kennedy defeated Richard Nixon a year ear-lier? In Wednesday's column, Murray came up with the explana-tion. He had been examining Public Document 75452 from the subcommittee of the Senate Committee on Commerce, labeled "The Joint Appearances of Senator John F. Kennedy and Vice President Richard M. Nixon and Other 1960 Campaign Presenta-tions." Kempton quoted from an exchange on the NBC network's *Tonight Show* with Jack Paar.

Vice President Nixon: Could I ask you one favor, Jack?

Jack Paar: Yes sir; you can ask any favor you'd like.

Vice President Nixon: Could we have your autograph for our girls?

"That was September 11, 1960," Kempton noted, "and Nixon had packed [for the White House]. The Kennedys rallied two weeks later."

CHARLES COLLINGWOOD [OF CBS, ADDRESSING JFK'S TWO-YEAR-OLD DAUGHTER]: Hello, Caroline.

MRS. KENNEDY: Can you say hello?

CAROLINE: Hello.

MRS. KENNEDY: Here, do you want to sit up in bed with me?

MR. COLLINGWOOD: Oh, isn't she a darling?

MRS. KENNEDY: Now, look at the three bears.

MR. COLLINGWOOD: What is the dolly's name?

MRS. KENNEDY: All right, what is the dolly's name?

CAROLINE: I didn't name her yet.

Kempton concluded: "But the mystery of [Nixon's] collapse taunts us yet. Still it was a terribly close election and who can say what small mistake cost him it? There is this one clue:"

BILL HENRY, OF NBC: I am so fascinated with that little kitten. Does the kitten have a name?

JULIE NIXON: Yes, its name is Bitsy Blue Eyes.

"Maybe," Kempton concluded his column, "Caroline saved the package when she held off naming the doll."

My next Kempton Law was based on his column the day after he analyzed the reason for Nixon's defeat. He wrote about the Dominican Republic's famous playboy/politico, noting that Porfirio Rubirosa, sometime son-in-law of General Trujillo, had been fired from his diplomatic post after twenty-four years of—as Kempton put it—"carrying his diplomatic passport into some of the most distinguished boudoirs in the architecture of international relations."

What happened was that a U.S. grand jury was looking into the mysterious death in New York City of a Dominican opponent of the dictator and had written out a subpoena for son-in-law Rubirosa. But Rubirosa declined to go. The evidence against him was, as Kempton put it, "admittedly wispy and arose from the unfortunate coincidence that any member of the Dominican Republic's tiny middle class is apt to be related either to a victim or to an assassin or to both."

My Fourth Law: All sociologists could learn from Kempton how in one sentence to capture an entire culture.

I then devoted a minute or two to Murray Kempton as Chronicler of the American Right.

"He is fascinated by the Right," I said, "especially the hard Right. 'I have discovered the definition of a radical,' he told me once over the telephone. 'It is anyone whose name is preceded by "so-called."'

"Kempton had had difficulty, a few days before, persuading a Montgomery, Alabama, taxi driver to take him to the home of Martin Luther King. He solved the problem by asking a driver to take him to the home of *the so-called Martin Luther King.*' Kempton is the principal chronicler of hard-Right activities, and makes his way about the Right labyrinth with ease. He has no trouble at all mixing easily with those whom the next morning he will berate with a passionate wit. As a matter of fact, Kempton has *no* enemies, and that is an unusual estate for a man with so active a tongue. '*Everybody likes me,*' he told me mournfully at the political convention in Chicago. 'That is one of my major failings. For instance, take my book *America Comes of Middle Age*—it got only favorable reviews!' His book was not seriously criticized because it is hard seriously to criticize Kempton, as it is difficult to criticize seriously—whom else? I have given the matter five minutes' thought and I can't come up with anyone so intensely partisan to whom all is forgiven, and whose most outrageous statements are allowed to rest in peace.

"But back to Kempton and the American Right. 'Sharonology,' he writes, 'is the study of the internal struggles of the American Right, as Kremlinology is the study of the internal struggles of the Politburo, the materials in both cases being incomprehensible documents and speakers' lists at dinners. It takes its name from Sharon, Connecticut, birthplace of . . .' your visitor tonight. '[Conservative columnist George] Sokolsky has taken after Dr. Fred Schwarz, director of the Christian Anti-Communist Crusade. Schwarz is an Australian, and Sokolsky feels that anti-Communism is an American enterprise; he is high tariff in all things.' Conservative radio commentator Fulton Lewis Jr., Kempton observes, has become a security risk in some quarters of the hard Right because 'as an honored speaker at the *Human Events* Forum in Washington the other day…he abused the privileges of the rostrum to attack certain unidentified flying objects who confuse the issue by thinking that everybody is a Communist.'"

Straining for a hundred-proof dollop of Kempton applejack, I concluded my essay by examining his column on the Communist Party. "Here Kempton is at his absolute, unbeatable worst. It has been said there is no theological question Billy Graham cannot vulgarize; so there is no issue touching the Communist problem that Murray Kempton cannot sentimentalize. The Communist enterprise, or at least that part of it that goes on in this country, is in his opinion opéra bouffe. I have never seen a pointed sentence by Murray Kempton on the subject of the Communist problem at home: always the systematic refusal to face the systematically demanding question [philosopher] Sidney Hook has tried to face up to in his book, *Heresy, Yes—Conspiracy, No.* 'The trouble with

Kempton,' Hook once said, 'is he thinks with his stomach.' The trouble with Hook, your visitor admits, is he doesn't think often enough with his stomach.

"But Hook is right here. I give you the locus classicus, Kempton's report on the election of the new chairman of the Communist Party of the United States of America. 'It is impossible to look at Miss [Elizabeth Gurley] Flynn [the CPUSA chairman-elect] without collapsing into the molasses of the American dream. She is the aunt Dorothy longed to get back to from Oz....If the old-fashioned virtues really had any impact on our culture, the disenchanted of our society would rush to this dear sister's bosom. [She has] a face that would be irresistible on the label of an apple pie mix.' Had enough?" I asked rhetorically. "Well, I don't care. You will have more. 'You could sum up the domestic history of a dozen years just by printing a picture of Elizabeth Gurley Flynn and putting under it the caption, "From 1948 to 196– a great nation was afraid of this woman." But what generation unborn could possibly be expected to believe that?'"

I ended my essay/introduction gravely. "There are other problems more likely to urge themselves on generations unborn. The incumbent young generation in Cuba will wonder less why some Cubans were afraid of Fidel Castro, than why other Cubans were not.

"Kempton's glands are, alas, no substitute for the humorless appraisal of the role of the Communist parties in the free world. He is foremost among those the burden of whose thought is that it is the grave responsibility of the free world to ensure the serenity of those in their midst who would subvert their freedom. E. Flynn's face is, after all, no more pleasing than poor Kerensky's. One has the feeling that the poet Kempton, whose grasp of reality so often surpasses that of the ho-hummers who have been charged with the evolution of our destiny, is resigned to turning over the future to the prosaic men who are poetically benighted, just so long as he can be around to write the requiem for our time. And your visitor, to the extent he is ever tempted, where such solemn issues are involved, would care greatly to read that requiem, for it would be grand. But it would be easier reading if one knew that unborn generations would wake free, into free countries, unbewitched by such as Elizabeth Gurley Flynn, who once worked for Lavrenty Beria, who is less than apple pie mix."

Well then, that was stirring stuff in 1962, and even in 1989—Murray and I, at the Y, performed five months before the Berlin Wall came down. But one hour after my long introduction, Murray, wandering from subject to allied subject to not-quite-allied subject, from aphorism to jollity to reminiscence to questions self-directed, to reflections on the Byzantine experience, had the audience eating out of the palm of his hand, as also his interrogator.

℘

On my seventy-first birthday he sent me the complete sonatas of Scarlatti, performed by Scott Morris. And a letter that began, "I pray your forgiveness for having waked one morning a while back to the revelation of how much I missed you. There's little enough to say beyond that foolishness, and nothing of wisdom except to report that the years between 78 and 80 are quite shockingly depleting and to warn you to brace yourself for their leakage with an early commitment to the disciplines of Geritol."

The discipline Murray Kempton embraced was the Christian faith, as embodied in the Episcopal Church. "My church was inspired by a languid but dutiful zeal to serve the royal will with a bill of divorce. The Book of Common Prayer—the envy even of you Romans, who deserve to be envied for everything else—was established as the foundation of this shadowed faith; and every line and comma was passed through the gimlet eye of Elizabeth I. For centuries thereafter congregants ingested mighty cadences, sweet solaces, and the necessary adjurations to pull up their socks."

He reiterated that he was weary, but that he hoped to stay clear of unheavenly inducements. "I cry your mercy for divagating but, when people haven't talked for so long, degrees of loss of touch do assert themselves. I do, as I first said, very much miss you but"—Murray's witty cheer surfaced, as it always did—"I am otherwise content with having grown too old for further steps on the road to Avernus,* which, as Virgil soundly observed, is a slope so easy that the Germans had but to begin it by underpaying Bach to travel straight down to the Holocaust."

He was a great artist, and a great friend.

---

* Rendered in Dryden's Virgil as:

Smooth the descent and easy the way
(The Gates of Hell stand open night and day);
But to return and view the cheerful skies,
In this the task and mighty labour lies.

Henry Regnery, 1912–1996

His publishing firm in Chicago was only a few years old when I sent him, in 1951, the manuscript of God and Man at Yale, *which he published in the fall. The firm was relocated to Washington, D.C., in the eighties, headed by Henry's son Alfred.*

In 1972, I was asked to speak at a dinner in Henry's honor, given in his beloved Chicago. The topic on everyone's mind was Richard Nixon's visit to Red China, two months earlier. I had been one of the journalists on that trip. ⟶

When I learned that I would be preceded by Russell Kirk and David Collier and Jack Kilpatrick and Vic Milione and Stan Evans and Eliseo Vivas, I wondered why master of ceremonies Louis Dehmlow hadn't, while he was at it, arranged to produce Ezra Pound. To present me at the end of this list of speakers is, to say the least, dramatically insecure. Kirk, Kilpatrick, Vivas, and Buckley. It was Abraham Flexner who remarked that "For God, for Country, and for Yale" was surely the greatest anticlimax in the English language. But I am here, as we all are, to register our solidarity with a man who has been important to all of us in one way or another, indeed to some of us in a combination of ways: as a friend, a publisher, a mentor—in my own case all three. I have not only read books he suggested I read, but even written books he suggested I write: and this requires a very special relationship.

It is a night for reminiscences, and I think it is accurate to say that I have known Henry longer than any of the other speakers, having met him even before Russell Kirk did. I am especially happy about the fecundity of his noble house, inasmuch as I remember, during the very dark days just after *God and Man at Yale* appeared, that Henry was wondering whether any writer would ever again consent to write for a publishing house which had midwived such an outrage. It is characteristic of Henry that when he reached this slough of despondency, he didn't do what most of us incline to do— call out for help or reassurance from our friends. I still have the letter from him advising me that he had devoted the night before—after seeing the first rash of reviews—to rereading my book. He concluded that he had been correct to publish it and, so far as I know, never gave another thought to his decision to launch the book, not even when the University of Chicago took the occasion to discontinue its Great Books contract with the Henry Regnery Company.

It is hard to recall, in the light of later experiences, how much fun it used to be to publish a book. When I came to Chicago to meet Henry and discuss such matters as jacket design, it was automatically assumed that I would stay at his big house in Hinsdale, where over the course of several years I, and subsequently my wife and I, spent so many evenings. I should pause, in deference to historical accuracy, to record that there was a certain risk at that time in spending the night with the Regnerys. To begin with, it was during the years of their martial Quakerism—if Professor Vivas will permit the oxymoron. Translated, that meant: No booze. This was a quite awesome prospect for a young author only a few months away from Fraternity Row at Yale University. But providence has a way of stringing out its little lifesavers—and, sure enough, it transpired that across the street from Henry, in another big house, lived a most informal and exuberant gentleman, an artist named

Kenneth, who had befriended Henry and, by the expansiveness of his temperament, Henry's friends, known and unknown, ex officio. So that at approximately six o'clock in the afternoon, Kenneth would throw open his shutters and, at the top of his lungs, cry out, "If Henry has any guests staying with him, thee-all can come over for a drink." That disposed of *that* problem.

The other problem was that Henry's guests tended to sleep later than Henry's four children. Depending on my mood, I give different answers to the question I am sometimes asked: When did you stop publishing with the Henry Regnery Company? When I feel provocative, I say: Sometime after I stopped sleeping with the sister of the company's president. In due course I chivalrously divulge that Susan was then six years old, and she and her two brothers and her little sister would all four of them come into my bed at about six o'clock in the morning and giggle with apprehension when they heard the footsteps of their mother coming to relieve the beleaguered guest. I would do my sleepy best to entertain them, but they were thoroughly spoiled. Because the bed in question was often occupied by Roy Campbell, and he would begin instantly, on being boarded by the children, to improvise great tales of giants and giant-killers; and it was not long before they would find themselves under the covers with Russell Kirk, who would tell his tales of ghosts, in accents baroque and mysterious. I could not hope to keep them so much excited by tales of Keynesianism at Yale.

They were as I say very happy days, in which book publishing was something of a personal partnership between publisher and author. I remember hustling for *McCarthy and His Enemies*—a speech in Milwaukee, driving up in Henry's car with Regnery officials Bill Strube and Kevin Corrigan, Henry at the wheel, the trunk loaded with books, which we hawked shamelessly after the speech was concluded. I think we sold seventy-five books that night, and when, long after midnight, we finally reached Hinsdale, exhausted, it was with grins on our faces, as if we had drilled a gusher.

Henry has written, in a published piece, about the "dismal" sixties, which is how he refers to the decade that introduced Camelot, the Playboy Philosophy, and Mario Savio. Usually when one designates an unhappy decade, it is in order to highlight a happy contrast with the succeeding decade. But on that score, Henry is not optimistic, not at all. "The threat of extinction," he surmises, "is now much greater than it was then: those bent on destroying civilization are better organized, and the defenses are weaker." He tells us that there won't be—I use his language—any "money or glory" in it, but, he says, "we have inherited a great and noble tradition, and it is worth fighting for."

On that proposition we are all, I assume, agreed—at least, all those of us who paid twenty-five dollars to attend this dinner. On the other hand, it is also obvious that by no means everyone is agreed that this is so. It was ten years ago that I heard the most succinct statement on this point, by a fashionable young literary iconoclast who put it this way: Once upon a time, it was worth dying—for two reasons. The first, that heroism was rewarded in another world. The second, that heroism was rewarded by the memory of man. However—he said—now that we know from the scientific evidence that there is in fact no other world, no Christian heaven; and now that we have invented weapons which are capable of destroying all mankind and therefore all human memory, what reason is left to run the risk of death in war?

This is a blunt way of saying it, and by no means suited for mass consumption. After all, the average man is not absolutely convinced that H. G. Wells was that much more on top of history than, say, Christopher Dawson; or that George Bernard Shaw had the better of the argument with G. K. Chesterton or C. S. Lewis. And besides, to make the point that we have weapons enough to vaporize mankind is not to dispose of the point that just as after a war there would almost surely remain weapons unused, so would there remain human beings unkilled: so that the potential uses of heroism survive even in the secular context.

The accent is quite clearly discernible. The sharp edges of the arguments nowadays stress not so much the nuclear war that would abolish mankind, as the senselessness of war; indeed, derivatively, the senselessness of a convincing defense system. Why the Pentagon? What would be the point of it?

It used to be, finding oneself in such a corner, that one had merely to reach into one's quiver and pull out the arrow that had "Freedom" written on it. Touch it down on the skeptic, and he would waste away, like the witch come in contact with water.

You will have noticed that this does not work any more. Freedom is increasingly a subjective condition, in the assessment of the thought-leaders. Professor Ross Terrill, writing the two most influential articles on the subject of Red China, is to be distinguished from the famous apologists for Stalin's Russia, who made their way by simply denying the crimes imputed to Stalin.

Terrill denies nothing. Although he does not in fact dwell on the atrocities—the mass executions, the terrorism, that kind of thing—he does not disguise the conditions of life in China today. After informing us that there is no freedom to practice religion there, or to vote, or to express oneself freely, or to read books or periodicals one desires to read, or to change one's job, or to travel to another city, let alone another country, he says ingenuously: "People ask me, is China free?" He answers them, incredibly, with great difficulty. Depends what you mean by freedom, he says. Freedom is always defined with reference to the limitations on the group, and whereas the operative group in the West is the individual, or the corporation, or the labor union, in China it happens to be the whole state.

And he illustrates: Consider the writer Kuo Mojo. In the thirties he wrote books for a mere four or five or at most eight thousand people, and now he is required by the state to write books that will appeal to twenty, thirty, or fifty million people. "Is that wrong?" the young professor asks. Then there is the scientist whose affinity was for abstract science but who was recently directed to concentrate exclusively on pest control. "Is that wrong?" Terrill asks, anaphorically: as we begin to understand the lethal quality of the ideological egalitarianism that rushes in after practical diplomacy, such that Richard Nixon, who went to China to establish a dialogue with Mao Tse-tung, ends by likening Mao's revolution to America's revolution—ends by saying that we will have a "long march" together. And there is Nixon seated next to Madame Mao Tse-tung, watching a ballet which has become agitprop, a violation of art as well as of taste; it was as if we had invited the presidents of the black African republics to the White House to show them a ballet on the theme of Little Black Sambo. And Mr. Nixon, returning to the United States, proclaims the great enthusiasm the Chinese people feel for their government. Indeed. The Chinese government has many ways of generating enthusiasm, and no doubt Mr. Nixon is professionally fascinated by them, even as Henry Regnery would be fascinated by methods of teaching authors how to write books that sell not five thousand but fifty million copies.

We see then the movement of Western opinion: What, really, is so bad about Red China? Their ways are not our ways, to be sure, but is it seriously proposed that we should be prepared to die if necessary in order to avoid living by their word, rather than by our own—which is in any case corrupt, racist, and decadent?

Henry is right when he generalizes that it will be hard to teach people to oppose the effronteries of the modern world. Henry published a book called *In Defense of Freedom*, by Frank Meyer, who would have been here tonight except that he died two weeks ago. Even in the early sixties, Meyer's metaphysical defense of objective freedom was—somehow—just a little bit embarrassing, even to the finest of people, the finest of friends, the most ardent of counterrevolutionaries.

"If the Republican Party does not find a way to appeal to the mass of the people," Whittaker Chambers wrote me after the election of 1958, "it will find itself voted into singularity. It will become, then, something like the little shop you see every now and then in the crowded parts of great cities, in which no business is done, or expected. You enter it and find an old man in the rear, fingering, for his own pleasure, oddments of cloth (weave and design circa 1850), caring not at all if he sells any. As your eyes become accustomed to the gaslight, you are only faintly surprised to discover that the old man is Frank Meyer."

Those oddments of cloth, by a familiarity with which a few men know to hesitate not at all when someone asks the question: Is it wrong for the state to tell the writer what to write? Is it wrong for the state to tell the scientist what to study? Those few do not hesitate for a moment to say: *Yes, it is wrong. It was always wrong, is now wrong, and will forever be wrong.* The old man with the oddments of cloth is fingering some of the truths that Henry Regnery has endeavored over the years to propagate: yes, in books, some of them, that sold only five or eight thousand copies; some that sold even less. But what more can a man do than give himself to making available a book to the man who hungers for it? In Russia it costs what for many is a month's wages to buy a novel of Solzhenitsyn on the black market. And there are old men—and old women, and young men and young women—who in the far reaches of that vast country transcribe by hand, from Radio Liberty, which they risk prison by listening to, the new novel of Solzhenitsyn, word after word, sentence after sentence, a process that takes months to complete: resulting not in thousands of copies, but in dozens or perhaps a few hundred: the oddments of cloth, circa the golden age of civilization, viewed synoptically. It is worth *everything* to preserve those oddments, to make them available to those who are graced with a thirst for them: that, or—nothing is worth anything at all. Henry Regnery was never confused on this point. As long as people are free to remember, there will be those who will give thanks to those who thought, as Henry has done, with loving care to preserve the tokens of hope and truth.

National Review, b. 1955

I chose the magazine's thirty-fifth-anniversary banquet, on October 5, 1990, to announce my retirement as editor. ⟶

I *suppose that if there is a single occasion* on which a professional will be indulged for speaking personally, it is when he retires. (If that isn't the case, then *National Review* will establish yet another precedent.) When my father first saw the offering circular with which in 1954 I traveled about the country attempting to induce American capitalists to invest in our prospective journal, he spotted only a single sentence that disturbed him. I had written in the circular that I pledged to devote ten years of my life to *National Review* should we succeed in giving it birth. My father, who was very...formal about personal commitments, told me he thought this exorbitant. "Ten years is simply too long," he said. "Suppose you decide you want to do something else with your life?"

Well, the warning became moot, because there never was anything else around seriously to tempt me. For the fun of it I divulge that in 1970 I was approached by a very small delegation of what one is trained to call "serious people" whose proposal was that I should run for governor of New York; I should expect to win the election, I was told, thus positioning myself to run for the presidency. I was nicely situated to say two things, the first that anyone who had run for mayor of New York City and received only

13 percent of the vote shouldn't be too confident about winning a general election for governor. And I finally silenced my friends by adding that I didn't see how I could make the time to run for governor, given my obligations to *National Review*. My friends couldn't understand my priorities. But I was very content with them.

Oh yes, I won't cavil on that point. The magazine has been everything the speakers tonight have so kindly said it was—is. It is preposterous to suppose that this is so because of my chancellorship. How gifted do you need to be to publish Whittaker Chambers and Russell Kirk, James Burnham and Keith Mano? But, yes, the journal needed to function. Somehow the staff and the writers had to be paid—if an editorial note is reserved for me in the encyclopedias, it will appear under the heading "Alchemy." But the deficits were met, mostly, by our readers: by you. And, yes, we did as much as anybody with the exception of—Himself—to shepherd into the White House the man I am confident will emerge as the principal political figure of the second half of the twentieth century, and he will be cherished, in the nursery tales told in future generations, as the American president who showed the same innocent audacity as the little boy who insisted that the emperor wasn't wearing any clothes, back when he said, at a critical moment in history, that the Union of Soviet Socialist Republics was an evil empire. It is my judgment that those words acted as a kind of harmonic resolution to the three frantic volumes of Solzhenitsyn. *The Gulag Archipelago* told us everything we needed to know about the pathology of Soviet Communism. We were missing only the galvanizing summation; and we got it from President Reagan: and I think that the countdown for Communism began then.

Since you were so kind as to ask about my personal plans, I disclose that I intend to continue to be active on other fronts. Early this week I performed a harpsichord concerto with the North Carolina Symphony and resolved—with the full acquiescence, I am certain, of the orchestra and the audience—that I will not devote my remaining years to performing on the harpsichord. One month from today I will set out, with my companions, on a small sailboat from Lisbon, headed toward Barbados via Madeira, the Canaries, and Cape Verde, forty-six hundred miles of decompression at sea, the cradle of God; inevitably, a book will come out of this. But on reaching the Caribbean, unlike the Flying Dutchman, I will jump ship, to get on with other work. I have not scheduled the discontinuation of my column, or of *Firing Line*, or of public speaking, or of book writing. But these activities by their nature will terminate whenever the Reaper moves his supernatural, or for that matter democratic, hand, whereas *National Review*, I like to think, will be here, enlivening right reason, for as long as there is anything left in America to celebrate.

And of course, it will always crowd my own memory. One thousand fourteen issues of *National Review*. The hour is late, nearing five in the afternoon of press day, and the printer's messenger is already waiting, so we move into the conference room, the only room at *National Review* in which more than four people can fit, and Priscilla reads out the editorial lengths, and I enter them on the paleolithic calculator I bought in Switzerland in 1955, and Linda checks to see that I have got the right count. We have 1,259 lines of editorial copy but space for only 718. We absolutely need to run something on the subject of Judge Souter's testimony, but I see we can't afford the 78-line editorial I processed earlier in the day. "Rick, would you shorten this?"

"To what?" he asks, as matter-of-factly as a tailor might ask what the new waistline is to be.

The copy is spread about the room, occupying every level surface, and you walk about, counterclockwise, turning face down any editorial that can wait a fortnight to appear, and subtracting on your little calculator its line count from the rogue total. We need to cut 541 lines. First your eyes pass by the editorials and paragraphs that deal with domestic issues, Priscilla having grouped them together; then those that deal with foreign countries or foreign policy; then the offbeat material. You look down at the calculator, having made the complete circuit of the room, returning to where you began: it shows 854 lines, and so you start the second counterclockwise circuit, the killer instinct necessarily aroused: you have got to cut another 136 lines. "Jeff, shrink this one by ten lines, okay?" At *National Review* the editors always answer "Okay" when a deadline looms.

So it is done, down to length. And then you ask yourself: Which paragraph is just right for the lead? The rule: It has to be funny, or at least piquant; directly or obliquely topical; engaging of the broader imagination. I remember one from years and years ago: "The attempted assassination of Sukarno last week had all the earmarks of a CIA operation. Everyone in the room was killed except Sukarno." And, during the days when we feuded almost full-time, "Gerald Johnson of *The New Republic* wonders what a football would think of football if a football could think. Very interesting, but not as interesting as, What would a *New Republic* reader think of *The New Republic* if a *New Republic* reader could think?" Last week there wasn't anything absolutely, obviously preeminent, but ever since it came up on the dumbwaiter at 2:00 P.M. from Tim Wheeler's fortnightly package, this one about colors had burrowed in the mind.... Time is very short now. Okay, we'll lead with it. It reads:

"Iraq and the budget are as nothing compared to the firestorm following the retirement of maize, raw umber, lemon yellow, blue grey, violet blue, green blue, orange red, and orange and their replacement by vivid tangerine, wild strawberry, fuchsia, teal blue, cerulean, royal purple, jungle green, and dandelion, by the makers of Crayola crayons."

Nice, no? Orson Bean used to say that the most beautiful word combinations in the language were "Yucca Flats" and "Fernando Lamas"; though Whittaker Chambers, along with Gertrude Stein, preferred "Toasted Susie is my ice cream."

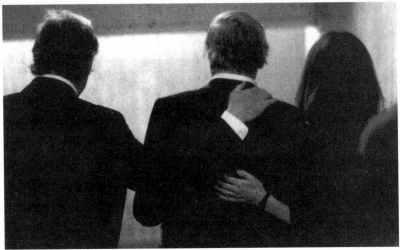

HELENA A. MARTEMUCCI

DEPARTING THE ANNIVERSARY BANQUET,
ESCORTED BY SON CHRISTO AND DAUGHTER-IN-LAW LUCY

And then you need the closing eye-catcher, the end paragraph, traditionally very offbeat; usually nonpolitical, but not necessarily. You knew which would be the end paragraph the moment you laid eyes on it, early in the day—another by Tim Wheeler, whose reserves of mischief are reliable—and now you find it and designate it as such. It reads:

"This week's invention is a sort of miniaturized zapper, battery-powered, to be inserted in the cervix for contraception and, the inventor hopes, prophylaxis. If you aren't shocked by this, you will be."

The editorials are now in order, and the line count is confirmed.

Another issue of *National Review* has gone to bed; and you acknowledge—the thought has ever so slowly distilled in your mind—that the time comes for us all to go to bed, and I judge that mine has come, and I leave owing to my staff, my colleagues—my successors—my friends, my muses, my God, an unrequitable debt for having given me so much, for so long. Good night, and thanks.

Blackford Oakes, b. 1975

On accepting the challenge to attempt to write a work of spy fiction, I had to produce a leading man. This was what went through my mind in coming up with my protagonist.　⌒

I have frequently been asked what was the genesis of Blackford Oakes, the protagonist of my novels. Critics are divided on the question whether these novels are political. There is a sense in which they are necessarily that. Politics is an affliction of the twentieth century, in which more and more power is concentrated in fewer and fewer hands, so that it becomes more and more difficult to keep politics outside in the cold, where one would like it to be.

The historical genesis of Blackford Oakes, however, was certainly nonpolitical, and I suppose that a quick recounting of the circumstances of his birth, as the catalyst of a point of view on current spy-novel conventions, belongs here.

It was October of 1974, and I had been invited to lunch by a genial editor at Doubleday, my friend Sam Vaughan. He had with him three colleagues, and we enjoyed a vinous lunch with discursive conversation in the course of which I expressed admiration for a suspense novel I had just finished reading called *The Day of the Jackal*.

"Why don't you," Sam said smiling, "write a novel?"

"Why don't you," I replied with that wit for which I am famous, "play a trumpet concerto?" Everyone laughed, sort of; the subject matter changed, and the next morning on my desk I found a signed contract for a novel.

So I would write a novel. Or attempt to do so.

I arrived in Switzerland with only a single idea in mind. And that idea was to commit literary iconoclasm. I would write a book in which the good guys and the bad guys were actually distinguishable from one another. I took a deep breath and further resolved that the good guys would be—the Americans.

I had recently seen a movie called *Three Days of the Condor*. Perhaps you will remember that Robert Redford, a CIA agent of Restless Intelligence, working at a CIA front in New York City called the American Literary Historical Society, goes out one day to buy a hamburger, comes back to the CIA brownstone, and finds all nine of his colleagues quite dead. Murdered. By pistols firing ice pellets. In due course we discover that Mr. Big, who ordered the killings, is very high up in the American government. Indeed, by the law of compound interest, if the movie had gone on another half hour, one would have been satisfied only on discovering that the evil spirit behind the killing of Robert Redford's CIA colleagues was the President of the United States.

Thus the movie went, deep in suspense. Mr. Big might have been exposed, finally, as a conventional double agent: posing as an American patriot, but actually a spy working for the Soviet Union. It transpired, however, that Mr. Big was a 100 percent American, period. And there was nothing at all unusual about him. He had routinely made the decision to eliminate all those nice people at the American Literary Historical Society because they were about to stumble on a secret contingent CIA operation—by following a lead turned up by Robert Redford's Restless Intelligence.

So finally, in a dramatic sidewalk confrontation, Mr. Jr.-Big—on instructions from Mr. Big—explains to Redford that the unfortunate killings were really all to do with high patriotism; that they were a necessary safeguard against the discovery of a top-secret plan to protect America against a shortage of oil. Stressing the importance of Redford's keeping his knowledge to himself, Mr. Jr.-Big now invites Redford to come back into the Agency and simply accept the imperatives of life...as an intelligence agent...in the modern world.

But Redford, taking off his glasses, says, "No, *never*. This very day, I have told everything to..." the camera slithers up to a marquee above the two men and you see the logo of...the *New York Times*. The director of *Three Days of the Condor* neglected only to emblazon on it, "Daniel Ellsberg Slept Here."

Mr. Jr.-Big reacts like the witch come in contact with water. He snarls and shivers and slinks away, after muttering half-desperately: "*Maybe they won't print it!*" But Redford has by now seeded the audience with his Restless Intelligence, and we all know that the *New York Times will* print it, and thus we shall all be free.

The film's production notes state, "Over a year ago, Stanley Schneider, Robert Redford, Sidney Pollack, and Dino De Laurentiis decided to create a film that would reflect the climate of America in the aftermath of the Watergate crisis."

"The climate of America" is a pretty broad term. They really meant, "the climate of America" as seen by Jane Fonda, the Institute for Policy Studies, and *The Nation* magazine. One recalls Will Rogers returning, in 1927, from the Soviet Union, where he had witnessed a communal bath.

"Did you see all of Russia?" a reporter asked.

"No," Rogers said, weighing his answer carefully. "But I saw all of *parts* of Russia."

Redford–Pollack–De Laurentiis had shown us the climate in all of parts of America. It is very cold out there.

✣

And so I thought to attempt to write a book in which it was never left in doubt that the CIA, for all the complaints about its

performance, is, when all is said and done, not persuasively compared with the KGB.

I was myself an agent of the CIA—for nine months, beginning
in 1951 when I left college. My admiration for the mission of the
CIA has never been diminished by any evaluation of its overall
effectiveness.

The point I sought to make—and continue to do so in the series
of novels that has followed the initial one—is that the CIA, whatever its failures, seeks to advance the honorable alternative in the
struggle for the world. We have had not only Robert Redford starring in a movie the point of which is that the CIA is a corrupt and
bloody-minded secret instrument of an amoral government. We
have also had novels by Graham Greene, and John le Carré, and Len
Deighton, for instance, their point being, really, that there is little
to choose between the KGB and the CIA. Both organizations, it is
fashionable to believe, are defined by their practices. I said to
Johnny Carson, when on his program he raised the question, that to
say that the CIA and the KGB engage in similar practices is the
equivalent of saying that the man who pushes an old lady into the
path of a hurtling bus is not to be distinguished from the man who
pushes an old lady out of the path of a hurtling bus: on the grounds
that, after all, in both cases someone is pushing old ladies around.

The novelistic urge of the great ideological egalitarians who
write books with such titles as *The Ugly American* has been to
invest in their protagonist in the CIA—or in his counterpart in
Britain's MI-6—appropriately disfiguring personal characteristics.
So that the American (or British) spy had become late-middle-
aged, a paunchy alcoholic, a cuckold who ruminates late at night
when well along in booze that—after all—who really is to answer so
indecipherable a question as whether the United States is all that
much better than the Soviet Union? The KGB and the CIA, when
all is said and done, really engage in the same kind of thing, and
what they do defines them, not why they do it, right?

So that when, having no preset idea of where I was going, I sat down in Switzerland to write that first novel, it suddenly occurred to me that it would need a protagonist. The alternative of trying to persuade Doubleday that I might create a new art form and write a novel featuring *nobody* struck me as unprofitable; and so by the end of the day I had created Blackford Oakes, the principal character in a book called *Saving the Queen*.

A year later, the editor of *Vogue* magazine wrote to me to say that many reviewers had denominated Blackford Oakes as being "quintessentially" American. She invited me to explain, explicitly, the "American look." I thought to reject the invitation, because I reject the very notion of quintessentiality, as here applied. The reason you cannot have the quintessential American is the very same reason you cannot have a quintessential apple pie, or indeed anything that is composed of ingredients. In all composites there has got to be an arrangement of attributes, and no such arrangement can project one quality to the point of distorting others. This is true even in the matter of physical beauty. A beautiful face is a comprehensive achievement.

So, Blackford Oakes is not the quintessential American, but I fancy he is *distinctively* American, and the first feature of the distinctively American male is, I think, spontaneity. A kind of freshness born of curiosity and enterprise and native wit.

Would you believe that three days after meeting her, Blackford Oakes was in bed with the Queen of England? (Not, I hasten to elucidate, the incumbent queen. Blackford Oakes, as the distinctive American, is a young man of discretion, who sleeps only with fictitious queens, thereby avoiding international incidents.) There is something distinctively, wonderfully American, it struck me, about bedding down a British queen: a kind of arrant but lovable presumption. But always on the understanding that it is done decorously, and that there is no aftertaste of the gigolo in the encounter. In that novel, the queen was the seducer, Blackford the seduced.

I remember even now my trepidation when my novel came out in London. The first questioner on the television show there was, no less, the editor of *The Economist*, Andrew Knight, and he asked me a question, I thought, quite un-English in its lack of circumspection: "Mr. Buckley, would you like to sleep with the queen?"

Now such a question poses quite awful responsibilities. Just to begin with, I am a married man. And then, there being a most conspicuous incumbent queen, one could hardly wrinkle up one's nose as if the question evoked the vision of an evening with Queen Victoria on her Diamond Jubilee. The American with taste has to guard against any lack of gallantry, so that the first order of business becomes the assertion of an emancipating perspective which leads Queen Elizabeth II gently out of the room, lest she be embarrassed. This was accomplished by saying, just a little sleepily, as Blackford Oakes would have done, "*Which* queen?" And then quickly, before the interrogator could lug his incumbent monarch back into the smoker, "Judging from historical experience, I would need to consult my lawyer before risking an affair with just *any* British queen."

The American male must be tactful, and tact consists mostly in changing the subject without its appearing that you have done so as a rebuke.

Blackford Oakes appears on the scene in my first novel at age twenty-one; so I stuck him at Yale, which gave me the advantage of being able to write about a familiar few acres, and, I suppose, Blackford Oakes emerged with a few characteristics associated, in the literature, with Yale men.

Like what?

Principally, I think, self-confidence; a certain worldliness that is neither bookish nor in any sense of the word anti-intellectual. Blackford Oakes is an engineer by training, the kind of engineer who learns how to build bridges, and his nonroyal girlfriend is doing her doctoral dissertation on Jane Austen. *She* is not expected to

dwell on her specialty in conversation, let alone show any curiosity about how to build bridges. The American look wears quite offhandedly its special proficiencies. If one is a lawyer, one does not go about talking like Oliver Wendell Holmes, any more than Charles Lindbergh went about sounding like Charles Lindbergh. Though Blackford quite rightly shows a qualified, if not extensive, curiosity about Jane Austen, and probably has read (actually, reread: one never *reads* Jane Austen, one *rereads* her) *Pride and Prejudice*.

Blackford Oakes is physically handsome. Here I took something of a chance. I decided not only to make him routinely good-looking, but to make him startlingly so. I don't mean startling in the sense that, let us say, Elizabeth Taylor is startlingly beautiful. It is hard to imagine a male counterpart for what we understand as pulchritude. An extremely handsome man is not the *equivalent* of an extremely beautiful woman, he is her *complement*, and that is very important to bear in mind in probing the American look— which is not, for example, the same thing as the Italian look. When Schopenhauer exclaimed that a sixteen-year-old girl is the "smash triumph of nature," he made a cosmic statement that could only have been made about the female sex. So when I decided that Blackford Oakes should be startlingly handsome, it was required that he be that in a distinctively American way, and what does that mean? Well, it doesn't mean you look like Mickey Rooney, obviously. But it doesn't mean you have to look like Tyrone Power, either. I think the extremely handsome American male is made so not by the regularity of his features, however necessary that regularity may be, but by the special quality of his expression. It has to be for this reason that, flipping past the male models exhibited in the advertising sections of the local newspaper or of *Esquire* magazine, one seldom finds oneself pausing to think: That man is startlingly handsome. But such an impression *is* taken away, from time to time, from a personal encounter, or even from a candid photograph. Because the American look, in the Startlingly Handsome man, requires: animation, but tempered by a certain reserve.

I thought of Billy Budd. I have long since forgotten just how Melville actually described him, but Melville communicated that Billy Budd was startlingly handsome. But looks aside, his distinctiveness was not that of Blackford Oakes. Billy Budd is practically an eponym for innocence, purity. Oakes, though far removed from jadedness, is worldly. And then, and then...

Billy Budd, alas, is humorless. Correction: not *alas.* "Do not go about as a demagogue, encouraging triangles to break out of the prison of their three sides," G. K. Chesterton warned us, "If a triangle breaks out of its three sides, its life comes to a lamentable end." Give Billy Budd a sense of humor and he shatters in front of you into thousands of little pieces, which you can never reconstruct. Blackford Oakes doesn't go about like Wilfrid Sheed's protagonist in *Transatlantic Blues*, or John Gregory Dunne's in *True Confessions*, being hilariously mordant. The American look is a leavened sarcasm. But careful, now: Escalate sarcasm and you break through the clouds into the ice-cold of nihilism, and that is my last word on the American look. The American must—*believe*. However discreetly, or understatedly. Blackford Oakes believes. He tends to divulge his beliefs in a kind of slouchy, oblique way. But at the margin he is, well—an American, with Judeo-Christian predilections; and he knows, as with the clothes he wears so casually, that he is snug as such; that, like his easygoing sweater and trousers, they—fit him. As do the ideals, and even most of the practices, of his country.

I remember with delight reading a review of that first novel, published in the *Kansas City Star*, written by a professor of English from the University of Missouri, I think it was. I had never heard of the gentleman, but he made it quite clear that he had spent a considerable part of his adult life abominating me and my works and my opinions. He was manifestly distressed at not quite disliking my first novel, which he proceeded to describe. He salved his conscience by concluding, "The hero of *Saving the Queen*, Mr. Blackford Oakes, is tall, handsome, witty, agreeable, compassionate, and likeable, from which at least we can take comfort from knowing that the book is not autobiographical."

꙳

What is attempted, in the tales of Blackford Oakes, is to make the point, so difficult for the Western mind to comprehend, that counterintelligence and espionage, conducted under Western auspices, are not exercises in conventional political geometry. They are a moral art.

Consider one hypothetical dilemma and reason backward, from the particular to the general, a posteriori. I give you a question and ask that you wrestle with it, confining yourself, if you can, within the maxims of the conventional morality.

Is it wrong to effect the execution of the chief of a state with which you are not at war?

Answer: Yes, it is wrong to do so.

Question: *Is it wrong to countenance a destructive event of such magnitude as conceivably to trigger a world war?*

Yes, it is wrong.

What then do you call it when it appears to rational men that the second injunction cannot be observed save by defying the first?

Scene: Uganda. Colonel Idi Amin has got possession of a nuclear bomb and plans at midnight to dispatch a low-flying plane to drop that bomb on Jerusalem. A CIA agent in the field communicates to Washington that Idi Amin will lie between the crosshairs of the agent's rifle at the airport before the bomber is dispatched. Should he then squeeze the trigger?

There are those, and Blackford Oakes is one of them, who would answer that morally wrenching point by saying two things: (1) As to the particular question, yes: authorize the agent to shoot, in order to abort the destruction of Jerusalem, and all that might then follow. But (2) do not then require as a condition of this decision that rules should subsequently be written, and then codified, that attempt to make lapidary statutory distinctions. It is not possible to write such judgments into law, any more than to specify to the artist the exact arrangement of circumstances that call for a daub of Prussian blue; or, to the composer, the exact rules that admit the striking of an A augmented seventh chord.

Blackford Oakes lives in an age when what matters most is the survival of basic distinctions. America faces grievous problems; we are beset by unfulfilled hopes and awesome difficulties. Even so, that which distinguishes us from those awful political cultures in the Soviet Union and the People's Republic of China, in which human beings are treated as mere aggregations of random clinical circumstance, to be dealt with according as said human phenomena further, or hinder, the surrealistic visions of totalitarian superpowers that acknowledge no role whatever for morality in the formulation of public policy—*that* difference, between Us, and Them, is the difference that matters. And any failure by beneficiaries of the free world to recognize what it is that we have here, over against what it is they would impose upon us, amounts to a moral and intellectual nihilism. To founder there is more incriminating of our culture than eristic scruples of the kind that preoccupy so many of our moralists.

Blackford Oakes has weaknesses spiritual and corporal. But a basic assumption guides him. It is that the survival of everything we cherish depends on the survival of the culture of liberty; and that this hangs on our willingness to defend this extraordinary country of ours, so awfully mixed up so much of the time, so schizophrenic in its understanding of itself and its purposes, so crazily indulgent of its legion of wildly ungovernable miscreants—to defend it at all costs. With it all, this idealistic republic is the finest bloom of nationhood in all recorded time, and save only that God may decide that the land of the free and the home of the brave has outrun its license on history, we Americans must contend, struggle, and if necessary fight for America's survival.

In due course we will all die. But when we die, let us resolve that we shall have died confident that those who follow us will live freely; and that they, living as free men and women, will be grateful that, at the threatened nightfall, the blood of their forefathers ran strong.

William Shawn, 1907–1992

The renowned editor of The New Yorker. *I met him only twice. He published five of my books in his magazine.*

The day the newspapers carried the news of his death, a letter from him arrived at the office. It was handwritten and had been mailed the day before he died. I quote it in full:

Dear Mr. Buckley:

Thank you for sending me copies of *WindFall* and *In Search of Anti-Semitism*. Since you are the author of both books, I am confident that I will not be disappointed. I have not yet read *Anti-Semitism*, but I've had enough of *WindFall* to see that I can read the rest with confidence. The Buckley style, the innate goodness, is intact, and the humor is undiminished. I'll go on reading. Meanwhile, I send you warmest regards,

William Shawn

Obviously he was "Mr. Shawn" to me, as he was Mr. Shawn even to authors who were older than I, and who had had much closer associations with him. From the beginning he was in his own way so very courteous to me that I took extravagant pains never to suggest that I was urging on him a familiarity he might have found uncomfortable. With almost anyone else with whom I've had fairly extensive personal dealings, I'd have got around pretty early on, never mind how I addressed him/her, to signing off as "Bill." Never with Mr. Shawn. Always, "Wm. F. Buckley Jr." I can't help believing that he knew what I was up to, and liked it.

I don't remember what it was that prompted me to send the manuscript of *Cruising Speed* to him in 1971. The odds against *The New Yorker*'s running an intensely personal journal of a single week in the life of a youngish (I was forty-five) right-wing journalist were overwhelming. We all remember the usual things, the day Kennedy was killed, V-J Day; I remember the afternoon I reached Camden, South Carolina, to visit with my mother. Frances Bronson had left word to call her at the office. I did, of course, and she told me breathlessly that Mr. Shawn had *called her up* and told her that he very definitely wished to publish "Mr. Buckley's" book— which, he told her, was "wonderfully well written and amusing"— and that he would himself be editing the excerpts run by *The New Yorker*. No other professional experience in my lifetime has so buoyant a place in my memory.

He had assigned himself, I gather from reading about him and talking with a few *New Yorker* professionals, the job of personally editing one book manuscript every year, I think it was, and whether he selected me because, by lot, my manuscript came up at the time his turn had come to serve or because, for whatever reason, he wished to edit it specifically, I don't know. But the experience was unique, a word he would frown upon unless it was used with great precision.

I use it with great precision. Others have written about the experience, but it is ever so hard to believe, even having lived through it. That part of your book Mr. Shawn has elected to reproduce arrives one day in galley form. A single column, two inches wide, running down the middle of a long sheet of paper, clipped to the next galley. The appearance is identical to cutting out a column

A WEEK'S JOURNAL
CRUISING SPEED—I

MONDAY, NOVEMBER 30TH. The car pulls in at ten, and my wife, Pat, undertakes to supervise the loading of it. This is an operation, because it has been a long weekend, during which a lot of clutter accumulates that we'll need in New York, and there is the fruit and the cheese and the flowers that would spoil if we left them in Stamford until next weekend. Angela, the maid, will go with us; and our house guest, Peter Glenville; and three dogs, *my* Rowley and *her* Pepper and Foo, the last an ill-tempered, eccentric Pekinese, a gift from Marvin Liebman, one of the two or three people I would forgive for

lem, smoothed out earlier this morning over the telephone. Sister Elizabeth did not want Manhattanville to be referred to as a "Catholic college." But, I said to the producer, Warren Steibel, that will hardly do, since the purpose of the television program is to bring together two college heads who are disagreed about the role that religion should play in the curriculum: Father Baker being outspokenly in favor of palpably Catholic Catholic higher education, Sister Elizabeth believing something else—a decision that, the research suggests, she was perhaps necessarily driven to by the Blaine Amendment, which is a part of the Constitution of the State of New York and says that no

tion of Manhattanville's Catholicism on the program, because, after all, that's the kind of thing the program is about, and if she wants to drop out, we'll go with Father Baker alone, if need be. The word comes back. Sister Elizabeth will take her chances.

We head out for New York. Pat and Peter chatter on, giggle, exclaim, while the dogs bound about, and I read the recent court decisions that have left so many people so confused about what the law demands, let alone the Constitution. I had written, earlier in the morning, the [syndicated newspaper] column I must write every Monday (and Wednesday, and Friday), and in it I thought to rebuke the House Com-

from the *New York Times* and pasting it on a long sheet of paper eight inches wide. There was no apparent reason at all for the extraordinary extravagance (in the precomputer age) of the procedure: Why did it not come to you typewritten and double-spaced, cheaper to execute, and easier to edit? One did not ask.

In the roomy spaces to the right and to the left appeared Mr. Shawn's handwritten "queries." He wondered whether this was the correct spelling of a name, whether, on reflection, one wished to say exactly this, worded exactly so, about that phenomenon, or that statement, by that man or woman. He questioned the use of a comma there, of a paragraph break somewhere else.

The author confronted also the queries of the "fact checker." No "fact" was ever taken for granted, if it could be independently verified. I remember that in one passage in my book I made a reference to a speech given by Ramsey Clark, with whom I was debating before the annual conference of the National Association of Manufacturers. I had written that Clark's opening speech was "a half hour" long. On the side, a tiny note from the fact checker: "Listened to tape. He spoke for twenty-two minutes."

But this was the first of three drafts of the thirty thousand words *The New Yorker* would publish in two installments. The second and the third drafts were completely reset by the compositor, assimilating alterations. And *they* arrived with fresh queries and suggestions. Then the great moment came when Frances told me that Mr. Shawn had called her to ask if I would lunch with him at the Oak Room at the Plaza. He liked to talk to your secretary, much preferred doing this to talking to you; or in any event, that was so in my own case. For every conversation I had with him over the telephone, Frances had a half-dozen. I acknowledge that this probably says something about Mr. Shawn, but conceivably says something about the relative advantages of talking to Frances Bronson instead of to me.

I went to the Plaza, of course, and we ate behind a small screen. I don't remember what Mr. Shawn had to eat but do remember that the waiter knew what to bring him, and I think I read somewhere that he pretty much always ate the same thing. He was genial only in the sense that his courtesy was absolute. There was only the barest amount of small talk. He wished to talk about the book he was editing, and to ask me a question or two concerning this point or the other. In particular I remember his telling me, in the most mild-mannered tones, that on reading the proofs I had returned—in most cases I had stuck by the punctuation I had originally used, rejecting the proffered alternatives—he had concluded that I was given to rather…eccentric uses of the comma. He said this by way of imparting information. It was not a reproach; or rather, not exactly a reproach, yet I could feel the tug of his great prestige, and so told him I would go back and look again at my footloose commas.

The lunch ended fairly quickly and most agreeably, and a week or two later he called me on the telephone, as he did four or five times before the manuscript finally appeared in print, to tell me, "Mr. Buckley, I really do not think that you know the correct use of the comma." I can't remember what it was that I replied, but do remember that I resolved not to fight à outrance over the remaining ambiguously placed commas in the essay.

It is not everywhere known that, under Mr. Shawn, the author was given the final say as to what parts of his book would run, subject to the space allotted for that book. On some points Mr. Shawn would not give way—animadversions, for instance, which he thought for whatever reason unfair or unjustified. "Mr. Buckley, I do wish you would eliminate that paragraph about Mr. [Jones]. You see, we do not run a letters page, and it isn't quite fair to leave him without an opportunity to defend himself...." I don't know how other authors handled him, but in almost every case, I yielded. His style was to cause the author to acquiesce in the change, rather than to dictate the change. With me this worked, though I remember a few cases in which, on other of my books, I pleaded my case through an intermediary editor, and, in all but one of these, Mr. Shawn yielded.

Three years later I wrote him to say that I had completed a book about the United Nations, but doubted he would wish to read it because United Nations life was intolerably boring. He replied instantly by phone and one week later wrote to say he wished to publish my United Nations book. I made the dreadful mistake of declining, finally, to release it to *The New Yorker* because of the magazine's ruling that no book published there could appear in the trade press until six months had gone by. My publisher didn't want to let six months go by, and so I hurried out with it, only to discover that not more than sixteen literate people in the entire world are willing to read any book about the United Nations. I was pleased to hear from Mr. Shawn that I had written the only book about the United Nations that was both "literate and readable." I appreciated the compliment even though it was not hard to make, inasmuch as at the time there were no books about the United Nations, literate or illiterate, of any kind, except an odd Brazilian memoir and a kind of coffee-table book by Conor Cruise O'Brien, designed to promote the work of some artist.

Two years after that, I sent him the first of my sailing books, *Airborne*, once again thinking the possibility remote that he would himself read it, let alone publish it. But he did, passing along, through Frances, some nice words about my prose.

Five years later I wrote Mr. Shawn to say that I had cruised again across the Atlantic, and did not suppose that he would wish to consider yet another book on yet another transatlantic sail. Oh but he would; and he proceeded to publish *Atlantic High*.

In 1983 he published *Overdrive*, a sequel of sorts to *Cruising Speed*, in that it too was the journal of one week in my life. It was greeted as a most provocative, outrageous book, and was bitterly criticized by many reviewers. I winced at the review that said that Mr. Shawn's literary judgment was manifestly deteriorating, as witness his publication of *Overdrive*. When a few months later I wrote the introduction to the softcover edition of the book, a long essay examining the criticisms of it, I sent him a copy. He telephoned to say, in gentle accents but without running any risk of my misunderstanding him on the subject, that the critics of my book had had other things in mind than the quality of the book, which he was pleased to have sponsored.

Four years later I told him that only out of courtesy was I mentioning to him my manuscript *Racing Through Paradise*, as it was inconceivable that *The New Yorker* would wish a third book by me with an ocean cruise as background. Inside of one week he advised me he wished to publish it, the last book of mine that he published.

I mentioned that he liked to speak to Frances. When *The New Yorker* check arrived for *Overdrive*, she called me in San Francisco to report jubilantly that the check was for more than we had expected. But later in the afternoon she called and said with some dismay that Mr. Shawn had telephoned her. "What he said was,

'Oh, Miss Bronson, our bookkeepers have made a most embarrassing mistake on the check for Mr. Buckley, and I would be grateful
if you would simply mail it back to us, and we will mail the correct
check tomorrow.'" That could only mean, we both reasoned, that I
had been overpaid. The following day a check arrived—for a larger
amount than the first check. Mr. Shawn had his own way of twinkling at the world he treated so formally.

An interesting postscript. When at age seventy-nine he was
forced to retire from *The New Yorker*, there were vigorous protests
from his adamantly loyal staff, all in vain. About nine months later
I said to myself: Should I write and invite him to lunch with me?
I'd never have done any such thing while he was still the editor of
his magazine, with powers of life and death over you. Such an overture might have been thought a venture in ingratiation. So I put it
very carefully in my little note to him, saying merely that it would
give me great pleasure to lunch with him but I recognized that he
didn't go out very much and that when he did he almost certainly
had on his mind a professional objective. He called Frances a day
or so later and said he would be most pleased to lunch, and a week
or so later we met at the Carlyle, and talked together animatedly.
He had read that week's issue of *National Review*. I couldn't
believe that he (a hardy political liberal) read *NR* as a matter of
habit, but I could easily persuade myself that he had made it a
point to read the current issue in order to prepare for our lunch.
(He read, by the way, with the speed of light. Everything that
appeared in *The New Yorker* he had himself read, some of it two and,
as with my books, three or even four times.) The hour went quickly
and pleasantly, and there was a total absence of ambient pressure,
I thought.

The difficult decision came one year later. What went through
my mind was this, that if I did not invite him one more time to
lunch, he might think that the first invitation was done out of a

sense of duty to a retired editor who had acted generously to me, and that now that he was so far away from the scene, I had no further interest in him. I decided to invite him again to lunch. He replied to Frances that he would like very much to have lunch, and suggested that perhaps sometime in the fall would be good. That was summer 1989. In the fall, he called Frances to say that he still looked forward to our lunch but would rather not set a date for it right away; would this be agreeable? I wrote back that of course that would be agreeable; any time would do. I did not hear again from him until the letter I received the day he died.

He was a mythogenic character, a man totally taken by his muse and by his determination to hold to the standards he respected. I hope someone, perhaps one of his talented sons, will one day produce, if not exactly a "life" of William Shawn,* then a book about his priorities, his literary manners, his immense effect on our culture, and his enormous impact on such devoted admirers as me.

---

* Several books have been written in which Mr. Shawn is the principal figure, including Gardner Botsford's *A Life of Privilege, Mostly*, Renata Adler's *Gone: The Last Days of The New Yorker*, Ved Mehta's *Remembering Mr. Shawn's New Yorker: The Invisible Art of Editing*, and Lillian Ross's *Here but Not Here: My Life with William Shawn and The New Yorker*.

Firing Line, 1966–1999

I launched my weekly television program in 1966, and ended it as the millennium came in, almost thirty-five years later. The program typically presented a single guest, every now and then two or three guests, to discuss a single topic. Three or four times a year, Firing Line *produced a two-hour live debate. One in particular I remember, from January 1978. The topic: Resolved, the Senate should ratify the Panama Canal Treaties. The guests: Sam Ervin, Ronald Reagan, Ellsworth Bunker, Elmo Zumwalt, Patrick Buchanan, James Burnham, John McCain, Roger Fontaine, George F. Will.* ⟶

President Carter's signing of the Panama Canal treaties in 1977 was vigorously opposed by most conservatives. (The most visible exceptions, among highly perched conservative figures, were one sometime presidential candidate, and one actor with a mass following: Barry Goldwater and John Wayne.) Ronald Reagan, campaigning for the presidential nomination in 1976, lost narrowly in the New Hampshire primary and then again in Florida against the incumbent president, Gerald Ford. But in North Carolina, Reagan thought to make his opposition to the treaty the center of his campaign—and he won. This propelled a heavy political movement toward him. It proved too late to wrest the nomination from President Ford. But Reagan did not forget the impact, especially among conservatives, of his stand on the Panama Canal.

My own initial opposition to the proposed treaty (actually two treaties, but always referred to together) changed after a five-day visit to Panama in 1976. From then on, after I had recorded my change of mind in a series of columns and in *National Review*, Ronald Reagan and I would from time to time genially disagree on the subject, in public and in private. Late in 1977 I thought to ask him, in a telephone conversation, whether he would debate the subject on a special two-hour *Firing Line*. At first he was reluctant ("Why should I want to debate with you?"). But a few days later, after he had contemplated my proposed format, he said yes.

Some have assigned to this debate something of historical significance. Whether this is to inflate its effect I do not know. Certainly it was of consequence in my own career—I received disparaging mail for having deserted first principles, and the stand I took is still here and there cited as evidence of my unreliability as a conservative.

One objection cited bitterly by friends and colleagues was that my public departure from orthodoxy, even though assisted by other important conservatives, shattered the notion that opposition to the Panama treaty was a position that bound all conservatives. The defections of John Wayne and Barry Goldwater were excused on the grounds of eccentricity. I happen to believe, as I wrote elsewhere, that Reagan's conspicuous position on the treaty, combined with the treaty's ratification by the Senate, made possible his election as president four years later. My thesis is that if he had favored the treaty, he'd have lost his hard initial conservative support (Senator Howard Baker suffered crucially for his support of the treaty). But—I speculated—if the treaty had *not* passed the Senate, which it might not have done if the conservative opposition to it had been hegemonic, uprisings in Central America during the 1980 presidential campaign might have frustrated Reagan's hopes.

I had suggested to Reagan that each one of us bring along two debating partners, and also one military expert, and that the principal treaty negotiator, Ambassador Ellsworth Bunker, be present to answer technical questions concerning the treaty put to him from either side. And that former senator, former judge, Samuel Ervin, recently retired from the Senate, where he had presided over the liquidation of Richard Nixon, should act as moderator.

I picked my team, and Reagan picked his.

It was after I had stared at the roster of names signed up for the debate that I recalled something the late Herman Kahn, futurist and theoretician, and founder of the Hudson Institute, had once told me. It was what I came to call Kahn's Theory of Contiguous Dialogue.

A, who believes in preemptive war against the Soviet Union.

B, who believes in tough, inventive opposition to the Soviet Union, short of war.

C, who believes in restricting any action against the Soviet Union to diplomatic initiatives.

D, who believes in generous gestures of conciliation toward the Soviet Union, attempting always to forge détente.

E, who believes in unilateral nuclear disarmament.

F, who believes that the use of any military force, in any circumstance, is wrong.

Kahn's declaration was that A could argue with B, and possibly stretch over to argue with C. Similarly, F can argue with E, and perhaps with D. The implicit challenge is to the cozy rationalist superstition that dialectical exchanges are profitable even between positions totally removed from each other.

In going over the names of Mr. Reagan's allies and my own it struck me that, to use Clare Boothe Luce's phrase, "you couldn't slide a piece of Kleenex between any two of them" as regards our antipathy to Communism and our wholehearted belief that the

United States was, and should continue to be, the principal engine by which to oppose world Communism.

And yet there was not only a division on the tactical question before the house, it was a division so deeply felt as to take on emotional intensity.

It ought to be, I thought, a perfect debate, given Kahn's Theory of Contiguous Dialogue. And its participants were very bright people.

On my side were my colleague James Burnham, the foremost (in my judgment) anti-Communist strategist in the free world; and George Will, a sometime colleague at *National Review*, one of the nation's premier polemicists, a journalist of high style and learning. My military expert was Admiral Elmo Zumwalt, former Chief of Naval Operations, and a stalwart and resourceful anti-Communist.

On Ronald Reagan's side were Patrick Buchanan, the talented author, columnist, and polemicist, former assistant to Richard Nixon; and Professor Roger Fontaine of Georgetown, a highly informed anti-Soviet expert whose field is Latin America. Reagan's military expert was Admiral John McCain Jr., former CINCPAC, the (theoretical) supreme commander of our military forces during much of the Vietnam War, and the father of future senator John McCain.

All the participants, excepting Fontaine, whom I hadn't known, were personal friends, many of them colleagues in one or another enterprise.

The question before the house: "Resolved, That the Senate should ratify the proposed Panama Canal treaties."

Reagan was the first speaker. He performed eloquently for fifteen minutes. I followed for fifteen minutes. Each one of our seconders made a briefer statement. Then the time came for the cross-interrogation.

JAN LUKAS

THE PANAMA CANAL DEBATE. FROM BEHIND WFB, AND TRAVELING CLOCKWISE: ADMIRAL JOHN MCCAIN, ADMIRAL ELMO ZUMWALT, GEORGE F. WILL, JAMES BURNHAM, AMBASSADOR ELLSWORTH BUNKER, SENATOR SAM ERVIN, PROFESSOR ROGER FONTAINE, RONALD REAGAN. (PATRICK BUCHANAN IS HIDDEN BEHIND WFB.)

ERVIN: At this time...the chair will recognize Governor Reagan and give him the privilege of questioning William Buckley.

REAGAN: Well, Bill, my first question is why haven't you already rushed across the room here to tell me that you've seen the light? [*Laughter and applause.*]

BUCKLEY: I'm afraid that if I came any closer to you the force of my illumination would blind you. [*Laughter and applause.*]

REAGAN: Well, all right. The United States has run the Canal at no profit. We have maintained its neutrality throughout the history of the Canal. We have certainly vastly benefited Panama. What do we gain by making this change?

BUCKLEY: Well, what we gain by making this change, to quote myself, is increased security and increased self-esteem. I understand the arguments you use in opposition to the treaty, but I do think that some of them are based on factual misconceptions. It would be useful to ask Ambassador Bunker to straighten you out— if I may put it thus bluntly.

BUNKER: The question which Mr. Buckley addressed, and which you mentioned, Governor Reagan, had to do with the question of our [continuing] right to take any action necessary to protect the Canal, and to protect the neutrality of the Canal, and the question of our rights of passage for our ships. Now, as you'll recall, the Declaration of Understanding agreed to by President Carter and General Torrijos in October [1977] specifically spells out the right—*our* right—to take *any* action against any threat to the Canal or *any* action against [any threat to] the neutrality of the Canal, and [specifies] that we [alone] are the judge of that. It does not include the right of [U.S.] intervention in the internal affairs of Panama, and that we made clear because [any such intervention] is against the United Nations Charter. With regard to expeditious passage of ships, the declaration stipulates that our ships are entitled to expeditious passage and, in case of emergency, to go to the head of the line, which lets them move in ahead of *any* of the other ships.

BUCKLEY: So, Governor, put *that* in your pipe and smoke it! [*Laughter.*]

REAGAN: To simply sign a statement between the current two presidents, outside the treaty, I think, has no bearing whatsoever. It has no legal weight, and what's to happen when there are two different presidents, and someone is running Panama who never was a party to all of this?

BUNKER: Our legal opinion is that they do have weight in the interpretation of the treaties.

REAGAN: Okay, we're in disagreement on that. Am I still asking questions? Thank you, Mr. Ambassador.

ERVIN: You have about two more minutes.

REAGAN: Bill, the next question is, If the Canal is so unimportant to us commercially, defense-wise, or whatever, why don't we just *give* it to them? Why do we *pay* them to take it off our hands? And if it *is* important to us, why don't we *keep* it?

BUCKLEY: You have outlined nonexclusive alternatives. In the first place, under the projected treaty there would be a net income to the United States for the next twenty-two years. In the second place, under the projected treaty, there would be a period of orderly transition during which power gradually accumulates in the Panamanian government. I would like to, if I may, supplement my answer to your question by reasserting that there *is* an importance to the Canal, but that its importance is precisely *protected* by that treaty. And let me ask Admiral Zumwalt to give the military reasons why this is so.

ZUMWALT: The military reasons why...?

BUCKLEY: Why it is so that our security is *enhanced* by this treaty.

ZUMWALT: The situation, in thumbnail, is the following. The United States has surrendered strategic nuclear superiority to the Soviet Union. This means that *conventional* military war is likelier. It means that, as both you and Governor Reagan have said, the need for the Panama Canal is *vital*. We *must* be able to deploy ships from one ocean to another in choosing which of our allies we will save, because we can't save them all. The best security—the best certainty—the likeliest probability of being able to use that canal is to have a friendly regime in support of the operation rather than a hostile regime. Those of us who have had to deal with insurgencies—as I did in Vietnam—can tell you that it is impossible to defend that canal, as all the Joint Chiefs have agreed, against a hostile insurgency and that the odds are greatly increased that that insurgency would occur if the United States fails to ratify these treaties.

> Ronald Reagan had so far focused his fire on two general points. The first was that the canal historically and legally belonged to the United States (on this I think he was indisputably correct). The second was a series of tactical objections to deficiencies in the treaty, among them what he thought was the preeminent right of the United States, acting unilaterally, to move to protect the canal against abuse. Although Ambassador Bunker dented his second argument, Reagan profited by clinging closely to his first.

ERVIN: The chair now extends to Mr. Buckley the right to interrogate Governor Reagan for seven minutes.

BUCKLEY: Governor, do I understand you to say that you are considerably influenced in your opposition to this treaty because of your dislike of Torrijos? [Omar Torrijos was the left-leaning strongman, undisputed boss of Panama.]

REAGAN: No, but I think we have to recognize that we're talking about the thing that our country has always deplored. We're talking about a dictator, and we have no assurance that he represents the thinking of the people of Panama.

BUCKLEY: Well, let me ask you to give me the answer to a question which you cannot document, but in which I permit you to consult only your insight. Would you guess that the Panamanian people would prefer, or not prefer, to exercise sovereignty over their own territory? Take as long as you want to answer that. [*Laughter and applause.*]

REAGAN: I was just sitting here wishing that I had with me the transcript of the impassioned plea that was made to United States senators at a meeting of the Civic Council a week or so ago in Panama. The Civic Council is made up of representatives of all the towns in the Canal Zone. The speaker was a black—a Panamanian, not an American. His father, a West Indian, worked on the canal, in building the canal. The speaker had worked all his life on the canal, and his impassioned plea was, even though he was a Panamanian, "Don't! Don't do this! Don't ratify those treaties!"

I could quote the *Chicago Tribune* reporter who did a man-on-the-street thing in Panama with many Panamanians—some refused to give their names, but they answered. But many of them were so outraged that they didn't care. They gave their names even though relatives and friends were pulling at their sleeves and saying, "Don't answer! You'll go to jail!"

BUCKLEY: If what you're saying, Governor, is that Torrijos has *enemies*, it seems to me that you do not need to say that at any length because I concede that he does. Among his enemies are yourself and myself and anybody who has any respect for human freedom. But it is a worldwide phenomenon that irrespective of the ugly character of the ruler, people do desire independence. They do desire sovereignty. There were Russians who fought even under Stalin and fought to the death to defend their territory. Why is it that those impulses which you so liberally recognize as beating in the breasts of people all over the world should suddenly stop beating in Panama because of Torrijos?

REAGAN: Well, I have to ask, Bill, whether this [urge for independence] is all that strong on the part of the people. As I've said before, we deal with a government that does not represent the will of the people. The people never had a chance to express their will, and—

BUCKLEY: But it was before Torrijos became the dictator that the initial riots took place demanding an assertion of that sovereignty. How do you account for that?

REAGAN: I think the first time that it was expressed was in 1932 in the charter of the new Communist Party of Panama. They put as one of their top objectives the taking over of the canal.

BUCKLEY: Are you saying that the Communists invented patriotism in Panama?

REAGAN: No, no.

BUCKLEY: Yes. Well, you really tried to say that.

REAGAN: No. [*Laughter and applause.*] No, Bill, I really didn't, but I also have to point out something else about this. The canal and Panama are Siamese twins. Neither one could have been born without the other, and ninety percent of all of the industry and the population of Panama is on one side of that canal. We have the right to sovereignty, as we say, by that treaty. Panama had the worst riots of all in 1964. More than a score of people were killed. Yet not one move was made to attempt to sabotage the canal. Business didn't stop for one second, and a statement was made about those riots that said, "Led by persons trained in Communist countries for political action." The government of Panama, instead of attempting to restore order, was, through a controlled press, TV, and radio, inciting the people to attack and to violence.

BUCKLEY: Who was it who taught the people who did the Boston Tea Party how to exercise violence?

REAGAN: Well, the gentleman who [recounted what was done] is Mr. Bunker, and I think it's a very eloquent statement and description of what took place in 1964. [*Applause.*]

BUCKLEY: In making that statement Mr. Bunker was reiterating a statement made at some length by Professor James Burnham in his book *The Struggle for the World*, showing exactly how the Soviet Union would attempt to take over patriotic movements. But to attempt to take them over does not mean necessarily to contaminate them, and the notion that someone who wants freedom for Panama wants freedom for Panama because he is being manipulated by the Communists is the kind of talk that belongs in Belmont, Massachusetts [home of the John Birch Society, renowned at the time for imputing pro-Communist motivation to liberal movements], not at the University of South Carolina [whose facilities we were using]. [*Applause.*]

REAGAN: But I think—to answer your question, Bill—I think that there are alternatives which would benefit the people of Panama, at the same time that we preserved our right to protect the canal for our own national security, and the security of the hemisphere. And so far no one has suggested any way that this can be done unless we retain the right of sovereignty that we have in the Canal Zone.

I recognize that there are irritation points. I was going to suggest that I think long before now the Americans should have offered the people of Panama who are arrested for crimes in the Panama Canal Zone the choice of whether they wanted to be tried in our courts or be returned to their own country for trial in their own. I think it would be offensive to us to have our people tried in Panamanian courts, which they will be as soon as the treaties are ratified.

BUCKLEY: Well, Governor, the Status of Forces Treaty—

ERVIN: The chair hates to interrupt, but the chair will now be compelled by the compunction of time to recognize Patrick Buchanan to interrogate William Buckley.

REAGAN: Thank you, Mr. Chairman. [*Laughter.*]

BUCHANAN: Mr. Buckley, you've spoken eloquently, as usual, about Panamanian pride and Panamanian patriotism. Now I'd like to ask you about American pride and American patriotism. As you've suggested, those treaty negotiations were begun in 1964 by virtue of Panamanian riots which were or were not Communist-inspired. They've been concluded under a threat of sabotage and guerrilla warfare, which has been discussed [earlier] this evening. Now, is it realistic to suggest that American prestige will rise if, *under these conditions*, the United States walks away from that canal, surrenders money, territory, military bases, the Canal Zone, and the canal itself? Secondly, is it realistic—

BUCKLEY: No, no. One at a time, please.

BUCHANAN: All right.

BUCKLEY: The answer to the first is that if *you* were the president of the United States and concluded the treaty—handed over the instrument of ratification to General Torrijos with such a statement as you just finished making—the answer is, No, American prestige would not rise. On the other hand, if *I* were president and I handed over the identical treaty, my answer is, Yes. The prestige of the United States is increased, in my judgment, when we show by our acts that we believe in our own rhetoric.

BUCHANAN: Was the prestige of Great Britain enhanced after it turned over the Suez Canal to Egypt?

BUCKLEY: It didn't turn it over. One of the confusions of Governor Reagan has to do with that. What happened was that the Suez Company was an Egyptian corporation whose shareholders were Englishmen and French. It was nationalized. There is a general understanding that you can nationalize a corporation registered under the laws of your own country. What we're talking about is not a corporation. It's a United States agency. The Panamanians would no more have the right to nationalize the Panama Commission, as specified under this treaty, than they would the Statue of Liberty.

BUCHANAN: One final comment—or question, rather. Given the conditions under which we're departing—the threat of sabotage and the like—is it realistic to think that the United States would send the Marines into the Panama Canal Zone after Panama takes control of the Zone in 1980 if, for example, Panama then closed the canal, or blacklisted vessels going to and from such pariah states as South Africa, Chile, and Taiwan?

BUCKLEY: It would if we had a self-respecting president. If you ask will we have a self-respecting president [after] 1980, the answer—

BUCHANAN: Do we?

BUCKLEY: —is I don't know.

BUCHANAN: Do you *know* who will be in the office [after] 1980?

BUCKLEY: Do you mean, Would President Carter, as commander in chief—

BUCHANAN: And would the Senate support him?

BUCKLEY: —would he assert American rights in the Panama Canal? In my judgment he would. Yes, sir.

BUCHANAN: With regard to South Africa and Chile?

BUCKLEY: Excuse me?

BUCHANAN: With regard to South African and Chilean vessels, or vessels going to and from those two pariah countries?

BUCKLEY: We have a guarantee that antedates this treaty to see to it that nondiscriminatory passage is guaranteed. It's the Hay-Pauncefote Treaty.

BUCHANAN: Right, but do you think American Marines would *go in* to guarantee passage to vessels headed for South Africa?

BUCKLEY: You're asking me a question that has nothing to do with the language of the treaty.

BUCHANAN: It has to do with Panamanian control of its own—

BUCKLEY: Because whether they would or they wouldn't has nothing to do with what we're discussing tonight. If we *don't* pass the treaty, we have identical obligations in respect of the question you ask as if we *do* pass the treaty. Am I correct, Mr. Bunker?

BUNKER: That's correct.

BUCHANAN: In 1980 Panama will have full control, as I understand it, of both sides of the Canal Zone. Is that correct, Ambassador? In 1980—if the treaty is passed, in thirty months Panama gets full control of both sides of the Canal Zone?

BUNKER: Full jurisdiction.

BUCHANAN: Jurisdiction, right.

BUNKER: Yes.

BUCHANAN: Suppose they say—in response to a call of the General Assembly—that this canal is to be closed to all vessels that travel to and from South Africa. Do you think the United States would really act under those circumstances, having left Panama under the circumstances under which we're leaving right now, which is in response to riots in '64, to threats of sabotage and threats of guerrilla warfare?

BUNKER: Panama will have jurisdiction over the Zone, but we will have rights to use the lands and waters necessary to protect the canal.

BUCHANAN: Do you think we would—again, in response to my question—do you think the United States *would* send in the Marines under those conditions, given the conditions under which we've departed?

BUNKER: I think they would, yes.

BUCHANAN: Do you think *Carter* would send in the Marines?

Buchanan had a pretty good point there. It would be easier, in the future, for any president to assert operational control over an area he already commanded than to send down the Marines to do it afresh. A legitimate objection, I thought.

ERVIN: The chair will now recognize Mr. Burnham.

BURNHAM: I'd like to try to single out one specific question and put it as just a single actual event—not in terms of abstraction. Now, we've said a good deal about this matter of the priority of our vessels under an emergency, so let's try to see what might happen. Suppose that a red alert or ultimate emergency was declared and the naval forces in the Caribbean were ordered to transit the canal immediately, and let's say that Ronald Reagan is the commanding admiral. Now, how would he proceed?

Will he send a message to the Port Authority and say, "Well, I'd like authorization to send my ships through on the double, and sort of get to the head of the line?" And then if he hears in reply, "Well, I'm very sorry, but under my interpretation of the treaty that was signed in 1978, I don't interpret it to give you that right, and I'm afraid we've got eighty-three shrimp boats and we've got nineteen tankers and we've got a number of ships and we've got three canoes that are ahead of you, and if you'd just sign the list, then you'll be in line here, and it'll take about sixty-four hours." Now, is the reply of the commanding admiral going to be "Oh, yes, sir. Thanks very much. I am following your instructions; please let me know a couple of hours ahead of time when our turn will come"?

REAGAN: Well, Mr. Burnham, I think you're ignoring a physical fact that those other ships aren't sitting on a shelf waiting to go through. They're in the way of those American ships. A captain is going to have to pull up an anchor and move to get out of the way, and how does an American naval officer— And incidentally, thank you for the promotion. I was a captain of cavalry—horse cavalry. There is a very physical fact that ships will be in the water, in the roadway, off the entrance of the canal, in the canal itself, in the locks going through— and what do we do about them? We can't blow them up.

BURNHAM: If I may ask, then, what does the treaty have to do with it one way or another?

REAGAN: Well, no, no. If the American ships had the right, then those ships that were there in the way would *have* to turn, reverse course, and get out of the way to let us through. But if the American ships don't have the right, the captain may order it, but I'm quite sure the captain's not going to fire on an unarmed merchant vessel or tanker.

BURNHAM: Well, I've known admirals who sometimes give those orders, too.

> Burnham, I thought, had also scored. It usually doesn't matter, in the chaos associated with an emergency, whether there is or isn't a treaty.

ERVIN: The chair will have to interrupt and recognize Dr. Fontaine for a question.

FONTAINE: Thank you, Senator. Mr. Buckley, let me see if you share a worry—another worry—that I have. I know you are, in fact, worried about the character of public enterprise in Panama, but another worry—and that's this. Under the treaty, we will have a gradual phasing out of American technicians and managers. Within thirty months they will fall under the jurisdiction of Panamanian courts and police—perhaps I could say, "fall into the clutches of," because that's how the American workers view it. Now, at this point, some twenty-five or thirty percent of the work force in the Canal Zone are Americans. They're also the top managers and the most skilled technicians, dredge operators, canal pilots, and that sort of thing. According to reliable polls, some seventy percent of that American workforce will leave on treaty day. Are you concerned, as I am and some others in the Senate, that the guarantees to the American workforce provided under the present treaty are not very adequate and that perhaps radical surgery of the present treaty would be wise?

BUCKLEY: Mr. Fontaine, I was asked tonight whether I would vote for the treaty or against it, and my answer is I would vote for it. If you say, "Are there ways in which it might be improved?" my answer is, Obviously there are certain ways in which it might be improved. For instance, rather than give the Panamanians ten million dollars, I would rather give them nine million. Rather than give them nine million, I'd give them eight million. The fact of the matter is that we have come out of a *negotiation*. We have not come out of a situation in which Mr. Bunker went down there and said, "I am going to vouchsafe you the following." If you are suggesting that Mr. Bunker acted unreasonably, then you are required to say that the Status of Forces Treaties under which our men overseas have operated for thirty years [are] unreasonable, and you also have to say that it is unreasonable for Ambassador Bunker to have worked into the treaty a provision that allows Americans convicted of crimes under Panamanian law to serve out their sentences in United States jails.

FONTAINE: But you're not saying that the possibility or even the probability of—well, let's not even say seventy percent, let's say fifty percent—is a detail like the difference between one or two million dollars. For example, if fifty percent of the highly skilled technicians and managers left, there would be *no* functioning and operating canal.

BUCKLEY: Well, may I set your mind at ease? Seventy percent of Americans are not going to quit, and one of the reasons they're not going to quit is because they did something very smart down there— something that as of October of last year they hadn't thought to do. The [U.S.] guaranteed the American working force permanent employment for the rest of their working lives under similar, if not exact, conditions. That is what the people in [the] Panama [Canal Zone] primarily wanted. That's what they told me they wanted when I went to several meetings down there [in September 1976].

FONTAINE: Who arranged the meetings?

BUCKLEY: People who are violently opposed to any change in the status quo. [*Applause.*]

ERVIN: The chair recognizes George Will.

WILL: Governor, I think we're all struck by how narrow, really, are our differences here and that we all accept that the world is dangerous and the canal is essential, and both are apt to remain the same. But in that regard, I'd like you to address yourself to a statement made earlier by Admiral Zumwalt, which is—if I can embroider it just a bit—that there's a sense in which, given the widespread technology for freelance violence in the world and the ideology of terrorism, isn't it the case that it's easier for the United States to protect Europe than it is to protect this canal—to keep it functioning? That is, of all the crucial waterways, the choke points, as it were, that Admiral McCain mentioned, only the locks on the Panama Canal make it so terribly vulnerable. Therefore, is it not conservative, reasoned, hardheaded prudence to rewrite the treaties, as Mr. Bunker and others have done, to give the Panamanians a greater psychic and economic stake in maintaining and defending those [locks]?

REAGAN: Well, no, and I don't think it's all that difficult. The Panama Canal is not something—as one of the advocates of the treaty said—that a man with a stick of dynamite stuck in his belt can disable. There are some vulnerable points. The locks, of course, and the dams for the lakes that provide the water, the tens of millions of gallons of water that it takes to put a ship through the locks, but you're talking about something—a lock gate is made of steel. It's about seven feet thick. They've survived an earthquake, a very severe earthquake, virtually right after they were installed.

ERVIN: The chair is going to have to interrupt. Personally, I wish this debate could go on till the last lingering echo of Gabriel's horn trembled into ultimate silence, but we are prisoners of time, and at this time, the chair is going to call on Governor Ronald Reagan for his rebuttal and going to give the very sad advice that it has to end at strictly 10:44.

REAGAN: I have how long?

ERVIN: It's about ten minutes.

REAGAN: Oh, for heaven's sake. I don't know if I've got that much to say, Mr. Chairman.

Well, Mr. Chairman, and ladies and gentlemen: I think, again, we come back to the original premise that I was making here, and I would start, I think, with the question that I was unable to answer just now—the defensibility of the canal. If we're talking nuclear defense of the Panama Canal—if a missile is to come in aimed at the Panama Canal—then no [you can't defend it]. But you have to ask yourself, in the event of a nuclear war, who's going to waste a missile on the canal? They'll be dropping missiles on New York, Chicago, San Francisco, Los Angeles, and so forth, and it would be a waste of time to use that. So we come down to conventional warfare and we come down to sabotage.

I claim that the United States, with a military force trained on the ground, which has defended the canal against any attempt at sabotage through four wars, recognizing the fact that it's going to take more than a single saboteur slipping in in the night with a hand grenade or an explosive charge—it's going to take a trained demolition team, with plenty of time to work and no interruption, to do something to disable the gates, the locks, and so forth. Or the other means of sabotage would be to assault the dams that hold back the lakes—a two-hundred-square-mile lake, for one; there're three lakes—that provide the water that, through gravity flow, floods these locks. Now, I submit that with an American armed force on hand guarding those vulnerable points, they are far safer than if the Panamanians are in charge and the Americans are not there, and the sabotage we could expect would come from people within the ranks of the Panamanians. I don't know who else it would be.

We do also know that there are elements in Panama who have said that these treaties are unsatisfactory to them because they take twenty years [before Panama gets full sovereignty], [that] they want the canal *now*, and that they're going to riot and cause trouble unless they're given the canal now. But I think we come back to the point that is at issue. Yes, there is a problem—sensitivity to the Panamanian people, to what they want, to their pride. I agree with that, but also, on our side, is a responsibility we cannot abdicate—to protect and make sure that the canal remains open to all shipping and that it is there for the defense of this hemisphere and of our own nation.

Now, we have to face the Panamanians in a negotiation, *not* because we've been threatened that they're going to cause trouble—I say that this is one of the first things that should have called off the negotiations. When they threatened violence, I believe the United States should have said to them, "We don't negotiate with anyone under threats. If you want to sit down and talk in a spirit of goodwill, we'll do it." [*Applause.*] But we go back now and say, "If we can find a way that ensures our right to the security the canal must have, we'll do everything we can to find a way to erase the friction points"—some of which I pointed out and was pointing out there in my previous remarks. The canal is not a natural resource of Panama that has been exploited by the United States. We haven't taken minerals out of the Canal Zone. We haven't plundered it. We've gone in for one purpose and one only—the one the treaty called for: to build and operate a canal, and I don't know of anyone who has benefited more than the people of Panama. Their ships even have an advantage in the tolls that they must pay, as do the ships of Colombia.

We're dealing with a government that, as I've said repeatedly here, has not been elected, and with a dictatorship that has accumulated the highest per capita debt in nine years of any nation in the world. Thirty-nine percent of the Panamanian budget goes to service that debt. If our debt was comparably that size, it would have to be five times as big as it is right now,* and it's already seven hundred million dollars—seven hundred billion. That was a big slip. [*Laughter.*]

I don't believe that in Latin America we would do anything to strengthen our position by, again, yielding to this unpleasantness in this treaty. I think, if anything, we would become a laughingstock by surrendering to unreasonable demands, and by doing so, I think we cloak weakness in the suit of virtue. This has to be treated in the whole area of the international situation. The Panama Canal is just one facet of our foreign policy, and with this treaty, what do we do to ourselves in the eyes of the world, and to our allies? Will they, as Mr. Buckley says, see that as the magnanimous gesture of a great and powerful nation? I don't think so, not in view of our recent history, not in view of our bug-out in Vietnam, not in view of an administration that is hinting that we're going to throw aside an ally named Taiwan. I think that the world would see it as, once again, Uncle Sam putting his tail between his legs and creeping away rather than face trouble. [*Applause.*]

I think that Professor Fontaine was right to question the ability of the Panamanians to run this. This particular administration of Panama has started three sugar mills, a hydroelectric project, an airport, a public transportation system, a resort island, an agriculture

---

* By 1987 U.S. debt was three times our debt in 1977.

development program, and an exploration for natural resources, and has failed in every one of them.

But, again, I come down to the basic argument of whether we, as a great nation, return to Panama and say, "We cannot forsake this one responsibility. Now here are the things that we are prepared to do, and if you have any other suggestions do them in negotiation." But I submit, with all due respect to those who negotiated, I think they were put in an untenable position. I think our negotiators did the best they could under a circumstance in which they were sent there not to negotiate, but literally to concede as little as they had to in order to pacify the demands of the dictator and to avoid violence. [*Applause.*]

ERVIN: The chair recognizes William Buckley, and he has to do like he did to Governor Reagan. He's got to give you a warning. You've got to stop at exactly 10:54.

BUCKLEY: Mr. Chairman, Governor Reagan. James Thurber once said, "You know, women are ruling the world, and the reason they're ruling the world is because they have so insecure a knowledge of history." He said, "I found myself sitting next to a lady on an airplane the other day who all of a sudden turned to me, and she said, 'Why did we have to pay for Louisiana when we got all the other states free?'

"So," he said, "I explained it to her." He told her, "Louisiana was owned by two sisters called Louisa and Anna Wilmot, and they offered to give it to the United States, provided it was named after them. That was the Wilmot Proviso. But President Winfield Scott refused to do that. That was the Dred Scott Decision."

She said, "Well, that's all very well, but I still don't understand why we had to pay for Louisiana." [*Laughter.*]

Now, intending no slur on my friend Ronald Reagan, the politician in America I admire most, his rendition of recent history and his generalities remind me a little bit of that explanation of how the state of Louisiana was incorporated into this country.

He says we, in fact, don't negotiate under threats, and everybody here bursts out in applause. The trouble with *that* is that it's not true. We *do* negotiate under threats. Ninety-nine percent of all the negotiations that have gone on from the beginning of this world have gone on as a result of threats, as the result of somebody saying, "If you don't give me a raise, I threaten to leave my job." That's a threat, isn't it? What do you call what we did to George III? It was a most convincing threat. The fact of the matter is that there are people in Panama who don't accept the notion of Governor Reagan about the undisputed, unambiguous sovereignty that the United States exercises over that territory.

In 1948, the Supreme Court of the United States, in one of its decisions—*Vermilya-Brown Co.* v. *Connell*—made the following reference. "Admittedly, Panama is territory over which we do not have sovereignty." 1948. In 1928, in the Luckenback Steam Company case, the Canal Zone was referred to by the Supreme Court as a place in which there were no foreign ports. William Howard Taft said to Panama that we had "not the slightest interest in colonizing." [John Foster] Dulles said to the United Nations in 1946, "Panama is sovereign." In 1936, we reaffirmed the titular sovereignty of Panama. Children born of foreign parents in Panama don't become Americans. We do have there the absolute right, which I do not deny and which my colleagues do not deny, to stay there as long as we want. But to say that we have sovereignty, as Governor Reagan has said, is to belie the intention of the people who supervised our diplomacy in the early part of the century, and it is also to urge people to believe that we harbor an appetite for colonialism which we shrink from, having ourselves declared in the Declaration of Independence principles that were not only applicable to people fortunate enough to be born in

Massachusetts or in Connecticut or in New York or in Virginia, but people born everywhere.

And all of a sudden we find that we resent it when people say that they're willing to fight for *their* freedom. There was fighting done within a hundred yards of where we're standing here because the people of the South felt that they wanted their freedom from the Union. We fought back, and it continues to be an open question whether there was successful diplomacy in the course of resisting that insurrection. But who is to [say] that the people who backed up their demands for freedom by saying they were willing to die for them are people for whom we should feel contempt? I don't feel that contempt, Mr. Chairman, and I don't think the American people feel that contempt either.

I think that Governor Reagan put his finger on it when he said the reason this treaty is unpopular is because we're tired of being pushed around. We were pushed out of Vietnam because we didn't have the guts to go in there and do it right, just as Admiral McCain said. [*Applause.*] We're prepared, as it was said, to desert Taiwan because three and a half Harvard professors think that we ought to normalize our relations with Red China. [*Applause.*] We are prepared to allow sixteen semisavage countries to cartelize the oil that is indispensable to the entire industrial might of the West because we don't have a diplomacy that's firm enough to do something about it, and, therefore, how do we get our kicks? How do we get our kicks? By saying no to the people of Panama. [*Laughter and applause.*]

I say: When I am in a mood to say no, representing the United States, I want to be looking the Soviet Union in the face and say no to the Soviet Union, next time it wants to send its tanks running over students who want a little freedom in Czechoslovakia. I want to say no to China when it subsidizes genocide in Cambodia on a scale that has not been known in this century, rather than simply forget that it exists. I don't want to feel that the United States has to affirm its independence by throwing away its powers—by saying we must not distinguish between the intrinsic merits of rewriting the treaty in Panama and pulling out of Taiwan because it is all a part of the same syndrome.

Who in this room doubts that if the President of the United States weren't Jimmy Carter but, let us say, Douglas MacArthur, and if the chairman of the Joint Chiefs of Staff were Curtis LeMay, and if the Secretary of State were Theodore Roosevelt, and this instrument was recommended to the Senate—who doubts that the conservative community of America would endorse it? We are allowing ourselves to be beguiled not by those ideals to which we profess allegiance every time we meditate on the Declaration of Independence. We are allowing ourselves to be pushed around because we express a quite understandable bitterness at the way we have been kicked around. We ought to be mad not at the Panamanian students who are asking for nothing more than what our great-great-grandparents asked for. We ought to be mad at our own leaders—for screwing up the peace during the last twenty-five years.

But do we want to go down and take it out on people who simply want to recover the Canal Zone? What we have done to Panama is the equivalent of taking the falls away from Niagara. Is it the kind of satisfaction we really feel we are entitled to, to proceed on that basis in order to assert a sovereignty which is, in any case, not a part of the historical tradition on the basis of which the Panama Canal was opened?

No. Let's listen to reason. Let's recognize, as Admiral Zumwalt has so effectively said, that we are so impoverished militarily as a result of so many lamentable decisions that we need the Panama Canal, and that we need the Panama Canal with a people who are residents of Panama, who understand themselves as joined with us in a common enterprise, because when they look at the leaders of the

United States they can recognize that, not as a result of our attempt to curry favor with anybody, but as a result of our concern for our own self-esteem, we were big enough to grant little people what we ourselves fought for two hundred years ago. [*Applause.*]

ERVIN: Tonight we have had the privilege of hearing a great debate between two great Americans, and I would just like to say this. As long as this can go on in America, America will remain free, and I would like to give all Americans the admonition that Daniel Webster gave us. He said, "God grants liberty only to those who love it and are always ready to guard and defend it." And I trust that the American people will remember that and also remember what John Philpot Curran said—that "the condition upon which God grants liberty to mankind is eternal vigilance." I thank you very much. [*Applause.*]

The postdebate reception was chilled by (a) the teetotalism of our host, the governor of South Carolina, and (b) the sad news (everyone had known for weeks that it would not be long delayed) that Hubert Humphrey had died.

❧

A few months after the debate I was headed for the Reagans' house in Beverly Hills for dinner. "Drive carefully as you approach the house," he had warned me over the telephone. "I have special instructions for you on my driveway." I did as I was told. At intervals of twenty yards there were cardboard strips hand-painted with huge block letters. They read, in sequence,

WE BUILT IT.

WE PAID FOR IT.

IT'S OURS!

Well, the Panamanians got the canal, and Reagan got the White House.

CHAPTER SEVEN

LANGUAGE

The Dictionary, Ready at Hand

I have engaged energetically in the world of language, defending some practices not everywhere applauded. The larger scene is recorded in Samuel Vaughan's book, Buckley: The Right Word. *In this section I register a few particular points, starting with the bliss of a quarry of words sitting there for us all, easily accessible by an inanimate contrivance widely scorned as the apotheosis of aridity. Of course I mean the computer, which, as repository of The Word, gives immediate gratification. I wrote about my introduction to the dictionary-on-line two years after acquiring it.* ⟶

E*ver since computers entered my life,* and in some respects came to dominate it, I have from time to time quite accidentally tripped upon a program that caused a glint in the eye of the possessor. I found, too, that he/she wasn't always all that eager to communicate the discovery. It can be that way with a special joke. Some people just don't want indiscriminately to toss it around, perhaps on the grounds that a universal knowledge of it would cause it to lose its flavor.

It is through such experiences, plus also the comprehensive generosity of one or two experts, that I've come upon programs which had the effect on me I'd have expected if suddenly, in Peru in the sixteenth century, someone had said, "Here, why don't you try this when you move all those rocks around? It's called a wheel."

It was about two years ago [i.e., 1994] that someone casually mentioned the *American Heritage Dictionary*. Years earlier I had bought the *Oxford English Dictionary* on one CD, paying an appalling nine hundred bucks for it. But it isn't that often that you build up the etymological hunger that absolutely requires you to know when, under the scrutiny of lexicographers, was the first use of "bacterial" (1871). And to check it out meant a considerable interruption in your work, or at least in my work, because I can't simultaneously use my word-processing program and my CD. What happened is that I neglected the *OED*, and indeed sometimes went to the volumes rather than bother with the CD version.

Along came this retiring soul who said to me that, really, I should get "the *AHD*." I was polite enough to keep him from hearing my groan, anticipating he'd talk about another CD. He paused just for a moment, and then went on. What he was talking about, he said, was fifteen floppy disks which you'd enter as a subdirectory in your hard drive, and instruct your working program to stand by to access it. What then happens, he said, is that you can with one (or two) strokes stare at the dictionary meaning of the word you have just finished typing.

"How long does that take?" I wanted to know.

"How fast is your computer?"

"Well, I have a 486."

"It will take about one-tenth of a second."

Even now, I am awed at reciting the conversation. Quickly I got the *AHD* and, as I installed it, found myself wondering whether it would be a kid's version of a dictionary, of no particular use to those who have passed the John–Jane–Gyp vocabulary level.

You will have guessed it is nothing of the sort. There are 361,000 entries in this magical device. If you choose, you can call in the thesaurus. You misspelled it "thesorus"? A column of fifteen words on the right gives you the nearest thing to what you were looking for, and you spot "thesauri" and "thesaurus." You can either rewrite the word or coast the cursor down to the correct spelling and press Enter. It is also a mini-encyclopaedia. When was Xerxes? "(519?–465 B.C.)". A captivating aspect of it is its spare stylistic elegance. No italics, no boldface, minimum quotation marks, a definitional lucidity hard to match.

I was so struck by its effective displacement in my life of the major dictionaries (*OED*, Webster's Third), I began to record the words I asked the meaning of which it did not have. Here is the fruit of my first two years' experience. The computer version of *AHD* doesn't have: *seakindly, apopemptic, outrance, angelism, jesuitry, roadkill, ipsedixitism, potvaliant, instantiate.* Two years' search!

And then there is the USAGE feature. After the word "hopefully" you get an essay of about five hundred words which absolutely says it all, acknowledges that the *AHD*'s board of consultants weighs in against using the word to mean, *Let us hope that*—and proceeds in a respectful, scholarly way to make the permissive case.

My opinion for years has been that the nonusers of word processing simply have to be abandoned: they are Luddites and there isn't, really, any point, after the third or fourth try, in saying to Alistair Cooke, Look, old boy, you really must do away with that typewriter...

Leave 'em alone, I say to myself. But then I think of my *AHD*. It changes your habits in this sense: most words you don't look up (a) because you already know what they mean, and (b) because looking up a word is an athletic exertion, for us sedentary types. But what the *AHD* has done to me is cause me to look up quite ordinary words, to reflect on their etymology, or usage, or whatever. I mean, I don't have idle hours to spare, but I can give you a tenth of a second *any* time, just try me. And if you question my opinion on this, don't think, after all these years, you can dismiss me simply as flushed with bridal-night enthusiasm. It is the greatest clerical blessing of my lifetime, excepting only of course, Word Processing itself, the King of Kings.

❧

Not long after I acquired the *AHD*, I was in a radio exchange with the senior U.S. liberal, Professor Arthur Schlesinger Jr., who in a casual survey of technology stunned me by saying that, in his judgment, "word processing is the greatest invention in modern history." Suddenly I was face to face with the flip side of Paradise. That means, doesn't it, that Professor Schlesinger will write more than he would do otherwise?

The Conflict over the Unusual Word

I am perhaps too stubbornly defiant of the strictures of such estimable critics as James Jackson Kilpatrick, who wars against the use by journalists of words not recognized immediately by everybody. ⟶

The editor [of Sky *magazine],* Duncan Christy, having bombarded his readers for eleven months with words judged "unusual" taken from my opera,* has decided to end his regular blurts in his magazine and has invited me to write in general about words. ("I hope such an essay would be an encomium to words, alloyed with some direct observations about why we should not let words like 'encomium' and 'belletristic' and 'valedictory' go.")

---

*DEAR SIR: What does he mean, "opera"? As in *Madame Butterfly*? CURIOUS

DEAR CURIOUS: He means "works." The word is the plural of opus—"a creative work." Best, ED.

DEAR SIR: Well, why didn't he *say* "taken from my works"? CURIOUS AND ANNOYED

DEAR C&A: He was asked to write an essay about *words*, so you shouldn't be surprised if he starts out by using an unusual word. Let's hear him out, okay? ED.

Well sure, so let me get a few things off my chest, since the question of me and words has come up before.

1. Two people of the same approximate age and similar education won't have identical vocabularies. John will know the meaning of maybe one hundred words that Jane doesn't know. But Jane will know an equivalent number of words that puzzle John, when and if he runs into them.

2. The reader's attitude toward an unusual word often depends on the context in which it is used. Two stories hang on this point. Years ago a classmate took me delicately to one side and said, Bill, *National Review* would have a much larger circulation if you would just forbid the use of so many arcane words. I told him it was his imagination that so many such words congested my magazine, and I made him a bet. Sight unseen—I said—here's ten dollars that says the next issue of *Time* magazine will have more words you judge unfamiliar than you can target in any back issue, you take your pick, of *National Review*.

Well, you can guess I would not be telling you this story if I had lost the bet. Question: Why was my friend under an illusion that cost him ten bucks?

Explanation. If a sentence or paragraph of prose is analytical in nature, an unusual word springs out at you. But when the identical word appears in a passage in which the writer is describing something, or telling a story, the eye leaps over a word otherwise arresting. Since *National Review* is a journal of opinion, most of its articles and features are, as one would expect, analytical and critical. An unusual word, in a verbally demanding environment, comes at you more aggressively.

An example.

"She was a ravishing beauty, from the sunlit hair to the limpid eyes to the full lips, sparkling teeth, and curious, tectonic smile." What kind of a smile? The reader doesn't know, exactly, and isn't going to ask,

not unless whatever the writer goes on to say about the beautiful lady can't be understood without knowing exactly what it is that makes up a "tectonic" smile, whatever the hell that is.

"In that plane the practiced eye can discern the tectonic disruptions of an early geological age." The word "tectonic" ("Relating to, causing, or resulting from structural deformation of the earth's crust") reaches out at you, and you see in its eyes the candid stricture: Buddy, unless you know what a tectonic disruption is, you can't swing with me on this one. Go read something else, or—if you want to—stick with me and see if you can follow what comes next.

The context often establishes whether the unusual word can coast by without interrupting the reader's thought.

3. The law of the advantage of flexing your muscles. The following episode is my all-time favorite, though I have never set it down before.

Thirty-five years ago my hosts took me, prelecture, to dinner at the large hotel in Garden City, New York. Our waiter, a man of about fifty, was visibly excited by my presence. At the end of the meal he drew me to one side to disclose the reason. He belonged, it turned out, to a militant labor union to which he was required to pay dues. Every month the union newsletter featured proudly the union's most recent political activities on behalf of its membership. "They are *terribly* Democratic," he complained, "and I am a *Goldwater Republican*. So when I saw you come in I really cheered."

I thanked him, and then he leaned over and whispered into my ear. "Let me tell you something, Mr. Buckley. I subscribed to *National Review* just a month ago. Now if you would do something about all those long words, you will"—he stretched out his arms expansively—"double...no, *triple* your circulation."

My friend Swifty Lazar was a very famous and, all bald-pated five feet of him, instantly recognizable mogul movie agent. He could not patronize a fancy restaurant without running the risk that somebody, usually a young pretty woman—maybe a patron, maybe a waitress—would corner him and beg for an audition. "Can I call you at your office?" she would typically ask.

"*Always say yes*," counseled the worldly Irving Lazar, "to that or *any other* request.... There isn't any civil alternative. You're not going to be able to explain to the applicant, in the middle of a restaurant, why, in the world we live in, and the way the world works, you can't just agree to give auditions, etc. etc. etc., every time somebody asks for one. So, just say yes, and let her nudge up against reality when she actually calls the office for an appointment."

"*Do you agree with me, Mr. Buckley?*" the waiter persists.

"Yes, sure," I reply. "We'll certainly try to do something about those words."

Flash forward, one year. Same dining room, same waiter (different speech). He beams when I come in. Both his hands close on my right hand. "You took my advice. It's made the magazine! Everybody can read it now!"

I was carried away by the underlying meaning of it all and smiled back exultantly. I thanked him. "It was *very* good advice you gave me."

The moral here is really liberating. The unused muscle begins to work out. In January it hurts awfully, looking at all those unfamiliar words—like the first day of skiing, or tennis. In February, the incidence of such unknown and offensive words is a little less, and you feel the relief.

In March it still happens to you, but only now and again. By June?—yes! You feel no pain at all. It isn't necessarily that your vocabulary has increased at a geometric rate. It is that the words you used to think of as alien and intimidating are less and less that, as they continue to crop up, and your mind and imagination are gradually including them in your immediate visibility range. If you are assigned the job of sportswriter (my sister Priscilla was, age twenty-two, by United Press), you gradually become comfortable with any number of words you simply could not have defined before. Exactly the same thing happens, or has happened, to the reader of the sports section. Or of the financial section. After a while you feel quite at home.

4. It's fair to distinguish between different categories of unusual words. I like the late Dwight Macdonald's nomenclature. Some words, he wrote in a celebrated review of Webster's Third, belong in the "zoo section" of the dictionary. I.e., the words do exist, but the need for them is so remote, you can—and should—keep them caged up in the zoo until it is absolutely necessary to take one out, which may be never. I know a word that describes the feeling you have in the roof of your mouth when peanut butter sticks to it, but I will never use it; in fact, I decline to disclose it.

On the other hand, it is important to remember that every word berthed in the dictionary is there because at some point one of three things happened. Either an objective thing or a concept or abstraction came on the scene which hadn't been descried before and now just had to be given a name ("cyberspace"); or an artistic hand closed in on what had been a void and the new word survives the infidelity of the season, earning its way into the dictionary ("seakindly"); or an authoritative writer simply uses the word and such is his prestige that his mere enunciation of it validates its legitimacy ("tushery").

Leading to my conclusion, 5., which is that while one can be very firm in resisting people who spout zoo words, one should be respectful and patient with those who exercise lovingly the wonderful opportunities of the language. I went downtown some years ago to hear a black pianist about whom the word had trickled in that here was something really cool and ear-catching, besides which his name rolled about the tongue releasing intrigue and wry amusement, and so I heard Thelonious Monk. He struck some really sure-enough *bizarre* chords, but you know, it would never have occurred to me to walk over and say, Thelonious, I am not familiar with that chord you just played. So cut it out please.

On Writing Speedily

The questions arise, Who writes speedily? What's lost? What did Trollope leave out? ⌣

I f, *during spring term at Yale University* in 1949, you wandered diagonally across the campus noticing here and there an undergraduate with impacted sleeplessness under his eyes and coarse yellow touches of fear on his cheeks, you were looking at members of a masochistic set who had enrolled in a course called Daily Themes. No Carthusian novice embarked on a bout of mortification of the flesh suffered more than the students of Daily Themes, whose single assignment, in addition to attending two lectures per week, was to write a five- to six-hundred–word piece of descriptive prose every day, submitting it before midnight (into a large box outside the classroom). Sundays were the only exception.

For anyone graduated from Daily Themes who went on to write, in journalism or in fiction or wherever, the notion, a few years later, that a burden of five hundred words per day is the stuff of nightmares is laughable. But caution: five hundred words a day is what Graham Greene produced, and Nabokov wrote 180 words per day, devoting to their composition (he told me), four or five hours. At that rate, neither Greene nor Nabokov could qualify for a job as a reporter on the *New York Times*. Theirs is high-quality stuff, to speak lightly of great writing. But Georges Simenon is also widely considered a great writer, and he wrote books in a week or so. Dr. Johnson wrote *Rasselas* in nine days. And Trollope...We'll save Trollope.

~

I am fired up on the subject because, to use a familiar formulation, they have been kicking me around a lot since it has got out that I write fast, which is qualifiedly true. In this august journal [the *New York Times Book Review*], on January 5 [1986], Mr. Morton Kondracke of *Newsweek* took it all the way. "He [me—WFB] reportedly knocks out his column in twenty minutes flat—three times a week for 260 newspapers. That is too little time for serious contemplation of difficult subjects."

Now that is a declaration of war, and I respond massively.

To begin with: It is axiomatic, in cognitive science, that there is no correlation between profundity of thought and length of time spent thinking. JFK spent fifteen hours per day for six days before deciding exactly how to respond to the missile crisis, but it can still be argued that his initial impulse on being informed that the Soviets had deployed nuclear missiles in Cuba (*Bomb the hell out of them!*) might have been the strategically sounder course. This is not an argument against deliberation, merely against the preposterous suggestion that to think longer (endlessly?) about a subject is necessarily to probe it more fruitfully.

Mr. Kondracke, for reasons that would require more than twenty minutes to fathom, refers to composing columns in twenty minutes "flat." Does he mean to suggest that I have a stopwatch which rings on the twentieth minute? Or did he perhaps mean to say that I have been known to write a column in twenty minutes? Very different. He then goes on, in quite another connection, to cite "one of the best columns" in my new book—without thinking to ask: How long did it take him to write that particular column?

The exercise, you see, is without validity. Every few years, I bring out a collection of previously published work, and this of course requires me to reread everything I have done in order to make that season's selections. It transpires that it is impossible to distinguish a column written very quickly from a column written very slowly. Perhaps that is because none is written *very* slowly, such interruptions as I have, during column-writing time, being in the nature of stopping to check a fact, or answer a telephone call. I write fast—but not, I'd maintain, remarkably fast. If Mr. Kondracke thinks it intellectually risky to write 750 words in twenty minutes, what must he think about people who speak 750 words in five minutes, as he often does on television?

The subject comes up now so regularly in reviews of my work that I was prompted to do a little methodical research on my new novel. I began my writing (in Switzerland, removed from routine interruptions) at about 5:00 P.M., and wrote usually for two hours. I did that for forty-five working days (the stretch was interrupted by a week in the United States, catching up on editorial and television obligations). I then devoted the first ten days in July to revising the manuscript. On these days I worked on the manuscript an average of six hours per day, including retyping. We have now a grand total: ninety plus sixty, or 150 hours. My novels are about seventy thousand words, so that averages out to just under five hundred words per hour.

Anthony Trollope rose at five every morning, drank his tea, performed his toilette, and looked at the work done the preceding day. He would then begin to write at six. He set himself the task of writing 250 words every fifteen minutes. Indeed, it is somewhere recorded that if he had not, at the end of fifteen minutes, written the required 250 words, he would simply "speed up" the next quarter-hour, because he was most resolute in his insistence on his personally imposed quota: 3,500 words per day.

Now the differences between Mr. Trollope's circumstances and mine are enumerable and nonenumerable. I write only about the former. *He* needed to write by hand, having no alternative. I use a word processor. Before beginning this article, I tested my speed on this instrument and discovered that I type more slowly than I had imagined. Still, it comes out at eighty words per minute. So that if Mr. Trollope had had a PC, he'd have written, in his three and one-half hours per day, at my typing speed, not 3,500 words but 16,800 words.

Ah, you say, but could anyone think that fast? The answer is, Sure, people can think that fast. How do you suppose extemporaneous speeches get made? Erle Stanley Gardner composed his detective novels nonstop to a series of secretaries, having previously pasted about in his studio three-by-five cards reminding him at exactly what hour the dog barked, the telephone rang, the murderer coughed. He knew where he was going, the plot was framed in his mind, and it became now only an act of extrusion. Margaret Coit wrote in her biography of John C. Calhoun that his memorable speeches were composed not in his study but while he was outdoors, plowing the fields on his plantation. He would return then to his study and write out what he had framed in his mind. His writing was an act of transcription. I own the holograph of Albert Jay Nock's marvelous book on Jefferson, and there are fewer corrections on an average page than I write into a typical column: clearly Nock knew exactly what he wished to say and how he wished to say it; prodigious rewriting was, accordingly, unnecessary.

❧

Having said this, I acknowledge that when I begin to write I do not know what exactly I am going to say, or how exactly I am going to say it; and in my novels, I can say flatly, as Mr. Kondracke would have me say it, that I really do not have any idea where they are going: which ought not to surprise anyone familiar with the non-stop exigencies of soap-opera writing or of comic-strip writing or, for that matter, of regular Sunday sermons. It is not necessary to know how your protagonist will get out of a jam into which you put him. It requires only that you have confidence that you will be able to get him out of that jam. When you begin to write a column on, let us say, the reaction of Western Europe to President Reagan's call for a boycott of Libya, it is not necessary that you should know *exactly* how you will say what you will end up saying. You are, while writing, drawing on huge reserves: of opinion, prejudice, priorities, presumptions, data, ironies, drama, histrionics. And these reserves you enhance during practically the entire course of the day, and it doesn't matter all that much if a particular hour is not devoted to considering problems of foreign policy. You can spend an hour playing the piano and develop your capacity to think, even to create, and certainly to invest yourself with a feeling for priorities.

℘

The matter of music flushes out an interesting point: How is it that critics who find it arresting that a column can be written in twenty minutes, a book in 150 hours, do not appear to find it remarkable that a typical graduate of Juilliard can memorize a prelude and fugue from the *Well Tempered Clavichord* in an hour or two? It would take me six months to memorize one of those numeros. And mind, we're not talking here about *Guinness Book of World Records* types. Isaac Asimov belongs in *Guinness*, and perhaps Erle Stanley Gardner, but surely not an author who averages a mere five hundred words per hour, or who occasionally writes a column at one-half his typing speed?

There are phenomenal memories in the world. Claudio Arrau is said to hold in his memory music for forty recitals, two and a half hours each. *That* is phenomenal. Ralph Kirkpatrick, the late harpsichordist, actually told me that he had not played the Goldberg Variations for twenty years before playing it to a full house in New Haven in the spring of 1950. *That* is phenomenal. Winston Churchill is said to have memorized all of *Paradise Lost* in a week, and he is reported to have been able, throughout his life, to memorize his speeches after a couple of readings. (I have a speech I have delivered fifty times, and I could not recite one paragraph of it by heart.)

So cut it out, Kondracke. I am, I fully grant, a phenomenon, but not because of any speed in composition. I asked myself the other day, Who else, on so many issues, has been so right so much of the time? I couldn't think of anyone. And I devoted to the exercise twenty minutes. Flat.

CHAPTER EIGHT

GETTING ABOUT

1001 Days on the Orient Express

The trip from Peking to Moscow on the Luxury Trans-Siberia Orient Express was too good to pass up. ⌐

I*'m sure it has happened to you,* the special invitation—however conveyed—to a trip, perhaps even an adventure. You stare at it for a little while, then pull up an Uzi and blast away at your calendar, leaving not one living trace of what had been commitments trivial and solemn, some of them months old. It had happened to me three times before. The first was an invitation to come along as a guest of the Argentine navy aboard their four-hundred-foot cadet sailing ship (Santo Domingo to New York). Again when I was asked, would I like to travel to the South Pole with the secretary of the navy? And then the phone call, would I like to travel down in the little deep-water sub to ogle the *Titanic*? Now the brochure from Yale University described a trip on the "Nostalgie Istanbul Orient Express Via Trans-Mongolian and Trans-Siberian Rail Lines." Breathlessly, I showed the brochure to my wife, declaring my intention to go. She scanned it, and shook her head in disbelief.

Three months later, twenty-four hours after boarding the Russian train, I wrote the following sentences.

Just in case I should forget, though I won't: Don't even *consider* sharing a compartment with your wife/husband on the luxury Trans-Siberia railway trip, Peking–Moscow or vice versa. It is hard enough on one person, even of moderate agility. They tell you these are luxury compartments—designed and built, to be sure, in the thirties. When I read that, I nodded my head acquiescently...Nine nights on such a train? So? What could be so austere about the thirties Orient Express? The swells who traveled about the world with their valets didn't really notice Wall Street suicides or the grapes of wrath. These were trains designed for them to enhance their pursuit of luxury. Indeed, the word is formally used on the company's stationery: "Orient Express/Luxury Private Train."

The temperature in the compartment, as I write, is eighty-nine degrees. There is no air conditioning. There is no toilet (there is one toilet per sleeping car—i.e., for nine compartments). There is no hanging locker. There are no drawers. In the bathroom, which is a sink, there are two ledges, one eight inches across, the other four inches: enough to hold one-tenth of your (my) toiletries. (There is ten times more vertical wall space, but it goes unused.) Above the electric socket is printed, "110V, Razor." You have anticipated a need for an alien plug for your razor, and you confidently whip up, from your kit, the appropriate one. Nothing happens. You call the Russian attendant. "Oh yes, the electric outlets. Well, they don't work. Don't work anywhere on the train." You pull out your laptop to situate it on the little desk/table, which only just accommodates it. You look about for convenient spaces to place such sundries as pens and paper clips and diskettes, but the window ledge is without a fiddle. (A fiddle is the guardrail that keeps objects like eyeglasses or ashtrays from falling off the ledge.) Forward of the table, at waist level, there are two tiny ledges that *do* have fiddle protection. But they lie athwartship. Since railroad cars, when they tilt, do so from side to side, not from back to front, these fiddles are useless; and anyway, they are out of reach when you are sitting (the only place you *can* sit). Although there is no hanging locker, you are given hangers. They are usable on the steel webbing of the luggage racks overhead. Everything you hang—jackets, pants, overcoats—dances about in the kinetic frenzy of your luxury private cabin.

SHUT UP! What *dumb* things to fret over, freshly embarked on a 4,500-mile trip across Eurasia with sights to see—great plains, tundra, mountains, lakes, rivers—that even the Great Khan never saw!...The Voice I hear is dead right.

So you crumple up your disgruntled notes and look for the wastebasket.

Only you can't find one!

So you *uncrumple* your notes and try to sleep in the heat. The little electric fan does work, and in your misery, eyes closed, you force yourself to wonder what it must be like for the wretched living outside, the herdsmen of the Gobi Desert, dry, menacing, sullen from wasted history. Meanwhile it is difficult, with the seeing and sawing, to read. You have the impression you are racing down the tracks at 110 mph. Actually we never go over fifty-five mph. How do I know? Because I do not venture outside without my GPS [Global Positioning System], and I can stick it out of the window and get speed and geographical location. Sleep eventually rescues you.

❧

It is a pretty overpowering thought, to do the great trip on the fabled rail route completed as recently as under Czar Nicholas II. The first night of travel, after three nights in a Peking hotel, we would spend on the Chinese Siberian train. It operates on a narrower gauge than the succeeding Russian train. I would learn from Alan, a fellow traveler from Palo Alto who knows quite simply everything, that the reason different countries have different gauges is to discourage invasion. When the Spaniards set out to rebuild their railroad system, in the early 1800s, they intentionally selected a different gauge from the French, to guard against another Napoleon.

After the first night's train travel we would arrive in Mongolia, about whose vivid history we would hear vividly from Professor Hal Kahn of Stanford. He told us about the Great Khan's genius as a warrior and organizer, and of the awful, workaday brutality of life & times under him and his successors (defiant cities under siege were often made an example of by simply killing, after the city was taken, all its men, women, and children). At Erenhot we board the Russian-gauged Nostalgie Istanbul Orient Express, arriving on Day 3 at Ulan Bator, the capital of Mongolia.

Depending on the seniority of your application, you are berthed next door to the bar car and three dining cars, or as many as nine cars away, in which case you must be prepared for three alpine expeditions every day. The little aggravations dog you. The electrical outlet in the compartments having failed, you needed to find juice for your computer, and there is only one live plug—in the shower car, in the same little office from which the tour guide and the lecturers address you, once or twice or more every day. But in order to hear them you have to leave your cabin and stand in the narrow passageway, because there are no speakers inside the cabins. After coping with the computer problem for the first time on Day 2, I trudged on to the bar car and ordered a gin and tonic. No ice. Why? Because, sir, the water in Mongolia is not pure. You ask why they don't use non-Mongolian water to make the ice. No answer. The air in the bar car is impossibly fetid. You think, Never mind: I will swallow my lukewarm gin and tonic and have a little smoke and forget it all; but you can't smoke. *In a bar car in central Mongolia you cannot smoke a cigar!*

You take your warm drink to the dining car. Surely there will be candlelight, indispensable to your vision of choo-chooing in the night across vast dark spaces. No. Only bright overhead lights— you might be dining at one of those buffets in Penn Station still open at 3:00 A.M. for staff and stray travelers. It is dismally hot and you ask why the windows aren't raised. You try to understand exactly what it is that the Russian steward is telling you. It has something to do with the absence of a crank handle, without which those windows simply stay shut. You sit down, and close your eyes, and say to yourself, repeatedly, *I am on the Luxury Trans-Siberian Orient Express beginning a 4,500-mile romantic expedition covering ground it took Marco Polo a lifetime to traverse. I am just now in Mongolia, where the Great Khan found himself, in the thirteenth century, master of practically the entire known world. Think about it!* If you don't succeed in igniting the enchantment of the venture in your fancy, you ... will ... go ... nuts.

ॐ

At Ulan Bator we saw the museum, viewed and heard some native song and dance, and ended the afternoon with a visit to a yurt ("a circular domed portable tent used by the Mongolian nomadics in Central Asia"). Once inside we had succor from the sudden biting cold, a wind that shrilled in from the mountains to the west. The little fire burned sheep dung. We had been warned by Management not to eat or drink anything proffered us, under pain of instant death, and so had to cope with the diplomatic problem: We accepted bits and pieces of the hard gruel especially prepared for us by the patient, heavy woman in the little tent, her four children at her side. Surreptitiously and with much evasive action we disposed of them, in my case in the deep pocket of my parka.

It was at Ulan Bator that we lost Mr. Metcalfe.

Having been almost three days without any news, except from Professor Kahn of happenings seven hundred years ago, we were riveted to learn that when time came just now to pull away and head toward Russia, a quick poll of the sixty-eight passengers revealed that Mr. Metcalfe was simply not there. Earlier in the afternoon he had elected to forgo the yurt excursion, but when Mrs. Metcalfe, his Ph.D. wife, returned with the rest of us, he was not there. She assumed he had gone out for a ten-minute walk. A frantic forty-five-minute search was undertaken, of the railroad station and points of conceivable interest in the immediate vicinity; but soon a desperate Mrs. Metcalfe was informed by Management (the principal official on the excursion was Mr. Amstutz from Zurich, superintending the Swiss-owned train) that there was no alternative to simply going on. Our train's track reservations are hallowed, negotiated with Peter the Great or whomever, and there is no *way* a thirteen-car train can just dawdle someplace waiting to find Mr. Metcalfe. So Mrs. Metcalfe grabbed an overnight bag and went off in the night in central Mongolia looking for her husband.

The business about the rigidity of the train's scheduling was forcefully communicated to us the following morning when, as told to do, we awaited a knock on the door of our compartment at "about 4:00 A.M." It came, and one of the three uniformed customs officials handed me a form. Our instructions were to complete it and await a second call about a half hour later, when we would give the Russian officer our passports. One hour after that, approximately, there would be a third knock: our declaration form, stamped, would be returned, as also our passports.

I remember remarking at breakfast to Sam Vaughan, my dear old friend, who occupied the compartment next door, that if I had the resources of the *New York Times*, I would assign a cub reporter to explore the question: Why do the Russian immigration and customs people put Trans-Siberian passengers through that early-morning ordeal? Are the officials all otherwise occupied before 4:00 A.M. and after 6:00 A.M.? Or is it just a Marxian twitch, *déranger le bourgeois*? After all, you can arrive at the airport in Moscow and do immigration and customs in a half hour, so why on the Mongolian border two hours? And before dawn? But Sam and I were becoming listless. He had contracted a dogged stomach disorder, while I tried, as it happened unsuccessfully, to subdue an energy-consuming cold. There were no complaints to be made on board. We had been thoroughly chastened, and, besides, we had Metcalfe to worry about.

Siberia. In the mind's eye it is primarily the vast frozen part of the world that Stalin thought providentially designed by God for forced-labor camps. Much of it is permafrost, too cold, in the higher latitudes, ever to let the ground thaw out. To contend with Nature's oppression, some of Siberia's factories are built on stilts. Shrewdly cut fissures are exploited as canals for the heavy east–west traffic. Siberia is immense, larger than the United States, though its population (twenty-five million) is less than California's. Its natural resources are huge: fuel, gold, timber, diamonds, furs, all together accounting for one-half of Soviet hard-currency receipts (in 1988, a net of $20 billion). Its citizens are, we learn, bitterly resentful of Russian exploitation (We Siberians, writes Valentin Rasputin, are "a barge moored to Russia that brings in its wealth of goods and then is pushed away from the shore"); but from all appearances they are resigned to another millennium or two of satellite status.

Everything about Siberia is huge. We paused at Ulan-Ude. Its most immediately memorable feature is the largest extant head of Lenin (twelve feet, nape to pate). The Russians have a difficult time coping with Lenin. On the one hand they know he is a not-so-good historical character. On the other hand, without him somewhere in the picture, they are ugly historical ducklings. In Moscow, before the happy events of 1991, there were sixty-two statues of him, reduced now to eight—it is an asymptotic exercise, the culmination (zero statues of Lenin) never quite taking place. The day is yet unknown when all of imperial Russia will be clean of any monumental memory of V. I. Lenin, whose cosmetic remains we would view a week later in Moscow.

From Ulan-Ude we went on and dallied at Lake Baikal, traversing it by hydrofoil, learning that the lake is four hundred miles long and one mile deep, and that there is as much fresh water there as the entire world consumes in five years. It nicely reflects the Siberian metabolism to hear that the lake widens by one inch every year. "So we only measure it every seventeen years."

We would spend three more days before reaching the Urals, which separate Europe from Asia, and my memory is of day after day of large open areas with birch trees, thinly populated and unsupervised, yet here and there transmuted as if tended acre by acre, making great British gardens, with soigné fir trims and decorative finger lakes. Our passage over Siberia was as long as coast-to-coast travel in the United States.

Irkutsk, the gold capital of southern Siberia, is a great cultural and scientific center. It sprang neatly to shape early in the nineteenth century, though only after some prodding—it was for a while disorderly, in the tradition of gold towns. In 1808, a governor brought in forced labor and filled in the muddy streets. Then they looked around for a professional engineer to oversee what more needed doing, but there wasn't one around. Nature abhorring a vacuum, one Gushya, an exiled convict, took over. "He terrorized the householders, especially when their wooden buildings failed to conform to the new street plan," our guidebook informed us. "If a corner or wall stuck out too far, he would have it chopped off, causing some half-sawn-off rooms to be open to the elements, sometimes for years. By 1822, Irkutsk had a new look, with fifteen thousand citizens and two thousand houses." City planning, direct approach.

It was at Irkutsk that we learned that Metcalfe lived! A native, espying a lost Western soul, had gently directed him to the U.S. Consul in Ulan Bator, to whom Mrs. Metcalfe was subsequently directed, and by the time we had news of them, they were flying home; to be sure, without their baggage, which traveled with us on the Trans-Siberian Express. I remembered that our tour instructions had included advice on how to secure insurance against missing out on the trip for whatever reason—in the case of Mr. Metcalfe, a little inopportune vagueness.*

𝛡

We had yet ahead of us Novosibirsk, the great industrial center, with its great opera house and prodigious local market, which stretches out for acres. We were being taken now to the Church of the Holy Cross. Its life had more than once been threatened. At one point, soon after he began exercising total power, Stalin had

---

* How much would such insurance have returned? The cost of a compartment on the Trans-Siberian excursion was eight thousand dollars double occupancy, but if there are empty cabins well into the countdown, you could get an entire compartment (for one) for about a thousand. (These are 1996 dollars.) Absolutely all expenses are covered, including three nights in Peking (where you see the usual sites: The Forbidden City, the tombs, the summer palace, the Great Wall, and Tiananmen Square, where the great clock tolls out in huge neon numbers how many seconds remain between now and the reannexation of Hong Kong, at midnight the last day in June 1997). And two days in Moscow, where you can more or less make up your own itinerary. Air travel is supplementary, and ranges in price from $2,500 to $5,000, depending on the class of service selected.

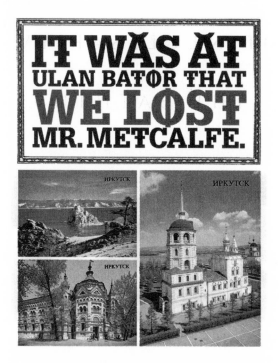

decreed that all churches and synagogues should be razed, and many were. But many also remained standing, some of them put to secular use, as granaries or whatever. As we approached the church, Olga, our guide, using the loudspeaker in the bus, described the once-threatened church as if it were a member of her immediate family. At one point in the thirties an emissary was conscripted to travel to the Kremlin and plead for the church's survival. He had been carefully prepared: he was not to make any mention of any spiritual concern for the church. He was to express his wish for its survival only because of the church's antiquity and its ornamental importance to the city. It was truly a miracle, Olga said, though there had been the downside. The church was spared, the emissary disappeared.

We entered it, high-ceilinged, the walls crowded with paintings and statues, the glass stained. And immediately on closing the church door we heard music seemingly divine: one woman's voice, one man's, with organ, it turned out to be, as the background. Three bearded priests were at the altar, saying the Orthodox Mass. I sidled over to the nave to observe the musicians more closely. He was perhaps thirty, not older; she, with her unerringly pitched bel canto, in her mid-thirties. The priests were all three of them young men. The parishioners (it was not Sunday) were about twenty, at least half of them young. There were more people at Holy Cross that day than we found waiting to view Lenin, three days later.

Some of us were ready for a little culinary diversion. The food provided on the tour was always substantial, but not much more could be said for it. At one market stand I tried to make headway, but failed to get my request over to the smiling young woman on duty. Unaccountably, a word flashed into my mind from the Russian vocabulary list passed around that morning at breakfast, and I found myself saying: *"Ikra?"* Instantly she ducked down under the counter and bounded up with two round tins, four hundred rubles. I shot a triumphant glance at Sam. *"Tonight we shall feast on caviar,"* I solemnly announced. To which end we roamed the market and collected sour cream and onions and lemon and an aromatic high-priced vodka and great cylinders of fresh bread. That night I handed the cans to the waiter to take back to the kitchen, open, and serve. I sliced the onions, poured the vodka, exchanged toasts with Sam, and waited for the plate of black gold. The waiter came back and placed our booty down on the table. We stared down at globs of emetic raw sturgeon. We tried to give it away, without much success. Do not order *ikra* behind the Iron Curtain.

Our traveling companions were about one-half of them associated with Yale, the other half with Stanford. They were mostly, like Sam and me, of a certain age. With no exceptions they were genial men and women. Social energies were, however, pretty well consumed after a day's travel and sightseeing, and the pianist who performed in the bar car found it unattended most of the time after nine o'clock (time changes were eccentric and incessant—we traveled through seven time zones). We passed by Ekaterinburg, where Lenin exhibited his Bolshevik manhood by ordering soldiers to pump lead into one czar, one czarina, their four daughters, and their teenaged son, so now we had reached the Urals. And, on the same long day, before reaching Moscow at midnight, Yaroslavl, leafy and old and self-confident, astride the Volga River, with pre–Civil War mansions and a professional choir of thirty-six singers who performed for us, overwhelming in their discipline and musicianship; then on to Moscow.

ॐ

Robert and his wife, Candy, both much younger than I, were progressively more fatigued by our exertions and those of the train, and when we got to Moscow, Robert stormed United Airlines for two seats on the nonstop to New York, where his Lear would pick them up and return them to Dallas. Robert has a wry look on his face, the special look of resignation of the Jewish comedian, cultivated most notably by Jack Benny. During the tender and charming last-night-together banquet (in the exquisite dining room of the Savoy Hotel with, however, overhead lights more appropriate to a surgical operating room), he left for a few moments to converse on the phone with his brother in Brussels. He returned and whispered out his amusement to our little company. "I told my brother about the awful trip. He said, 'Robert, you oughta know that our people shouldn't travel on trains in Europe.'"

Definitive Vacations

Asked to write (for Private Clubs *magazine) about vacations, I pondered the special joys of spontaneity.* ⌐

There is an inbuilt problem with vacations, which is that when they are carefully planned—weeks, months, sometimes years ahead—they run the risk of losing the element of spontaneity that gives them that special lift. If you know at Christmas that you are going to take off August 1–15 for a vacation touring the Carlsbad Caverns and the Painted Desert and the Grand Canyon, you have, yes, the advantage of plenty of time to plan ahead, but also the disadvantage that during July you begin a countdown that makes the magic day when the vacation actually begins just a little routinized, like when Gary Cooper polishes off the last of the bad men after shooting the first three: the wedding night, contrasted with the seduction. My father led a very busy life, as so many Americans do, and when I was a boy he confided to me his rule: "There is never a convenient time for a vacation." So? "So take a vacation whenever you feel like taking a vacation."

Granted, that's easy to say, but less easy to execute. Obstetricians can count nine months ahead and turn down patients for the period of their proposed vacation, their means of central planning. But however completely you think you preside over your own schedule, there are always inflexibilities there. Inflexibilities which

not even one of Ayn Rand's heroes could do very much about. If
you have just been elected president, for instance, you really can't
take a two-week vacation beginning on January 15 of the year
ahead, though, come to think of it, nothing in the Constitution
specifies where exactly you have to be standing when you take the
oath of office. LBJ stood in the saloon of Air Force One on the
ground at Dallas and presto! he was the thirty-sixth President of
the United States.

Extemporaneity in vacation planning is wonderful. For thirty
years I practiced a little ritual with my older sister Priscilla, who
served as hardworking full-time managing editor of the magazine I
served as editor. Priscilla is a woman who radiates a sense of fun
and humor and the excitement of a secretly shared plot. Our
exchanges over the telephone would go like this:

Me, calling either from my office upstairs or from home, in a
solemn voice: "Pitts [her nickname], what *were* you planning to do
next Wednesday?"

She always caught the signal, never mind how burdened her
schedule. It was always—without a trace of hesitation—"Next
Wednesday? Why [it didn't matter that she had a magazine closing that afternoon, a cocktail party before dinner, and opera tickets for that night]—nothing."

"Terrific!" I would respond. "I've booked you to go to Tahiti
with me and Pat for a week's sailing."

It inevitably worked, whatever it meant for her in terms of
evenings working until midnight before the next Wednesday, or,
after Wednesday week, struggling to catch up. She found it fun to
treat me, her baby brother, that way, and baby brother adored her
approach to vacations. Do you know anybody like that? The kind
of person who says, Sure! Why not! If you don't, try to cultivate
such a friend, though I guess they're rare, and of course there are a
lot of pit bosses around who don't put the same high marks on
spontaneity.

One reads that Roman slaves had no vacations. If that is true, then their regimen would appear to defy what Americans take for granted as, quite simply, a metabolic requirement. The political prisoners in the Gulag had no "vacation," but Solzhenitsyn, in *One Day in the Life of Ivan Denisovich*, made mention of the ten-minute reprieve to celebrate Stalin's birthday, or whatever, a reprieve suddenly announced in the early morning after roll call, a ten-minute delay before the daily forced march to the frozen work area. *Ivan Denisovich* is about how a human being living, eating, and working in circumstances almost unimaginably cruel spots in his schedule little fireflies of hope and surcease: the day in which two extra ounces of bread slipped to him by a retiring guard bring a carnal joy almost orgasmic; an extra piece of coal stumbled upon on the march back from forced labor, which means that for an hour that night the barracks' cold will be mitigated by a sense of almost voluptuous warmth. Such events are, in such circumstances, a "vacation" from the iron schedule of life.

We've got used to vacations, and indeed during the 1940s vacations worked their way into the United Nations Universal Declaration of Human Rights, which demands a vacation with pay for everyone. Some societies anticipated the United Nations by generations. Costa Rica, a touring political scientist counted a few years ago, had 187 days' vacation every year, the accumulation of Sundays, Holy Days of Obligation, national holidays, and saints' days, plus personal vacation time.

In such situations one might even talk oneself into thinking of a day at work as a day on vacation, my thesis being that nothing kills a vacation more surely than endlessness. This, of course, is to round the corner, when the vacation suddenly looms as a great stretch of emptiness, which is what often happens, we are informed, when the very busy very important man (seldom woman—women are more resourceful) wakes up a month or two after his retirement party to realize that all that golf and leisure and Caribbean cruising have begun to cloy. Yesterday he was a divisional commander and what seemed like all the world was there for him to deploy, whether to bring him a cup of coffee or to launch an offensive against the enemy, and now, now—they keep him waiting on the f-ck-ng phone! He can't find a porter at the airport! He forces himself to acknowledge a creeping indifference to his golf score.

The point, really, is that vacations are primarily there to interrupt the quiet, understated, indeed often unacknowledged pleasure you take from work. However routine, work is a fortifying experience, your intimate sense of your own productivity. Charlie Chaplin made himself grotesque in *Modern Times* standing by a conveyor belt that moved faster and faster while he attempted to tighten a fleeting nut or whatever; and his movie about assembly-line work made all the world laugh, including men and women who stand for lifetimes in such assembly lines and live full and happy lives. And for them, of course, there is the vacation, which might include going to the movies and seeing Charlie Chaplin in *Modern Times*.

Winston Churchill defined a vacation as "doing something different." He liked to paint, but no one who has painted has ever suggested that to paint requires less concentration of the mind than tightening an infinite series of nuts on an assembly line. A professional pianist will spend five or six hours every day at the keyboard. Here is a secret: The professional musician almost *never* plays for himself. He plays for *other* people. When he plays for himself, he is *practicing*—to play for other people. For Bach virtuoso Rosalyn Tureck, a vacation means *not* playing the piano. What would be a vacation for the politician fully engaged in his profession? Cincinnatus twice left his farm to fight for his country, but happily turned his sword into a plowshare when the fighting was over. He was not a very good politician, by modern understanding.

They don't all come that way. Hubert Humphrey's sadness came only after the public narrowly declined to make him president of the United States. He had never really taken a vacation before, hurtling from mayor of Minneapolis to senator to vice president to presidential candidate. Some friends, colleagues, and observers speculate that if he had permitted himself the experience of a vacation, he might have lived longer and might have served more effectively in high office. For some legendary people the very idea of a vacation is somehow alien. Charles de Gaulle building a sand castle on the beach? In exile on the forlorn island of St. Helena (*"ce damnable rocher!"*), Napoleon would lie five hours in his iron bathtub dictating to his amanuensis stuff nobody ever after read: for the glory mongers, there is no such thing as a vacation.

For others, there is nothing like it. I have coveted my share of this & that in life, but nothing so much as what kept me awake at night as a thirteen-year-old at boarding school in England for weeks before it was scheduled to happen. Vacation! It would mean joining my two sisters, coming in from their own boarding school nearby, and being driven to Southampton, there to catch the majestic *Normandie*, a five-day passage to New York, one month at home over Christmas! Two weeks before we were scheduled to sail, there was the rumor, communicated to me by the headmaster: a threat of a shipping strike. If it materialized, that would mean canceling the passage, and—I'd learn from my father's London agent— there was no other steamship on which we could secure passage to New York in December 1938.

The suspense was all but unendurable, but the ship did leave on time. You feel it still, the sudden relief from what you did yesterday and the day before and the day before. You are Antaeus, the Greek god whose strength dissipates menacingly until, at intervals, he touches his feet down on the ground, getting from the mere touch of the earth that jolt of life and energy that make bearable his mus-clebound mission on earth.

But I am carried away. In need, obviously, of time off. Of a vacation.

A Pilgrimage to Lourdes

I had never before gone to Lourdes. What … actually … happens there? ⸺

I *went to my doc and told him* that for five days I hadn't done any-thing much except sleep, that I had even had to abort a long-planned weekend in Nassau with my wife. "I assume it's the same old thing," I said—my refractory sinuses punishing me, this time around, for having spent twenty-one consecutive days on airplanes, flying here and there on the lecture circuit. He went through his customary motions, took maybe his 150th throat culture, and told me to come back the next day with a set of sinus X-rays, and I told him, No, that was not possible, because I had to fly the next day, and he said I was positively not to fly until after he had seen the X-rays, and I said to him, Look, doc, I have to go to *Lourdes* tomorrow and I can't believe Our Lady would make me sick en route to Lourdes, that would make no sense. He said why didn't I leave one day later, and I told him that was not possible because I was flying non-stop as the guest of a friend with a private plane.

We struck a bargain: I would agree to submit to a big-deal MRI on the spot, ten blocks away; he would examine it and (presum-ably) tell me if one more flight would be lethal. Later that after-noon I heard from his assistant. Her exact words were, "The doctor said since you're going to go anyway, we may as well let you go."

So off I went, equipped with antibiotics and auxiliary medications. If you have an eye for piquancies, here is one—that the first two nights at Lourdes I slept cumulatively not more than four hours. On night three I decided it was time for a shoot-out with whatever neurological hobgoblin was playing degenerative games with me, and so at bedtime I took not one sleeping tablet but *two*. From my experience with this drug I had long since concluded that it must have been the stuff they gave to Juliet, so effective is it. I reckoned that if the next morning I did not wake up at all, I would be left with a serious theological problem. But I slept the whole night through; and when I woke, prepared to resume the scheduled program of our pilgrimage, theological questions were on my mind anyway, indulging as I was not only the experience of a pilgrimage to Lourdes but a corollary curiosity about what exactly goes on there and what would be its impact on one first-time visitor.

One reason we don't hear so much about Lourdes these days (compared, say, with a generation or two ago) has to be that people don't really know what more there is to say. The inquirer whose mind turns for the first time to the subject begins by asking the questions one would expect, the first of which is, of course, "Was there really an apparition?"

This translates to, "Did the girl called Bernadette Soubirous actually *see* something? Or was what she reported no more than the product of an inflamed imagination?"

That question was first posed on February 11, 1858, to her family, whose reply was plainspoken—Bernadette's mother spanked her and put her to bed.

But there was something about the dogged sincerity in the fourteen-year-old's recounting of her experience that brought on a grudging acknowledgment—not that Bernadette had in fact come face to face with an apparition, but that *something* was going on worth investigating, even if it turned out to be nothing more than her mental health. Accordingly, three days later her mother gave her permission to return. Back Bernadette went, to the little grotto alongside which, on Day One, she, a younger sister, and a friend had been foraging for firewood.

That was when Bernadette had suddenly stopped, immobilized for a full half hour. When she came out of her trance she excitedly described the lady in white, with the blue eyes, the smile, and the blue belt-sash hanging down the front of her white robe.

On the second day at the grotto, once again in the company of her sister and their friend, she again lost her composure while in communion with the apparition. The trance over, she opened her eyes and said that the lady in white had come and gone. But Bernadette could not rise, nor could her companions lift her up from the ground. They called on a neighboring miller for help. He handled her as a muscular aide would handle a heavyweight boxer who had been knocked insensate in the ring. Bernadette's family ruled that the phenomenon was ridiculous and profane and once again forbade her to return to the grotto. But of course she did. And her third visit, four days later, proved special because, for the first time, the lady in white spoke to her.

What had she said?

She had said that Bernadette should return to that site every afternoon for the next two weeks.

Bernadette did so. As one might expect, with each visit a larger number of villagers accompanied her, curious to witness the girl's catatonia and to hear from her own lips, after she came out of it, what it was that she had seen and heard.

❧

Lourdes was (and still is, really) a small town, situated in the foothills of the Pyrenees. Charlemagne is said to have fought over it, laying siege to its imposing fort in the eighth century when the

Moors occupied it. He struck a bargain with them: They would be permitted to survive the siege provided they converted to Christianity. In the years that followed, Lourdes, like the islands of the Antilles, became a musical chair: France had it, Spain had it, England had it. Permanent French occupation came only in the fifteenth century.

Lourdes withstood attacks during the religious wars, remaining stoutly Catholic, so that Bernadette's neighbors were indisputably French Catholic. But notwithstanding the fabled Gallic skepticism, they were themselves hypnotized by the transfiguration, before their own eyes, of the miller's eldest daughter. Whatever it was that was inducing those trances, the consensus gradually consolidated that they were not *self*-induced. For one thing there was nothing in the least theatrical in Bernadette's disposition, and certainly nothing in her background that would encourage anything of the sort. Her father was a casualty of the Industrial Revolution, well on the way to bankruptcy because technology had come up with more economical ways of making bread than by grinding flour with roughly the same tools that had been used at the time of Christ. In the single room that made up the home of M. Soubirous, his wife, and their four children, histrionic episodes, one confidently deduces, were neither expected nor countenanced.

And when Bernadette woke from her trances, her accounts were always direct and unambiguous. The lady in white usually did not speak to her, emitting only a smile. Seven times, during the eighteen apparitions, she broke silence. On one occasion she called on Bernadette to relay her plea for repentance—hardly an irrelevant request, in the south of France in 1858, or for that matter in the north of France in 1958. Then came the second declaration: Bernadette was to pass on the word to the clergy—they must construct a chapel alongside the site at which the apparition was taking place. Next, she instructed Bernadette to dig in the earth a few feet away. She did so, and a stream of water sprang out. It continues, 145 years later, to flow, at a rate of up to fourteen hundred gallons per hour; water from the Pyrenees mountains that empties into the river Gave. It fills the thousands of receptacles in which it is collected by pilgrims. It also fills the baths in which over one million pilgrims have immersed their bodies, their motive to experience a cure for an infirmity, or else merely to perform a devotional act, even as, in the secular world, a line might form to kiss the emperor's ring or curtsy to the queen.

The elders of Lourdes were now prepared to acknowledge that Bernadette was seeing "something." But they were resolute in disbelieving that the lady in white was the Madonna: whatever the chimera was, it was surely something other than the mother of Christ. The parish priest, a hardy skeptic during the entire fortnight, said repeatedly to Bernadette that she must ask the apparition to give herself a name: Who was she?

The priest's request was compliantly transmitted, but the lady only smiled in response—until the sixteenth apparition. This time the lady in white answered Bernadette. She said, "I am the Immaculate Conception." Bernadette dutifully reported these words to the priest and the general company. The reaction was electric: the lady in white had declared herself to be the Blessed Virgin, the mother of Christ. The awe increased when Bernadette was closely questioned and it transpired that she (a) had never before heard the term "Immaculate Conception" and (b) had no idea what it meant or to whom it referred.

What followed was the usual sluggish reaction to any extraordinary event (Thomas Edison brought on no headlines when he announced that he had harnessed electricity). But the First Stage was now complete. No one associated with her any longer doubted that Bernadette—who went on to a novitiate in a nearby nunnery, where she died early from tuberculosis and the asthma she had contracted before the apparition—had truthfully described what she had seen and reported what she had heard.

In due course the chapel she had been instructed to propose was realized: the basilica is very large, its satellites numerous. The lady in white had given no intimation that the little spring she had brought to life would have therapeutic effects on many who touched it or were touched by it, but in fact it did. And even when her story had become nationally and internationally accepted, well before her death in 1879, at age thirty-five, few gave any thought to the canonization of Bernadette Soubirous (this happened in 1933). Certainly no one had any idea that more than a hundred years later several million people every year would travel to Lourdes to see the grotto where the lady in white appeared, to feel the waters that continue to flow from the spring she unearthed, and to return from their visit to Lourdes substantially—in many cases, critically—affected by the experience. It is a matter of record that there are cases of the lame and the halt who have returned whole from Lourdes, and for every one of them there are tens of thousands who return affected in other ways.

&

Oddly, English-speaking visitors to Lourdes cannot find there literature in their own language other than photographic books with slender textual matter. My sister Patricia Bozell and I looked diligently for more, but unsuccessfully. The French, yes—their Lourdes library is copious. But even the cosmopolitan bookstores don't carry copies of *The Miracle of Lourdes*, written in 1955 by Ruth Cranston, and more or less updated in 1986. It is a useful volume, written by a Protestant who became a devotee of Lourdes. The book is valuable primarily for its inclusion of basic data about the shrine. It records in considerable detail, for instance, a dozen of the cures attributed to Lourdes.

FELLOW TRAVELER, SISTER PATRICIA BOZELL.
THE GROTTO IS VISIBLE IN THE BACKGROUND.

It is not surprising, but worth stressing, that there is no tribunal in existence more skeptical than those through which you need to pass if your claim is to have been cured at Lourdes. One faces first the so-called Medical Bureau. It is a cadre of doctors who donate their time, spending periods of various lengths in residence at Lourdes. Their duty is to examine—their opportunity is to learn from—the phenomena that pass by. Only a minority of these men of science are professing Catholics.

On the extraordinary occasion when the Bureau, after exhaustive investigation, places a stamp of approval on the claims of a "*Curé*," it is saying formally that there is no known or hypothetical scientific explanation for the physical transformation the doctors have documented. The case goes then to a second medical examining body, an international committee whose headquarters are in Paris. If this body concurs, the validation is then referred to a canonical commission in the diocese in which the candidate lives, and the skepticism here is not only scientific but theological. The

Church has almost always been the last to believe that a miracle actually took place, but of course prepared to believe that what took place *was* a miracle. In this respect the Church learns from Thomas, who declined to believe in the resurrection until the palpability of Christ's wounds was experienced. Do not ask the ecclesiastical tribunal at Lourdes to acclaim that you have been miraculously cured unless you have been. You would have better luck appearing at that bank in London that continues to store remnants of the Czar's treasury and announcing yourself as Anastasia.

Before the International Medical Committee will agree to pursue your case further, sixteen questions (I am not responsible for the English rendition) have to be answered satisfactorily—questions such as: Has the diagnosis been established by adequate objective examination? Does the comprehensive clinical picture rule out psychogenic overlay? Does the prognosis rule out the possibility of spontaneous remission, natural cure, significant improvement, or long-term remission? Has the sick person noticed the disappearance of subjective symptoms? Did the cure appear completely contrary to the prognosis? Was the cure sudden and consistent with the disappearance of objective pathological signs?

A completed questionnaire with answers to every one of its taunts would still not satisfy everybody. Emile Zola, a devout, indeed consecrated, atheist, went to enormous pains, practical and poetic, to affirm his animating axiom, which he once reduced to simple words: "Even if I *saw* a miracle, I couldn't believe it." So eager was he to affirm his disbelief that he based one work of fact/fiction on a Lourdes pilgrim. The story was taken from life, and he coped with his problem by simply falsifying the documented record, poor Zola. Every now and again a dedicated body of skeptics engages somebody to apply his theatrical energies to faking his way through the Lourdes accreditation process in order to discredit it. My favorite of these stories is that of the young lady who arrived at Lourdes complaining of a lifelong affliction, getting worse as the years went by: an anal fistula. She took the baths and on emerging announced herself triumphantly as cured! She was taken to the Medical Bureau, where the doctors proceeded to put together her record—her family history, the history of the illness, the history of the cure. The paperwork having been done, the doctors were ready to go on to the next stage, a physical examination. The record gives us the ensuing exchange:

"Examine me—but why?"

"In order to verify your cure, madame."

"And all that I have been telling you—that is for nothing?"

"For nothing, madame, if we do not examine you."

"But I do not wish to be examined."

"In order to verify a cure, we must examine the patient. If you do not consent, we shall tear up the record."

"Then I shall not be verified?"

"No, madame."

The dear lady faced a problem, and the chronicler, Mrs. Cranston, tells in her book of the proceedings: "After much protesting and objecting, finally she yielded, and the examination took place, five or six doctors assisting.

"There was nothing whatever the matter with the woman, and never had been—certainly not the malady she described. When the doctors asked her to show them where the anal fistula was, she pointed to a little white scar (the vestige of an old cyst operation) quite high up on the back and in a spot where certainly no one ever had an anus."

Well, one does try. After protracted questioning the lady broke down. "She had been purposely sent, by an anti-religious organization of one of the big departments in the middle of France, to bring back a personal document showing that at the Medical Bureau of Lourdes they recognized miracles without even examining the patients." It is really quite charming, this certainty of the young lady impostor that no gentlemanly doctor would propose to examine...that part of the body...in search of mere medical evidence.

❦

Fewer than one hundred cures have been certified by the Church as miraculous. This number is drastically smaller than the number of cures plausibly claimed by men and women who have traveled to Lourdes but who for whatever reason (they did not care; they had not kept records; their own doctors would not cooperate) didn't submit to the rigorous examinations required; or else did so, and did not pass these tests. Mrs. Cranston, who spent many years in residence at Lourdes and engaged in meticulous record-keeping, estimates at ten thousand the number who have declared themselves cured. But even if her calculations are correct, that leaves us with one cure per ten or fifteen thousand pilgrims. The odds, one supposes without actually going to statistical laboratories, are not very different from those one might expect on buying a lottery ticket. People go to Lourdes, then, for other reasons than miraculous cures, and if my own experience is representative, they leave profoundly affected.

The book by Mrs. Cranston gives the record, as noted, of many documented cures. I select one, not because it is singular but because it is, in essential respects, typical. Marie Bailly was a patient of a French doctor who, when finally he complied with the family request that he accompany her to Lourdes, wrote down, for the record, what would be the transformation he would need to see before acknowledging that any cure had taken place. He confronted, first, a general question: What kind of ailment would qualify as miraculously treated? His answer: "An organic disease: a cancer disappearing; a bone regrown; a congenital dislocation vanishing."

He went on in his notes to describe the plight of his patient, a young woman in the last stages of tuberculous peritonitis. "I know her history," he recorded. "Her whole family died of tuberculosis. She has had tubercular sores, lesions of the lungs, and now, for the past few months, peritonitis diagnosed by both a general practitioner and the well-known Bordeaux surgeon, Bromilloux. Her condition is very grave. She may die right under my nose. If such a case were cured, it would indeed be a miracle."

One hour before Marie Bailly was carried to the grotto, her doctor examined her yet again at one of the adjacent hospitals, remarking in his notes the white, emaciated face, the galloping pulse—150 beats a minute—the distended abdomen, the ears and nails turning blue. He told the sisters, "She may last a few more days, but she is doomed. Her heart is giving out. Death is very near."

The doctor accompanied Marie Bailly to the grotto. There he saw her face change color, losing its ashen hue. Her swollen abdomen flattened out under the blanket. Her pulse became calm and regular. She requested a glass of milk. Her respiration had become normal. Mrs. Cranston records the doctor's reaction. "The sweat broke out on his forehead. He felt as though someone had struck him on the head. His own heart began to pump furiously. It was the most 'momentous thing' he had ever seen."

The doctor roused himself from his trance and took his patient back to the hospital, where he examined her in the company of three other doctors. They confirmed what he knew already from his intimate knowledge of her case. His patient had been—cured. The doctor told a colleague: "When one reads about such things one cannot help suspecting some kind of charlatanism. But here is a cure I have seen with my own eyes. I have seen an apparently chronic invalid restored to health and normal life."

Of course. One can't go any further than to say that (a) there was a cure, and (b) there is no *scientific* explanation for it. You cannot conclude, using scientific methodology, that the transformation was a "miracle." To do so would be to place yourself in the hands of the theologians. "MIRACLE 1. A marvelous event occurring within human experience, which cannot have been brought about by human power or by the operation of any natural agency, and must therefore be ascribed to the special intervention of the Deity..." (*OED*).

The word is casually used in the modern world. "*Miraculously, Silky Sullivan came from last place and won the race by a nose.*" But the dominant meaning is as given in the *Oxford Dictionary*, something caused by an act of divine intervention. If one is required to describe what happened to Marie Bailly as other than a "miracle," one needs to use words that don't come easily to the tongue. Was it a...*thaumaturgical event*? In ruling out a natural cause we are required to acknowledge a supernatural cause. In formal logic, it would not need to be a Christian agent that brought about the miracle, but given the story of Bernadette, Christianity does, well—come to mind; and anyway, the secular humanist has a problem because in his etiology there has to be a natural cause for every phenomenon. Those who seek relief from the quandary *If it wasn't a natural cause that effected the cure, what did?*—will need to come up with a superforce of some sort. Who was it at the grotto in 1858? Madame Allah? The skeptics run the risk of being ambushed by: God/Christ/the Immaculate Conception. The whole Christian package.

But the Christian too is without *explanation* for what happens at Lourdes, because we cannot reason to why Marie Bailly found relief while so many others do not. Yet this only reminds us that what in the secular coinage we would think of as stochastic (Why the death-dealing volcanic eruption here? the pestilence there?), religion ascribes to a divine order that countenances extemporaneous afflictions, natural and personal. God's ways are inscrutable.

So where is the skeptic left? I thought of the liberating sentence of Chesterton in which he recounts how, in his desperate search for a suitable cosmology, he had stumbled upon orthodoxy. It was chance that I stumbled, the second evening at Lourdes, on this paragraph in a Chesterton essay. GKC was an ardent admirer of W. B. Yeats; indeed he and the poet were personal friends. Chesterton is here reflecting on the endless search for timelessness on earth. "A very distinguished and dignified example of this paganism at bay is Mr. W. B. Yeats." He quotes a passage from Yeats's "delightful" memoirs:

> I think it [Christianity] but deepened despair and multiplied temptation...Why are these strange souls born everywhere today, with hearts that Christianity, as shaped by history, cannot satisfy? Our love letters wear out our love; no school of painting outlasts its founders, every stroke of the brush exhausts the impulse; pre-Raphaelitism had some twenty years; Impressionism, thirty, perhaps. Why should we believe that religion can never bring round its antithesis? Is it true that our air is disturbed, as Melarme [sic] said, "by the trembling of the veil of the temple," or "that our whole age is seeking to bring forth a sacred book"? Some of us thought that book near towards the end of last century but the tide sank again.

"Of course,"—Chesterton moves in—

> there are many minor criticisms of all this. The faith only multiplies temptation in the sense that it would multiply temptation to turn a dog into a man. And it certainly does not deepen despair, if only for two reasons: first, that despair to a Catholic is itself a spiritual sin and blasphemy; and second, that the despair of many pagans, often including Mr. Yeats, could not possibly be deepened. But what concerns me, in these introductory remarks,

is his suggestion about the duration of movements. When he gently asks why Catholic Christianity should last longer than other movements, we may well answer even more gently: "Why, indeed?" He might gain some light on why it should, if he would begin by inquiring why it does. He seems curiously unconscious that the very contrast he gives is against the case he urges. If the proper duration of a movement is twenty years, what sort of a movement is it that lasts nearly two thousand? If a fashion should last no longer than Impressionism, what sort of fashion is it that lasts about fifty times as long? Is it just barely conceivable that it is not a fashion?

ॐ

Pilgrims who travel to Lourdes make up their own schedules, in cooperation with the Administrative Office there. The routine of our group began one afternoon with Mass at the upper Basilica, one of the many churches. An odd sense of tranquillity settled on us. I can't offhand remember when last, other than at sea, I felt so little concern for timetables. On Friday there was a "Morning of Recollection" and the anointing of the sick at another chapel (St. Joseph's). There are three hospitals—more properly, hospices—all of them administered by volunteers. Few of us were sick, but we were reminded that, from the day of birth, we are on our deathbed. In the afternoon, Mass at the Salle Notre Dame, and in the evening a candlelight procession in front of the Rosary Basilica. It is not easy to imagine twenty thousand candles shaping a cross, but we saw it. The ensuing four days included daily Mass in different churches; easy access to confession, heard in six languages throughout the day; the Stations of the Cross, twice-life-sized bronze statuary, rising up a steep hillside, invoking the travail of Calvary. The schedule left several hours every day during which one could do as one chose (there are historical sites, including the birthplace of

Bernadette, and the great, massive fort built during the Middle Ages), and one tends to walk about, and to take keen pleasure in casual encounters.

A sense of the visit is rapidly communicated. There are thousands of gurneys (*voitures*, they are called) for the *malades*, the all-inclusive French word for the sick—again, propelled exclusively by volunteers. Perhaps every *malade* harbors the hope that he or she will be cured, though it is not reasonably expected; yet somehow being cured seems irrelevant as larger perspectives take hold. It is a part of the common faith that prayer can effect anything (*"Remember, most gracious Virgin Mary, that never was it known that anyone who fled to thy protection, implored thy help, or sought thy intercession was left unaided"*), but incantatory hyperbole is simply a ritualized form of docility. The sick travel to Lourdes, yes, because of the undeniability of recorded miracles, but that isn't what brings as many as fifty thousand people a day to Lourdes, the great majority of them healthy. The reason so many people come, many of them on their second or tenth visit, is that what is effected is a sense of reconciliation, if not well-being. Hardly miraculous, unless one chooses to use the word as most appropriate for that buoyancy experienced on viewing the great processions, sharing with almost thirty thousand people an underground Mass, being lowered for three bracing seconds into one of the baths; suddenly noting the ambient serenity. These are Christians feeling impulses of their faith, and intimations of the lady in white.

They are at Lourdes because of this palpability of the emanations that gave birth to the shrine. The spiritual tonic is felt. If it were otherwise, the pilgrims would diminish in number—would, by now, have disappeared, as at Delphi, which one visits as a museum, not a shrine. What it is that fetches them is I think quite simply stated, namely a reinforced conviction that the Lord God loves His creatures, healthy or infirm; that they—we—must understand the nature of love, which is salvific in its powers; and that although we are free to attempt to divine God's purpose, we will never succeed in doing so. The reason is that we cannot know (the manifest contradictions are too disturbing) what is the purpose behind particular phenomena, and therefore must make do with only the grandest plan of God, which treats with eternal salvation. To keep the faith: to do this (the grammar of assent) requires the discipline of submission, some assurance that those who are stricken can, even so, be happy; and that the greatest tonic of all is divine love, which is nourished by human love, even as human love is nourished by divine love.

Waiting to board the airplane to Paris I found myself in the company of three *malades*. They could walk, else they'd have been on one of the trains, on stretchers. One young man had a face wretchedly distorted—it brought to mind one of the unpleasant pictures of Picasso. Around his neck the attendant had placed a plastic folder, his ticket inside, his travel arrangements upon landing at Orly explained. With heavy use of a heavy cane he could, so to speak, walk. He was treated, by this company returning from Lourdes, as a member of the family. Which he was, as Lourdes manages to make plain.

The Stupefaction of the New England Coastline

I have spent, gratefully, more days on or around the New England coastline than anywhere else on earth. ◠

I *know—everybody knows, there's no arguing* about it—the most beautiful part of the world is wherever you grew up, so there's that egalitarian formality.

Now let me tell you about the most beautiful part of the world, which is the New England coastline. Writing about it isn't to exclude New England's inland, but you can't have both at the same time, and if you pull in at Saybrook, Connecticut, and resolve to stick to the shoreline until it runs out, you'll be traveling, by car or by boat (preferably by boat), all the way to the easternmost tip of the United States in Eastport, Maine, which is opposite Campobello, where Franklin Delano Roosevelt was hit with polio—but we have to leave history out of it, otherwise we'd never get any further than Boston.

Coastal New England begins in Connecticut, in Greenwich. Before you reach the eastern end of Connecticut, you have passed by more harbors than the whole of California gives you along its thousand-mile coastline. It's as if New England were beckoning to you at every possible moment, to come on in out of the rain.

We're talking about the same coastline our way-back fathers happened upon and proceeded to colonize. In Plymouth the old burial ground is still there, which tells us who really did come over on the *Mayflower*. You have glided by the old white churches and the fishing nets of Gloucester and New Bedford, and the Cape Cod Canal, which saves you forty miles of roundabout travel if you are headed Down East. You can take in a thousand inlets and little havens and major ports, cold and luminously green in the spring, challengingly hot in midsummer; and then, when the fall comes, the premonitory little pulsations of cold in the early morning. And then is when the leaves begin to turn, and you know what the forests would look like if they were painted by all the fauvists in France, using googols of red and orange and yellow and traces of green and umber. At York Harbor, where Maine begins, was the great inn that opened its three hundred rooms for only ten weeks, after the reluctant springs, and before the autumn freezes. It wouldn't be fair, one starstruck old-timer said, to let New England's coastal season last any longer—nature has to give other people a little time of day.

So you sail up the coast, making a major daily stride or two (thirty, forty miles), and fuss a little with wind and tide, and every day resolve to immerse yourself in the ocean with water temperatures as cold (in midsummer) as fifty degrees. Then, perhaps in midafternoon, perhaps later, you noodle into one of those great bays. You can linger as long as you like at Casco and Muscongus, Penobscot and Frenchman, framing Mt. Desert Island, famed for splendid summerhouses and overnight accommodations for tourists. There are deep waters and sheer promontories, great rocks and pine woods, and the little villages, whose settlers, during the century and a half after the pilgrims came, struggled to make snuggeries where life could be sustained, drawing on the ocean to one side, the soil and wildlife and forests on the other. They dreamed a great deal, but could not have anticipated that on top of taking care of the problems of Indians, the British king, hunger, and cold, they were also bending the great natural resources of coastal New England to give passing pleasure to all who come to experience it, and lifelong pleasure to those who come in out of the rain there permanently.

A Performance with the Symphony, Coming Up

The date, ineluctable, was only a week or so ahead of me, the stomach-churning challenge of an appearance as soloist with the Phoenix Symphony Orchestra. I chose the self-interview mode to tell how I got into this mess. ⌐◦

Q. *What made you decide to play* a concerto with the Phoenix Symphony Orchestra?

A: That's easy—I was invited. The interesting question is, What made the Phoenix Symphony Orchestra decide to invite me?

Q: Well, do you have the answer to that?

A: After my first few months of shock, little hints drifted in on the disorderly beach of my correspondence. Yes, I now know how the idea began. In one of my books I made a reference to the singular pleasures it must give a musician to be able to play, night after night, masterpieces written by great composers, by contrast with the fate of the public speaker, who needs to be satisfied with reiterations of his own inventions. But that blissful alternative, I commented, is available only to the artist, which is what I hoped to be up until about the age of fifteen, when I was precocious enough to recognize that I didn't have the talent to become one.

Q: But you decided at age sixty-three that you had enough talent, after all, to play with a symphony orchestra?

A: Well put. But we need to make distinctions. If in the letter I received, in September 1988, the managing director of the Phoenix Symphony had invited me to take up a career as a performing keyboard artist, I'd have replied without any difficulty.

But he didn't do that. His challenge was excruciatingly finite. What he said, and the words are engraved in my memory, was, "Would you play any Bach concerto any time in 1989 or 1990 with the Phoenix Symphony?"

That was not an invitation for me to take on a profession at which I knew I would be a failure. It was a challenge which, transcribed into the language in which I read it, said: "Do you think you could manage to cultivate the technique and the savoir faire to play any one Bach concerto with a professional orchestra on a public occasion if we give you two entire years in which to practice?"

That was a very different invitation.

Q: What was your immediate reaction?

A: At first I thought, No, it is quite simply impossible. My fingers have been rusty for generations, the butterflies-in-the-stomach problem is not one I could predictably overcome, and anyway, the endeavor would consume entirely too much time. I wake up every day and, roughly speaking, work until I go to bed—there is never any time just "left over," let alone the kind of time it takes to attack the keyboard at a professional level.

Q: So then what did you do?

A: I called Fernando Valenti. You don't hear his name as a recitalist so often nowadays, as he has retired from the professional circuit because of health problems. But I first heard him play when he was a senior at Yale University, only a few years before *Time* magazine made a casual reference to him as the "best living harpsichordist." Years later we became very good friends, so I called and told him about this crazy offer. I had the advantage of talking to someone who knows (a) that I revere music, and (b) that I am lucky if I get through "Chopsticks" without playing a wrong note.

Q: What did he say?

A: Well, he said it was a very "interesting challenge"—nobody was going to say anything different from that, by the way, right up to the present moment. So then I asked him which was the briefest concerto Bach ever wrote, and he said, "The F Minor takes only eight and one-half minutes."

Eight and one-half minutes! I was being given, potentially, twenty-seven months to discipline my fingers to play for eight and one-half minutes, which comes down to just over three per minute, or about one week per note. Hell, figuring it out that way, I could perform "The Flight of the Bumblebee" in a couple of years!

Q: What was Mr. Valenti's reaction?

A: He said: Why don't you try working on it for a month or two and see if anything happens?... Well, that is exactly what I did, only first I called Rosalyn Tureck, who is also a very close friend. She knows by heart everything Bach ever wrote for the keyboard and is as incomparable at Bach as Valenti is at Scarlatti. And I said, What do you think about the F Minor Concerto? And she said, "Well, everybody knows the famous Largo, the slow movement from the concerto. But my advice to anyone who sets out to conquer it is: Start with the third movement. Then go to the first movement. If you can manage those, you can manage the second movement."

Q: Did you follow her advice?

A: No, actually. I lined up my teacher. Rick Tripodi is an organ virtuoso at a local church whom I had come to know and who is a very gifted musician. Together we listened to a recording by Trevor Pinnock, and I decided the first movement was as difficult as the third. So...we set out. My idea was to give the experiment a two-month trial, practicing one half hour a day, and taking a one-hour lesson every week. Getting to hit the right notes was sheer hell.

Q: But obviously, you didn't give up.

A: No. But I came close to doing so. After I'd been working on the first movement for about two months a friend told me about a musician who lived in the neighborhood with whom my friend was studying. "The wonderful thing about Mrs. Josephson," she said to me, "is that every five or six lessons, she just stops me and reteaches me how to practice. She's great on teaching you how to practice."

This I needed special training in, because over the years, if your technique is quite awful, you get used to slurping your way through whatever little piece you are engaging, and time after time you make the same dismaying errors. I needed someone who could coach me in the correct gymnastic basics. So I finally prevailed on Mrs. Josephson to give me a lesson.

She was genial and quite stern, and told me to play the first movement no faster than 90 on the metronome until New Year's Day—that was six weeks off. I had been playing it at about 110.

I persuaded her to give me a second lesson, during which I played the first few bars of the third movement. She listened patiently. And then she said, "Have you made a commitment to the Phoenix people?" And I said, Well, I had a telephone conversation just a week ago with the managing director, and I told him I was practicing every day and I had a premonition that I would be accepting his challenge. I told her rather excitedly that I had asked him one specific question: How late in the day could I actually pull out? His answer was: "Ninety days." They would not schedule the concert until ninety days before. If I said yes at that time, I would need to go ahead with it. So, I said exuberantly, I've decided I can't possibly devote two years of my time to learning the F Minor Concerto so I am going to perform it in mid-October, thirteen months after attacking it, which means that I have until mid-July to say yes or no definitively to Phoenix.

That was in January.

"You may as well say no now," said Mrs. Josephson.

"Oh?" I asked, probingly.

"You will never be able to play the F Minor Concerto. Not ever. Not unless you stop everything and practice three hours minimum per day, for two years."

That was a very sobering statement, and I recounted it not only to my first teacher, Rick Tripodi, but also to my second teacher, Barbara Cadranel (Mrs. Fernando Valenti #2), herself a harpsichord recitalist, who had undertaken to coach me an additional one hour per week. She was indignant at this expression of fatalism and flatly contradicted it. The following day I had a telephone call from Fernando Valenti on his sickbed—he too was passionately aroused by the categorical pessimism of Mrs. Josephson. I felt suddenly as though I were listening to Knute Rockne during the half, when Slippery Rock U. was leading 50 to 0.

Q: So what did you do?

A: I persevered. I resolved that a day would not pass without my giving the concerto at least the half-hour. Now this, for a peripatetic Modern Man, was a considerable commitment. I had to buy, of course, a Yamaha traveling five-octave keyboard instrument, which is designed for rock bands but which will give your fingers the requisite daily workout. Let me see. In the months that followed, I played bits and pieces of the F Minor Concerto in

Antigua, St. Lucia, Martinique, Bequia, Switzerland, England, Mexico, Greece, Turkey, California, Hawaii, Tahiti, New Zealand, Australia, Sri Lanka, Kenya, South Africa, aboard my little sloop en route to Bermuda, and on a ketch touring Corsica and Sardinia. As I say, not a day went by—

Q: Had you at that time decided whether to perform on the piano or the harpsichord?

A: I was amused early on, struggling through the first movement in front of my original piano teacher, Marjorie Otis Gifford, age seventy-nine, whom I adore above all living people. She suggested I play it on the harpsichord. When next I played it for my harpsichord teacher, she suggested perhaps I ought to play it on the piano. Amusing. But I came early on to the decision to do it on the harpsichord for two reasons. The first, that Bach wrote it for the harpsichord, which is also the instrument I love beyond all others; the second, that my fingers, which are structurally weak, can handle the muscular requirements of the harpsichord with less strain— the harpsichord key depresses more easily than most piano keys. The disadvantages, on the other hand, are manifest.

Q: What are they?

A: There simply isn't any doubt that there is less room for dynamic interpretation when playing the harpsichord than when playing the piano. You cannot control the volume, and your articulation of the notes is less easily discerned.

I discussed the whole question with Trevor Pinnock, who came to lunch one day. He is a great performer and scholar, and he had recently played the F Minor in Berlin and had recorded it—that was the recording Rick Tripodi and I listened to at the beginning of this enterprise. He dismayed me by referring to it as "a treacherous body of music." Which it is, by the way: your fingers never

get any time off, and if your fingering goes askew, it can only be
compared to your parachute failing to open. And then Mr. Pinnock, whose (very brief) cadenza, by the way, he was kind enough
to copy out and send to me so that I could use it—it comes in just
a few bars before the end of the concerto—told me that he has no
hesitation in using the sixteen-foot pedal during the tutti passages
(i.e., when the harpsichord and the chamber orchestra are playing
simultaneously). On this point the musical world is furiously
divided. The purists say, No!—Bach did not even know of the existence of the sixteen-foot (which gives you a register one octave
below the register you are playing). Others say: Nonsense. He
would certainly have availed himself of it had it been around.

And then there is the question of amplification. Mr. Pinnock
agrees that his own recording of the F Minor underplays the harpsichord sound to the point where it sometimes just plain gets lost
in the ongoing commotion. The idea of one of my precious eight
and one-half minutes getting lost is more than I can bear, so that I
have put in for plenty of amplification, and hope this will not
become a point of contention between me and Mr. James Sedares,
the distinguished conductor who is indulging all of this.

Q: An interesting point. What's in it for Phoenix?

A: I have pondered that. There are two extreme possibilities,
from either of which Phoenix would profit. Suppose I go out there
and—freeze. Or, perhaps, hit a few notes, and then dismember the
rest. Just turn in an absolutely memorable godawful performance.
Now that wouldn't be all bad for Phoenix, frankly. People would
remember it, and write about it. "Were you there when the
Phoenix Symphony Orchestra gave Buckley that chance-in-a-life-
time and he fell on his right-wing arse? It was spec-*tac*-ular!" You
don't really get mad at Barnum and Bailey when one of their tra-
peze artists misses and goes down, down, down to ... Exactly.

Progress photo by David G. McIntyre

Tuxedo-clad and admittedly nervous, conservative columnist William F. Buckley Jr. performs J.S. Bach's F-minor concerto Tuesday with the Phoenix Symphony Chamber Orchestra before an enthusiastic audience of 550 at the Scottsdale Center for the Arts.

Buckley's debut positively propitious

By Mark J. Scarp
Progress Staff Writer

It was a sweaty, jittery performance, similar to what it would probably be like to observe Johann Sebastian Bach beating out a newspaper column on a computer terminal.

But William F. Buckley Jr., columnist, magazine editor, talk-show host and noted conservative thinker, celebrated the culmination of 13 months of practice Tues-day with a harpsichord rendition of Bach's Concerto in F minor with 35 members of the Phoenix Symphony Chamber Orchestra at the Scottsdale Center for the Arts.

Buckley performed the 8½-minute concerto, Bach's shortest, to the satisfaction of conductor James Sedares, who regarded the experience of sharing the stage with Buckley as fun, but scary.

The audience of 550 embraced the columnist's performance with a standing ovation, to which Buckley responded with an encore.

Buckley has described the experience with self-deprecating humor and with his trademark command of English vocabulary that sends even college professors listening to him heading for the dictionaries.

He told media representatives Friday that "nobody in the history of the world has attacked the F minor concerto of Bach as I have done, extruding my exiguous musical resources with the kind of care you would take with a quart of water embarking in a life raft across the ocean.

"But I rejoice that I have three days ahead of me in which to redouble my efforts not to sound . . . like a stuck horn on a Rolls-Royce."

In addition to the concert, Buckley taped a segment of his PBS-TV talk show, *Firing Line*, at the Center for the Arts Monday.

The other extreme possibility—and I'd say the first is infinitely more likely than the second—is that the local critic will say that last night was definite proof that all those years spent by Mr. Buckley writing and speaking were wasted, given what he might have bestowed on the world as a harpsichordist.

Now, even if I perform creditably, no critic is likely to say this who knows what I have been through, because it would take me longer than I expect to live to be able to perform Bach's other half-dozen concertos, at the rate at which I learn, let alone the whole of the harpsichord literature.

In between the two extremes, if I hit most of the right notes and prove that I understand what Bach was trying to do, people will say, That was a nice little stunt Phoenix pulled off. They ran risks, granted; but they weren't embarrassed. And it was fun finding out that a lapsed amateur can, if he is willing to spend lots and lots of time on the problem, manage to draw on a lifetime of devotion to a composer and play creditably for eight and one-half minutes one of his beautiful concertos. Besides, think of all the books and articles and speeches Buckley might have done in the hundreds of hours he devoted to solitary practice! We may have been spared the equivalent of another six months of Reaganomics.

Who knows? The Phoenix Caper might become an annual event. Now, if anybody wants to start a scholarship that would make it possible for John Kenneth Galbraith to devote all his spare time to mastering the Minuet in G, why, I will contribute to that fund, and maybe even organize a picket line around his house in Cambridge to guard against any distraction. You know, don't you, that he has pledged never to cross a picket line?

The Life of the Public Speaker

I was still on the lecture circuit, though on a reduced schedule, when I wrote for The New Yorker *of the memories I took with me from my years of public speaking.* ⌒

A *generation ago Bernard De Voto,* Harvard historian, novelist, and wit, resolved to give up public lecturing. After so many years of it, he had had enough. Besides, there were those books he wanted to get written, those books still left to read. But he had a valedictory in mind on the subject of public lecturing, and he devoted his column, "The Easy Chair" in *Harper's Magazine,* to it. He gave the reader an instructive and amusing account of pitfalls in the trade. Much of what he wrote lingers in the memory of the present-day lecturer, which is not surprising, because the basic arrangements are unchanged.

For instance, you have agreed to lecture six times during the month of May. Your agent discloses a few months ahead where the lectures will take place. A week or two before each event, you receive detailed marching orders. Up until then, though, you will find yourself putting off specific attention to mainstream lectures, i.e., those where one isn't asked to devote attention to special, ad hoc concerns. The reason for this, I suppose, is that one generally puts off thinking about any sort of heavy duty ahead; you tend to avoid looking down the calendar when you know it is heavily stocked with looming

obligations, whether professional or social. If you project that iner-
tia a step or two you will, I hope, understand why, as often as not, I
do not actually examine, until the plane has set down, the page in the
folder that describes my exact destination and the name of the spon-
soring body. I tend to do this when, upon landing, I rise from my
seat, pull out the folder from my briefcase, and fall, at the end of the
gangway, into the arms of my host or his representative.

Now vagueness of that order can get you into trouble when successive economies of preparation accumulate. A few years ago I left
my hotel in St. Louis, where I had spoken the night before, to go to
the designated hangar at the airport where a little chartered plane
waited to take me to a college a hundred miles or so away, where I
would speak that evening. I had been counseled to travel light on
the Cessna four-seater and accordingly brought along only a book
and my clipboard with my speech, leaving my briefcase at the
hotel, to which I'd return late that night.

When I arrived, two charming students, a young man and
young woman, whisked me off to a restaurant for a quick prespeech
dinner. I was suddenly confronted with the fact, as we chatted
merrily along, that I had no memory of the name of the college
whose guest I was. I attempted to maneuver the conversation in
search of the institution's identity.

When was "the college" founded? I tried. I got from my hosts
the year, some of the history, some of the problems, the year coed-
ucation was introduced—but never any mention of the college's
name. And so it went, right through the crowded evening. To this
day I don't know where I lectured that night, other than that it
was a couple of airplane hours north (I must have looked at the
compass) of St. Louis, Missouri.

I assume that my experiences, over the forty years I have been
on the circuit, are fairly typical, though there is of course this difference: as a conservative controversialist, I could not reasonably

expect to be greeted onstage as, say, Jacques Cousteau would have been. In pursuit of my apostleship, and the attendant revenue flow to *National Review*, I used to do seventy engagements a year; I now attempt to limit myself to twenty. There are several motives for lecturing. One of them is the redemptive impulse: you feel you have to get your message out there. Another is the histrionic bent: some wish always to lecture, to teach. Then of course there is the economic factor. Most successful lecturers will in whispered tones confide to you that there is no other journalistic or pedagogical activity more remunerative—a point made by Mark Twain and by Winston Churchill. Yes, one can find exceptions. James Clavell and James Michener no doubt earned as much in a day spent on their new novel as they would giving a lecture. But forget the half-dozen exceptions. The working professor or journalist will spend two or three days reading a book and reviewing it for the *New York Times* for $450; or—at the most lucrative level—three or four days writing an essay for *Playboy*, for ten times that sum. A night's lecture will bring in better than commensurate revenue. And sometimes the host at this college or that convention—for whatever reason—wants you and no one else, and the offer proves irresistible.

To De Voto's reflections, in any case, I append my own, starting with Buckley's Iron Law of Public Lecturing. It is that no matter what they tell you, between the time when they pick you up at your motel and the time they return you to your motel, a minimum of five hours will have elapsed. How so? Didn't the contract call simply for a forty-five-minute address, followed by a fifteen-minute Q&A? Forget it.

Well no, it isn't exactly an Iron Law, because there are exceptions: the dream dates. These happen when you are asked to lecture between 11:00 and 11:45, and please do not go over your time period, Mr. Buckley, because the next lecturer comes in at noon and there must be a coffee break for the convention subscribers between you and him. You arrive, as requested, fifteen minutes before the hour; the host/hostess leads you to an anteroom of sorts in which, by closed-circuit TV, you can hear the tail end of your predecessor's speech and get some sense of the audience. Promptly at 11:00 you are introduced, and promptly at 11:50—the master of ceremonies had said there was time for only three questions—you leave the stage, shake hands with somebody or another, go out into the street, and rejoin the free world. But interaction at such a mechanical level is rare.

A few performers we get to know about on the circuit are abrupt in their dealings with their hosts. Evelyn Waugh was the Great Figure in this regard. It is said that his agent would shrug his shoulders and warn the prospective lecture host that there was simply no shaking Mr. Waugh from his ways. No, he would give no press conference. No no no, no dinner before the lecture. No! No! Absolutely no signing of books. No-receiving-line-no-questions-after-his-speech. If that sounds awfully austere, it is absolutely convivial in contrast with what Mr. Waugh would proceed to do, which was remain in his limousine outside the hall until after he had been introduced. Only then would he lumber onstage, deliver his speech, and return to his limousine, whose door, one supposes, was held open for him. We do not know whether he paused to say good night to his host.

To behave that way and somehow get invited to deliver more lectures, you need to have a reputation as a grouch so entrenched as to become mythogenic; indeed, in a way, endearing, like the temperament of the Man Who Came to Dinner in the famous movie. The lecture public is titillated before such a character's appearance by tales of his eccentricities, and would be disappointed if he behaved other than as advertised.

Those who aren't given to misanthropy, natural or cultivated, simply can't get away with it, and wouldn't want to if they could. They oblige. Both because good nature impels you to do so, and because it is, in the long run, easier to comply than to resist. Your agent tells you that the sponsors who put up the money for the engagement are having a private dinner, at which your presence is... expected. A letter comes in, a week or two before the event, from the student who has led the threadbare conservative movement at the college, and life and death—the future of the Republic!—hang on your agreeing to meet with his group for a mere half hour sometime before or after the engagement. After the lecture, there is to be a public reception—it is a fixed part of a hundred-year-long tradition at the Xville Forum, and any failure by you to attend it would quite shatter the evening and demoralize the dozens of people who had a hand in making it a success. The lecture will be so widely attended that there won't really be a proper opportunity for the twenty brightest students at the college to interrogate you, so surely you wouldn't mind an hour's seminar at five, well before the lecture? It would mean so much to the students to have this opportunity.

Most people, as I have suggested, are good-natured. We give in, up to a point, and what finally makes it difficult to protest is the attentiveness and kindness of most of one's hosts and hostesses, who have put in fifteen hours of hard work for every hour's work of the visiting speaker. Notwithstanding good intentions, however, the speaker's priorities aren't always intuited, let alone observed. I have mentioned the ancillary activity with which you will inevitably become involved. That is a burden. So also is the absolutely distinctive fatigue that goes with the experience. This doesn't have anything to do with stage fright (I don't get this). And it is not alone a product of anfractuous travel schedules (flight to Louisville, feeder flight to Canton, car meets, hour-and-a-half drive to lecture site; reverse procedure the following morning, which means you will need to leave your motel at 6:15 in order to catch the only flight that will get you securely to where you are headed).

What sets in, and I think my experience is not unique, is a quite situation-specific exhaustion. You are back at the hotel at 10:30. You are not a television watcher, so that form of decompression doesn't work on you. You have a briefcase bulging with undone work, but reading manuscripts at that hour induces only a conviction that nobody who writes manuscripts can hold your attention in your current mood. If it had been fifty years ago and you were reading Hemingway's "The Killers," you'd probably have wondered, after page two, why in the hell he hadn't got to the point. You pour yourself a glass of wine from the bottle provided by your thoughtful host, nibble at a cracker, and read the back-of-the-book of *Time* or *Newsweek*. You then get around to calling the hotel operator. You tell her that the world itself hangs on her dependability in waking you at 5:15. That is too early for coffee, so you will use your wife's hot-wired, hair-curler type thing, which brings a cup of water to the boil in a minute. You might pop a sleeping pill, read two or three pages from your current book, and go to sleep.

What can happen then is a lecturer's nightmare. When your escort, often an undergraduate, tells you he/she will be there at 7:30, about one-half the time no one is there at 7:30. "Dear Josie," I began my letter to my student hostess at the University of Colorado a few years ago. She had been incensed, on arriving at my hotel, to find me in a cab, about to drive off. "Let me explain the events of yesterday morning so that you will not think me rude to have acted as I did," I wrote. "You had said the night before that you would pick me up at 7:30 to drive me to the Denver airport. You weren't there at 7:30. At 7:35 you still were not there. What passes through the mind in such situations is this: If Josie is not there at 7:30, when she contracted to be there, when in fact *will* she be there? It is possible that she overslept. Or that she has had a flat tire. In which case, she might not be there for a half hour—which would mean missing your plane. Precious time, dear Josie, is slipping through your fingers, so you go to the porter and say, Can you get me a taxi to drive me to the airport at Denver? He calls, and the lady driver arrives, and the two of you have just completed loading the luggage when Josie drives up, at 7:41. Now the point you made—that there was still plenty of time to get to the airport at Denver—isn't what goes through the mind of the lecturer. If I had absolutely known that you would materialize at 7:41, I'd have waited. But if you weren't there when you said you'd be there—at 7:30—how could I absolutely know that you would be there in time for me to make my plane? Having brought in the lady driver, negotiated the fare to the airport, and put all my luggage in her cab, I thought it would be unseemly to pull out the bags, dismiss her, and go with you. I do hope you understand."

Josie never acknowledged my letter. I guess she's still mad. Make it a point to say two things, ever so gently, to the people who are going to pick you up. First, be clear that punctuality the next morning is very important to you. Second, stipulate an offbeat time for the rendezvous. Never an easygoing 7:30. Rather, 7:25. Or 7:35. If you were back with the CIA, you'd say 7:33. Nobody is ever late if told to be there at 7:33. Dear Josie would have been on time at 7:33, but she would have thought it positively weird.

The whole operation is, as I say, strangely fatiguing. The compensation, however, lies not alone in the fee and the satisfaction of passing along the Word, but also in the relative ease of preparation. For some of us, writing out an entire speech is intensely laborious work, in part, I suppose, because most journalists are accustomed to writing thousand-word bites, or else three-hundred-page books. But if your lectures come in orderly sequences, the major effort is made once a season, either a calendar season or a political season (the inauguration of Bill Clinton, for example, constituted the beginning of a political season). I have a half-dozen offbeat speeches in my portfolio: "The Origins of Conservative Thought,"

"The Case for National Service," "The Genesis of Blackford Oakes"—that kind of thing. If the scheduled engagement calls for a debate (there are about five or six of these per year), that requires hard hours of ad hoc study, but there is no need to write anything out—debates call for extemporaneous handling.

Otherwise, I give out as my title (it is always the same) "Reflections on Current Contentions." The advantages are manifest. There are always current contentions, and pundits always reflect on them—indeed, as in the troubles of Mr. Clinton, revel in them. Every weekend during the two lecture seasons (fall and spring; I do not lecture in the summer), I pull out last week's speech and go over it line by line—search out anachronisms; insert fresh material; add or subtract a proposition; decide which contentions to analyze at a college, which at a business meeting or civic association. It makes for a busy few hours on Saturday or Sunday, but then you have in hand a speech which, as far as the audience is concerned, might have sprung full-blown from your imagination that very morning.

Some professionals frown on reading a speech. Mine now are mostly read. It requires experience to do this without appearing to be glued to the text. I have that experience. But I also know that there is going to be a question-and-answer period, and that during that period I will establish to the satisfaction of the audience that I can handle myself (and my interrogators) extemporaneously. The statement "Mr. Buckley has graciously agreed to answer a few questions," which inevitably precedes this part of the program, would more correctly be put as, "Mr. Buckley demands that there should be time for questions." Sometimes a Q&A is necessarily excluded—the hall is too large, the occasion too ceremonial (for instance, a commencement)—in which case you simply make do. But you are left feeling both underexploited and underappreciated, a singer of great range whose upper and lower registers were never tested.

And then whether there is to be a Q&A can depend on the hour, and here is a Great Grievance. I speak of the dinner that begins at eight. At about nine o'clock you start looking down at your carefully drafted forty-five-minute speech. As the clock moves relentlessly on, you start fidgeting with your text. Got to cut something! Maybe cut that section? Contract the beginning? Maybe eliminate it? Got to do something, because it's getting very late.

The enemy of the after-dinner speaker is identified with remarkable ease. Yes, sometimes there are too many cards to be played: awards given out, accounts of activity during the preceding year. But most often, the enemy is—the salad course. I can think of fifty salad courses that came close to ruining the evening, and that is because serving a salad, waiting for it to get nibbled away, removing it, and coming in with the main course is going to consume a half hour. During that period (a) everybody is eating up finite reserves of energy; some people are getting a little sleepy; (b) many are assuaging their anxiety/ennui/irritation by drinking more copiously than they otherwise would; and (c) the speaker is sitting there knowing that every minute that goes by is a minute that increases the natural torpor of active Americans at the end of a working day, inevitably affecting the keenness of their disposition to listen to his subtleties. And it is a law of nature that when something goes on for too long, management tends to chop off that which can be chopped off. If a Q&A was unscheduled, forget it; if a Q&A was scheduled, the master of ceremonies is likely to eliminate it ("Due to the lateness of the hour, we will need to do without the question-and-answer period Mr. Buckley had so graciously agreed to").

Speaking of booze, I am reminded of one of Professor De Voto's major complaints, namely the dry host. In 1972, many years after reading his jeremiad, I had Harold Macmillan on *Firing Line*. He insisted on a half hour's preparatory interview the day before, designed to explore the ground I intended to cover. After touching on Winston Churchill's disappointments, on the perils of the Normandy landing, on the winds of change in Africa, Mr. Macmillan got down to business: he would expect some champagne in the room to which he would be conducted before going into the studio. Harold Macmillan was a pro.

There are several stratagems for dealing with The Problem. Entering senior citizenship, I have become blunter than I was as an apple-cheeked circuit rider. So, on the way from the airport to the motel, I will say to my escort, "I see dinner is at six. Will they be serving wine?"

The chances are about six out of nine these days that the answer will be yes. But it might well be no, especially if you are eating in a dining hall located on the premises of a state college, or if you are in a dry county, or, of course, if you are in Mormon country. Some hosts/hostesses instantly understand, and those who do will vary their responses all the way from inviting you to the president's house for "a little wine" before the dinner, to inviting you to their own house, to delivering a bottle of wine to your room. People really are kind and obliging. But the trouble with any of these expedients is that some of us are indisposed to have a drink at 5:30, when dinner is scheduled for six, the lecture for eight. The kind of stimulation one is looking for won't keep for two and a half hours; and then, too, however happy you might be to find yourself with extra moments of unscheduled privacy, you desire privacy least during the cocktail hour, which is inherently convivial.

Might a lecturer abuse the cocktail hour? Rarely, I believe. I am aware only of the lurid exception of Truman Capote. Arriving in New Orleans twenty years ago I was picked up by the chairman of Tulane's annual Academic Week, during which the college sponsors five different lectures or debates on consecutive nights. On the way to the hotel from the airport I found my young host in high dudgeon. He and other members of the undergraduate committee had put hundreds of hours of work into planning the Academic Week, and what was the fruit of it all last night? he asked dramatically, as we threaded our way through New Orleans traffic.

"We knew Mr. Capote had this problem," the tall, angular, blond prelaw student explained, shaking his head slightly. "So during the cocktail hour I handed him a drink that was about one half jigger bourbon and one gallon of soda water. It didn't work. Mr. Capote said, 'Heh heh, lit'l man, you cayan't get away with that, no sir, not with Truman Capote!' He handed me back his glass, and I had to give him a regular drink. Then another. Then another. And he was already bombed when he arrived. By the time he got to the seminar, he couldn't even talk! We had to rely on the other lecturer, Edward Albee, who carried the whole ball. And then...and then"—my host was throbbing with indignation—"after the main talk, you know from the last time you were here, we all go over across the street for the informal talk. Well, Mr. Capote's aide came to me and said, 'Mr. Capote is too tahhred out to engage in the second pahht of the proceedings.' So I said to him, 'Well, you tell Mr. Capote if he doesn't come to the second part of the engagement, he's not going to be paid for the first part.'"

What happened? I asked.

"He made it. But there wasn't much for him to say, I mean, nothing much he *could* say."

I consoled my host. "Ten years from now," I promised him, "the Tulane audience will remember only one thing about your Academic Week. It was the week in which Truman Capote got tanked and couldn't speak." I was right, as usual.

Then there is the matter of the introduction. A few months back I listened with mounting horror to an introduction of me that Demosthenes would not have merited. I wish I had it in my power to restrain the enthusiastic introducer—particularly the one who wants to justify the special pains the committee went to in getting you there by dwelling on the discursive dreamland that lies ahead for the audience. He (or she) might feel that to do less than advise the audience to expect the wit of Oscar Wilde, the eloquence of Abraham Lincoln, and the profundity of Aristotle would suggest that he held you in less than the esteem owed ex officio to any guest selected by the Lackawanna Annual Forum Series. The thing to do—it works about one-third of the time—is to write out and send ahead a suggested introduction to yourself, making the usual high points sufficiently to justify your presence there and the audience's, but carefully refraining from hyperbole. Having said this, I have to add that some hosts take extraordinary pains in composing their words and indite truly elegant introductions.

If the beginning of your talk is unchanged and you have tested it out on a dozen audiences in the past ten weeks, you will know very quickly the speed of this assembly, as also something of its disposition. Audiences are generally a little nervous, starting out: they don't quite know what they will make of you, and they often fear that their reaction may be ploddish. If you are talking to undergraduates, they will wish to be wooed; but they tend to be nicely disposed, except for those whose fidelity to antithetical politics is a matter of deep principle. I remember lecturing at noon at the University of California at Long Beach during the Vietnam frenzies of the late sixties. Two thousand students lay stretched out on the lawn (that was the convention at the weekly lectures). A few months before, they had permitted Senator Vance Hartke of Indiana to get through only ten minutes of his speech unmolested, notwithstanding that the senator was against the war and had been from the beginning. After that, the students began talking to one another, laughing, walking about. I had no problem, none at all, getting through my talk, some of it stoutly defending the policies of Lyndon Johnson. After it was over, I said rather complacently to my host, a professor from the Department of Psychology, that it

was reassuring that I had the power to compel a college audience to listen to me on so excitable a subject. His comment was wonderfully deflating: "Don't you understand, Mr. Buckley? When you speak, they treat you as they would a man from the moon. They don't care what you say. They are just biologically curious."

People who wonder about the subject at all (they are mostly press interviewers writing about your talk, past or scheduled) tend to wonder whether I have been given a hard time for taking positions usually (especially when speaking at colleges) at variance with those of my audiences. But the shock to the listeners was always reduced by the foreknowledge that they would be listening to a conservative. At the beginning, in the fifties and sixties especially, college students, and of course faculty, were surprised, not to say aghast, at the heterodoxies they were hearing from the Right. But there was never (almost never) disruption.

The demands of courtesy tend to prevail. But sometimes someone just can't take it. Sometimes a public point is intended. Last May in Wilmington, with Delaware's Democratic governor sitting on the dais, I devoted the whole of my time to the problems that had arisen from the Lewinsky–Clinton business. My analysis was sharply to the disadvantage of the president. When I finished speaking, the governor rose and walked swiftly from the dais, manifestly in order to avoid social contact with the speaker after the evening's formal closing.

If the ambient mood is doggedly skeptical, then do not equivocate unless you have extraordinary seductive powers. I have seen Hubert Humphrey, and indeed Bill Clinton, draw blood from a stone in public speeches, attacking the skeptics in the manner of Jimmy Durante, who would, if necessary to entertain his audience, take an axe to the piano. Such as these have very special skills. The other way is to strive to communicate to your audience that if they exhibit the curiosity and the attentiveness to hear you out, their favors in attending will match yours in appearing; and both parties will leave the hall with a sense that neither wasted its time.

It is a grueling business, though obviously easier on those who are happiest when operating from a podium. The late Max Lerner, a learned evangelist, who was truly contented when instructing others how to think and what to believe in, told me that a perfect life for him would involve lecturing every day of the week: the rabbinical itch. Others cherish their afflatus but are more happily engaged when sweating over blank sheets of paper. What would be ideal for us would be an audience of people who sat there while you wrote and told you, after every paragraph or so, whether you were succeeding in reaching them.

Going Down to the *Titanic*

In 1987, I ventured two and a half miles down to the ocean floor to explore the mythogenic remains of the great ship that had gone down seventy-five years earlier. ⌁

T here comes a time when the nature of one's interest in a tragedy becomes historical, to use the word loosely, not human—to use *that* word loosely. When I was thirteen I was taken to Pompeii, and the guide spoke about the phenomenon and dealt only macrocosmically with the human tragedy. The people who died because Vesuvius belched up its firestorm of molten lava were entirely anonymous "victims," like the victims of Napoleon's march on Russia, or the men and women slaughtered day after festive day in the Roman Colosseum, or the cavalrymen of the Light Brigade. That doesn't mean any of these events is wrenched forever from the creative attentions of the artist whose design is to reconstruct the human story and therefore to reevoke sympathy for the suffering at Pompeii; the artist who declares eternal war against the routinization of death that followed in the wake of Napoleon's retreat; the writer who strives to capture the majestic nobility of the naked Christian, praying as he is prepared for the lion, or the mordant scorn owed to the bureaucratically homicidal idiocy of Lord Cardigan, who ordered his men to charge into suicide.

But the time comes when one's interest is taken by other aspects of these phenomena. Such times must come, else we'd be consumed by our preoccupation with our personal sorrows and by our knowledge of the suffering endured in so many historical events. Zero Mostel could not have given us his version of *Fiddler on the Roof* if the audience had been permitted to ponder only the pogroms in Russia, and the final solution they would lead to in Nazi Germany. If I went tomorrow to the mausoleum at Verona, I would probably find myself asking the guide whether there actually existed such a drug as Juliet took, brilliantly to feign death while all that was really happening was a profound sleep, pending her reanimation by Romeo. I would not, by asking that question, deaden myself to the poetry of one of the great romances in literature.

If you want one item (there are thousands to choose from) that will recall the awful poignancy of the death of the *Titanic*, I offer you this. A day before the *Carpathia* reached New York, on April 18, 1912, with the 705 survivors it had picked up on the lifeboats a few hours after the *Titanic* had gone down, the *Mackay-Bennett*, a cable ship, set out from Halifax in search of corpses, men and women and children floating on the Atlantic in life preservers, dead from exposure (this is how most of the *Titanic*'s victims died). Several hundred were retrieved. Some, because of decomposition, were forthwith buried at sea, but painstaking efforts were made to identify all the dead and, where successful, to advise relatives of their fate and to itemize any personal effects that had been retrieved with the corpse. Notification went to one couple concerning their son, a young sailor. This is the text of the letter received back by the authorities in Halifax:

I have been inform by Mr. F. Blake Superintendent Engineer of the White Star Line Trafalgar Chambers on the 10th that the Body of my Beloved Son Herbert Jupe which was Electrical

Engineer No. 3 on the Ill-Fatted *Titanic* has been recovered and Buried at Sea by the Cable Steamer "Mackey-Bennett" and that his Silver Watch and Handkerchief marked H.J. is in your Possession. He bought him half a doz of the same when he was at Belfast with the R.M.S. Olympic to have a new blade put to one of her Perpellors we are extremely obliged for all your Kindness to my Precious Boy. He was not married and was the Love of our Hearts and he loved his Home but God gave and God has taken Him Blessed be the Name of the Lord. He has Left an Aceing Void in our Home which cannot be filled.

Please Send along the Watch and Handkerchief marked H.J.

Yours Truly C. Jupe.

His Mother is 72 Last April 4th.
His Father is 68 Last Feb 9th.

A bystander reading that letter in the spring of 1912 (if indeed the letter was read other than by the recipients—it is unearthed in Michael Davie's *Titanic: The Death and Life of a Legend*, outstandingly the best book afloat on the *Titanic* apart from Walter Lord's) could have been expected to feel sheer civic rage against the executioners of Herbert Jupe; and moral historians are always free to cry out that justice was never really pursued after the great ship went down.

True, the White Star Line had had to pay out two and one-half million dollars, which is a lot more than it sounds, if you close your eyes for perspective. Captain Edward J. Smith of the *Titanic* was the highest-paid seaman in the world, receiving £1,250 per year.

Oh yes. Captain Smith. He paid a stiff price for ignoring four Marconigrams (as they then called wireless messages) warning of circumambient ice. After all, he went down with his ship. But that was incomplete consolation for the relatives of the other 1,500 who went down. Then there was Captain Stanley Lord of the nearby *California*. He chose to ignore eight distress flares on the extraordinary grounds (a judgment he reached in his cabin, half asleep) that the color of the sighted flares probably meant that they had been set off as a sort of festive handshake in mid-ocean, one merchant vessel spotting another from the same line off in the distance. Captain Lord turned over and went back to sleep in his immobilized liner (he had ordered the engines stopped because of ice conditions). Captain Lord, who might have saved 1,500 people from drowning, walked into historical obloquy, though his professional career was unobstructed. Indeed there gathered to defend him what appropriately were called "Lordites," who stress inconsistencies in the *Titanic* narrative in order to justify Captain Lord's insouciance.

Who else was punished? Not Harland & Wolff, which had built the largest moving object ever created. The great Ulster shipyard had complied with the nautical specifications of the British Board of Trade, and no one at H&W had ever said the *Titanic* was "unsinkable." That unsinkable business was nothing more than the creeping vainglory of a jingoistic age in which the leading sea power in the world, the U.K., was out to make a public demonstration of her infinite resources in order to assert her clear dominance over the brash competitor on the other side of the Atlantic, and, at the same time, to impress the Kaiser, who in 1912 was beginning to stir. It was not advertised that the British champion was financed, and in effect owned, by American bankers.

What about the Board of Trade itself? Why were there lifeboats for only 1,200 people, given that there were 2,200 people on board?

Well you see, the Board of Trade reasoned that any ship that had watertight bulkheads which could be raised to sequester an accidental inflow of water didn't *need* the traditional ten cubic feet of lifeboat space per passenger. The contingency simply hadn't been considered that raising the bulkheads wasn't enough if those bulk-heads weren't designed to rise to the ceiling of the topmost deck. As it was, what happened in the *Titanic* was that water under pressure flowed bustily from one compartment to the next, even as water flows from one cube in a tilted ice tray into the next.

What was one to do to the Board of Trade?

You could give it a little rhetorical hell. Senator William Alden Smith and his investigating committee did so. If Senator Smith was a moral slouch, then so was Cotton Mather. Smith subpoenaed all the surviving officers of the *Titanic* and twenty-nine members of the crew. When he learned that five crew members, ducking the subpoena, had sailed furtively out of New York aboard the *Lapland*, Smith responded by sending a vessel to bring them back. (Senator Smith simply asked President Taft for a naval ship; request granted; *Lapland* stopped.) The tenacity with which Senator Smith challenged the behavior of British officers, British architects, and British administrators was undiminished by his ingenuous ignorance of the sea or of shipboard terminology (he did not know that a ship's "bow" was different from a ship's "head"). The investigation so provoked (and titillated) the popular press in Great Britain that a derisory invitation was issued to the senator to come to London to lecture at the Hippodrome on "any maritime subject."

And, of course, the British had their own investigation, conducted by Lord Mersey. It is fair to generalize that the Mersey board concluded in effect that although the North Atlantic route taken by the *Titanic* on its fateful passage ought not to have been taken, in fact it was the workaday steamer route; that binoculars should have been available to the lookouts, though binoculars are not necessarily aids to spotting objects at a distance; that more lifeboats should have been available, though it is not justified to indict the Board of Trade for failure to foresee that which was unforeseeable; that the behavior of the officers and crew would have been more orderly if clearer instructions had been given and if a lifeboat drill had been conducted, but that under the circumstances they performed well, indeed in some cases heroically.

Leaving the parents of Herbert Jupe with what? Concretely, with £100, the per-seaman settlement from the civil lawsuit concluded in 1916. Civic rage had to satisfy itself by other means, and to that rough end, an entire literature sprang up, each book, or article, with a slightly redistributed gravamen. There came, early on, the philosophizing of it all. By conceiving a vessel of such arrant luxury and size, we Lilliputians had stirred the attention of the gods, who had stretched out an admonitory finger, casually but sternly to remind us that we are mortals, and ought not to engage in extrahuman conceits.

The great war came, and gradually the memory of the *Titanic* receded, though always there were the full-time coroners, however sparse at times they seemed (the first issue of the journal issued by the *Titanic* Historical Society had only forty-five subscribers). But the legend was rekindled by Walter Lord's stirring *A Night to Remember*, and by the movies and the television reenactments of that night. The Philadelphia Maritime Museum became the formal collector of Titaniana.

And then, in 1985, the great bell rang. The little, pilotless submarine *Argo*, under the direction of the naval exploratory vessel *Knorr* from Woods Hole, Massachusetts, had been "mowing the lawn" over an area of one hundred fifty square miles in the neighborhood of where it was calculated the ship had actually gone down. The anxious operation was conducted under the direction of a French and an American scientist. The process had been going on tediously, day and night, ever since July 11. It was then that the fancy little sub, with its congeries of surrealistic technological devices designed to permit objects on the ocean floor to be seen, began its slow sweep. At 1:40 in the morning of September 1, 1985, the excited French scientist found himself staring at a ship's boiler. The *Titanic* had been found.

ॐ

Two years later, at eleven in the morning, on the identical site— 963 miles northeast of New York City, 453 miles south of New-foundland—after being asked one final time whether I suffered from claustrophobia, I was placed over the shoulder-wide opening of the little submarine *Nautile* and made my way down the vertical iron ladder into the tubular control center.

The *Nautile* is the twenty-million-dollar jewel of IFREMER, a scientific offshoot of the French government. It is an underwater exploratory vessel built with titanium, weighing eighteen tons, six feet in diameter at its widest point. It can descend to depths of twenty thousand feet below sea level. The chief pilot occupies a berth on the port side. Behind him, sitting on an abbreviated seat, is the copilot. The starboard berth is for the "observer," in this case me. Each of us has a porthole built of one-foot-thick glass. The copilot, in addition, has two pairs of eight-inch television screens, attached to video cameras. One of the cameras is trained to look dead ahead, a second to pivot. The other pair of cameras portrays at close range and at longer range the movements of the mechanical arms operating from the side of the *Nautile*. These are designed to pick up objects from the seabed. With the aid of the video, the operator can exactly instruct the arms.

The overhead hatch is now tightly sealed, and you close your eyes slowly, hoping this will not be the moment you contract claustrophobia. The *Nautile* is dragged by cable to the launching end of the *Nadir*, the mother ship, then lifted by halyard, lowered into the ocean, and towed by frogmen on a rubber Zodiac out a short distance. The descent begins.

ENSCONCED . . .

. . . WITHIN THE NAUTILE. DESTINATION: TITANIC

At about 2:20 A.M., two hours and forty minutes after it scraped the iceberg, the *Titanic* lost, finally, its fight to stay afloat. Its stern rose up so high, the huge ship was almost vertical over the water. It paused there; appeared, in the description of some witnesses in their lifeboats, to shudder; and then eased back to an angle of about forty-five degrees, as if cocking itself to spring ahead on its long descent. Seconds later it catapulted into its plunge, with its live company of 1,500 people, including the eight-piece band which had been performing for the condemned right up until it was no longer possible to stand up. Like everyone else, the band members were wearing life preservers. It is calculated that it took the *Titanic* approximately ten minutes to reach bottom and that it was traveling, when it hit the ocean floor, at a speed of twenty miles per hour.

To descend the same distance, the *Nautile* takes ninety minutes, which means a descent at just under 1.7 miles per hour. You try to sit up, which requires you to raise your knees six inches or so—there isn't room to stretch them out. You had been advised not to eat breakfast, and dutifully you did not. It is now 11:30 A.M., thirty minutes after our descent began, lunchtime aboard the *Nautile*. The copilot, Pierre Yves, brings out little packages wrapped in aluminum foil. The first course is a hard-boiled egg. Did I wish any salt?

"*S'il vous plaît, oui.*"

Then there is cold roast beef and French bread. Followed by cheese and a plum or a peach.

"Do you have anything to drink?" I ask abstractly. Answer: Yes. They have water. But it is not thereupon proffered, though you are left believing that if you directly ask for it the plastic bottle will be handed to you. It isn't any lack of French hospitality, it is just that it would be such an awful *dérangement* if the observer along the way experienced an undeniable call of nature. Just the physical gyrations necessary to bring this off call to mind a Marx Brothers three-in-a-bed sequence. You pass.

What to do, as the pilot and copilot exchange rapid technical French? You had arrived at the *Nautile* with two plastic bags, causing the chief pilot, Georges, to frown and ask, Did you really need all that—*équipage*? Embarrassed, you pulled out and left on shipdeck the largest of your three flashlights, and three of your six cassette tapes. But that did leave me with (1) two small flashlights; (2) a book—a thriller, to distract me during the long descent and ascent; (3) a little dictating machine (I might want to make notes, and there is hardly room for even the smallest laptop); which machine serves also as a Walkman, for which (4) I had three cassettes. The second parcel contained (5) a thick white sweater, to augment protection from the thirty-eight-degree cold at ocean-floor level (I had on long winter underwear, my regular sweater, and the fire-resistant coveralls required by the French); (6) a little can of Right Guard, in case the chill exercised less than all its usual functions; and then (7) a set of knee pads furnished by Ralph White, my new best friend, an American professional jack-of-all-trades, a genial member of the entrepreneur's team who knows more about diving, history, geology, mechanics, ships, airplanes, and the sea than anyone I had ever met. Why knee pads? You will see, Ralph said; and indeed I would see. When you are lying with your nose against the porthole you need to put your left knee somewhere, since there is no room to stretch out. So it ends up on the narrow knurled ice-cold titanium bottom strip between you and Georges. Try then bringing up your knee for relief when it is protected only by underwear, pants, and fire suit for a half hour against the cold grid; and then give thanks to the Lord for Ralph.

The knee pads, plus (8) gloves for hands that would become cold and (9), perhaps most important, an inflatable rubber pillow, this to lay over the little metal bar that runs either under your chest while you are lying down, or else under your back during the vertical passages. There are moments when I wonder whether an extra million dollars might not have been dredged up to cushion that bisecting rod.

But the great moment was coming. We would reach bottom at 3,784 meters, and Georges would turn on the outside beam lights when we reached 3,550 meters. We were in place, on guard by our portholes. The lights flashed on. Nothing to see, though the water is startlingly clear, diaphanous to the range of our light's beam, an apparent twenty-five to thirty feet ahead.

Then, gradually, it happens: You are descending slowly to what looks like a yellow-white sandy beach, sprinkled with black rock-like objects. These, it transpires, are pieces of coal. There must have been a hundred thousand of them in the area we surveyed, scattered between the bow of the ship and the stern, a half-mile back. On the left is a man's outdoor shoe. Left shoe. Made, I would say, of suede of some sort. You cannot quite tell whether it is laced up. And then, just off to the right a few feet, a snow-white teacup. Just sitting there, thank you, on the sand. I would liken the tableau, in its sheer neatness, to a display that might have been prepared for a painting by Salvador Dali. Would we, I asked Georges anxiously, be pausing to scoop up the shoe?

No. The expedition does not pick up articles of personal clothing. What about the teacup?

Only if it is bordered in blue. The distinction, I learn, is that the blue-bordered tableware is rarer than the plain white used by the 712 steerage passengers. First-class passengers (337) had the fancier, blue-bordered cups. Enough of the former had been picked up in the twenty-six previous dives. Time was limited, and we would not use it up on redundancies.

On & on we floated, our bottom suspended sometimes six inches from the ocean floor, sometimes a meter or two. We were looking for targets of opportunity, which is why I was expected to keep my eyes hard to starboard, but we were also looking specifically for a piece of the command mechanism from the *Titanic*'s bridge, the signal handles brought sharply back by First Officer William Murdock when he was told to reverse engines, moments after the iceberg was sighted dead ahead. The control mechanism had been photographed lying on the ocean floor in the area we were now covering, and instructions were being radioed from above ("*130 degrees. Proceed for sixty meters*") directing us to our quarries. And then a portion of a leaded window. They wanted that piece. It was missing from a reconstruction of an ornamental *vitrine*, one of the luxurious decorations in first class. And a man's leather satchel, contents unknown.

℘

We were below, searching and scooping, for six and one-half cold hours. Ralph had said I would find it surprising how quickly the time would pass. That was not exactly what I found after two or three hours. But the sensation, in microcosm, was vivid, exhilarating, and uncomplicated by any philosophical misgivings about our mission. I did not feel any kinship to the voyeur; no more than when, three years earlier, I had ogled at the tombs in the Nile or, a dozen years ago, at the catacombs in Lima beneath the great cathedral, where the bones of thousands of Incas lie.

I was a passive part of an archaeological venture which was also a personal adventure—only one hundred people in the world have dived as deep in the water as I have now done. The exploration is singular because it is being conducted in a part of the planet heretofore thought totally inaccessible, let alone accessible to men who have in mind actually collecting an inventory of items that, for seventy-five years, have lain on the ocean floor, objects last seen by men and women two-thirds of whom died a quite awful death,

victims of an assortment of hubristic naval architects, cocky seamen, and mindless moneymen.

Finally the moment came to terminate our sortie and begin our
slow ascent. After a few minutes, permission was requested over
the radio (permission granted) to jettison one of our two lead-
weight ballasts, permitting a sharp increase in our rate of ascent.
You attempt to sit up, just to find something different to do with
your bones. But you have to lean just slightly forward. Otherwise
you might lean just slightly back, in which case you might brush
up against one of those hundred toggle switches behind you and,
who knows, flip the one that would toss you out between the shoe
and the teacup—the pressure out there is six thousand pounds per
square inch.

Time to use the Walkman? But in order to do that you need to
recover the satchel, dig out the relevant parts, and wire your ears,
and suddenly that mounts up to a series of exertions on the order
of stopping to change your socks while climbing to the very top of
Mt. Everest.

So you half-freeze, half-continue trying to read your stubbornly
unprepossessing thriller with your flashlight between your teeth,
your hands behind you, supporting your arched back, and you
exchange every now and then a drollery, in your kitchen French,
with the pilots.

You look for the one-hundredth time at the fast-changing depth
meter. This time it joyfully tells you that you have just about
reached the surface. You know you are within fifty meters when
the little sub begins to roll, reflecting surface turbulence. It seems
an age before the frogmen are there to secure you to the halyard
coming down from the ship's crane. But eventually you are airborne into the mother ship's womb. The hatch is turned, and you
climb out; a Superman grin on your face, you have to admit.

Aboard the *Sea Cloud*

We traveled from Tahiti to Easter Island, stopping in at Pitcairn Island, where the descendants of Fletcher Christian will sing to you on their longboat. ⟋

When *Marjorie Merriweather Post,* in Bermuda for that purpose, first laid eyes on her new boat waiting there for her (we will skip the varied names the boat has sailed under and just call it the *Sea Cloud*), she might reasonably have concluded that the million dollars she paid for it would, in 1931, get you *anything.* True, in the next twenty years or so she would spend five to seven million dollars just to maintain the boat, and when finally she sold it, she got less than a million (General Trujillo traded her a second-hand Viscount turboprop for it). On the other hand, who wants—can afford?—is willing to pay for?—a 360-foot boat requiring a crew of about sixty, which is what it takes to mount twenty-nine sails, with all those nice things that go with a vessel of such dimensions?

The answer is a German syndicate called Hansa Treuhand. In purchasing and refitting the *Sea Cloud* in 1979, Hansa acquired the most seductive commercial ship at sea. And, evidently, Hansa operates her successfully, for her calendar is robust. In 1988, the year the *Sea Cloud* came to my attention, you could sail on her to Malaga, Casablanca, Tenerife, Mallorca, Corsica, Nice, Sardinia, Monaco, Plymouth, Aberdeen, Bergen, Copenhagen, Stockholm, Leningrad,

Gothenburg, Hamburg, Amsterdam, St. Malo, Lisbon, Gibraltar, Piraeus, Patmos, Corfu, and Venice, and, if stretching your legs at sea is your bag (it is mine), you might take the final marathon of the season, Las Palmas to Antigua, nonstop, fourteen days.

For us (my wife and me), the circumstances of our arrival on the *Sea Cloud* were ideal. Just before boarding a boat for a trip that by its comprehensive hedonism would numb a Puritan's soul, it helps to have struggled a bit with workaday tribulations. You would not, after all, want to start in on Scheherazade's *Thousand and One Nights* rising from your couch, interrupting only your consumption of bonbons. The preceding twenty-four hours, in our case, were created fully to exercise a syllabus of self-abnegation. Pat was nearing the end of an eternally long recuperation following hip replacement, and the end of (we like to think) the most hectic social/civic week of her career in New York City.

We would meet at the Continental Airlines gate in Los Angeles in time to board the ten-hour flight at 11:50 P.M. for Papeete. In Tahiti we would have a leisurely thirty-six hours before boarding the *Sea Cloud*. During the twenty-four hours preceding the flight, I would preside at a two-hour television debate in Houston featuring the six Republican candidates for president. The following morning, I'd attend a breakfast given by the sponsors of the debate. This would be followed by two one-hour tapings for *Firing Line* reflecting, in the company of specialists, on the performance the night before of the candidates and on the political issues raised by them. A chartered airplane would guarantee my arrival early in the afternoon in San Francisco, giving me plenty of time to rehearse for a long-planned public social event at which I'd serve as MC and perform two pieces on the harpsichord. A second chartered plane would guarantee my arrival at the airport in Los Angeles "with over an hour to spare."

You guessed it. (1) En route to San Francisco, the winds required an unscheduled stop, in Albuquerque, for refueling. Delays at the

S.F. Airport, another hour of waiting. (2) Arrived in S.F. only just in time to dash to the harpsichord, already on-stage, and, sick with nervousness, rush through a rehearsal. Cocktail reception, dinner, the affair...(3) I slaughtered Bach's Chromatic Fantasy. Was rushed out to the airport to learn (4) that we were fifty-fifth in line for takeoff (two of the runways were out). (5) It wasn't a jet, as promised, but a turboprop.

However, a car *was* waiting at LAX when finally we landed, which drove me at feverish speed to Continental at the other end of the airport, where I checked my bags. I was carrying one carry-on bag, a porter another two. Together we sprinted through one of those endless LAX passages from check-in counter to departure gate—arriving at the gate at 11:45 to face hysterical wife, her face lit up with fear & loathing, delivering at virago speed her standard lecture on how Husband Cannot Manage His Life Properly Going at Overdrive....All I needed; except (6) the ensuing announcement of an hour's flight delay. Followed by the announcement of a second hour's delay. Followed by the announcement of the flight's cancellation and news of the unhappy coincidence that, the fuel pump and the hydraulic gear having been fixed, this last, and conclusive, delay was caused by the refusal of the cargo door to close. Any cargo door that cannot close, we were told, a fortiori, can't open: which meant that (7) our six checked bags might as well have been in Tahiti. Following a scramble at 2:20 A.M. for Continental's emergency toothbrush kit, a bus takes us to a motel, where we collapse into bed. Followed three hours later by a 6:00 A.M. phone call: the plane is fixed, will depart in exactly forty-five minutes, all but precluding even somnambulistic toilet duties. But we are there in forty-five minutes to hear (8) the announcement of an hour's delay. Followed by the announcement of a second hour's delay. Followed by the announcement of the flight's fresh cancellation. Back to the motel. We order lunch, Pat steps gratefully into bath, phone rings: plane fixed, immediate departure, quick, hurry up. We get there, and this time are led to our seats on the plane and given a glass of champagne, Château Triomphe, here's looking at you, baby. Followed by a second glass. Followed by…the sorrowful notice of (9) the flight's newest cancellation. We are led to the Air France waiting room, having been resignedly advised by Continental to switch allegiance. Air France flight (10) delayed. Two hours.

But it does then leave, and our baggage is waiting for us in Papeete (Continental finally made it), we get to bed, rise, have three hours to survey war-torn Papeete (this was the week after a riot, and curfew was still in force), quick lunch, and on to: the *Sea Cloud*.

There was a moment when we thought our curse had traveled with us. The captain said that a shipment of provisions from Australia was delayed and we might not be leaving the harbor until midnight. But one hour after he said that, bells & whistles began to sound, and the *Sea Cloud* zigzagged its way from the dock, turned laboriously, clumsily about, and headed out of the busy, cosmopolitan harbor in balmy, cloudy weather. We were aboard the largest sailing boat in the world, the most luxurious commercial boat in the world; and we were setting out to visit the remotest little insular notoriety in the world, a full sailing week ahead of us, east, a little south; followed by a second week's sailing to the second-most-remote island in the world, again, east, a little south.

The bags unpacked, I surveyed the pleasantest bedroom (with private fireplace) I have ever sailed in. It was Mrs. Post's—excuse me, "Marjorie's"—prime guest quarters, less the adjoining room, which had been her prime guest's boudoir, now a separate cabin. (On the *Sea Cloud*, Mrs. Post is always "Marjorie," even to people born after she died, as in, "This is where Marjorie used to sit.") We walked out into the corridor, which looks like a high Colonial Williamsburg reproduction, to the main deck, and climbed up to the Lido deck, where champagne was being distributed to the fifty-seven passengers. The moon was out, four days short of full, and the lights of Tahiti gave us a modest, gradually evanescing perspective. The boat's engines (we wouldn't hoist sail till the following day) were nicely unobtrusive, the generator practically soundless. Back down the stairway into the main lounge, with four or five rectangular tables set up for dinner, as also another four or five tables in Marjorie's adjoining dining room. The two rooms are of intimate dimensions, exquisitely furnished; there was candlelight, and good cuisine. After dinner we walked out to the stern, to the area they call the Blue Lagoon (I don't know what Marjorie called it, perhaps that). It is a quarter-acre of blue cushions set along the rounded stern of the boat. You can sprawl out on them and see the moon and the stars and the waves going by, and you will say, or at least I did, *This ship is a wonderful idea.*

𝕻

Marjorie had a roaring good time aboard the *Sea Cloud*, it is generally agreed. Her then-husband was E. F. Hutton, a big, romantic Wall Streeter who loved to sail, causing the *Sea Cloud* to spend much of the next four years at sea. But, it appears, E.F.H. loved not only sailing and Marjorie, but also some of Marjorie's friends and at least one of her servants, which led to his being jettisoned, and to the ensuing wedding with Joseph Davies, a journalist, businessman, lawyer, politician, and Roosevelt backer who was appointed ambassador to Stalin's Russia.

That was a very good deal for Stalin, inasmuch as Joe Davies a few years later published one of the most sycophantic pro-Stalin books (*Mission to Moscow*) ever penned this side of Izvestia, Inc. That book more than atoned for the anachronistic appearance in Leningrad, five years earlier, of Ambassador and Mrs. Davies, arriving for duty on the *Sea Cloud*. I swear, you would have thought it was the overture to the Romanov Restoration.

But Ambassador Davies didn't particularly enjoy sailing, so the *Sea Cloud* was used primarily as a place to entertain, in Leningrad and, subsequently, in Brussels, where Davies went for his next tour of duty as ambassador. Marjorie divorced him, one forgets exactly why (maybe she read his book?), and then the world war was upon us, and Marjorie of course turned her boat over to the Coast Guard, which removed the masts and used it vigorously as a sub spotter, among other things. By coincidence, the *Sea Cloud* was in the vicinity when the Normandy invasion took place, and the relevant admiral invited it to come along behind his command vessel; which it did, so that for a historic twenty-four hours, the *Sea Cloud* was there, a part of Operation Overlord.

In 1944, the Navy concluded that the facilities of Marjorie's vessel were not really needed anymore, and the *Sea Cloud* was decommissioned. Refurbishment was scheduled, and that would last four or five years, costing about two million. There was a brief revival of the *Sea Cloud* as of the old days—the Duke and the Duchess of Windsor deftly suggested that a cruise to Havana would be nice; they had never been to Havana, poor dears—but Marjorie's mind was on other things, and she offered the boat for sale, $1 million bare, $1.2 million with its exquisite furnishings and decorations.

There were no takers. Eventually General Trujillo, overlord of the Dominican Republic, came along. In order to qualify the *Sea Cloud* as an official part of the Dominican Navy, the resourceful Generalisimo mounted one (1) machine gun on it, and it was thereupon incorporated into his happy entourage of cars, planes, castles, and plantations. A while later, they shot Trujillo. His son Ramfis inherited the Dominican Republic and the *Sea Cloud*, which he used with hectic joie de vivre. A journalist observed that aboard Marjorie's former boat, "star-studded parties became so raucous that one morning, painted on her gleaming white sides, appeared the graffito: 'Zsa Zsa Slept Here.'" When the reformers went after Ramfis, he tried to escape on the *Sea Cloud* with lots and lots of gold bullion. He made it as far as Martinique, but there he was stopped, and after protracted negotiating, the Dominican Republic got back the *Sea Cloud* plus the gold, and Spain got Ramfis.

The *Sea Cloud* sat about unused for years, sold finally to a company in Miami that thought to convert her into a commercial liner, or perhaps a floating college of sorts. This didn't work out, and the boat found herself, unloved, in Panama for yet another stretch of idleness, until the little German syndicate decided to go to work on her and try her out on the luxury trade.

I don't know how much they spent, but boats require endless sums of money. In this case, furthermore, it was necessary, for commercial use, to expand the cabin area. What amounts to a whole extra floor of cabins was plunked down on the deck, in front of the Blue Lagoon. This hurts, but does not deface, the original profile; and of course there was the added weight and windage for the sails and engines to cope with.

I tried, without obtrusive zeal, to probe the ship's economics. The focus turns on the accommodations. These range from indescribably luxurious (Marjorie's cabin and E. F. Hutton's) to utilitarian. I give here the descriptions exactly as given in the official literature, with the price for the fortnight (Papeete–Pitcairn–Easter Island) we spent on board:

SUITE—Original owners' suite. Outside with double bed, private bathtub, shower. Suites 1, 2—$8,195 [single occupancy—i.e., that figure is paid twice, once by husband, once by wife]

SINGLE DELUXE—Original outside stateroom with lower bed, shower. Stateroom B—$8,295

DELUXE—Original outside stateroom with double bed or two lower beds, private bathtub, shower. Staterooms 3, 4, 7—$6,795

SINGLE SUPERIOR—Original outside stateroom with lower bed, shower. Stateroom 11—$7,895

SUPERIOR—Original outside stateroom with double bed, shower. Staterooms 5 (bathtub), 6, 10, 14—$6,395

TYPE A—Outside stateroom with two lower beds, shower. Staterooms 19, 22, 31, 33, 34, 35, 36, 37, 38, 39, 40, 41—$5,695

SINGLE TYPE B—Outside stateroom with lower bed, shower. Staterooms 29, 32—$5,295

TYPE C—Outside stateroom with one lower bed and an upper berth, shower. Staterooms 15, 17, 18, 20—$4,895.

I did a little arithmetic, rounding the figures, and calculated that if the entrepreneurs of the *Sea Cloud* sold out every cabin at the price designated, the ship would bring in a *weekly* income of $366,000. Almost by definition, this cannot happen. The lecturer (there is one for every trip, sometimes two), for instance, gets a double cabin free. (I was a lecturer.) On the other hand, on our run there was only one unsold double cabin. Sometimes the ship's company is light, but we are talking about special circumstances. (When, in June 1986, we attacked Qaddafi and he countered that he would retaliate against Americans in Europe, prospective passengers on the *Sea Cloud* cancelled their bookings all but unanimously.) The syndicate does not give out the figures, but informed speculation holds that the vessel pays its way and returns a profit, which is as it should be, and reassuring news for those who like to be propelled by sail, and who tend to associate sailing with the strenuous life but hope it can, at least every now and then, be otherwise, as it is aboard the *Sea Cloud.*

஧

Now on the matter of sailing. If you travel from Tahiti to Pitcairn to Easter Island, you will be traveling for the most part into light head winds. This was known to whoever laid out the course, but management knew too that the ship's passengers would not acquiesce in two weeks aboard a sailing boat without ever setting sail. Accordingly, provision was made for laying off the wind during the day, permitting the sails to go up and fill out. Late in the afternoon, the sails would come down, and the boat would proceed under power for the next sixteen hours, on course; and, day after day, the routine would be repeated. This could have meant that to go the 1,350 miles, Tahiti–Pitcairn, you might in fact have traveled 1,600 miles. So what?

There was an unpleasant surprise in store for us. It was the peculiar effect that Pacific underwater glop had on the *Sea Cloud*'s bottom. Quite unlike anything ever experienced in the Atlantic, in the Mediterranean, or in the Caribbean, observed Captain Edward Cassidy (a Coast Guard retiree, a man of huge charm and ability, and emphatically not the kind who would deceive a serious questioner). There was no *way* for a frogman to scrape off those hard Pacific barnacles, and they cost the ship as much as two knots in speed, whether under power or sail. The impact of this was comprehensive. Now it would take much more time under power to make up the time lost under sail. And while under sail in a light wind, you would come pretty close to the sensation of no forward movement at all.

Concretely, we had to average 8.2 knots to reach our destinations on schedule. A piece of cake, for a boat that can power at eleven to twelve knots. But using the preferred, quiet two engines, we were now making under power only eight to nine knots. And sailing at four to five knots.

There was no moment, during the 2,500-mile journey from Tahiti to Easter Island, when the great *Sea Cloud* traveled under sail as fast as my thirty-six-foot sloop would have done. So that we ended up sailing on only five of the fourteen days, thanks to the burdened hull. Sailing at snail speed, however, was not without pleasure and excitement. There was, for example, the spectacle of eighteen deck hands (fourteen boys, four girls) concerting one of the truly complicated and heroic surviving anachronisms at sea: the hoisting of twenty-nine sails on a brigantine bark. The sight of twenty young seamen aloft on the spreaders, some of them one hundred feet above you, lingers in the memory.

And then at whatever speed you make, a boat under sail simply gives off different sensations. It's probably relevant to remark that no one goes up for a ride in a sailplane intending to set speed records. The sensation is distinctive whether you are traveling at ten knots or at five. Ten is more exciting, and the *Sea Cloud* is easily capable of making ten knots when the bottom is clean and the wind is coming in at an accommodating angle (best: just aft of the beam). The rule of thumb, Red Shannon, the relief captain, told me, is this: the *Sea Cloud* can travel at one-half the speed of the wind. But there is this caveat: If the ship heels over more than ten degrees, sail is reduced, to make the passengers comfortable.

More than ten degrees! God! (I sputtered), my wife is scared by white mice, yet when she laid down the law on my first ocean sailboat, and affixed her sticker, "Patsy Gets Off," she placed it on the inclinometer at thirty-five degrees! *Ten* degrees!!... Knowing smile. Management knows best what elderly passengers like, what they do not like. "Make that twelve degrees," the captain corrected. But if the wind is all the way aft, then the heel isn't athwartship, the boat is steadier, and you can *move*. With, say, a twenty-five-knot wind, you can go twelve or more knots, and then you are *really* racing along. I can only imagine, when that happens on the *Sea Cloud*, thinking truly sweet thoughts about Marjorie.

❧

Everybody—*everybody*—one ran into among the professional crew was obliging, attentive, good-natured. Such things can never be laid down to coincidence, but what does one do to make it so? Court-martial anyone caught saying No to any passenger, whatever his/her request?

Such situations have got to reflect the personality of the captain. "Cas" Cassidy was everywhere, greeting and mingling and laughing with the passengers, running the ship, and telling us, in about as many words, that there was nothing we were not permitted to do except fall overboard ("It creates a great deal of paperwork"). Only one area of the ship is out of bounds, the forepeak, where the young deckhands stroll and sunbathe. But if we wish to go there—say to take a photograph of the ship under sail from an advantageous site—why, we need only ask at the bridge and a deckhand would be deputized to escort us to the area.

Call in at the sacrosanct bridge? "We have an open bridge. Everyone is welcome." Some of us took full advantage of this, and one sleepy afternoon I even inquired into the exact formula for descrying the distance between longitudinal lines as you travel south from the Equator toward the Pole. One would think that since one minute of latitude measures exactly one mile at the equator, and exactly zero at the South Pole, it would measure one half mile at forty-five degrees south. Wrong. Captain Shannon dug up his Bowditch, which vouchsafes the formula, the inditement of which would fill an inscrutable paragraph.

There was, for instance, Johnson, the young and experienced Anglo-Indian radio officer. To meet editorial responsibilities in New York I needed to send out two or three telex communications every day. I undertook to type these myself, rather than have Johnson retype them from my computer screen. Fine. He would yield me his little seat in the tiny radio room he shared with the purser, and I would type away. Now, my typing is done at whiz speed, but my bane is typographical errors. Because the telex tends to be a sluggish machine with a miserably insensitive space bar, my messageswouldtendtoreadinthisway. This made no difference at all to me, and it wasn't a surreptitious design to cheat Telex Inc., since they charge not by the word, as with Western Union, but by the minutes and seconds required to transmit a message (very expensive, by the way: a 250-word telex cost about fifty dollars). But Johnson could not *stand* such typographical imperfections, and so he would patiently go over my copy and meticulously, and after a while delightedly, insert a space between each pair of elided words.

We became fast friends. The night before the trip ended, I left him a message:

MR.BUCKLEYJR.WISHESTOEXPRESS
HISENDURINGGRATITUDETOOFFICER
JOHNSON RAPHAEL
FORHISINVALUABLEHELPINMAKINGMR.
BUCKLEY'SGARBLEDCABLESLEGIBLE
TOALLTHECORNERSOFTHEEARTH.

The next morning, on the tender heading into Easter Island, the tour director handed me a telex message. I opened it:

DEARSIR
MANYTHANKSFORYOURAPPRECIATION...
WISH YOU AND MRS. BUCKLEY A HAPPY AND SAFE JOURNEY
BACK HOME. ALL THE BEST.

The time at sea was heavily unplanned, but with just enough way-points to give the days a little punctuation. At first I wondered that there was no movie. But on day five, we could see *Mutiny on the Bounty* after lunch, in the lounge; and every day after that there was a movie, mostly comfortable old-timers (*Some Like It Hot*), some more modern (*Tootsie*). Every night, on your bed, a printed schedule of the following day's activities would lie. The day began with a half hour's calisthenics led by cruise director and pianist Tom Hook. If

there was a lecture that day, it was scheduled at eleven. In the course of the fortnight there was a Trivial Pursuit tournament, skeet shooting, a treasure hunt. Lunches were buffet, served on the main deck. Depending on the weather, you might take your tray up to the Lido deck (more exactly—since this required steadiness of foot, especially if we were under sail—a steward would materialize to take the tray up for you), or else consume it on the main deck outside, or in the air-conditioned lounge. After dinner, Tom would play the piano, and generally there were those who would accompany him in song. One night, twelve deckhands came up to sing for us, four girls, eight men, each one of them a fit subject for a cover picture of Young America (or Sweden, or Norway, or New Zealand, or India). Their singing was indescribably awful; they were only episodically in unison and never, absolutely never, in harmony. A charming unprofessional, indeed antiprofessional, performance. (CAUTION: If you care about music, bring along a cassette player and tapes.)

So it went, fourteen days of high relaxation, twelve of them sunny, eight nights with a moon, my occasional sextant sights checking in nicely, thanks; thanks to WhatStar, which gurgles for ten seconds and then yields me the name of that arcane star I shot (Archenar), and then graces me with a navigational fix, one-half of it based on Archenar's sturdy leg.

§

So it went, day after day. But there were high moments, two of them.

The first was the end of the day at Pitcairn Island. There are fifty-eight people who live there. We had foraged about the two-mile-square island where, the year before our John Adams left the White House, *their* John Adams (the only surviving mutineer from the *Bounty*) took charge: a minuscule colony that mysteriously survives notwithstanding two corporate attempts (1831, 1856) to move it lock, stock, and barrel elsewhere (to Tahiti, to the Norfolk Islands). Forty-eight of the "Islanders" now come to us in their sturdy longboats, and board the *Sea Cloud*. Four generations, some haphazardly offering this or that artifact for sale, all of them talking, laughing, listening; the children obsessed with the toilet (they have VCR and television on Pitcairn, and outhouses). They are Seventh-Day Adventists who do not drink, unless you offer them a drink.

The time comes for the *Sea Cloud* to leave. Three-quarters of the entire population of Pitcairn go down the gangway and pack into the longboats. But, before casting off, they pause alongside and sing to us. Four songs—I swear they sounded as good and as full as the Mormon Tabernacle Choir. The last words of their apopemptic hymn were,

> *In the sweet bye and bye,*
> *In the beautiful land beyond the sky,*
> *We shall part never more, when we meet*
> *On the be-yoo-tee-fool shore...*

Returning to their little acre in the South Pacific, the Islanders managed to leave our urbane company of sixty sailors and sixty passengers, headed out on our luxury vessel toward civilization, feeling lonely.

And then that moment the first announcement of which found most of us routinely blasé. It just happened, we were informed, that headed in our general direction, bound west, was: the *Eagle*. It is a three-masted bark manned by Coast Guard cadets, a vessel Captain Cassidy had once commanded. We would effect, we were told—if all went well—a union at sea! A thousand miles from the nearest point of land! Very well.

At dinnertime the disappointing news was passed around that the *Eagle* was hopelessly off our course, and would pass by sixty miles south of us. But then, just after eleven, we were told the *Eagle* would heave into view in fifteen minutes.

Everyone did as one would expect: we lined up along the port deck. The moon was nearly full but was playing tag with the clouds, so that only momentarily did we have its illumination. Came the magical moment when we spotted the dull yellow blur, two or three miles ahead.

It was a full half hour before the *Eagle* was abeam, a few hundred meters away. Its sails were distinctive, each bearing a Maltese Cross. So it must have been, in these waters, two hundred years ago, when approaching ships were spotted and one wondered, in those bloody days, whether the ship was manned by pirates; or by the sailors of a nation at war; or by privateers, with letters of marque and reprisal.

But there was never, ever, a more fraternal bypass than that night's, two sailing ships, one with its sails full, the second headed into the wind under noiseless power. The cadets' cameras popped in the night, opposite our own, doing the same thing, a ghostly simulacrum of cannon flashes exploding at each other at sea. An unplanned moment, breathlessly beautiful in the off-again-on-again moonlight, the indulgent northeast trades blowing balm over the elated participants.

CHAPTER NINE

POLITICS

My Own Secret Right-Wing Conspiracy

I acknowledge my one involvement in what one might fancifully call covert political life, namely, my trusteeship in the oddest bequest in memory. In that capacity I served with the most concentrated aggregation of American right-wingers, fitted into a single room, in modern times. There we suddenly were, eight of us, distributing the legacy of one businessman who had rooted himself and his deputized trustees in Wichita, Kansas. We met in Wichita once a year for ten years, to do our bit to affect American politics through adroit and sometimes eccentric disbursements of a few thousand dollars. ⟶

O*n November 4, 1964,* Barry Goldwater woke in his desert home in Phoenix, encircled by cactus and other asperities. He did not need to be reminded that one-half of the national press was waiting outside to hear him pronounce, after putting it off the night before, his surrender to Lyndon Johnson; and to hear him convey—if he felt like it (he didn't, but he went through the motions)—his congratulations to the political figure who had won the most sweeping electoral victory since Franklin Delano Roosevelt's demolition of Alfred Landon in 1936. Goldwater was sore (though not—at that point—surprised) about the magnitude of his defeat. He divulged to his friends, and wrote about it in successive autobiographical accounts, that he was simply disbelieving that the positions he had taken before and during the campaign appealed decisively only to the voters in Arizona and a few Southern states.

But that was the conclusive judgment of the establishment: The right-wing critique of American liberalism had now had a final exposure on the national political auction block. The bitter-enders could now go back to their lairs and sing to themselves their tribal songs of nostalgia and recrimination and fancy, and maybe convene every now and again to hold testimonial dinners in honor of Barry Goldwater. History would record simply that he was the candidate returned by Lyndon Johnson to the parched earth of Phoenix, where dwelled only millionaires seeking dry air to breathe, and the Indians Barry Goldwater could now resume photographing. But then of course sixteen years later history was made to stand on its head when Ronald Reagan was swept into office on a platform indistinguishable from what Barry had been preaching.

What happened? On their little cat feet, the conservatives—with myriad committees, seminars, assemblies, documentaries, scholarships, leaflets, and prayer and fasting—had crept back onto the scene and found themselves in the Oval Office. *What happened?*

My own explanation is: John T. Gaty.

ॐ

I first saw his name on quick-reading what I initially judged to be merely a quaint letter. It was dated July 27, 1967, and it came from a Mr. Jack Shane, Vice President and Trust Officer of the Fourth National Bank of Wichita, Kansas. Mr. Shane was advising me that I had been named one of nine trustees given the responsibility of disposing of the residual estate (amounting to about half of the total estate) of the late John T. Gaty.

I read on. The letter included a four-page biography. John Gaty had graduated from Cornell University, where he had studied mechanical engineering. He had been employed as General Manager of the Beech Aviation Company in Wichita. On the side, he managed some modest oil explorations. He retired from Beech at age sixty, and at age sixty-one—in 1961—he contemplated a negative medical prognosis. He died in 1963. It was not easy (I would learn) to burrow into the private thoughts of the diffident bachelor, but we now know that he brought forth an extraordinary will.

The first part of it was conventional, bequests to individuals (a Mr. J. Arnold Dowd received $100,000 "for his unflagging effectiveness in helping me accumulate my fortune") and to the usual charities. It was Article 23 that caught the eye. "My trustees are directed to distribute one-tenth ($\frac{1}{10}$) of the corpus and all of the income the first year, one-ninth ($\frac{1}{9}$) of the corpus and all of the income the second year"—and so on for ten years, at which point the corpus would be exhausted. The money would go to such "religious, charitable, scientific, literary, or educational purposes as met the requirements for exemption under the present and future Internal Revenue Code of the United States." John Gaty then narrowed the focus of his design. *"I request that in making such distribution my Trustees give special consideration to the purposes which will promote individual liberty and incentive as opposed to socialism and communism."* He went on to name his selected trustees.

Any list, however devised, that sought in 1963 to identify the twenty most conspicuous right-wing figures in the United States would have included the nine names given by John Gaty. His list included three senators, the director of the Federal Bureau of Investigation, the founder and president of Harding College, a conservative radio publicist, the elder brother of President Eisenhower, and the founder and editor of *National Review*. What were they supposed to do, these guardians of the tablets?

Mr. Gaty's memo specified certain procedures. The trustees would meet once every year in Wichita. I blinked. Those nine people, with their schedules, foregather on the same day? Every year for ten years? *In Wichita?* But Mr. Gaty's artfulness unfurled: Every trustee would receive a stipend of $1,000 for attending the meeting (about $6,000 in current money). And every trustee would have unimpeachable authority to distribute $10,000 (again, the equivalent of $60,000 today) to the recipient of his choice. Not only that, but to cast a vote on how to allocate the rest of that year's portion of the corpus.

ॐ

A stroller with a trained political eye who happened to find himself at the intersection of Douglas and Market Streets in Wichita, Kansas, at 9:00 A.M. on Saturday, October 28, 1967, would have rubbed the eye in astonishment. *What was going on in Wichita?* What was it, hidden from general view, that brought these troglodytes to town? Barry Goldwater, as antecedent candidate for president, the ranking national Republican. John Tower, the hard-line first Republican senator from Texas since Reconstruction. Frank Lausche of Ohio, former governor, senator, Democratic mugwump. Strom Thurmond, senator from South Carolina, sometime presidential candidate. Clarence (Pat) Manion, sometime Dean of the Notre Dame Law School, weekly radio broadcaster delivering Catonic messages on the Communist threat. George Benson of Harding College, full-time conservative evangelist and educator. Edgar Eisenhower, the rightwardmost of the three Eisenhower brothers. And then the ubiquitous Buckley. What were they up to? A putsch?

Our paths had, mostly, crossed before Wichita. I hadn't met Edgar Eisenhower, tall, stocky, balding, traces of freckles, formally dressed, his smile as magical as that of his brother, who had arrived, smiling, at the White House in 1953. Several of us hadn't met George Benson, the soft-spoken, solemn educator/evangelist, or else had forgotten that we had. Everyone else was old-hat in the fraternity of the Right.

We sat in an ornate boardroom, the eight of us (J. Edgar Hoover had declined to serve), plus Jack Shane and two other executives of the bank. At each place there were pencils, a yellow pad, a water glass, a list of the trust assets, a copy of the will, and a folio on the Fourth National Bank. The first order of business was the election of a chairman. Barry Goldwater nominated Strom Thurmond, who was senior in rank, politically invincible, and also—it seemed even then—biologically evergreen. At the time of our first Gaty meeting he was sixty-five years old, and had been a widower for seven years. One month after our second Gaty meeting, he would marry a twenty-two-year-old and sire, to be sure after a decorous interval, a child, the first of four. A States' Rights Democrat in 1948, whose hand President Truman had refused to shake, he had evolved after twenty years into a Republican on genial terms with the Democratic White House; reelected, term after term, with wide support from the black community of South Carolina. Strom Thurmond accepted his unanimous election as our chairman and suggested that before the meeting proceeded, a moment of prayerful reflection was in order. He bowed his head and spoke a few words in the unapologetic and melodious accents of the native South Carolinian.

Handed the agenda, Chairman Thurmond told us that the next order of business would have to do with the J. Edgar Hoover question. In declining to serve, Mr. Hoover had reminded the bank that he accepted no secular offices, directorships, or trusteeships. We were not required to replace Mr. Hoover, Mr. Shane, in his quiet voice, informed us, inasmuch as the will called for replenishing the body of trustees only if death or resignation had reduced the number to less than five.

I spoke, to proffer the name of Louis Nichols. Until his recent retirement, he had served J. Edgar Hoover as a senior aide. As an undergraduate, I had had personal experience of him when he came to Yale at my invitation, at a groundbreaking event: he had publicly defended FBI policies against all questioners, performing brilliantly before a hostile house. Having retired, Lou Nichols was now an executive with Schenley Industries, Inc., and served as president of the J. Edgar Hoover Foundation. Was he not a plausible substitute for the prince? A motion carried; though John Tower, diminutive, sharp, half smiling, mischievously reminded us that adding 12 percent to the board of trustees meant diminishing by 12 percent the loot at our disposal. By our votes, we scorned his fratricidal distraction, however ruefully.

Senator Thurmond then proposed that each of us should speak in turn, and include in our remarks the name or names of the beneficiaries to which we wished our inviolable ten thousand dollars to go, reciting their qualifications. After which we would discuss to whom, and in what amounts, to send the money left over for this year's distribution.

The first man called, seated to the left of the chairman, was Pat Manion, an engaging Irish-American who had fifteen years earlier retired as Dean of the Notre Dame Law School to practice law independently. He had a considerable reputation as a spellbinding and witty right-wing orator and had struck gold in 1960 when he persuaded Barry Goldwater to write a book-length personal political testament. When assembled, *The Conscience of a Conservative* proved spectacularly popular, its success having much to do with the Goldwater presidential movement. Manion now presided over *The Manion Forum*, a syndicated weekly broadcast devoted to forwarding the conservative and anti-Communist agenda.

Manion spoke now in a voice that commanded instant attention. The voice of a litigator, a sometime dean, a general accustomed to addressing units large and small. Pat Manion said it would be a good idea to consider a half-dozen young conservatives

STANDING, FROM LEFT: AN EXECUTIVE OF THE FOURTH NATIONAL
BANK OF WICHITA; TRUSTEES FRANK LAUSCHE, WFB, AND LOUIS
NICHOLS; TRUST OFFICER JACK SHANE; CLARENCE MANION AND
GEORGE BENSON; TWO MORE BANK EXECUTIVES. SEATED: STROM
THURMOND, JOHN TOWER, BARRY GOLDWATER, EDGAR EISENHOWER

competing for Congress. Why not give them a leg up? A few thousand dollars contributed to their campaigns?

A soft but commanding harrumph came from Trust Officer Shane,
a serious, high-buttoned, faded-blond executive in his fifties whose
private passion (I learned) was oil painting. He was seated behind
the chairman and flanked by the two other executives of the bank.
Jack Shane was always deferential in addressing the trustees, but he
said now most firmly that he did not believe it possible, under the
Internal Revenue Code, to give money from the estate to a political
candidate.

How could that be? asked Manion. He had in hand a copy of a
letter written by John Gaty himself to John Wallace of the Fourth

National Bank in August 1963, in which he had enumerated, as one of the purposes of his trust, contributing to "the campaign fund" of any candidates "designated by each of the persons" present at the annual meeting.

"I know, *I know*," said Mr. Shane patiently; but when Mr. Gaty wrote that letter, he was just plain unaware, or else he had forgotten, that money from his estate could not be given to a politician seeking office without forfeiting the tax-exempt status of the whole trust fund we were here to distribute.

There was spirited discussion, but the language of John Gaty, correspondent, ceded to the language of John Gaty, testator. The will had authorized gifts that "met the requirements for exemption" under the IRS Code. It was not a light rebuke, handed down to a former dean of a law school, and in the presence of four politicians whose every instinct is to clear the way for those willing to lighten campaign expenses.

Clarence Manion reassembled his thoughts and turned to the Sino-American Amity Fund, which pleaded the cause of a Free China and U.S. familiarity with Taiwanese affairs. George Benson, fluent in the exercise of mendicancy, then spoke, meticulously and passionately, about the National Education Foundation, which sponsored scholarships and activity at the two fundamentalist colleges with which he was especially associated, Harding and the Oklahoma Christian College. I spoke about the Educational Reviewer.

Most of us had a cause close to the heart, and the hearth. Mine, obviously, was my indigent magazine, *National Review*. The Educational Reviewer, a tax-deductible enterprise, contracts for educational research using the special facilities of the magazine. Louis Nichols (when he came on board) wanted to patronize the J. Edgar Hoover Foundation, which in turn patronized the Valley Forge Freedoms Foundation, which gives out little prizes every year to encourage lively conservative editorial enterprise. Barry Goldwater settled on helping finance the Goldwater Chair at the University of Arizona, and John Tower the John Tower Chair at Southwestern University in Georgetown, Texas. Only Edgar Eisenhower had no specific beneficiaries in mind when he arrived, and accordingly distributed his ration among several enterprises.

When we turned to selecting beneficiaries for the uncommitted portion of the estate, we looked in two directions. All of us—again excepting Mr. Eisenhower—had a second recipient in mind. We spoke about these, incidentally demonstrating our cosmopolitan knowledge of conservative activity. Circumspect horse-trading began. If George clucked acquiescently for a few thousand for Pat's Cause #2, perhaps when Pat's turn came, he would see the special merits of George's Cause #2. And if, after all that, there was still a little left over, wouldn't it then be seemly to augment George's Cause #1 and—why not?—also Pat's?

A second obligation was to consider applications from the dozen or more enterprises that had got wind of the Gaty operation and written to the bank, or to individual trustees, soliciting patronage. These were screened, and one or two of them graced. But this was time-consuming, and none of us had come to Wichita to take up residence. At the second meeting, a year later, it was resolved to limit consideration to organizations that had already been sanctioned. This of course did not impinge on the right of individual trustees to reallocate their personal allowances as they saw fit. Nobody was about to repeal the Bill of Rights that had brought us all to Wichita in the first place.

We lunched on sandwiches and coffee and brownies at the same table where we had done business, and conversation turned to matters of general interest. Would Nixon easily sweep the Republican primaries next spring? How unequivocal would Lyndon Johnson, seeking reelection next year, be on the progressively more

divisive question of South Vietnam? Exactly how far were the student protesters willing to go? What were the effective means of
mobilizing counterprotests? Was there a growing acceptance in the
academic community of such as Milton Friedman?

Edgar Eisenhower, sitting next to Pat Manion, sipped his coffee
and touched down on "right-wing crazies." "Did you know, Dean
Manion, that there's a feller up in the Boston area"—his chuckle
was one part mirth, one part indignation—"who thinks that Ike is
a Communist agent?"

Manion's reaction was faultless. "You don't *mean* it?" He managed utter astonishment. But he caught my wink, and winked
back. There was indeed such a feller up in the Boston area, his
name was Robert Welch, he had founded the John Birch Society,
and Dean Manion was at that moment a member of the society's
national board.

Poor Pat. Like so many others, he had stayed on as a director of
the Birch Society for no other reason than that he could not, as a
matter of temperament, retreat under fire. He had never given a
moment's serious notice to this lunatic conclusion of Robert Welch,
set forth in a Birch publication given only discreet circulation (*The
Politician*). Goldwater looked on with pain. Two years before, he
had signed a manifesto I had written and published in *National
Review* disavowing the Society, but it had been difficult for him. For
a season or two, in Phoenix in the early sixties, joining the John
Birch Society was on the order of joining the local country club.

After lunch, John Tower, urinal to urinal, confided to me that
the nascent Reagan for President Committee was preposterous.
Not only was there no possibility that it would succeed in derail-
ing Nixon in 1968, but Reagan manifestly didn't have the "intellectual capacity" to serve as president.

A couple of years later, I asked the warmhearted and stentorian
Frank Lausche at lunch if he had seen the book just published by

Professor John Kenneth Galbraith on his diplomatic tour in India. What was it about? Lausche wanted to know. Professor Galbraith was a very left-wing person, he averred. Yes indeed, I agreed. But Senator Lausche might be amused by the reference to him in Galbraith's book, which I had just finished reviewing for *Life* magazine. "It was a footnote," I explained. Galbraith had written in the text that when his name came up before the Senate Foreign Relations Committee for confirmation as ambassador, the committee was unanimous in his favor "with [only] Lausche abstaining." And the footnote: "In 1968, Lausche was defeated for renomination. Asked to comment, I hazarded the guess that it was the result of the lingering resentment of the people of Ohio over this action. The explanation was not widely accepted." Senator Lausche laughed, with a little less than full conviction, and promised to read the book. He was a massively built man who, as what later would go by the name Reagan Democrat, had dominated political life in Ohio for many years.

We disbanded. We had spent three hours at work, and that would reduce to two hours, approximately, in the succeeding nine sessions. The Fourth National Bank completed the year's work gracefully, by sending the trustees individual checks made out to the charities of our choice, so that we could personally address them to the beneficiaries, Santa Claus for a day. One small step for mankind.

ॐ

For seven years, full attendance at the annual meeting was unbroken. Whatever the hardship of the round trip (one needed to make a connecting flight in Kansas City), none of us was going to pass up the guaranteed ten thousand dollars for our protégés. There were distractions. In 1968, counsel for the bank sadly advised the trustees who were senators that under the most recent revision of the Internal Revenue Code, they were ineligible to continue to receive the thousand-dollar annual stipend; indeed, they'd have to return the thousand-dollar payment for the preceding year. Parsing this regulation, what it said in effect was that a tax-deductible organization is such by government decree, and therefore no member of government can accept a fee from such a government-sanctioned organization. There was real indignation about this, especially from John Tower. The Senate had recently voted to forbid senators to earn more than twenty-five thousand dollars per year in speaking fees, and Tower said he was feeling the pinch.

Pat Manion suggested that the least the trustees could do was to augment by one thousand dollars the grants to beneficiaries selected by the uncompensated senators. We voted unanimously to approve this motion, Senators Thurmond, Goldwater, and Tower fastidiously abstaining. George Benson, at one session, advised us in his quiet solemn voice that he proposed to put every one of us on the Harding College Honor Roll, otherwise restricted to individuals who had donated one thousand dollars or more to Harding. I thanked him, and declined the honor. The reason was that I received every week or so requests from conservative organizations for gifts, and I regularly wrote out checks for twenty or thirty dollars. If the solicitors spotted my name on a list of donors who had given one thousand dollars to Harding, they would think me miserly for offering them only nickels and dimes. Goldwater spoke up: he too declined, "for the same reason as Buckley." Other trustees nodded their heads. Dr. Benson withdrew his offer.

Beginning the third year, the bank gave a dinner on the Friday night, in honor of the trustees, inviting forty or fifty local clients. The trustees, in turn, were called on after coffee and dessert to say a few words about the national scene. John Tower hated unpaid social functions unrelated to his own purposes, and regularly overconsumed at the cocktail hour, fading away during dinner, to appear chirpily the following morning at meeting time. The rest did their duty and spoke, mostly in pessimistic tones appropriate to the beleaguered conservative minority that, in 1964, had been instructed, in the public understanding, to go home and stop getting in the way of the nation's business. Meanwhile we had had the reoccupation of Czechoslovakia by Khrushchev, Communist expansionism in Southeast Asia, mounting deficits and inflation at home. George Benson came close as primary doomsayer, but the supreme pessimist was always Pat Manion, year after year. For him it was something of a forensic challenge to create just the right admixture. He was the Irish eulogist undertaking at once to rescue the mourners from terminal grief, and to validate their conviction that the loss of the deceased made now inconceivable any prospect of a happy life.

At long and vinous dinners the competitive spirit is provoked, and I found myself, without objective grounds for doing so, predicting great sunrises ahead, not excluding the disintegration of the Soviet Union, the burial of socialist dogma, the quelling of the Woodstock Generation, and an American triumph at the next Olympics. But the modest objective at hand was merely to repay the hospitality of the bank's executives by providing a little postprandial political theater, and that was done. The meetings were strictly off the record, and we were ignored by the press. Soon the goodnights were said. We had work to do the next morning.

In 1973, we met two weeks after President Nixon's Saturday Night Massacre. That was when Mr. Nixon had (1) demanded that the attorney general fire the special Watergate prosecutor, (2) forced the attorney general to resign when he refused to do so, (3) dismissed the deputy attorney general when he refused to do so, (4) abolished the office of the special prosecutor, and, finally, anticipating a negative decision by the Supreme Court, (5) released his suicidal tapes to Judge John Sirica. After our work for the bank, Senator Goldwater and I were driven to the airport, he to fly back to Washington, I to New York. We sat quietly at the little coffee shop waiting for our flights to be called, but Goldwater's movements had been tracked by the local CBS television outlet, and five minutes after we sat down, a camera and several reporters crowded around. What did Senator Goldwater think about President Nixon's prospects for surviving Watergate?

"I have no doubt that President Nixon will be completely exonerated, just a matter of time. Now that, gentlemen," he raised his right hand to signal an adieu, "is absolutely all I have to say on the subject." They left reluctantly, and Goldwater addressed me in private. "There is absolutely no doubt Nixon is guilty." He put down his Coca-Cola and with his hands attempted to make his analysis graphically. "You know, if I had been beached ten years ago on an island cut off from the world, and a helicopter suddenly dropped down and the pilot described the mess in the White House, I'd say to myself: *Richard Nixon has got to be the President of the United States!*"

Goldwater and I had been friends a very long time. Every year, almost from the beginning, he had voted five thousand dollars at my special request to the little Philadelphia Society. It had been founded in 1964 and had only the one purpose of bringing together two or three times a year, in different cities, its members, mostly academics, journalists, and businessmen. They deliver papers and discuss substantive questions. I read to my fellow trustees the themes of recent meetings, which included "Civil Disorder—Who Created the Urban Crisis?," "Dimensions of the Protracted Conflict," and "Disorder in the House of Intellect" (among the speakers: Gerhart Niemeyer, Hugh Kenner, Eric Voegelin). And I quoted from a review of the Society's Tenth Anniversary Meeting, published in *National Review*. The few sentences I gave them suggested at once a seriousness of purpose and a nice idiomatic lightheartedness. "In the early years," the reporter had written, "the issues were more pressing and the arguments steamier. An urge to save the world was near the surface; how to do it was the question that divided the house. One group argued for restoring the traditional values of Western civilization; another pleaded the case for freedom. Others, holding that liberty and tradition were compatible, steered the Society towards the reconciliation of values. Someone tells me that a certain congressman has voted against aid to crippled veterans because they should stand on their own two feet."

When I first introduced the Society to my fellow Gaty trustees I passed around copies of its balance sheet for Year Four. It listed assets of $4,700 (mostly, dues owed), and liabilities of $9,100. "As you can surmise from the income statement," Henry Regnery, president of the Society, would later write me, "[a Gaty grant] is almost a matter of life and death." Our bequest to the Society probably amounted to 75 percent of its annual receipts; by contrast, the gifts to Harding and Oklahoma Christian College were, I'd guess, a small fraction of what they received from graduates and well-wishers.

The crisis came on Friday, shortly before I'd be leaving for Kansas for the eighth meeting. I learned almost by accident that Senator Goldwater would not be attending. His absence could mean the end of the little subsidy for the Philadelphia Society. I tried, before catching my flight, to reach him by telephone, but did not get through.

Sometimes you simply have to rely on mutual understanding. I took a deep breath and wrote out a telegram. "GENTLEMEN: DEEPLY SORRY INADVERTENT CONFLICT MADE MY PRESENCE IMPOSSIBLE. IF AGREEABLE TO YOU WOULD DEEPLY APPRECIATE YOUR VOTING FUNDS IN APPROPRIATE AMOUNTS TO THE SAME CHARITIES I FAVORED LAST YEAR. WARM REGARDS, BARRY GOLDWATER." I had it dispatched to every one of the trustees, in care of the Fourth National Bank of Wichita, including myself. A second telegram went to Senator Goldwater, telling him what I had done.

The next morning, Chairman Thurmond read out his telegram and said he assumed we had all got the identical request. We nodded. At least it can be said that I had promised myself I'd keep my mouth shut, leaving it to someone else to move the adoption of Senator Goldwater's request, or to speak in favor of it—or against it. I would say *nothing*. An affirmative motion was made. It carried unanimously. The Philadelphia Society lived! In due course I had word from Goldwater, thanking me for taking the initiative I had taken. I was glad to have this, and recalled that, years ago, some lawyer, in some connection or another, had remarked that a forgery isn't properly a forgery if the counterfeit has reason to suppose that the person whose name is being used would, if apprised of what had happened, ratify the act.

I did, however, feel a little pang about our benefactor, Mr. Gaty. As noted, he was a shy man, but in his will he had engaged in an act just a little bit exhibitionistic in character—summoning nine busy conservative leaders to Wichita every year for ten years. I didn't think it likely that he desired the physical union of the nine trustees on the grounds that only by human interaction would their collaborative judgment bear fruit, descrying hidden conservative enterprises that might otherwise have gone unnoticed and unpatronized. The only trustee who, in this sense, was genuinely instructed by the assembly was Edgar Eisenhower. The allocations, I'd guess, would not have been significantly different if we had made up our lists at home, and voted by mail on one another's nominations ("Please indicate on the enclosed list the order of your endorsement. Use '15' for your top choice, descending to '1'"). I did wonder whether the Goldwater precedent would bring on massive absenteeism in the last two years, telegrams flying about from everybody to everybody else, making the request to honor the preceding year's allocations.

But this did not happen. Dear Edgar Eisenhower, the world's most genial man, had died in 1971, and Senator Goldwater did not reappear, but there were no other absentees. On the tenth year, we voted the remainder of the funds. The John T. Gaty Trust ended its life. At the last meeting, Senator Thurmond gave thanks to providence, and bade us godspeed.

ॐ

So. Had the late John Gaty engendered the conservative victory of 1980? One seeks perspectives. In 1960 Norman Mailer explained that his essay in the *Village Voice* endorsing John F. Kennedy a few weeks before Election Day had made the critical difference, tipping the presidential scales. Correct? Then John Gaty was responsible for the election of Ronald Reagan. *Tout court.* We had sent funds to a total of fifty-six conservative enterprises. Distributing how much money?

One million three hundred thousand dollars. Okay, that isn't Rockefeller–Ford–Carnegie–scale money, especially spread out over ten years. And yes, it requires ten, one hundred, one thousand times that much to pay for the battleships of the getting-and-spending world. But it's always true that the people who think up how to build battleships and what to put in them are paid peanuts compared with the cost of the ship itself. And almost always the people who are paid the very least are those who work on public opinion, which decides where battleships should go, what they should aim at, and whether they should fire. Millions of words were printed, spoken, and preached by recipients of Gaty money. Sweaty work, over a period of ten years, but then revolutions take time.

Running for Mayor of New York City

My single non-covert involvement in politics was in the race for mayor of New York City in 1965. The New York Conservative Party had been founded three years before. It was the contention of the Conservative Party that no one who embodied Republican principles as generally understood could get nominated on the Republican ticket in New York in the age of Rockefeller. Therefore the Conservative Party would offer such candidates.

In 1965 the Republican candidate for mayor was John V. Lindsay; the Democratic candidate, Abraham Beame. When it was all over, I got 13 percent of the vote. Five years later, my brother Jim, who served as my campaign manager, would be elected to the Senate in a three-way race.

Following are some episodes from the campaign, in the form of a diary. There was bitter partisanship, here reflected. ⟋

GENERAL PULASKI

OCTOBER 1

It's 9:00 A.M. and I am at my apartment working on the speech I will deliver that morning at Fordham University when my assistant campaign manager, Neal Freeman, phones from headquarters. Chaos, absolute chaos. Press Secretary Kieran O'Doherty had melodramatically announced to the entire office that the story in the morning's *Herald Tribune* would cost us one hundred thousand votes. I told Freeman that that was probably more votes than we were going to get in the first place, and he remarked that, if I didn't mind, he would not convey this remark back to O'Doherty. The trouble:

Pulaski Parade: "No" by Buckley

...One of the ripest vote-gathering fields each autumn is the Pulaski Day Parade, but one mayoral candidate won't be on hand at harvest time this year. William Buckley Jr., the Conservative Party candidate, has rejected an invitation from the Pulaski Day Committee to review the parade this Sunday on the ground that he wants to avoid "ethnic appeals."...

In replying to the invitation from parade committee chairman Frank Wazeter, Neal B. Freeman, assistant campaign manager for Mr. Buckley, wrote: "I am sorry to report that Mr. Buckley will be unable to attend the annual Pulaski Day Parade primarily because he has pledged himself to make no specifically ethnic or nationalist appeals. I hope you will understand his policy: it is to treat the voters of New York as responsible adult-individuals and not as members of monolithic voting blocs. Thank you so much for your interest."

Of the three candidates, Mr. Buckley was clearly the favorite among some 300 members of the parade committee—that is, until his letter was read. The group—leaders of Polish communities throughout the Metropolitan area—met Wednesday night. They were relatively silent at the mention of Mr. Beame's and Mr. Lindsay's names, but applauded Mr. Buckley's, then groaned when they heard the letter.

I had not heard either of the invitation or of Freeman's refusal of it, and it went through my mind that I wouldn't myself have handled the invitation quite that way—although I understood,

and valued, Freeman's attempt to honor the no-bloc insignia of
the campaign. It comes down to a question of elementary diplomacy: it is one thing to decide not to go, on your own initiative,
into Italian or Jewish areas in order to eat pizzas or blintzes,
another to decline an invitation to join in paying friendly tribute
to a people who, once a year, parade their history-laden pride
before the people of their adopted city. Add the special consideration that the Poles have been a subjugated people for so much of
so many centuries, and compassion figures, along with the formal
requirements of courtesy. How, then, to maneuver, so as (a) not to
look too foolish; (b) to affirm confidence in one's staff; and (c) to
minimize the bleeding?

Freeman raced up and accompanied me to Fordham, and we
discussed the problem. He stoutly maintained that the letter
would help, not hurt, the campaign. But in deference to contrary
opinion, he volunteered to resign (ridiculous), or to accept the
humiliation of a public reprimand (unthinkable). I decided to
write a second letter to the head of the Pulaski Day Committee,
give copies to the press at the meeting that afternoon, and ride out
the storm.

> Dear Mr. Wazeter: I was not aware of Mr. Freeman's letter to you
> until I read it in the newspaper this morning. I endorse the main
> point Mr. Freeman has made, which is that too many politicians
> believe they can manipulate nationality groups by attending their
> parades. For that reason, I regretfully declined the invitation to
> attend the Steuben Day Parade, as I shall, also regretfully, decline
> the invitation to the Columbus Day Parade. If I had written the
> letter myself, I'd have added that I wish you every success with
> your parade, and that if you invite me next year to attend, when
> my presence would not be construed as politically motivated, I
> shall accept with pride and pleasure. And I might have added, as a

longstanding supporter of the American Friends of the Captive Nations, that my sympathy for the ordeal of your people is more than ritualistic. Yours faithfully, [WFB]

I got many letters, the burden of which was that my stand had been just plain stuffy. I tend to agree. Perhaps my dogmatic stand is excusable only in the sense that paradigmatic campaigns may every now and then be excusable—bending over backward in order to try to dramatize a point. At any rate, the Pulaski episode did force me to take a stiffer position, in application of the no-bloc rule, than in my heart of hearts I found reasonable, or easily defensible— politics, complexities thereof, Lesson X, in the long textbook I never mastered.

THE OTHER BUCKLEY

OCTOBER 5

A surprising number of people were writing and telephoning to HQ to ask (suspiciously) what exactly was my relationship to Charles Buckley, the failing Democratic boss of the Bronx, against whom John Lindsay had been directing broadsides for lo these many weeks. The easiest thing would have been to drive home the dissociation by a routine blast against Charles Buckley, easy enough since he is an orthodox Democratic politician. That would be ill-advised, I was told. The old curmudgeon is affectionately regarded by many people in the Bronx, who admire, if not the techniques by which over the years he has maintained himself in power, at least his disdainful treatment of the doctrinaire reform-ers. Many of these reformers have been concerned less with the fact of boss rule than with unexploited opportunities to accelerate the city's march toward socialism, and toward these reformers,

Boss Buckley's patience has been obscenely and endearingly short. Accordingly I made the following statement, which put a stop to the phone calls.

> Many New Yorkers have called this office to ask (a) am I the same Mr. Buckley who is said to preside over the Bronx; or (b) am I related to the said Mr. Buckley; or (c) am I a stooge of the said Mr. Buckley?
>
> I wish to record that I am not related to Mr. Charles Buckley, either politically or biologically.... I herewith request Mr. Charles Buckley to do me, and the voters of New York, the favor of ending the confusion by the simple expedient of changing his name. I would volunteer to do as much for him under reversed circumstances, but considering that I am running for political office and he is not, I think it natural, noblesse oblige, that he should take the initiative.

EPICENE DEMONSTRATORS?

OCTOBER 21

I arrived at headquarters ten minutes before the scheduled press conference, at which I was to release my position paper on air and water pollution. Kieran O'Doherty, my brother Jim, and Neal Freeman collared me to say that the press, already assembled, wanted above all commentary on the noisy anti-Vietnam demonstration that took place over the weekend. I was reluctant to extemporize an extended analysis of the demonstration and recalled that I had written a newspaper column six months earlier commenting on the anti-Vietnam demonstration outside the White House on Easter Saturday. From a file at headquarters, I pulled out the column, which had been published in New York City (and in 150-odd newspapers around the country), read it over quickly and removed a couple of anachronisms, ran it through the Xerox machine to produce a copy to read to the press, and handed over the file copy for stenciling and mimeographing.

I felt like an awful fraud, handing out a six-month-old analysis of another (though not significantly different) demonstration as if it were freshly minted, but I rationalized that such were the exigencies of a political campaign. The press, I reasoned, would probably give it little space anyway; and perhaps recognize it as having already been published and toss it away as secondhand.

But the next morning, page 1, the *New York Times*: "BUCKLEY ASSAILS VIETNAM PROTEST/Condemns Marchers Here as 'Young Slobs' Strutting 'Epicene Resentment.'" There followed a very long, carefully written digest of my six-month-old newspaper column—and, hundreds upon hundreds of words down the length of the story, a two-paragraph reference to my air- and water-pollution paper, on which I had lavished so many hours of work.

The *Times* appeared especially interested in my use of the world "epicene"... "Mr. Buckley said: 'I wonder how these self-conscious boulevardiers of protest would have fared if a platoon of American soldiers who have seen the gore in South Vietnam had parachuted down into their mincing ranks.' Noting that they would not die for Vietnam, he snapped [sic]: 'What *would* that group of young slobs die for? Their idealism?'" (I had gone on to say: "What *are* the idealisms of the young protesters? Freer education? More free speech at the University of California? Idealism is a hierarchy, if it is any idealism at all.")

The *Times* went on: "'It may be idealistic,' he said, 'to lay one's body across the street in order to protest the neighborhood slum where the tenants pay $50 for a $10 room.' But he asked how seriously could one take the gesture of that idealist who then protests against contributing his tax payment of $20 a year to save women and children in South Vietnam from murder by the Vietcong. 'Why did not a single one of the demonstrators denounce the Vietcong imperialists?' he asked." (I had added: "What goes on in the minds, always supposing that is the word for it, of the youth who fret and fuss and moan over a minimum wage of only a dollar and a quarter an hour, and strut their epicene resentment over a gallant national effort to keep an entire section of the globe from sinking into the subhuman wretchedness of Asiatic Communism?")

" 'Why [the *Times* account continued] do they demand that the United States withdraw, but fail to demand that the Communists withdraw?' he asked. 'These were no mere pacifists,' he declared. Rather, he said, they would 'have lit bonfires of jubilation if the President had sent Marines into Alabama to wipe out the Southern resistance.' In summary, he said the marchers were 'the kind of people who would have deserted little Anne Frank, if her tormentors had been Communists rather than Nazis.' " (I had added: "Their failing is intellectual above all; but intellectual in the sense that all true intellection is moral, because, disembodied from moral precepts, thought is misleading, empty, ugly.")

I am fascinated by the kind of attention that can be attracted to one's thought by the mere act of running for public office. My general position on Vietnam and on anti-Vietnam demonstrations was (a) widely known and (b) hardly relevant to the campaign for the mayoralty of New York. What induced the *New York Times*, I wondered, all of a sudden to give it that kind of coverage? The editors would not have situated on the paper's front page the views on Vietnam of any member of the Senate Foreign Relations Committee (excepting Senator Fulbright, its chairman)—unless they were dramatically heterodox. Why mine? Could it possibly be that by using the word "epicene" I had given scandal? Surely, surely nothing so square. Yet the *Times* had carefully defined the word it selected to use in the headline. "Webster's New International Dictionary," the reporter had dutifully recorded, "defines epicene as sexless, 'neither one thing nor the other,' and 'effeminate.'" Was that the operative communication in the entire story? I found it hard to believe.

But sure enough, incredibly, the very next day: "LINDSAY MEN TALK OF A 100,000 EDGE." And on down the story:

> Mr. Lindsay's associates said the candidate believed that part of his gain between now and the election would come from conservative Republicans who were becoming disenchanted with William F. Buckley Jr., the Conservative party candidate. The move away from Mr. Buckley, the Republican-Liberal has told friends, began with the Conservative's comments...in which he described Vietnam protest marchers as displaying their "epicene resentment" against the country's involvement in the Asian war. Mr. Lindsay is said to think that intellectual Republicans [hardly numerous enough to affect an election—WFB] who oppose him because of his refusal to endorse Barry Goldwater last year, would be repelled by suggestions that anti-war marchers were homosexuals or effeminate.

So help me, I could not believe my eyes. The sheer, utter, hopeless, humorless, philistine fatuity! Their resentment is epicene, therefore *they* are. Lindsay's befuddlement approximates Eleanor Roosevelt's, therefore he is a woman. To be so helpless amid the minor eddies and downdrafts of a language system as to be blown from the abstract noun ("resentment") that a metaphor ("epicene") characterizes, clear back to the class of people generating said resentment, and thus to suppose that the metaphor characterizes them...By Lindsay's Rule, "Jones uttered a feline snarl" would give Jones four paws; and if "Jones penned a heavenly ode to his mistress," that would make him divine.

The Problem of Principle

October 11
To: WFB
From: Neal Freeman
Re: Staten Island Speech
Date: October 11, 1965

Very seriously for a moment...if you even suggest that the fare be raised for the Staten Island ferry, our support there will evaporate. It is, literally, sacred.

The above memorandum was the sum total of my briefing for my single appearance on Staten Island.

Staten Island is a rather unlikely borough of New York City, green, removed, pacific, for generations connected to Manhattan only by the five-cent ferry, though now there is a great bridge—the Verrazano Narrows Bridge—to Brooklyn. (Goldwater quipped after the campaign that things were looking so bad for the Democrats in New York that Bobby Kennedy had put Staten Island in his wife's name.)

The memo gave me a wild delight. Needless to say, I could not bring myself to withhold it from the audience at the Staten Island rally, a packed house, which roared with (nervous?) laughter.

On getting the memo I was, as the saying goes, torn between principle and political expediency. Staten Island is, so to speak, my querencia; a relatively neurosis-free, ethnically reposed enclave in Greater New York, unsundered by ideology, tension, urban jitters. Here is where Hugh Markey is from, one of my running mates, the candidate for comptroller on the Conservative ticket. Markey is a bachelor businessman of retiring disposition, who runs now for public office because of his seignorial convictions about the requirements of peace and amity and order, a man about whom it could honestly be said that Norman Mailer would find him no less strange than he would find Norman Mailer. Must I now disappoint him, and his followers on Staten Island?

I didn't. Would I have, if I hadn't actually discerned an intellectually irrefutable defense of the five-cent ferry? I don't know. I can report that I did find it, in the nick of time, and Neal is pleased with me. It is this simple. Residents of all the other boroughs of New York City pay a flat fee for public transit. The city charges the same fare to bus and subway riders who come into midtown Manhattan from whatever point, whether from Pelham Bay, ten miles away, or from 67th Street, ten blocks away. A resident of Staten Island, although paying the same taxes, has not available to him the same public transit facilities at the same price. To travel to midtown Manhattan from the middle of Staten Island, he must pay fifteen cents for the bus to the ferry, then five cents for the ferry, then another fifteen cents for the bus or subway to his destination: for a total of thirty-five cents. Considerations of equity—for so long as Staten Island remains a borough of New York City—therefore easily justify the five-cent fare; indeed, would justify a free ferry-transfer. Whew!

I felt—understandably I think—a very special obligation to hew closely to principle—beyond the point to which I would have expected the most honorable man to go who had actually set his sights on election. Mine was conceived as what I have called a paradigmatic campaign—of what use would it otherwise have been? An additional one, or two, or three hundred thousand votes would not, I figured, mean very much if I lost the only caste I had, as the scrupulous—sometimes perhaps even perverse—adherent to principle.

This high resolution is not of the kind that requires any special kidney; if you do not expect to win an election, it takes minimal courage to defend unpopular points of view in public. Such courage as *is* shown is in the occasional encounters with your own associates, each one of whom is likely to feel—and, often, for the most plausible of reasons—about at least one unpopular position you appear consigned by your philosophical fates to defend, that the rationale actually exists for modifying it. It is much, much easier to disappoint a hundred thousand anonymous people than one colleague who sits next to you at a staff meeting and earnestly pleads the case, say, for supporting a subsidy for the subways, or for letting the city absorb the cost of installing water meters.

Then, too, nothing is more futile—or, for that matter, more anti-conservative—than to indulge the heresy of extreme apriorism. "Prudence is," I remarked to the Third Anniversary Dinner of the Conservative Party, "as the catechism teaches, a virtue. And you have exercised prudence most prudently. Prudence doesn't happen to be the virtue I am myself best at. But I do greatly honor it, and do believe that prudence plays, or ought to play, an important role even in the development of paradigmatic political platforms, such as ours have sought to be." On a dozen occasions, I admitted into the position papers I had drafted modifications, accommodations, emulsifiers, which, I thought, subtly, intelligently, humanely bent the doctrine to the reality: but each one of them, I happily believe, stopped short of the (admittedly impalpable) line between prudence and expediency.

The exception clings to the mind. At a policy meeting to discuss our position paper on education, I proposed that we should come out foursquare for the proliferation of private schools—by advocating such tax rebates as were often spoken of in theoretical literature (vouchers, we have come to call them) and, in Canada, were even then widely given to parents who desired to send their children to private schools. I know of no single educational reform that appeals to me more than this one, which might do so much to shield the student from the intellectual and moral monoliths of the central political orthodoxy. But my other running mate, Mrs.

Rosemary Gunning, the Conservative candidate for President of the City Council, was dismayed, pleading a point of personal privilege to which she was eminently entitled—namely, that as chief organizer of the Parents and Taxpayers Association she had been widely denounced as an Enemy of the Public Schools, which in point of fact she was not. To endorse the growth of private schools while she was on the ticket would appear to vindicate her critics, and would disappoint her friends. The proposal was dropped.

Did You Know Lindsay at Yale?

OCTOBER 11

I had the usual call at 10:30 A.M., from the member of my campaign staff who undertook every day to cover Lindsay's morning press conference. Incredibly, the *crise du jour* was: Did Lindsay and I actually know each other at Yale? "Seriously," my monitor told me from the pay phone, "that's all they seem to want to talk about. Lindsay says you're having delusions of grandeur."

It was true, I learned on arriving at HQ for my own press conference: that was all they wanted to talk about. The issue arose from a chance remark I had made on ABC television the day before. A reporter asked whether I had met John Lindsay while at Yale. Yes, I said, "As a matter of fact we did a little witch-hunting together." The next day:

REPORTER: John Lindsay says that you had illusions, that the two of you didn't even know each other at Yale and that you never went witch-hunting [together].

WFB: Illusions about what?

REP.: I gather, about knowing him at Yale.

WFB: I'm told he said I'm having "delusions of grandeur." Grandeur was not defined, while I was at Yale, as having the knowledge of John Lindsay. On the other hand, he hadn't yet announced himself as a big historical moment.

REP.: Mr. Buckley, Mr. Lindsay denies that he went witch-hunting with you at Yale.

WFB: Well, it's too bad to have somebody deny the highest glory of his career. I'm beginning to think he peaked too early.

REP.: How did you go witch-hunting together?

WFB: We heckled a fellow-traveling demonstration in New Haven. He and a guy called Bob Lounsbury, a guy called Hank Healy, and a guy called—me—the four of us.

REP.: You don't think Lindsay could have forgotten you, do you?

WFB: Well, he's supposed not to forget any potential voter.... Can *I* ask *you* a question? I wonder if people *care* about it.

REP.: I'll explain it very simply. In the course of a long, tedious campaign, everyone gets bored with everything that happens day in and day out, that's all there is to it.

WFB: Look, this is off the record now. Over there [I pointed] is my brother and campaign manager, whom you all know. He and John and David Lindsay were classmates at Yale. He [my brother] is the godfather of one of David's children. We overlapped at Yale for two years—the Lindsays and my brother at law school, I in the undergraduate school. You decide whether the probability was that I should have known my own brother's friends. I really wonder why John wants to press this.

REPS. [*in unison*]: Why off the record?

JAMES BUCKLEY: Because I don't want to trade on my friendship with Dave Lindsay, that's all.

The subject was finally dropped. ("Why spoil a good story with the facts?" said Gabe Pressman of NBC.) The *New York Times* published the names of the two men I cited as having been present at the heckling session. They were both Lindsay supporters. They were nowhere quoted as denying my allegation.

I had heard that Lindsay was greatly roiled when, at the Conservative Convention, I analyzed a couple of sentences from his keynote speech, about which his supporter Murray Kempton observed that it made the campaign speeches of Lyndon Johnson read like a collection of the parliamentary addresses of Charles James Fox.

> Mr. Lindsay [I had written], says of Mr. Beame that he "promises not progress but procrastination, not ideas but indifference, not energy but evasiveness, not advancement but apathy."
>
> What is wrong with that sentence—other than its suicidal search for alliteration? What is wrong with it is that it is unintelligible. How can an orderly mind maintain that Mr. Beame "promises procrastination"? And in what sense is "evasiveness" the opposite of "energy"?
>
> As for your servant, Mr. Lindsay accused me of seeking "to downgrade and vitiate, to divide, to negate, and to prey upon the tensions and fears among our people." Now (a) I would be very happy, indeed, to "vitiate" the tensions and fears among our people—that, in fact, is why I am running for office. So why should Mr. Lindsay (unless he favors validating the fears of the people) criticize this? And (b) how on earth does one "divide" a "tension," let alone a "fear"? And how can one simultaneously "vitiate" a tension, and "prey upon" it? Mr. Lindsay is constantly criticizing me as the candidate from Connecticut. I don't know

why he is so hostile to Connecticut. Perhaps he went there to be educated and, for manifest reasons, is displeased with the results.

It was as I put it at the press conference: "The feline phase of the campaign has started."

THE DEBATES

OCTOBER 22

There was much suspense in anticipation of the debates. It was widely speculated that, at that particular form, I had the advantage, having in pursuit of unpopular ideas been frequently required over the years to face the opposition. I suspect—an admission against personal interest—that those points I have scored are primarily on account of their own cogency, rather than on account of any personal adeptness at formulating them. And in dealing with politicians running for office there is, of course, a preternatural advantage. How can you lose, in a public debate with aspirants for the mayoralty of New York, by asking, nay, pleading with your opponents to join with you in, say, denouncing Adam Clayton Powell Jr. as a demagogue? I mean, it's almost unfair. They are not going to say: No, he isn't a demagogue—because to do so would be to fly in the face of a fact of New York as conspicuous as its skyline. On the other hand, they won't agree with you that that is what he is, because Adam's boys (approximately 90,000) are first and last Adam's boys, and they will not like that, not at all.

I first tried it on Paul O'Dwyer, in our mano a mano in August when he was contending for the Democratic nomination. It was very difficult for him to ignore the question, since we were able to speak back and forth to each other; but ignore it he did, time after time after time. I tried it with Beame and Lindsay. Beame ignored the challenge. Lindsay did too a half-dozen times, then finally—rather shrewdly—replied to it by saying, "I don't know why you ask *me* to renounce Adam Clayton Powell Jr., since Powell has come out for Mr. Beame." A classic example of what the logicians call ignoratio elenchi—I hadn't asked him whom Powell had come out for, but what he *thought* of Powell as a leading figure in New York politics and sociology. But it took him off the hook, I expect,

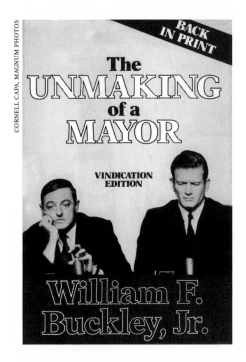

in the eyes of many listeners—as ignoratio elenchi frequently does, which is precisely why it was identified millennia ago in the first category of evasions.

I found the debates greatly constricting. The formula was always the same: round and round we went, whether posing our own questions or commenting on the moderator's: one candidate, the second candidate, the third candidate. The opportunity for evasion is enormous. Jones: How, Brown, are you going to raise the money to pay for that housing scheme you proposed? Brown: I want to answer Smith's ridiculous suggestion that I voted against the poverty bill. Smith: Jones has yet to make an original suggestion concerning traffic....

The moderators took pains to stay out of the way, except to clock the time periods exactly. None was ever heard to say to Jones: Honorable Jones, before you get off on that tangent, why don't you answer Smith's question about X? A three-man debate is not properly a debate but a forum. And unless its participants are permitted to colloquize, there is little engagement, infrequent resolution.

My associates urged, particularly in my opening and closing statements, that, instead of tangling with Beame and Lindsay, I should speak over their heads (as they were continually doing over mine and each other's) directly to the voters, giving them reasons why they should vote the Conservative ticket. I tried to do that, as often as it occurred to me; but often it didn't occur to me, my ungovernable instinct being to fasten on a weakness in the opponent's reasoning and dive in, or on a weakness in my own, and apply sutures—on the (Platonic?) assumption that voters will be influenced by the residual condition of the argument. A good debater is not necessarily an effective vote-getter: you can find a hole in your opponent's argument through which you could drive a coach and four ringing jingle bells all the way, and thrill at the crystallization of a truth wrung out from a bloody dialogue—which, however, may warm only you and your muse, while the smiling paralogist has in the meantime made votes by the tens of thousands.

Lindsay repeatedly accused me of collusion with Abraham Beame: "Buckley [me], Buckley [Chas.], and Beame" was his antidoxology during the last few weeks of the campaign. I sheepishly admit that there was one instance of such collusion. A very close friend of Beame's begged me, in October, to denounce

Beame during one of the debates as "the logical candidate of Roosevelt, Kennedy, and Johnson"—the triptych of the overwhelming majority of New York voters. I thought about it, and decided, Why the hell not? I had, after all, never said anything to suggest that the three gentlemen were my muses, and a whole lot to suggest otherwise. So, at the last debate, I dutifully suggested, while staring Beame in the face, that he was the logical candidate of Roosevelt, Kennedy, and Johnson. I wondered whether I would get a flicker of appreciation, a shaft of love. Nothing. Mr. Beame had probably never been told by his representative about our great collusion.

I had working for me, I repeat, an invaluable advantage, namely that I did not expect to win the election, and so could afford to violate the taboos. Lindsay and Beame had taboos' mother to observe: Beame could not afford to criticize Boss Powell or Boss Steingut; Lindsay could not afford to criticize Boss Rose or Boss Dubinsky. Neither would breathe a word of criticism against John Kennedy, or Mrs. Roosevelt, or Herbert Lehman, or Lyndon Johnson, the welfare state, the press, the voting population, labor unions, universal suffrage, or the Statue of Liberty. That left them precious little to criticize except inexperience (Lindsay's), fatigue (Beame's), crypto-Republicanism (Lindsay's), the bosses (Beame's)—and of course (all together, boys) me, Goldwater, and the nineteenth century.

Lindsay would arrive at the studio very tense, and instantly he would cover the desk area in front of him with a half-acre of three-by-five cards on which were graven in Magic Marker the salient points or statistics he intended to make and cite in the course of the fracas. (I had a mad impulse, one time when he went off for a moment to pose for a picture, to scramble the cards around, or maybe doctor the statistics, just a little, horrible bit.)

Always, when the camera first focused on the candidates, during the few seconds when we were being identified by the moderator,

my two opponents would manage a warming half-smile. Perfectly
proper, utterly professional—there isn't anyone in the business who
doesn't do it, whether Elvis Presley, Eric Sevareid, Lyndon Johnson,
or U Thant. Twelve years earlier I had signed up for what turned out
to be a half-hundred consecutive weekly television episodes, and I
noticed the other members of the panel regularly producing the
half-smile—I remarked it not with contempt but, increasingly, with
envy, because I simply could not, and cannot to this day, manage it.
At one point my wife, playfully, tried to make me practice, as if it
were a calisthenic; but there is no practicing it, because, inevitably,
you roar with laughter at yourself (try it). I have developed a sort of
anti-tic at such moments—my lips will simply not move, unless I am
moved by an elfin provocation, in which case I completely spoil the
intended effect of a sort of half-smiled reserved benevolence by
breaking out in a disconcerting sea of teeth.

Beame, so nervous that his hand shook when he reached for a
piece of paper, had several notebooks, and several brilliantly
memorized passages of rhetoric, one of which he never changed—
he always closed with it. "New York has done a great deal for me,"
he would rhapsodize. "It sent me through school. I love this city. I
owe a lot to this city. . . ." I commented about the third time around
that if he really desired to requite his obligation to New York, perhaps he should consider withdrawing from public office in favor of
me. He managed a wan smile. Lindsay's perorations changed verbally, but not in substance. Their thesis was that New York greatly
needed a change, and that here was New York's historic opportunity to effect that change. He used on more than one occasion a figure of speech which I found biologically disconcerting. It was what
we came to call at HQ "the three-handed pitch": "I ask all New
Yorkers to join me, to roll up their sleeves, to care, to adopt the
view that there must be from now on one hand for the self, one
hand for the family, and one hand for the city." He had clearly out-
bid all mortal men.

A Goldwater Operation?

October 8

At 11:45 A.M. I was still at home, working on a talk for Queens College that night. The telephone rang. It was Barry Goldwater. How was I, how was he, how was my wife, how was his wife, etc., etc. I asked if he could join me for lunch, which I had already scheduled with my brother Jim, my brother-in-law Brent Bozell (formerly associated with Senator Goldwater), and two members of the staff. He said he could join us for a drink, but would probably have to go off before lunch, to accommodate a crowded schedule. A few minutes later we met at Voisin, on 65th Street, and in short order the six of us were greatly enjoying ourselves—and G. stayed right through. He was in fine form, relaxed, sharp, detached. I had not seen him since the convention in San Francisco (and there only fleetingly). We had exchanged a number of letters, usually about matters tangential to our principal concerns. I had spoken to him over the telephone before announcing my candidacy. In the remoter past, I had visited with him more frequently, and I was glad to refresh my memory of him as among the world's most engaging men. To say nothing of most candid.

He was to be in New York for only a few hours, en route to Bermuda for a meeting of airplane enthusiasts. I asked him whether he was aware that Lindsay was to an increasing extent orienting his campaign on an anti-Goldwater basis, and he replied that of course he was—they have newspapers in Arizona too, perhaps not as few as absolutely desirable. Did he, I asked, feel the tug of organizational GOP loyalty to Lindsay? His answer was gloriously unambiguous: No. It wasn't, he said, just the matter of Lindsay's refusal to support him as the choice of the national Republican Party the year before, though that was a technical delinquency of heavy bearing on Lindsay's current claims to institutional Republican support. Lindsay, he felt, by his voting record and his public pronouncements, had identified himself as belonging outside the plausible limits of Republicanism as currently understood. Lindsay had under the two circumstances—organizational infidelity and infidelity to the most permissive expressions of Republican principle—disqualified himself from any call to loyalty from Republicans qua Republicans.

On we went to other matters. He talked most amusingly, I remember, about how Lyndon Johnson managed to upstage every meeting of the Republican National Committee in Washington, and how he had pleaded with Dwight Eisenhower to resist, on the occasions of National Committee meetings, invitations from Johnson to the White House, which inevitably overshadowed news of the GOP gatherings.

I began to notice a rather distracting sotto voce conversation on my left between my brother and my brother-in-law—less than absolutely courteous, I thought. Jim was scribbling something on a yellow legal pad. He suddenly interrupted Goldwater, in mid-sentence. "Senator," he said, "Brent tells me that since we're in politics, we've got to be terribly businesslike. I've written out a three-sentence statement. Do you mind if I read it to you?"

"Go ahead," Goldwater said.

"Throughout my public career," Jim began, "I have worked for unity within the Republican Party, regardless of shades of opinion, within the broad principles which characterize our Party. Today, in New York, there is only one candidate for Mayor who is running on Republican principles, and who is proud to identify himself with those principles. In my opinion, Bill Buckley is the only true Republican running for Mayor of New York, and I urge all good Republicans to support him this November."

"Would you sign that?" Jim asked.

"Sure," Goldwater said, quick as a shot—reaching with one hand in his pocket for a pen, with the other for Jim's notebook—and signed: "BMG"; and resumed his reminiscences.

We drove to the television station elated, a piece of front-page news in Jim's pocket. The newspapers were still on strike, but before the broadcast was over we were informed by the moderator that a settlement had just been reached, that the strikebound papers would resume publication the following Monday. That would be the moment to release the news!

Over that weekend, cooling down, we decided not to publish the endorsement at all.

Our reasoning: If we directly involved Goldwater in the campaign, post-election analyses would begin at the figure 800,000, the number of votes Goldwater himself had got in New York City in the 1964 presidential election. The difference between that figure and the inevitably lower figure the Conservative Party would score would prompt the refrain from the analysts that thus further had conservative fortunes fallen in the twelve-month interval between November 1964 and November 1965. In short, we calculated, neither the conservative movement, nor Goldwater, nor the Conservative Party stood to profit strategically from the publication of the endorsement.

I wrote Goldwater and informed him that such was our reasoning and our decision. Indeed he replied that he perfectly well understood. He must, as a politician of superior skill, have well understood what took us the whole weekend to fathom; undoubtedly he intuited it all in the moment it took him to reach casually for his pen and initial the endorsement. He initialed it anyway, because he is a valiant man and a faithful friend: and he was moved by our eagerness. Neither Lindsay nor the pro-Lindsay press ever learned about the proffered endorsement; though it hardly mattered to them in formulating their own public strategy, which was that I was the Goldwater candidate, on which theme improvisations were rendered reaching even to the suggestion that my candidacy was an intricate Arizona plot.

The accusations that Goldwater was a vindictive underworlder, managing my campaign for the purpose of evening a score with Lindsay, grew so frequent that I finally acknowledged them at a press conference: "The charge that Mr. Goldwater is running my campaign," I said on October 25, "seems to me quaint. I don't know who is running Mr. Lindsay's campaign, but I certainly don't blame him for guarding anonymity. I have talked with Mr. Lindsay more frequently during calendar 1965 than I have with Senator Goldwater, who in fact, as titular head of my party, the Republican Party, and as a personal friend, I have shamefully neglected, and to whom, wherever he is, I take this opportunity, through the public media, to transmit my affectionate greetings."

ELECTION NIGHT

NOVEMBER 2

It was 10:30 P.M. A reporter from the *New York Times* sent up word that he would like to talk to me, to record my impressions as the television returns began to show a slight edge for Lindsay and the spirits began to sag in the ballroom in which the Conservatives had gathered. I put the reporter off.

The *New York Times*! I thought back on a luncheon conversation I had had with, mirabile dictu, the editors of the *New York Times* four days earlier. I fondled, as the television was broadcasting the steady rise in Lindsay's plurality, the memory of the acutest pleasure of any I had experienced during the grueling weeks: arriving to keep my luncheon appointment and walking through the corridor of the *Times* building, past the information center, up the elevator to the august quarters of my hosts—and having to pause every step or two to shake gratefully the outstretched hands of porters, clerks, secretaries, elevator men, who, spotting me, wanted to wish me well, several of them whispering to me their subversive resolve to vote for me the following Tuesday. The irony elated me, that the maintenance force of this august newspaper, or at least those members of it who happened at that moment to stand between the street and the sanctum sanctorum, had, so many of them, been more greatly persuaded by the positions of the Conservative Party than by the thunder-machine of their employers.

I met with the editors and publishers, a disappointingly civil and charming assembly. They got down almost instantly to brass tacks as we dived into the first course of a superb meal. We touched on a number of things—on brutish instincts, of course (a *New York Times* editorial six days before our lunch had begun: "For weeks William F. Buckley Jr. has been pandering to some of the more brutish instincts in the community, though his appeals to racism and bigotry have been artfully masked"); on racism; on political courage; on New York's problems. And then toward the end of the meal, one of my hosts said to me gravely: "Do you *realize* that as a *practical* matter, your candidacy—which let us concede is idealistic from *your* point of view—is likely to result in a grave setback to the fortunes of New York City by depriving the city of a Lindsay Administration?"

"I have thought of that aspect of the business," I said. "And six weeks ago I went to someone whose judgment I profoundly trust—because his record of civic responsibility and of a shrewd devotion to New York's interests is, I think, unimpeachable. I asked him point-blank: Would New York fare better under Lindsay or under Beame? He answered, without a moment's hesitation: 'Under Beame.'"

The editors, tense, nevertheless spilled out traces of a smile, which they discreetly communicated to each other. "Who?" one of them finally asked, after a few seconds of silence. Who possibly could have come to such a conclusion? Robert Welch? General Walker? Mrs. Joe McCarthy?

"Is this lunch off the record?" I asked.

In unison they said: "Yes—absolutely—completely."

And I gave the name.

The effect was as if they had sat down comfortably at breakfast to read the morning editorial page of their paper, only to find it had come out for Goldwater for president. The dismay was paralytic.*

I wondered, still do, how, as practical men, they had succeeded in convincing themselves that the watershed of civic virtue drained only to Lindsay. James Farley, Peter Strauss, Robert Kennedy were not, by the *Times* editors' lights, evil men, but they were for Beame. All right, they are regular Democrats. But the editors of the New York *Daily News* also were for Beame. So also the editors of the New York *Journal-American*. They too would have to continue to do business in New York, to live in New York. And they weren't professional Democrats; on the contrary, their record was predominantly Republican. Why should *they* have come out for Beame, unless they reasoned that Beame would be a better mayor? And yet, somehow, the Conservatives, going only so far as to conclude that New York would fare about equally under Beame or Lindsay, were, in the eyes of my egregious hosts, motivated by a prejudice, by a desire for vengeance, by the gravitational pull of dark and brutish instincts....

On leaving the *Times* building I found a television crew waiting outside to ask me to comment on LBJ's sudden endorsement of Beame, which had just come in over the wire. We disposed of that subject, and Gabe Pressman, the cameras still rolling, asked me jocularly how I felt on emerging from the *Times* building, and I said—the kind of thing, I fear, that makes some people gray with anger—that it was as though I had just passed through the Berlin Wall.

"What is the first thing you would do if elected?" he pressed.

"Hang a net outside the window of the editor."

If I had been more conservative, less impulsive—more civic-minded?—I suppose I would have recommended a commission to investigate the desirability of suspending such a net.

---

* The name was that of New York City's patron saint, Robert Moses.

CHAPTER TEN

SOCIAL LIFE

Querencia: On Coping with Social Tedium

Writers and editors, like everyone else, live social lives, and our calling is occasionally to distill our reactions to what we see and do, and to own up to our own debilities and propensities, yea even our crotchets. ⸺

I *had a professor way back who* took to writing me four or five times a week, many of his letters seven or eight pages long and almost all of them describing his then-current plight. One of his plights lasted about nine months and had to do with his failure to pay enough money to the IRS a year or two earlier. He thought this failure the fault of his brother, a small businessman, who had always taken care of the clerical responsibilities of his older brother, the intellectual. I don't think Dante devoted more pages to the Inferno than my professor to whether, how, at whose expense, and with what recrimination he should come up with the one thousand three hundred dollars to pay Internal Revenue, plus interest and maybe a penalty.

His obsessive quandary became amusing enough, after six or seven months of it, to cause me to make mention of it at lunch to a friend in common. My tax-torn professor knew the great French political philosopher Bertrand de Jouvenel intimately; I, only in my capacity as a protégé of the professor. I recounted at lunch the agonies with which my friend belabored in his letters the question of his taxes. Jouvenel smiled and said, yes, he knew the professor was that way about all matters. He had always been that way. "And it astonishes me, for so intelligent a man. Because every subject in the whole world is more interesting than oneself," said M. de Jouvenel, some years before writing his autobiography.

The general social rule—don't talk about your personal concerns—continues to govern, especially at large parties, where social contacts are fleeting; especially at large parties of the kind that generally abound at holiday time. These parties exist for the most part because parties are an institutional imperative: so that just as the blossoms come out in May, so do the large parties constellate about the holiday season; and it is then that the percentage of people you know among the people who are there is likely to become smaller and smaller. It is then, entering the room, that you scan the horizon anxiously in search of a familiar face. And having found one?

There are several rules of thumb. One of them that it is easier and safer to approach a man, if you are a man, than a woman—unless the woman is, unaccountably, alone. This is hardly ever the case, and accordingly one's instinct is to let a woman engaged in conversation with someone else proceed uninterrupted. But men are more accustomed to being aggressed against. That means that with relative impunity you can edge over toward a man you know and either slither yourself into the conversation he is having with someone else, or preempt him. And talk about what?

Here is my point! Talk about *his* affairs! I think M. de Jouvenel quite wrong in this matter, and I will give you a hypothetical example. The man you recognize is a banker. Yesterday, the Labor Party beat Likud in a general election in Israel. The day before that, Ross Perot beat Bush and Clinton in a straw vote in California. The day before *that*, Gerald Ranck played thirty-one Scarlatti sonatas at the New York Ethical Culture auditorium, and John

McEnroe defeated Ivan Lendl in Paris. Question: Unless you know your mark extremely well, what reason do you have to suppose that he will discourse on any of these events (a) authoritatively, (b) originally, or (c) amusingly?

The answer is, you have no grounds for faith in the matter. But you *do* know that the man you have just approached is in banking. Knowing that, you can come up with something that encourages him to expatiate, there and then, on a subject he knows a great deal about at first hand, and your question will inflame his didactic spirit.

"About the discount rate. Is it possible in the futures market to gamble on the discount rate, say six months down the line, or maybe a year?"

As he winds into the subject, you can keep him wound up. The subject at hand will inevitably abut on another question (point, law, regulation, convention) and you skate right along with him. There is one thing you absolutely know—but for sure—which is that he will be saying more interesting things to you than in answer to the question, "How do you account for Ross Perot's appeal in California?" The reason for this is that you have in the past eight months read more about Ross Perot than about AIDS, the rich, and the homeless. So that the chances are infinitesimal that you will hear anything new or engaging on the subject. But you are talking to a banker, and he *does* know about the vagaries of the discount rate. Moreover, he can illustrate his point by recounting personal experiences. And the most interesting experiences are, really, personal. Would you rather read an account of the Battle of Austerlitz or an account of what Napoleon was thinking during that battle?

The British historian and diplomat Harold Nicolson was famous among other things for observing in his diary that ninety-nine people out of a hundred are interesting, and the one-hundredth is interesting because he is the exception.

But there *are* exceptions. It is therefore a good idea to develop means of self-defense for when, at a party, you find yourself locked in with the great bore. The first line of defense is of course to train your face to register appropriate responses—not to what the tedious guest is saying, because the whole point is that you are going to cease to listen to him. Instead, to what you reasonably *suppose* he is saying, to the extent that is required. The half-smile, following on his little wink; the eyebrows raised in suspense, as his voice indicates that what he is about to say is revelation; the barely enunciated, "I'll be damned!" when it is clear that he is saying something he accounts unusual. The French have the all-purpose word "*Tiens*," which is appropriate in absolutely every situation. Depending on the lilt you give it, you can use it to respond to news that your interlocutor's wife just died of cancer, or that he just married Miss America. ("*Tieeeens*." "*Tiens!*") The closest equivalent in English is "I'll be damned." ("I'll be daaaaaamned." "I'll *be*…" "I'llbedamned!")

These are the rudimentary skills to develop—some kind of facial and spoken reaction to what has been said—and if you have had a lot of practice, you can become very good at it. But there has to be a second line of defense.

You catch the word "Mabel," and you jump in. Now, you have to be dogged about this.

"Mabel?" you interrupt. "Is she related to Susan Mercer?"

He looks at you, surprised—he has never even heard of "Susan Mercer" (neither have you). He is maybe just slightly annoyed, because his narrative was interrupted. *You need to dig in.*

"Who is Susan Mercer? She was Mabel's half-sister, wasn't she? You remember, of course, the famous lawsuit? God, what a case! One of my best friends was working at the law firm that took Susan's case. He spent over a year on it, he said, tracking down all the evidence, what with the disappearance of the will, and the stepmother's adamant refusal to confirm that Susan had been legally adopted. I remember the lawyer saying that it introduced— the case, *Mercer* v. *Mabel Whatshername*, introduced the legal concept of 'pleading in the alternative': you know, lawyer stands up, addresses the court, and says, (1) Mabel never had the money; (2) Mabel had the money and it was her right to have it; and (3) Mabel had already given the money back to Susan." You look up for a reaction. Ah, but your friend has dematerialized.

But that course of action, needless to say, requires a certain histrionic resolve, and most of us don't have it, and so we need then to go to another line of defense. There are several of these, but the easiest to get away with is to gulp down your drink and then confess you must go to the bar and fetch another but you'll be right back, hahr hahr.

𝒫

There is the special problem raised by the party at which you have a social objective. There are difficulties here, because it might be necessary, having spotted your mark, for you to move over to him or her, passing by eleven people with whom, in the normal course of things, you would feel obliged to dally, even if only for a moment. And then in the adamant pursuit of your quarry you might find yourself guilty of behavior which, if not exactly boring, is certainly boorish.

I have a memory of this. Along with my wife, I arrived at a boat party with Mrs. Dolly Schiff, (a) whom I liked; and (b) who was among my employers (she published my syndicated column in the *New York Post*, the newspaper she owned); and (c) who was an important political presence in New York at a time when my brother Jim was the state's junior senator, preparing to run for reelection. Boarding the boat, Mrs. Schiff said to me, "Do you know, I have never even met your brother." Well, said I, I shall certainly cure that tonight—I knew that my brother was among the invited guests; in fact, he was already aboard.

A half hour later, chatting with my brother on the crowded deck, I spotted at the extreme other end of the deck the imperious forehead of Dolly Schiff. I grabbed my brother and told him we must forthwith maneuver past the eighty-odd people sipping champagne so that I could introduce him to Mrs. Schiff. Ignoring a dozen old friends, we reached her—at a moment when her head was slightly bent down, as she exchanged conversation with a petite woman whose back was to us. I charged in, "Dolly, this is my brother Jim, whom you wanted to meet. Jim, Dolly Schiff." The little woman we interrupted turned slowly around to us and smiled. She was our hostess, the Queen of England, but it was too late to undo the damage, so I proceeded with the introduction to Mrs. Schiff. (Jim had sat next to the Queen at dinner, and needed no introduction to her; the rest of us had been through the receiving line.) Jim said he was sorry to interrupt Mrs. Schiff, who smiled down at Her Majesty. I thought I'd break the ice by suggesting that the entire company join me in pleading with Mrs. Schiff to give me a raise. The Queen reacted with a half-smile, and excused herself to greet another of her guests. Anybody other than me. There can be casualties of a determined mission at a party.

❦

It is of course the objective of some guests to mingle with absolutely everybody at the party. I remember at the casual cocktail hour in California talking quietly at the edge of a social congregation with the president-elect of Yale University. I told him that a year earlier the outgoing president, Kingman Brewster, had been at this same affair. "The difference between King and me," Bart Giamatti said, "is that when he walks into a social gathering his eyes fix instinctively on the center of the densest social activity and he homes right in on it, the true social animal. My own instinct is to look to the farthermost edges of the gathering, and head softly in that direction. Where I am standing right now," he smiled.

Yes, and that raises the question of one's querencia, a favorite word of mine, one that I learned many years ago from Barnaby Conrad and have tirelessly used. The word describes a tiny area in the bullring, maybe fifty square feet, within which the fighting bull fancies himself entirely safe. The difficulty lies in the fact that every bull has his own unique idea of exactly where that querencia is, and it is up to the matador to divine, from a ferociously concentrated study of the bull's movements as he charges into the ring, the location of his particular querencia, because the matador must, at peril to life and limb, stay well clear of it when executing his critical passes. The bull who finds himself close to his querencia and is pained or perplexed will suddenly head for it, and in doing so may jerk his horns in an unpredicted direction, in which same direction the matador's groin or abdomen might find itself.

We all have, in any social situation, an undefined querencia, and we seek it out instinctively immediately on entering the crowded room. Most usually it is where one's spouse is—but that is a difficult sanctuary to avail yourself of, because it is deemed socially backward at a party to glue yourself to your wife. So you look elsewhere for your querencia. Generally, it is one human being: someone with whom you feel entirely comfortable, whom you can trust to greet you as if your company were the highlight of his day. You have tons to tell him, and he has tons to tell you, all of it of common interest. Is he...she...there? You look around.

No.

Is there an alternative querencia anywhere about?

Well yes. Somebody told you Algernon MacNair was going to be there. Not quite the company you *most* looked forward to attaching yourself to, but quite good enough to avoid the high stilt of tonight's social affair, and there is a specific point of interest. Maybe his op-ed piece this morning, in which he took those peculiar positions about taxation...But no. He is not there, nor is anyone else who will fill the bill in the same way.

Ah, but then the querencia can be greatly elastic. You can develop a consuming interest in the appointments of the sumptuous apartment. Every picture deserves close attention, worth at least three minutes of your time, as you look first this way at it, then that way, then examine the artist's signature. And the books! You pick up one from the fourth shelf and open it with delight transfiguring your face. *How is it that this neglected volume found its place into this library! How discriminating the taste of our hostess!* By the time you have examined that book, perhaps two or three others, and a dozen pictures and a score of family photographs—it is time for dinner!

With some apprehension you look down at your card (Table #23) and wonder who will be seated on your right, who on your left; and it is at such moments, as when in a foxhole, or in a sinking boat, that you rediscover God, and the need to utter a silent prayer.

The Threatened Privacy of Private Clubs

It was 1988, and the feminists had been leading the charge against the admissions policies of private clubs. The U.S. Supreme Court had just upheld a New York City law stating that clubs were public accommodations and thus bound by all the rules against discrimination. ⌒

T*he argument the Philadelphia* lawyers came up with that finally broke the back of the private clubs in New York City was this: that inevitably—never mind the fussy conventions governing members' behavior—if you have a private club, you have distinctive commercial opportunities. Thus the case against the Century Association of New York. Now, at the Century you are not permitted to pull a piece of paper out of your pocket and discuss it with your lunch companion, because the presumption, at the Century, is that the piece of paper has on it details of how to lance a mortgage, or execute a takeover. If it were absolutely establishable that the piece of paper had typed on it a sonnet by a forlorn seventeenth-century poet the case for whose rehabilitation you were arguing, the Century would be unlikely to have objections.

But, at the Century, there is great respect shown for your privacy, so that a steward would not be expected to come over and demand to examine the document in your hand, like the prep-school housemaster inspecting your fingernails. Under the circumstances, the presumption of guilt has to govern, and therefore: No papers.

Ah, but do you really *need* a paper in front of you in order to whisper to your lunch guest, "Joe, why don't you take your novel idea over to Knopf? I know Henry down there and I'm sure you will get a better deal." And, for that matter, who is to say that such conversations do *not* take place at the Century?—or at other clubs that fancy themselves engaged exclusively in fraternity? If a lawyer were to sit you down and wire you into a polygraph which turned itself into an electric chair if you answered a question falsely, would you be able to aver that you had *never*, at your club, asked a question, made a remark, opined a judgment, the impact of which affected in some way the commercial affairs, major or minor, of the man you were talking to?

But even admitting this, one wonders to what lengths the war against private clubs will go. The difficulty lies in part in the verbal apparatus that has silted up on the back of civil rights. Let us— in order not to burden the case with live models—suppose that there is a group of people called Blimphobians, and that these Blimps, as they are idiomatically referred to, appeal not at all to certain residents of Houston, Texas, who resolve not to admit to a particular eating club any Blimps.

Now never mind that I—or you, or the editor of *Private Clubs* magazine—would not wish to belong to any club that prejudged all Blimps. The point is, we have here a collision of two cultures, the culture of the private club, which deals in the (mostly) inexplicit attachments that bring people together when off duty; and the culture of civil rights, which is a government preserve. The first is saying that what it desires in its eating club is, however, inchoate, simply that which makes its members entirely comfortable, and

Blimphobianism somehow grates. The government, on the other hand, is saying that exclusion of Blimphobians is not to be tolerated in a club which—

In a club which what?

Well, it is not easy—in fact it is impossible—absolutely to demonstrate that anyone, let alone any institution, is wholly independent of government patronage. The Civil Rights Restoration Act of 1988 makes it clear that a college whose medical school is in any way subsidized by federal funds must expose its basketball team to the scrutiny of a Justice Department in search of evidence of discrimination. It isn't easy to see where the civil rightists' argument is logically contained. Most Americans, in the course of a year, send, or receive, a letter, or a piece of second-class mail. And we know that the post office loses money on its mail, from which it follows that all of us are federally subsidized, from which it could be made to follow that since we are federally subsidized persons, our affairs ought to be the object of government scrutiny to establish whether we discriminate in any way against any or all of the above.

A private club is increasingly viewed as an anachronism in an increasingly obtrusive society that objects to privacy except in fornication, which is why they said No to Justice Bork (we were invited to conclude that a Bork Supreme Court would take pictures every time Senators Metzenbaum and Kennedy did It). Private clubs are somehow suspected of harboring dark purposes (didn't even Adam Smith remark that when more than three men meet together, it is generally in order to conspire in restraint of trade?).

And private clubs fearfully stimulate the curiosity; and that curiosity, as a rule, is the curiosity of the envious. Not so much because we would necessarily enjoy the private club if given a key to it, but because there is envy of that which remains outside our reach. Some such envies cannot ever be mitigated (there isn't any way in which a woman can become a man, a commoner a king...).

But the arguments are floating all around us—the argument of commercial opportunity, for instance—which encourage us to disturb other people's satisfactions even if to do so by no means assures the multiplication of our own satisfactions.

Lesley Stahl, the super-bright CBS newsperson, came to interview me a while ago on the subject of private clubs, and we had a little infield practice on the question of whether women were being deprived of their "rights" by being excluded from men's clubs... Then she said, Oh, do you mind if we talk a little about the Bohemian Grove? And I said, Well, uh, you know, you're not supposed to talk about the Bohemian Grove, if you're a member. But, uh—

"Do you get used to seeing grown men running around naked?"

Well, I said, do you know, I've been a member for over twenty years, and I don't remember ever seeing any man naked at the Bohemian Grove except standing under a shower.

I paused then, melodrama written over my anxious face. Lowering my voice, a little gurgle of the highly-confidential-coming-up, I said to Lesley Stahl, leaning over breathlessly to take it in as the television camera whirred away: "—On the other hand, I think I *can* say this, that the Admissions Committee of the Bohemian Grove is *very* reluctant to admit to membership anyone who showers while dressed."

She laughed good-naturedly. But after she and the crew had gone, I wondered: How is it that people came by the impression that the Bohemian Grove is, in part at least, a nudist colony for men? It has got to be that mystique that we strain to assign to any institution that closes its doors to outsiders. What goes *on* there has to have a touch of mystery, to keep the curiosity lit.

What they hate to believe is that, as often as not, *nothing* goes on there, save an attempt to let individual men and individual women be free to be their own potty little selves (Chesterton's wonderful way of putting it), protected for the moment from the metropolitan juggernauts that were merely a gleam in the eye of Procrustes, back when nobody challenged the idea of a private club, let alone desired to hire a Philadelphia lawyer to come in and break one up. My favorite people don't belong to any club at all, for all I know. The best of all private clubs is the home. At home, I sometimes say to my wife, *everybody* is an outsider, except thee and me. And sometimes I wonder about thee.

Why Don't We Complain?

I conclude with an essay which is enduringly mysterious to me. I wrote it in 1961, and I am every month or so surprised— No, perhaps I am no longer surprised. A half-dozen times a year, every year, every decade, I am approached by one publisher or another for permission to reprint it, mostly in student-oriented collections and in anthologies. It is the only entry in this collection that I did not reread before choosing to include it. I didn't dare do so. I was afraid of failing to understand what it is about it that has struck so many publishers as memorable. But I place it here as, quite simply, in the judgment of the publishing world, my Hamlet, *my Gettysburg Address, my Ninth Symphony. I am certainly not going to complain about its ongoing life.* ⟶

It was the very last car and the only empty seat on the entire train, so there was no turning back. The problem was to breathe. Outside, the temperature was below freezing. Inside the railroad car the temperature must have been eighty-five degrees. I took off my overcoat, and a few minutes later my jacket, and noticed that the car was flecked with the white shirts of other passengers. I soon found my hand moving to loosen my tie. From one end of the car to the other, as we rattled through Westchester County, we sweated; but we did not moan.

I watched the train conductor appear at the head of the car. "Tickets, all tickets, please!" In a more virile age, I thought, the passengers would have seized the conductor and strapped him down on a seat over the radiator to share the fate of his patrons. He shuffled down the aisle, picking up tickets, punching commutation cards. No one addressed a word to him. He approached my seat, and I drew a deep breath of resolution. "Conductor," I began with a considerable edge to my voice.... Instantly the doleful eyes of my seatmate turned tiredly from his newspaper to fix me with a resentful stare: what question could be so important as to justify my intrusion into his stupor? I was shaken by those eyes. I am incapable of making a discreet fuss, so I mumbled a question about what time were we due in Stamford (I didn't even ask whether it would be before or after dehydration could be expected to set in), got my reply, and went back to my newspaper and to wiping my brow.

The conductor had nonchalantly walked down the gauntlet of eighty sweating American freemen, and not one of them had asked him to explain why the passengers in that car had been consigned to suffer. There is nothing to be done when the temperature outdoors is eighty-five degrees and indoors the air conditioner has broken down; obviously when that happens there is nothing to do, except perhaps curse the day that one was born. But when the temperature outdoors is below freezing, it takes a positive act of will on somebody's part to set the temperature indoors at 85. Somewhere a valve was turned too far, a furnace overstocked, a thermostat maladjusted: something that could easily be remedied by turning off the heat and allowing the great outdoors to come indoors. All this is so obvious. What is not obvious is what has happened to the American people. It isn't just the commuters, whom we have come to visualize as a supine breed who have got onto the trick of suspending their sensory faculties twice a day while they submit to the creeping dissolution of the railroad industry. It isn't just they who have given up trying to rectify irrational vexations. It is the American people everywhere.

A few weeks ago at a large movie theater I turned to my wife and said, "The picture is out of focus."

"Be quiet," she answered.

I obeyed. But a few minutes later I raised the point again, with mounting impatience.

"It will be all right in a minute," she said apprehensively. (She would rather lose her eyesight than be around when I make one of my infrequent scenes.) I waited. It was just out of focus—not glaringly out, but out. My vision is 20–20, and I assume that is the vision, adjusted, of most people in the movie house. So, after hectoring my wife throughout the first reel, I finally prevailed upon her to admit that it was off, and very annoying. We then settled down, coming to rest on the presumption that: (a) someone connected with the management of the theater must soon notice the blur and make the correction; or (b) someone seated near the rear of the house would make the complaint on behalf of those of us up front; or (c) the entire house—any minute now—would explode into catcalls and foot stamping, calling dramatic attention to the irksome distortion.

What happened was nothing. The movie ended, as it had begun, just out of focus, and as we trooped out, we stretched our faces in a variety of contortions to accustom the eyes to the shock of normal focus.

I think it is safe to say that everybody suffered on that occasion. And I think it is safe to assume that everyone was expecting someone else to take the initiative in going back to speak to the manager. And it is probably true that if we had supposed the movie would run right through with the blurred image, someone surely would have summoned up the purposive indignation to get up out of his seat and file his complaint.

But notice that no one did. And the reason no one did is that we are all increasingly anxious in America to be unobtrusive; we are reluctant to make our voices heard, hesitant about claiming our rights; we are afraid that our cause is unjust, or that if it is not unjust, it is ambiguous, or if not even that, then too trivial to justify the horrors of a confrontation with Authority; we will sit in an oven or endure a racking headache before undertaking a head-on, I'm-here-to-tell-you complaint. That tendency to passive compliance, to a heedless endurance, is something to keep one's eyes on—in sharp focus.

I myself can occasionally summon the courage to complain, but I cannot, as I have intimated, complain softly. My own instinct is so strong to let the thing ride, to forget about it—to expect that someone else will take the matter up, when the grievance is collective, in my behalf—that it is only when the provocation is at a very special key, whose vibrations touch simultaneously a complexus of nerves, allergies, and passions, that I catch fire and find the reserves of courage and assertiveness to speak up. When that happens, I get quite carried away. My blood gets hot, my brow wet, I become unbearably and unconscionably sarcastic and bellicose; I am girded for a total showdown.

Why should that be? Why could not I (or anyone else on that railroad car) have simply said to the conductor, "Sir"—I take that back: that sounds sarcastic—"Conductor, would you be good enough to turn down the heat? I am extremely hot. In fact, I tend to get hot every time the temperature reaches eighty-five degr—" Strike that last sentence. Just end it with the simple statement that you are extremely hot, and let the conductor infer the cause.

Every New Year's Eve I resolve to do something about the Milquetoast in me and vow to speak up, calmly, for my rights, and for the betterment of our society, on every appropriate occasion. Entering last New Year's Eve I was fortified in my resolve because that morning at breakfast I had had to ask the waitress three times for a glass of milk. She finally brought it—after I had finished my eggs, which is when I don't want it any more. I did not have the manliness to order her to take the milk back, but settled instead for a cowardly sulk, and ostentatiously refused to drink the milk—though I later paid for it—rather than state plainly to the hostess, as I should have, why I had not drunk it and would not pay for it.

So by the time the New Year ushered out the Old, riding in on my morning's indignation and stimulated by the gastric juices of resolution that flow so faithfully on New Year's Eve, I rendered my vow. Henceforward I would conquer my shyness, my unfortunate disposition to supineness. I would speak out like a man against the unnecessary annoyances of our time.

Forty-eight hours later, I was standing in line at the ski shop at Pico Peak, Vermont. All I needed, to get on with my skiing, was the loan, for one minute, of a small screwdriver, to tighten a loose binding. Behind the counter in the workshop were two men. One was industriously engaged in servicing the complicated requirements of the young lady at the head of the line, and obviously he would be tied up for quite a while. The other—"Jiggs," his workmate called him—was a middle-aged man, who sat in a chair puffing a pipe, exchanging small talk with his working partner. My pulse began its telltale acceleration. The minutes ticked on. I stared at the idle shopkeeper, hoping to shame him into action, but he was impervious to my telepathic reproof and continued his small talk with his friend, brazenly insensitive to the nervous demands of six good men who were raring to ski.

Suddenly my New Year's Eve resolution struck me. It was now or never. I broke from my place in line and marched to the counter. I was going to control myself. I dug my nails into my palms. My effort was only partially successful:

"If you are not too busy," I said icily, "would you mind handing me a screwdriver?"

Work stopped and everyone turned his eyes on me, and I experienced that mortification I always feel when I am the center of centripetal shafts of curiosity, resentment, perplexity.

But the worst was yet to come. "I am sorry, sir," said Jiggs deferentially, removing the pipe from his mouth. "I am not supposed to move. I have just had a heart attack." That was the signal for a great whirring noise that descended from heaven. We looked, stricken, out the window, and it appeared as though a cyclone had suddenly focused on the snowy courtyard between the shop and the ski lift. Suddenly a gigantic army helicopter materialized, and hovered down to a landing. Two men carrying a stretcher jumped out of the aircraft, tore into the ski shop, and lifted the shopkeeper onto the stretcher. Jiggs bade his companion goodbye and was whisked out the door, into the helicopter, up to the heavens, and down—we learned—to a nearby army hospital. I looked up manfully—into a score of man-eating eyes. I put the experience down as a reversal.

As I write this, on an airplane, I have run out of paper and need to reach into my briefcase under my legs for more. I cannot do this until my empty lunch tray is removed from my lap. I arrested the stewardess as she passed empty-handed down the aisle on the way to the kitchen to fetch the lunch trays for the passengers up forward who haven't been served yet. "Would you please take my tray?"

"Just a moment, sir!" she said, and marched on sternly.

Shall I tell her that since she is headed for the kitchen anyway, it could not delay the feeding of the other passengers by more than two seconds if she took away my empty tray? Or remind her that not fifteen minutes ago she spoke unctuously into the loudspeaker the words undoubtedly devised by the airline's highly paid public-relations counselor: "If there is anything I or Miss French can do for you to make your trip more enjoyable, please let us—" I have run out of paper.

I think the observable reluctance of the majority of Americans to assert themselves in minor matters is related to our increased sense of helplessness in an age of technology and centralized political and economic power. For generations, Americans who were too hot, or too cold, got up and did something about it. Now we call the plumber, or the electrician, or the furnace man. The habit of looking after our own needs obviously had something to do with the assertiveness that characterized the American family familiar to readers of American literature. With the technification of life goes our direct responsibility for our material environment, and we are conditioned to adopt a position of helplessness not only as regards the broken air conditioner, but as regards the overheated train. It takes an expert to fix the former, but not the latter; yet these distinctions, as we withdraw into helplessness, tend to fade away.

Our notorious political apathy is a related phenomenon. Every year, whether the Republican or the Democratic Party is in office, more and more power drains away from the individual to feed vast reservoirs in far-off places; and we have less and less say about the decisions which shape our future. From this alienation of personal power comes the sense of resignation with which we accept the political dispensations of a powerful government whose hold upon us continues to increase.

An editor of a national weekly newsmagazine told me a few years ago that as few as a dozen letters of protest against an editorial stance of his magazine were enough to convene a plenipotentiary meeting of the board of editors to review the policy. "So few people complain, or make their voices heard," he explained to me, "that we assume a dozen letters represent the inarticulated views of thousands of readers." In the past ten years, he said, the volume of mail has noticeably decreased, even though the circulation of his magazine has risen.

When our voices are finally mute, when we have finally suppressed the natural instinct to complain, whether the vexation is trivial or grave, we shall have become automatons, incapable of feeling. When Premier Khrushchev first came to this country, late in 1959, he was primed, we are informed, to experience the bitter resentment of the American people against his tyranny, against his persecutions, against the movement that is responsible for the great number of American deaths in Korea, for billions of dollars in taxes every year, and for life everlastingly on the brink of disaster. But Khrushchev was pleasantly surprised, and reported back to the Russian people that he had been met with overwhelming cordiality (read: apathy), except, to be sure, for "a few fascists who followed me around with their wretched posters, and should be horsewhipped."

I may be crazy, but I say there would have been lots more posters in a society where train temperatures in the dead of winter were not allowed to climb to eighty-five degrees without complaint.

EPILOGUE

Thoughts on a Final Passage

I *was asked by a friend and sailing companion* who read the manuscript of my book *WindFall* why I thought to subtitle it "The End of the Affair."

The voyage I chronicled in that book began almost immediately after my formal retirement as editor of a magazine I had founded as a very young man; and I would, on this passage, enter senior-citizenship. Practically the whole of my professional life had centered on that magazine, and when I left New York, having just then put my last issue to bed, I felt a certain sadness, a deracination almost, as one would expect to feel, even though at no point was it so keen as to make me wonder whether I had made an unwise decision in retiring.

Then, also, I couldn't predict whether, five years later, I would be in shape (physical, or psychological) to crank up the energy required to organize a fifth ocean crossing. The odds were against it, I felt, never mind whatever buoyancy continues to sustain me as I write. I am much struck by sentences in a letter I had from Whittaker Chambers (recalled in my portrait of him, pp. 299–317), the more so since it proved to be the last one I'd receive from him. "Weariness, Bill—you cannot yet know literally what it means. I wish no time would come when you do know, but the balance of

experience is against it. One day, long hence, you will know true
weariness and will say: 'That was it.'" I have very little in common
with Whittaker Chambers, having suffered so little by comparison,
my link to the heavy machinery of history so greatly attenuated
alongside his. He put it this way: "Our kind of weariness. History hit
us with a freight train. But we (my general breed) tried to put ourselves together again. Since this meant outwitting dismemberment,
as well as resynthesizing a new lifeview (grandfather, what big
words you use), the sequel might seem rather remarkable, rather
more remarkable than what went before. But at a price—weariness."
Even within that weariness, Chambers found the exotic content-
ment he believed Sisyphus to have found, though consigned to labor
every day to roll the huge stone up the hill only to see it roll back to
the bottom again, requiring him to renew his labor, indefinitely.

Yes, said Chambers, he thought Albert Camus correct, that in
manual labor, and in the "strangled cry" described by John Stra-
chey, who had fought his way free of Communism, there was satisfaction—better than that: Katow, who in the novel of Malraux
sacrificed himself by giving away his cyanide to a younger man,
must now, without alternative means of ending his own life, walk
into the fiery furnace prepared by his executioner. He "walks
toward the locomotive through a hall of bodies from which comes
something like an unutterable sob—the strangled cry. It may also
be phrased: 'And the morning stars sang together for joy.' It may
also be phrased: '*Il faut supposer Katow heureux,*' as Camus wrote:
'*Il faut supposer Sisyphe heureux.*' For each age finds its own language for an eternal meaning."

I do not anticipate a Sisyphean end, except in the sense that all
of us are condemned, always, forever, to renew our labors; and I
have never courted, let alone been stricken by, the sadworldiness
that afflicted Chambers. My life, on the whole, has been joyful, and
my passages at sea have been pleasures so marked that I thought it

2 Buckleys Become Best Sellers

By EDWIN McDOWELL

Being on the best-seller list is nothing new for William F. Buckley Jr. — but being on the list with his son is. And that is what will happen this Sunday, when the 60-year-old Mr. Buckley, who has written nine best sellers in the past 10 years, is joined on The New York Times fiction best-seller list by his 33-year-old son, Christopher.

The elder Mr. Buckley's "High Jinx" (Doubleday), will be No. 10. Christopher Buckley's "The White House Mess" (Knopf), a satirical first novel, will be No. 14.

It's a rare first novel that winds up on the best-seller list. But publishing industry officials say they cannot remember another instance of a father and son having simultaneous best-selling novels.

"I couldn't be more pleased," William Buckley said about the success of his son's novel. "I wish I weren't biologically related to him so that nobody could suspect that my enthusiasm for his book is self-serving."

Much of that pleasure is rooted in obvious parental pride, but part of it may also be rooted in surprise. Mr. Buckley said that as a reward for his son's doing well in school one year, he took him with him on an airplane trip to the West Coast. "He was listening to that dreadful music on the earphones," Mr. Buckley said, "and finally I said, 'Christopher, have you ever read a book?' He looked at me with a languid expression and said, 'Treasure Island.' If anyone had bet then he had a literary future, I'd have guessed 1,000-to-1 he had not."

Christopher Buckley wrote only one previous book, "Steaming to Bamboola: The World of a Tramp Freighter" (Congdon & Weed, 1982). It generated respectful reviews but only lukewarm sales. By contrast, "The White House Mess," a madcap romp through the corridors of pomp and power, has been racking up strong sales and warm reviews. "The delight of Mr. Buckley's satire," Christopher Lehmann-Haupt wrote in his review in The Times, "is that it not only sustains itself, it actually makes us laugh harder as it makes its outrageous way along."

The novel opens in January 1989, with President Reagan declining to attend the inauguration ceremonies for his successor, President-elect Thomas Nelson Tucker (TNT), and for the next 224 pages it heaps good-natured, bipartisan ridicule on the functionaries who maneuver for power and perks. (The White House Mess is actually a restaurant in the basement of the White House, in which all the aspiring movers and shakers desire membership.)

The author's insights into the corridors of power were acquired during the year and a half he spent as a speech writer for Vice President Bush, starting in 1981.

"I had agreed not to write about my experiences at the White House," the author said. "But I'd read about 10 or 12 White House memoirs, and I was somewhat appalled. The themes are generally, 'It wasn't my fault,' or, 'It would have been much worse if I hadn't been there.' Then one day, bingo, one of those light bulbs just went off. I said, 'Let's write a fake memoir.'"

Mr. Buckley, who with his wife recently bought a house in Washington, sent copies of the novel to President Reagan and Vice President Bush, both of whom appear to have enjoyed it.

"I had a letter from Reagan, whose sense of humor is as secure as his phone lines," Mr. Buckley said. "He thanked me and said he was delighted to share my new endeavor. Bush, who gets elected in my book, wrote to me a few weeks after George Will's attack calling him a smarmy lap dog. He said he was sorry to unseat my President, but the guy was such a smarmy lap dog that he deserved it."

The younger Mr. Buckley — an only child and, like his father, a graduate of Yale University — said that his father has been a constant inspiration to him, although he did not directly influence his wanting to be a writer. "I grew up in a house surrounded by typewriters," he recalled. "I used to sit on his lap and he taught me how to touch type when I was 6. I guess some of that enters the psyche."

Now both have graduated to word processors, although they compose at different speeds: the younger Mr. Buckley wrote his novel in about a year, his father typically writes his in 150 hours. "When I was in the middle of my book," Christopher Buckley recalled, "my father called me and said, 'Well, I finished my novel in 12 days.'"

William Buckley's best-selling novels — "Saving the Queen," "Stained Glass," "Who's On First," "Marco Polo If You Can," "The Story of Henri Todd" and "See You Later Alligator" — feature the exploits of Blackford Oakes, the intrepid American agent. In "High Jinks," Mr. Oakes sets his sights on the traitor who spoiled a plan to liberate Albania.

The Buckleys have often sailed together on the elder Buckley's yacht — William Buckley's nonfiction best sellers "Airborne" and "Atlantic High" are based on his trans-Atlantic voyages — and they telephone or write to each other several times a week. "It's a very brotherly relationship," the son said, "and now we can sort of talk shop."

Their one apparent disagreement is whether being William Buckley's son has been helpful or a hindrance.

"On the whole, I think his being my son negatively influenced his own chances, although perhaps not any-more, just as I think my novels have been negatively influenced by my having a political identity," the father said.

However, Christopher Buckley said that being William Buckley's son led to his being hired after college by Clay Felker at Esquire, where he is currently an editor at large, although he acknowledged there was a presumption that "because you're someone's son," a publishing house will publish your book.

"Martin Amis once told an interviewer he was pretty sure someone would have published his first book for being Kingsley Amis's son, but not his second," Christopher Buckley said. "Maybe now that my book is on the best-seller list people won't assume it was published because I'm William Buckley's son."

William F. Buckley Jr., right, and his son, Christopher, during a sailing trip aboard the elder Mr. Buckley's boat.

Christopher Little

impudent to suppose that, as though it required merely the setting of the clock, I might have yet another such an experience, with my friends, five years later.

And, as I related in *WindFall*, the nature of my companionship with my son had changed, as it ought to have done, and I had no clear sense of it that were I to suggest another passage to him in five years, he'd have joined me eagerly. At his age, one should expect he'd find alternatives that would be more beguiling. On the other hand, in the unlikely event of a prospective ocean passage, I might find his absence critically discouraging to the enterprise.

Oh yes, and there is the navigational point. About fifteen minutes after the appearance of my book, we could expect that navigation at sea would cease to be more than an antiquarian exercise. Probably a Trimble hand unit powered by a couple of flashlight batteries will tell you exactly where you are, day or night. And when that happens, what would I have to fret over on a long passage?... Ah, but the sea always has something lying in wait for you. Perhaps, in my last years, I'll deny it the opportunity to vex me.

But if so, how can I draw from it those fleeted moments? You have shortened sail just a little, because you want more steadiness than you are going to get at this speed, the wind up to twenty-two, twenty-four knots, and it is late at night, and there are only two of you in the cockpit. You are moving at racing speed, parting the buttery sea as with a scalpel, and the waters roar by, themselves exuberantly subdued by your powers to command your way through them. Triumphalism...and the stars also seem to be singing together for joy.

Acknowledgments

I *could not possibly come up* with the names of everyone who helped me when I wrote the fifty essays included in this book, and so I confine myself only to those who read the book whole, after it was put together. First, and always foremost, I am grateful to Samuel S. Vaughan, my longtime editor, for his care and for his advice.

And my thanks to my agent, Lois Wallace, and to André Bernard, my old friend and publisher. I am hugely indebted to Linda Bridges, editor-at-large of *National Review*, for her painstaking and illuminating work in going over this material sentence by sentence and giving it editorial attention. I am also grateful to Luba Kolomytseva, for her fine work in preparing the photographs for use in the book.

WFB

Stamford, Connecticut
October 2003

Index